W9-CFJ-446

DATE DUE		

HOLOCAUST SURVIVORS

HOLOCAUST SURVIVORS

A Biographical Dictionary

Volume 2: M–Z

Emily Taitz

GREENWOOD PRESS
Westport, Connecticut • London

Library of Congress Cataloging-in-Publication Data

Taitz, Emily.
    Holocaust survivors: biographical dictionary / Emily Taitz.
        p. cm.
    Includes bibliographical references and index.
    ISBN 978-0-313-33676-8 (set : alk. paper)—ISBN 978-0-313-33677-5 (vol 1 : alk.
paper)—ISBN 978-0-313-33678-2 (vol 2 : alk. paper)   1. Holocaust, Jewish
(1939-1945)—Personal narratives. 2. Holocaust survivors—Biography. 3. Holocaust
survivors—Interviews. 4. World war, 1939-1945—Personal narratives, Jewish.
I. Title.
    D804.3.T34 2007
    940.53'180922—dc22   2007006558

British Library Cataloguing in Publication Data is available.

Library of Congress Catalog Card Number: 2007006558
ISBN-10: 0-313-33676-8 (set)
ISBN-13: 978-0-313-33676-8
ISBN-10: 0-313-33677-6 (vol. 1)
ISBN-13: 978-0-313-33677-5
ISBN-10: 0-313-33678-4 (vol. 2)
ISBN-13: 978-0-313-33678-2

First published in 2007

Greenwood Press, 88 Post Road West, Westport, CT 06881
An imprint of Greenwood Publishing Group, Inc.
www.greenwood.com

Printed in the United States of America

∞

The paper used in this book complies with the
Permanent Paper Standard issued by the National
Information Standards Organization (Z39.48-1984).

10   9   8   7   6   5   4   3   2   1

Copyright Acknowledgments

To the survivors of the Holocaust:
those who wrote, those who told,
and those who remembered and were silent

CONTENTS

HOLOCAUST SURVIVORS

M

Mandelbaum, Sigmund (1910–) and Jack Mandelbaum (1927–)

Sigmund Mandelbaum and his nephew Jack began World War II in different Polish cities. During the war they were in different concentration camps. But when it was over, they found each other, the sole survivors of their large family, and together they came to America.

Sigmund Mandelbaum lived in Dzialoszyce, Poland, a town of 5,600 people, with his father, Chaim, his stepmother, Esther, and many siblings. The family ran a small factory in its home, sewing shirts and underwear and selling them locally. Chaim was also the cantor of the synagogue. About 75 percent of the population of Dzialoszyce was Jewish, and the Mandelbaum family was observant. On Friday evenings, people would often stop outside the window of their apartment to listen to the family singing Sabbath songs. But Sigmund found his town too small. He worked from the age of nine, and at thirteen he left for Lodz, where he was employed by his sister-in-law, also in the garment industry.

Jack Mandelbaum, a son of Sigmund's older brother, Mejloch, was born in the city of Gdynia, a port on the Baltic Sea. Given a secular education, he lived with his parents and two siblings in a large apartment near the beach with a maid and a private tutor to prepare him for his bar mitzvah. That life ended in August 1939, when Mejloch, fearing that Gdynia would be bombed by the Germans, sent his family inland to Dzialoszyce. There, Jack met his Hasidic grandfather for the first time.

The following month, when war broke out, Jack and his family remained in Dzialoszyce. Mejloch, who stayed behind in Gdynia, was arrested and sent to a concentration camp.

By 1939, Sigmund, already living in Lodz, had learned a trade. Rather than remain in the clothing business like his family, he became a painter. This choice may have saved his life during the war. Jack, only thirteen years old, earned some money in Dzialoszyce by substituting for other Jews who were conscripted for day labor by the Nazis. During one of those assignments, he worked as an electrician. A certificate affirming that he had worked for the mayor in that capacity may, have saved him from the gas chambers where his mother, sister, and brother were all murdered.

Sigmund was deported to Plaszow, a labor camp near Krakow. He was able to escape, and for a short time he hid with a farmer, but he left his hiding place because he feared that he would be turned in. He returned to Krakow and was recaptured.

Jack was not arrested until June 1942. He and his family were brought to an abandoned brewery, and the SS divided them into two groups. Jack was sent to one side with his brother and his mother. Hoping to save his family, he showed the soldier his electrician's certificate, but it did not help the others. "He grabbed me and put me on the other side," Jack told an interviewer many years later. He never saw his family again.

Both Jack and Sigmund spent the next three years being shifted from camp to camp. Jack was liberated from Dornhau in May 1945. Sigmund survived Auschwitz, Stuttgart, Stutthof, Buchenwald, and then Theresienstadt, where he was liberated. He soon discovered that, except for two cousins and his nephew, Jack, all his family had been murdered by the Nazis. His brother (Jack's father, Mejloch) had managed to survive for almost five full years from the time of his arrest in September 1939. He died in Stutthof just before the war ended.

As soon as the war was over, Jack and Sigmund applied for visas to America. Jack had heard that the United States was accepting only young people, so in order to increase his chances, he claimed to be the only survivor. When his visa came through, he returned to the American consulate claiming that he had just found his uncle and couldn't leave without him. He was able to cajole the officials into giving Sigmund a visa, too, and they left Europe together in 1946.

The Mandelbaums chose to settle in Kansas City "because it was not too big and not too small." Both men married quickly, and within two years of their arrival, both owned shops and were becoming more prosperous and established. Sigmund and his wife, Helen, had two daughters; Jack had a daughter and three sons. They thought they had put World War II and its terrible memories behind them until one of Jack's neighbors asked him what sports he played in the concentration camps. Realizing that most Americans knew little or nothing about the horrors of the Holocaust, Jack Mandelbaum became active in Holocaust education and was a cofounder, with **Isak Federman**, of the Midwest Center for Holocaust Education, established in 1993.

References

Dodd, Monroe, ed. *From the Heart: Life Before and After the Holocaust—A Mosaic of Memories*. Kansas City: Kansas City Star Books and the Midwest Center for Holocaust Education, 2001.

Fortunoff Archive for Holocaust Survivors, HVT 1649. Yale University Library. New Haven, CT. Interview with Jack Mandelbaum.

Markowski, Fabian (1906–1980)

Fabian (born Feibush) Markowski of Radziejow, Poland, was in the tailoring business with his father when the Germans invaded the country and World War II began. Because a minor infraction led to his early arrest by the Nazis, he escaped to Russia and was the only one of his large family to survive the Holocaust.

The thirty-three-year-old Markowski, the middle son of Elke and Eliyahu Markowski's five children, was engaged but had not yet married when the war began. He had learned his father's trade and was helping him in the family's clothing store when the Germans took their first census of Jews in the town of Radziejow. Their next project was to inventory all Jewish businesses and confiscate everything of value. Learning of this plan, Markowski hid some of their more expensive items, but the Nazis were alert to such methods and soon discovered the goods and the culprit. Markowski was immediately put in jail.

Within days, the mayor of Radziejow, a German-Pole who knew the Markowski family, intervened on his behalf and arranged for his release, but it was understood that Markowski was a marked man and was no longer safe in the town. With his parents' help, he hired a wagon and a driver. They filled the wagon with hay, and Markowski hid under it until he was safely out of the area.

Markowski was able to cross over into the part of Poland now occupied by the Russians, a division that had been put in place by the Soviet-German nonaggression treaty of August 1939. He settled in Bialystok, found work, and felt relatively safe until the summer of 1941, when the Germans broke their treaty with the Soviet Union and marched east to conquer more territory. Once again, Markowski was forced to flee, this time into Russia itself. In order to maintain himself, he became a trader of merchandise, buying and selling what the Russian people needed, mostly on the black market.

Thousands of Polish Jews had escaped to Russia when the German Army took over in 1941, and the Soviet government, now allied with Poland, offered Polish Jews the opportunity to accept Russian citizenship. It was a difficult choice. While Russian citizenship made them safer and allowed them to exchange their refugee status for that of permanent residents, they also ran the risk of not being allowed to leave Russia after the war was over. For Markowski, there was an ad-

Fabian Markowski, first on left, posed with his extended family just before the war. He was the only one who survived. Courtesy of Elaine McKee.

ditional factor. His fiancée was back in Radziejow, and he hoped to return to her. He refused the offer of citizenship, and the Russian authorities deported him to Siberia.

In Siberia, Markowski was assigned to a logging camp in a forest. However, he managed to get work there as a tailor, mending uniforms for the guards, and so he was able to avoid the more difficult physical labor and the cold weather that most of the prisoners endured. As a tailor, he needed only a needle and thread, but when he requested these supplies, the Russian guards told him he would have to obtain them himself. Always ingenious, Markowski traded his food rations for needles and thread. He went hungry for a few days, but he felt it was worth it in order to avoid cutting down trees in the bitter cold.

Even in Siberia, Markowski continued trading. The give and take of the marketplace seemed to be in his blood, and his skills at bargaining, buying, and selling often helped him to survive the worst conditions. He found that he could exchange some small item of value for having the server dip his ladle into the bottom of the pot, where the soup was thicker and more nourishing. Markowski often did that. Hungry as he was, however, he did have standards. Many years after the war, he told his daughter how he had once managed to get a particularly thick and nourishing serving of soup and then accidentally spilled it on the floor. In spite of what it had cost him, he refused to eat any of it and he watched while others salvaged what they could from his serving.

Markowski was held in Siberia for several years before being released along with other Poles. With a few friends, he traveled to southern Russia, where the weather was warmer. They first settled in Uzbekistan, where they found a community of Jews, many of whom had come from the camps in Siberia or its adjoining areas. Markowski continued buying and selling, and always managed to make a living. In Uzbekistan, he got typhus and almost died, but a friend stayed with him through the crisis, and he survived.

Most Polish Jews returned to Poland and their original homes after the war, hoping to find their loved ones; Markowski was no exception. Cut off from the news and with no mail service reaching him from any of his relatives, he knew nothing of the devastation that had befallen Poland's Jews. When he returned to Radziejow, he learned that his parents, his fiancée, and all his siblings had been murdered. From all that his family had owned, only a few pieces of real estate remained. He arranged with a friend to sell it for him and left for Lodz in western Poland. There, he organized a trading business with two friends who became his partners, but even then, antisemitism remained an issue; the group always used Markowski's name because it sounded less Jewish than the names of the others.

A year after the war, Markowski seized the first opportunity to leave Poland, which now had a Communist government, and escape to Paris. He arrived there on July 14, Bastille Day, the celebration of French independence. When he saw the festivities going on in the city throughout the night, he wrote to friends back in Poland, reporting that indeed, the Parisians did dance all night just as they had heard. From Paris, he paid a visit to cousins in London and attended the Summer Olympics in that city in 1948. Then he returned to Paris and set up a business manufacturing men's clothing.

Paris was not his ultimate destination, however; his goal was to leave Europe and go to the United States, Canada, or Australia. When he met and married **Marguerite Reich** (see **Schoenbrun and Markowski**) in 1949, he was even more determined to create a better life for them and their child, Elaine, who was born in 1950.

Markowski contacted everyone he knew living in North America and Australia to help arrange a visa for him and his family. Whichever visa came first, he said, would determine where they would go. It was the Canadian visa that arrived, and the Markowskis, with the help of the International Refugee Organization, were transferred to a displaced-persons camp in Bremerhaven. It took only five days for their passage to be arranged, and they sailed to Halifax, Nova Scotia, in 1951. From Halifax they took a train to Toronto, where friends were waiting to meet them.

Markowski first opened a manufacturing business with two friends who had been with him in Siberia and Uzbekistan. After two years, he left the partnership and ran his own menswear store, doing alterations and making custom suits. At his death at the age of seventy-four, he had two children and three grandchildren.

Reference

McKee, Elaine Markowski. Telephone interview by the author. July 2006.

Matathias family

The Matathias family of Greece was able to avoid the German dragnet by hiding in a cave in the mountains. Asher Matathias was born in that cave and lived there for the first two years of his life. Most of Nina Atoun Matathias's family was killed, but with the help of Christian friends, she, her husband, and her baby survived.

Jacob Matathias came from the Greek town of Volos. He was a *Romaniote* Jew whose ancestors had lived in that area for many generations and spoke Greek. A young businessman, he made a living as a peddler in the area and had many non-Jewish friends.

Nina was from Salonika. Her family's roots were in Spain, and her native language was Ladino, a form of Spanish spoken by Jews who originated from Spain and Portugal before the expulsion of 1492.

In spite of those differences in their origins, the Matathias and Atoun families were distantly related, and they sometimes got together for holiday celebrations. Nina and Jacob met at one of these events and eventually fell in love. Their decision to marry coincided with the Nazi occupation of Salonika in April 1941. They waited for over a year before setting the wedding date for September 6, 1942. After their marriage, they settled in Jacob's home in Volos, a town in southern Greece with a small Jewish community.

The Nazis had divided Greece into two sections. The southern parts were occupied by the Italians. Although the Italians were considered the enemy, Italian rule over the Greek people was relatively benign. The northern part of the country, including Salonika, was occupied by the Germans, and their regime was harsher and more brutal. Young Jews were drafted into labor brigades, and many died. Jews had to live in ghettos. However, deportations had not yet begun in 1942, and family life continued. Nina's father owned a restaurant in Salonika, and he was allowed to keep his business. The family hoped they would be able to remain in their homes. At the time of Jacob and Nina's marriage, the Greeks had not heard about the deportation and murder of the Jews of Eastern Europe. They assumed they would be relatively safe.

Nina was already pregnant with her first child when Italy surrendered to the Allies in 1943 and ended its alliance with the Nazis. German soldiers marched into Volos, taking over what was once the Italian-occupied zone and beginning a roundup of the Jews.

Jacob and Nina were cautioned by a Christian friend, Stamos, who insisted that they go into hiding in the mountain villages. That warning saved their lives and the life of their unborn child.

With other families, Jacob, Nina, and Nina's younger sister, Mendi, found refuge in a cave. Their gentile protectors brought them food daily, saw to their needs, and warned them when German patrols were on the way so they would have time to hide.

Asher was born in the cave in December 1943 without medical attention of any kind. There were no doctors available, and the local midwife was delayed by a storm and arrived three days later. During Asher's first year of life, German patrols made continual forays into the woods seeking Jews in hiding, but the Matathias family always escaped detection—except once.

Jacob and the other Jewish men worked with the Greek Underground and were away most days, returning in the evening. One day, a German soldier found their hiding place. When he entered, he saw only Nina and her baby. He stood there for a few moments in silence, then remarked that he had "a baby like that" at home in Hamburg. Nina did not say a word, and after a few moments the soldier left. Because Asher was told of this occurrence many times, he grew up without hating Germans. "Although Hitler had many willing executioners," he later wrote, "there were also Germans who protected Jews."

In 1945 the war ended, and the Jews emerged from their caves. Nina discovered that her family, along with 48,000 of the 60,000 Saloniki Jews, had been murdered at Auschwitz. Most of Volos's Jews had been saved, thanks mostly to the help of their Christian neighbors, but also to the Jews' ability to blend in with the rest of the Greek-speaking population.

Almost immediately after World War II, civil war erupted in Greece, and right after their second child, Miriam, was born, Jacob was drafted into the Greek Army to fight the Communist insurgents. He served until 1948.

By then, Israel had become independent. The growing Matathias family had originally planned to immigrate to Israel, but now they were settled in Greece. They had friends and a growing business. A third child, Rachel, was born in 1952. Then another disaster struck. Greece experienced a series of earthquakes that decimated the country. Aid came from America to help the Greek population, and one of the aid agencies was the American Jewish Joint Distribution Committee. Through the JOINT, as it was called, the Matathias family was offered a chance to start a new life in the United States.

Nina and Jacob, still a young couple in their thirties, with Asher, Miriam, and Rachel, arrived in New York on January 30, 1956. Although Jacob and Nina spoke Greek, Spanish, Italian, and French, they did not know a word of English. They settled in a Sephardic Jewish community in Brooklyn and learned to speak a new language. With the help of the Hebrew Immigrant Aid Society, they found an apartment and Jacob found work. Miriam died of leukemia, and a fourth child, Daniel, was born in America. The Matathias children grew up as Americans and prospered in their adopted country.

In 1970, the twenty-six-year-old Asher traveled back to Volos to meet with the Stamos family. Stamos, now an old man, had been responsible for keeping him and his parents alive, bringing them cheese and oil and bread daily, and fresh goat's milk for Asher when his mother could no longer nurse him. Asher had heard many stories about the Stamos family and wanted to meet them. They welcomed him happily into their home.

On that visit, Asher met his wife, Anna. She was visiting her family before her planned immigration to Israel. After they met, plans were changed, and within thirteen days, Asher and Anna married and returned together to the United States.

Asher, with an advanced degree in political science, taught in both secular and religious schools. He ran for political office and was an active member of the community. He and Anna had three daughters. Both of Asher's siblings, Rachel, a teacher, and Daniel, a pediatrician, also married and had children and grandchildren.

The Matathias family maintained a warm relationship with Stamos's children and grandchildren, visiting them regularly.

Reference

Glassner, Martin Ira, and Robert Krell, eds. *And Life Is Changed Forever: Holocaust Childhoods Remembered*. Detroit: Wayne State University Press, 2006.

Meed, Benjamin (1918–2006) and Vladka Meed (1925–)

Individually and together, Benjamin Meed and Vladka (originally known by her Yiddish name, Feigele) Peltel, both from Warsaw, rescued many Jews from the ghetto and helped to maintain countless others who were already in hiding. They met while they were working for the Jewish Underground, and after the war, amid the ruins of Poland, they married and began a new life.

Benjamin Meed (born Miedzyrzecki), his parents, and three siblings, Stella, Mordecai, and Genia, lived in a Jewish area of Warsaw, where his father worked in a tannery. The family was religiously observant and committed to Zionism, but from the age of eight, Benjamin was sent to a public school, and he became proficient in the Polish language. This proved vital to his later survival. He graduated from high school in 1938 and enrolled at a business school, but Germany's invasion of Poland and the beginning of World War II abruptly ended his studies.

By early 1940, Benjamin was invited to join a Jewish Underground that was being organized, and he accepted, becoming the leader of a small group that ran a Jewish lending library, an activity that the Nazis considered illegal. He continued his work with the underground even after he was conscripted into a forced labor battalion. Developing a relationship with one of the German guards, Benjamin was able to smuggle goods out of the ghetto. The German exchanged the goods for food, which was smuggled back in.

Vladka and Benjamin Meed in Lodz, Poland, in 1945. Courtesy of the Ghetto Fighters' House, Israel.

This friendship became widely known among the Jews of Warsaw's ghetto underground, and Meed's assistance was often sought when someone needed to leave or enter the ghetto. One of those who approached him for help in escaping to the "Aryan side" was Feigele, or Vladka, Peltel, who was starting her work as a courier for the underground.

Vladka, the daughter of Shlomo and Hanna Peltel, had a background similar to Benjamin's. Her father worked in a leather factory in Warsaw, and she was one of three siblings. She was educated in secular Yiddish schools rather than the Polish public schools, but her Polish appearance gave her an advantage that many other Polish Jews did not have. The oldest in her family, Vladka took the lead in supporting the others once the war began and especially after her father died of pneumonia in the ghetto.

In addition to her factory work, Vladka organized children's groups for the underground, but after her mother, sister, and brother were deported to Treblinka in 1942, she became even more committed to the cause. In the fall of 1942 she joined the Jewish Coordinating Committee led by Abrasha Blum, Menachem Kirschenbaum, and **Yitzhak Zuckerman**.

With Benjamin's aid, Valdka was smuggled out of the ghetto and worked as a courier for the Jewish fighting force, the *Zydowska Organizaria Bojowa*. Her first assignment was to smuggle a diagram of the Treblinka death camp to Jews outside the ghetto. In addition, she was to obtain weapons for the ghetto fighters, assist those already in hiding with money, food, clothing and false identity papers, and find hiding places for Jewish women and children. In this task, she worked closely with Benjamin, who was known as an expert in constructing hiding places.

By late 1942, after his older sister and her husband disappeared in a round-up, Benjamin also escaped from the ghetto. He brought out his younger brother and sister and his parents, and they all went into hiding. But even with Polish identity cards, they had to move from one safe house to another. At the same time, Benjamin's ties to Vladka, and through her to the underground, became closer. As increasing numbers of Jews escaped the ghetto, Benjamin's skill in finding or creating safe places was in great demand.

Benjamin and Vladka's romantic attachment blossomed during 1943 and 1944, but they kept it secret. Vladka feared that her colleagues would see her as less trustworthy if she had a lover.

When the Warsaw ghetto revolt broke out in April 1943, both Vladka and Benjamin were outside the walls and could only watch as the ghetto was destroyed. However, they worked tirelessly to help rescue the surviving ghetto fighters, finding shelter for them either in safe houses in Aryan Warsaw or in the forests and surrounding villages.

Shortly after the Jewish insurrection, Vladka was arrested and jailed along with fellow underground leader Abrasha Blum. A bribe by her Polish "foster mother" obtained her release. Blum was killed by the Gestapo.

> *I can still see before my eyes the flames from the burning Jewish houses leaping over the ghetto wall, and through the clouds of thick smoke, I can still hear the sounds of explosions and the firing of Jewish guns. . . . I can see the Jews of Warsaw. I see their life, their struggle, their resistance during all the years of Nazi occupation. For it was the Jews' daily struggle, their vibrant drive for survival, their endurance, their spirit and belief, which the Nazis failed to crush, even with their most dreadful atrocities. This was the foundation from which resistance in all its forms was derived.*
>
> —Vladka Meed in *"Ghetto" Dimensions Jewish Resistance in the Warsaw* 7, no. 2 (1993).

A year later, during the Warsaw Uprising of August 1944, both Benjamin and Vladka, still pretending to be Poles, joined the crowd in the streets in support of the first Polish-led rebellion against the Nazis, but they understood that liberation had not yet come. Benjamin took time to relocate the surviving members of his family, his parents and younger sister Genia, from a hut in the cemetery to a safer location. His brother Mordecai had been killed by the Germans in 1943. He then joined Vladka in her apartment.

When the Germans reestablished their rule in the city, they evacuated all the residents and sent many Poles to labor camps in Germany. In an attempt to avoid forced labor, Benjamin bandaged his head so he would appear to be wounded. He and Vladka walked out of the city, and the couple was picked up by a Red Cross wagon. They soon escaped from the wagon and found refuge on a large estate outside Warsaw, where they continued living as Christians. They were allowed to work on the estate, which was still under German control.

Liberation came to Warsaw on January 16, 1945, when the Soviet Army marched in. Benjamin was reunited with the remaining members of his family, and within a few days he and Vladka were married in a Jewish ceremony. With his family, Benjamin and his bride moved to Lodz and opened a leather-goods store. This, however, was only temporary. With antisemitism still rampant in Poland, the family knew it would be impossible to build a new life there. They made their way to Belgium in 1946, and Benjamin and Vladka were among a group of fifty Jews who were sponsored by an international relief committee and the Jewish Labor Committee. Within months they received visas to America. Benjamin's parents chose to remain in Munich and later immigrated to Israel, where they joined their daughter Genia.

A month after the Meeds' arrival in New York, Vladka was working for the Yiddish-American newspaper

> *Yes, we now stand at a distance from the events which shaped our lives and which reshaped history, and, standing at a distance, we look back and remember. For our memory is the ringing warning to all people in all times.*
>
> —Vladka Meed in *"Ghetto" Dimensions Jewish Resistance in the Warsaw* 7, no. 2 (1993).

The Daily Forward, and Benjamin had begun his own fur business. They had two children, Anna and Steven, and later five grandchildren.

Benjamin quickly became active in the community of Holocaust survivors. He was one of the founders of the American Gathering of Jewish Holocaust Survivors, representing more than a hundred thousand survivors and their families in the United States and Canada. He also served as one of the presidents of that organization. He helped organize the 1981 survivors' gathering in Israel with fellow-survivor **Ernest W. Michel** and was chair of the 1983 gathering in Washington, DC.

Vladka wrote a book, *On Both Sides of the Wall*, about her experiences in Warsaw's Jewish Underground. She was director of the Holocaust and Jewish Resistance Summer Fellowship Program and chaired the Education Committee of the American Gathering of Jewish Holocaust Survivors. She was also vice president of the Jewish Labor Committee and director of its Yiddish Culture Holocaust Program.

References

Del Calzo, Nick. "Benjamin Meed." *The Triumphant Spirit: Portraits and Stories of Holocaust Survivors*. Denver, CO: Triumphant Spirit Press, 1997: p. 103.
Meed, Vladka. "Jewish Resistance in the Warsaw Ghetto." *Dimensions* 7, no. 2 (1993).
———. *On Both Sides of the Wall*. Translated by Steven Meed. New York: Schocken Books, 1993.
http://academic.kellogg.cc.mi.us.
http://www.ushmm.org/uia-cgi/uia_doc/query/1?uf=uia_TzMeCC.
http://www.ushmm.org/uia-cgi/uia_doc/query/13?uf=uia_TzMeCC.

Mermelstein, Martin (1923–), and Susan Boyar (née Mermelstein) (1928–)

Martin Mermelstein and his sister Susan Mermelstein Boyar, originally from Czechoslovakia, were the only two members of their family to live through World War II. Because the area of Czechoslovakia where they lived was annexed to Hungary instead of Germany, the war and the wholesale arrest of Jews came much later. This historical fact, combined with luck, gave them a slightly greater chance of survival.

Solomon and Maria (Miriam) Mermelstein were from Racovec, a village in Czechoslovakia. Solomon was a tailor, and Maria a seamstress. They had six children in all, but three died at an early age. The remaining three included Martin, the oldest, Herman, who was two years younger, and Susan, the youngest.

Martin was six years old when the family moved from Racovec to Dorobratovo, which was in the Carpathian Mountains near the Ukraine. The Mermelstein children grew up in this area, attending first a Ukrainian and then a Czech school.

The Nazis took over Czechoslovakia in 1938. They annexed a part of it to Germany and allowed Hungary, an ally of the Germans, to annex the Carpathian region, including Dorobratovo. This political shift at first offered more opportunity to Martin, and he soon left for Budapest and found a position as apprentice to a cabinetmaker. Susan and Herman, only eleven and thirteen, remained at home with their parents.

In 1939 after the war broke out, Hungary adopted antisemitic policies similar to the Nuremberg Laws. They limited Jewish activity and access to education and restricted Jewish ownership of businesses. Although they barred Jews from serving in the Hungarian Army, young Jewish men were drafted into the labor brigades. These groups of workers were used as slave labor for the army. Conditions for these conscripts were terrible, and their treatment at the hands of the Hungarian officers was often brutal. Many of the Jews in the labor brigades died from disease or malnutrition, while others were killed by the soldiers for minor infractions. However, the Hungarian government did not deport its Jews to concentration camps then, and for the most part, Hungarian Jews were not aware of what was happening in the rest of Europe.

Because he was still young, Martin was not taken to a labor brigade. He continued living in Budapest, where he worked and participated in a Jewish youth group. He was hardly aware of the war until March 19, 1944, when the Germans marched into Hungary.

Martin Mermelstein in 1942 at age 19. Courtesy of Martin Mermelstein.

Almost immediately, the German SS, with the full cooperation of the Hungarian Nazis (the Arrow Cross), began rounding up Jews for deportation. The Mermelstein family was taken from its home in Dorobratovo and brought by train to Auschwitz. Solomon and Maria were sent immediately to the gas chambers, but Herman and Susan were allowed to work.

Martin, still in Budapest, was taken into a labor brigade working for the German Army. They marched westward toward Austria and away from the advancing Soviet Army. Their job was to dig traps to prevent the Russian tanks from coming through. The work was difficult physical labor, and they later found out that it was not at all effective in stopping the Russians.

Although the Germans had intended to bring their prisoners all the way to Mauthausen, a labor camp not far from Vienna, there was no time. The Russians caught up with the German Army inside Austria. Suddenly, the prisoners of the labor brigade realized that they were no longer supervised. The Nazis had fled, and the Jewish prisoners greeted the Russian liberators. It was April 2, 1945.

By April, Susan had already been liberated from Auschwitz. The Russians arrived there in January 1945 and freed all those who remained. Most of the prisoners, though, had already left, forced westward on a death march into Germany. Herman was one of those who was forced to march through the snow with no food or water. When he bent down to take a drink from a mud puddle, a German guard shot him to death.

After the war, Martin returned to Dorobratovo to search for his family. He found a neighbor living in what used to be the Mermelstein home.

The neighbor agreed to move out and give him back the house, provided that Martin intended to stay in Dorobratovo. He answered, "If another member of my family will return, he or she will decide."

Martin waited for two days. When no one else came back, he went to Budapest. At a shelter set up by the Jewish community, he found Susan and some other survivors from Dorobratovo. He also learned what happened to his parents and Herman.

With nothing left for them in either Czechoslovakia or Hungary, Martin and Susan began to think of America. They had several relatives living there and could make a new start.

Susan, still under eighteen, was the first to go. She arrived in the United States in 1946 with a group of war orphans and went to live with an aunt in Brooklyn. Martin, already considered an adult, was put on a waiting list. According to the American quota system, he had to wait for a visa.

Martin arrived in New York in 1949 and lived briefly with another aunt. Then he found his own apartment and worked as a cabinet marker for many years. In 1953, he married Lorraine Treiber, and they had a son and a daughter. Martin and his family remained in New York City, and he eventually had five grandchildren.

Susan married in 1950 and had two sons, but her husband passed away within a few years, and she was left a young widow. She later remarried but was again widowed. As of 2006, Susan Mermelstein Boyar lived in North Miami Beach.

References

Mermelstein, Martin. Unpublished memo.
———. Telephone interview by the author. June 2006.

Mettbach, Rosa (1924–)

Rosa Mettbach was born in Vienna into the Sinti branch of the gypsies. Among her entire family, she is the only survivor of the Holocaust. She escaped forced labor and prison many times and was caught and returned repeatedly, but she managed to stay alive.

Mettbach's father and brothers were musicians, performing in some of the best restaurants in Vienna. The family had lived in Austria for generations, and their lifestyle was similar to that of other Austrians. Mettbach's mother often invited non-Sinti neighbors to tea, and Mettbach played with non-Sinti friends. As a young girl she was unaware of the government policy that referred to her people as "the gypsy menace," but that would soon change.

In 1938, the Nazi Army marched into Austria, and with much local support annexed the country. This action was referred to as the *Anschluss,* and its immediate result was that the Nuremberg Laws were put into effect. At first only a thousand of the Austrian Roma and Sinti were arrested, but by August 1938 all eleven thousand had been registered and fingerprinted and had their records filed with the criminal police. Once recorded, the Roma and Sinti were subject to compulsory labor.

Mettbach was fourteen years old when the *Anschluss* occurred and along with other Sinti children, she was barred from school. A little more than a year later, she and her entire family were interned in a holding camp for six to seven months. From there, they were transported to Lackenbach, a camp near the Austria-Hungarian border. Although families were allowed to stay together in the camp, the conditions there were terrible. They slept in damp stables with no sanitary facilities and no comforts of any kind. It was a shock, Mettbach explained, because "we were taken there from . . . our clean houses and caravans into poverty and dirt." Prisoners were forced to work long hours and were beaten for no reason. There were epidemics of typhus, and many people died. Those who tried to escape were either deprived of food and beaten or simply sent off to concentration camps, where conditions would be much worse.

Mettbach and her family remained in Lackenbach labor camp for about a year before being transported to a place called Litzmannstadt, which was actually a separate area of the ghetto in Lodz, Poland. The prisoners were crammed into boxcars for the trip, and Mettbach realized they were going to their deaths. She and a few other young girls crawled out a tiny window in the boxcar just before the train left the station. She never saw her family again, and she later learned that they had all perished.

Mettbach and a friend found refuge in the home of her aunt, who had not yet been arrested, but they stayed there only eight days out of fear they would be discovered. Supplied with a little money that her aunt had given her, Mettbach and her friend lived in the woods, begging for food. One day, her friend went out and never returned. Now alone, Mettbach went back to Vienna and was hidden by her non-Sinti neighbors until she was caught, arrested, and returned to Lackenbach. Back at the camp, she was punished with twenty-five lashes and sent to work hauling rocks, but she was undeterred. After a few months, she escaped again, returning to Vienna, where she once again received help from her neighbors. They gave her food, clothing, and enough money to buy a train ticket to Munich, where she knew there was a large Sinti community.

Mettbach had no identification, and fearing capture again, she hid in the toilet every time the conductor came through the train to check the passengers' papers. Once, the conductor came in suddenly and she had no time to hide, so she pretended to be asleep. Just as the conductor was about to wake her, an old gentleman, realizing her predicament, said, "Let her sleep. You've seen her papers already." This kindness saved Mettbach's life, but there were many more challenges yet to come.

In Munich, Mettbach found what remained of the Sinti community. She was taken in by a family who had not been transported because their son was serving in the German Army. This son, Hamlet Mettbach, fell in love with Mettbach while he was on leave. They married according to the Sinti tradition but could not have a legal German marriage because Rosa had no papers and was an escapee.

For two years, Mettbach lived with her husband's family without being discovered. She became pregnant and gave birth to a son in 1943. By that time, most of Munich's Roma and Sinti had been deported to Auschwitz, but this branch of the Mettbach family remained safe because Hamlet was serving on the Russian front, where manpower was badly needed. Only Rosa, with no papers and a record of escaping, was still vulnerable. After her baby was born, both she and the child became sick, and Hamlet, home on leave, took her to a doctor, who treated her and then reported her to the German police. No amount of pleading or bribes could convince the police not to arrest her, but they did agree, in exchange for cigarettes, not to take the baby with her to prison. Hamlet left their ailing son at a local hospital. He returned to the front, and Mettbach was sent to Auschwitz, where she was tattooed and assigned to the gypsy camp at Birkenau.

Mettbach was in Auschwitz when the extermination of the Roma and Sinti began in late 1943, but a growing labor shortage enabled some of the younger prisoners to escape death. In one final selection, the SS guards were directing prisoners to the right, to work, or to the left, to the gas chambers. Mettbach was sent to the left, but she was not ready to die. She approached the guard and asked, "Why did you send me to the left? I can work." The guard answered, "You have a baby." "I have no baby," she insisted, and the guard sent her to the right. It was April 1944, and her life had been saved once again.

At first, her group was transported to Ravensbrück, but after two weeks, all the young Roma and Sinti women continued on to a factory camp in Germany. They worked twelve hours a day making airplane parts and slept above the factory. Very soon Mettbach figured out the nightly movements of the guards and made a plan to escape. With two other women, she waited until no soldiers were in sight, slid down the drainpipe, and ran. The next morning, they were discovered by the townspeople, turned in, and sent back to the camp.

Once returned, Mettbach was subjected to brutal punishment. First she was beaten, her elbow and head were fractured, then she was placed in a tiny room that was so small that she could not lie down but only stand or kneel. She remained there, in total darkness, for four weeks before being allowed out on Christmas Day. Somehow she survived this ordeal, too, and was still alive when the camp inmates, retreating from the Russian advance, were transferred westward. A friendly guard, a German woman named Sonia, whispered to her, "Hang on. It'll be over soon."

Once again, Mettbach escaped from the freight car and hid in town. This time, with the war nearing its end, she was helped several times by friendly Germans and then by American soldiers, but she trusted no one and made her way south to Munich and her husband and son. She found them alive and well and happy to see her, and with her own birth family all dead, she adopted the Mettbachs as her own.

In 1999 Mettbach, seventy-five years old, was in good health and still living in Munich. Although she gave birth to other children and had a new extended family with many grandchildren, she could not forget the pain of the war and the murder of her entire family. When she first learned of her loss, she cried for a year, Mettbach told an interviewer, and added, "When I think back, I cry again."

Reference

Sonneman, Toby. *Shared Sorrows: A Gypsy Family Remembers the Holocaust.* Hatfield, UK: University of Hertfordshire Press, 2002.

Michel, Ernest W. (1923–)

Ernest Michel, born in Mannheim, Germany, was arrested early in the war, survived five and a half years in many different concentration camps, including Auschwitz, Buna, Buchenwald, and Berga, and lived to become one of the most important leaders of the Jewish world.

Michel was in seventh grade when the Nuremberg Laws proclaimed that he was no longer permitted to attend school. A few years later, at the age of sixteen, he was sent to his first concentration camp. When he said goodbye to his parents, his mother's last words to him were, "Be a good Jewish boy."

From that time until 1945, when World War II ended, Michel was a virtual slave, shipped from one concentration camp to another, living under the worst conditions, surviving only by luck. Five hundred men slept in each barracks, three men to a plank bed, with only straw for mattresses. They did backbreaking work for twelve hours a day and were given only five hundred calories a day—barely enough food to live on. There were no toilets and no water. Life expectancy was four to six months, and Michel watched one friend after another die from starvation, overwork, or disease. He never knew whether he would live another day.

Michel's last transfer was to Auschwitz where he had a unique opportunity. Having gone to the infirmary for treatment of a head wound—the result of a beating by an SS guard—he heard someone asking: "Does anyone here have decent handwriting?" Michel's father had insisted that he practice calligraphy, and Michel tentatively raised his hand and was selected. His job was to register the names of all those due to be gassed in Birkenau (the death camp attached to Auschwitz), and it led to a permanent job in the Auschwitz infirmary and a reprieve from backbreaking manual labor. He did not find out until after the war that his parents were also murdered there in 1942.

In January 1945, as the war was nearing its end, the Nazi guards at Auschwitz marched 58,000 prisoners westward through the freezing cold. When they arrived at the next camp in Germany, twenty thousand were already dead. **Elie Wiesel**, who would later become a famous writer and an outspoken witness of Holocaust crimes, was also at the camp. Although not known to Michel, Wiesel wrote about the same "death march." In April 1945, a group of prisoners was marched out again, fleeing westward once more from Russian advances. This time, Michel and two friends managed to escape, and this saved their lives.

When the war ended, Michel worked briefly for the U.S. military government in Germany before becoming a correspondent for DANA, a German news agency covering the Nuremberg

Ernest Michel, a leader in UJA. Courtesy of Ernest Michel.

> *So here we are, all of us sharing memories of a horrifying past, carrying the evidence on our bodies, but proudly standing together to tell a world. We have survived.*
>
> *Touched by the madness of our nightmare, we have tried to live normal lives. Scarred by the acid of barbarous hatred, we have tried to give love to our children. Forgotten by a silent world, we have tried to avoid cynicism and despair. Despite all we have known, we affirm life.*
>
> —Ernest W. Michel, speaking at the Gathering of Holocaust Survivors in Jerusalem, 1981.

trials. He wrote for them regularly under the byline "Auschwitz Survivor #104995," which referred to the number that had been tattooed on his arm.

Michel later wrote that during the course of the trials, he often had the urge to shout, "Why? What had I done? Why did you kill my parents? My eighty-five-year-old grandmother?" But he knew he was a reporter and not a prosecutor, so he kept silent.

One day during the trial of the notorious Hermann Goering, Michel was approached by Goering's attorney and asked if he would like to meet Goering, who had been reading his articles regularly. Michel agreed, but when he was brought face to face with Goering, he found that he was speechless and unable to shake the hand that Goering held out to him. He left the room without uttering a word.

After the Nuremberg trials ended, Michel was offered a permanent job with the news agency in Germany, but he refused it. Instead, he came to the United States in 1946 as a displaced person. After briefly working as a reporter for a small newspaper, he became a speaker for the United Jewish Appeal (UJA) and worked his way up the ranks of that organization, ending as the executive vice president of the New York branch of UJA-Federation.

One of his main accomplishments was organizing the World Gathering of Jewish Holocaust Survivors that took place in Israel in 1981. The gathering was attended by six thousand survivors from all over the world.

In 1993, Michel wrote *Promises to Keep*, a book about his war experiences. He had committed himself to writing it while still at Auschwitz. As he comforted a dying friend he pledged that if he got out of the camp alive, he would tell their story.

After his retirement, Michel remained active and outspoken. He wanted to prove to the world that you can survive an event as terrible as the Holocaust and go on to live and to bring up a family. Ernest W. Michel had three children and as of 2005 six grandchildren.

References

Michel, Ernest W. "A Survivor and Nuremberg Journalist Recalls a Surreal Meeting with Goering." *Jewish Telegraphic Agency* (November 21, 2005).
———. *Promises to Keep*. Fort Lee, NJ: Barricade Books, 1993.
http://www.jta.org/page_view_story.asp?antarticle=16050&intcatego.

Migdilowitz, Mordecai (1909–2001)

Mordecai Migdilowitz of Lenino, Poland, spent the war years first as a prisoner, then as a partisan, and finally as a soldier in the Russian Army. The sole survivor of his large family, he searched for the remnants of the Jewish community and quickly established a family of his own.

Migdilowitz was the oldest child in the Migdilowitz family, which had three younger daughters and another son. They all lived in Lenino, a village that was at the time in Poland (it is now part of Belarus), where his father, Abraham Migdilowitz, was a carpenter. After attending a Jewish school for only four years, Migdilowitz also learned carpentry.

When World War II broke out and the Germans overran western Poland, Lenino, along with all the other nearby towns, was occupied by the Russians. It was not until the summer of 1941, when the Germans attacked the Soviet positions and drove the Russian Army eastward, that Lenino began to experience Nazi antisemitism.

By July 1941, most of the young men had been conscripted for forced labor, and Migdilowitz was among them. He was sent to Hanzovitch, a work camp near Luninitz. As the year came to an end, more and more young men were brought in, and Migdilowitz waited for his younger brother to arrive, but he never did. The men at Hanzovitch remained in the camp during the remainder of 1941 and throughout most of 1942. They had figured out almost immediately how to escape from the camp but did not do so. The Nazi guards had threatened that if anyone ran away, that person's entire family would be killed.

In the summer of 1942, the Nazis moved forward with their plan to exterminate all the Jews of Europe. They surrounded one town after another, arriving in Lenino in the early days of August. They ordered the peasants living outside the town to dig a pit, then they drove all the Jewish inhabitants of the town toward the pit. Those who refused to go were shot down immediately. The others, men, women, and children together, were lined up in front of the freshly dug trench. As the German soldiers shot, their victims fell into the pit, and then the mass grave was covered over. Among those killed that day were Migdilowitz's parents, his three sisters, and his younger brother.

Migdilowitz was not the only one in Hanzovitch who lost a family that summer. When the prisoners heard that all the Jews in the surrounding villages

---

EXCERPTS FROM "HYMN OF THE JEWISH PARTISANS" (TRANSLATED FROM YIDDISH)

Oh, do not let yourself consider this the end.
Though skies of gray above you threateningly bend.
The longed-for day will come at last, we have no fear.
Our steps will be like drums proclaiming we are here.

From lands so green with palms to lands all white with snow,
We shall be coming with our anguish and our woe.
And where a spurt of blood has fallen on the earth,
There our courage and our spirit have rebirth.
....
This song was written with our blood and not with lead.
It's not a little tune that birds sing overhead.
This song a people sang amid collapsing walls,
With grenades in hands they heeded to the call.

So, never let yourself consider this the end.
Though skies of gray above you threateningly bend.
The longed-for day will come at last, we have no fear.
Our steps will be like drums proclaiming we are here.

were dead, they realized there was no longer a reason to stay in the camp. It was time to escape.

At a prearranged hour, a hundred young Jewish men broke through the fence and ran in different directions. Migdilowitz could hear the German soldiers chasing them with dogs. Although many of the escapees were found and killed, Migdilowitz and several others managed to evade the search parties and disappear into the woods. Their goal was to join the partisans who were active in that area, but they knew that the price of admission was a weapon. Neither Migdilowitz nor his companions had any guns. In order to obtain a rifle, they would have to steal one from a German soldier.

Using his skills as a carpenter, Migdilowitz made a plan. He found wood and carved it to look like a rifle. Brandishing the fake weapon, he and a companion marched up to a Nazi guard. They knocked him down, took his gun, and killed him. With their newly acquired weapon, they repeated the same trick. Now they each had a rifle, and they were welcomed into the partisans.

Most of the partisan groups were Russians, both Christians and Jews. They lived together in the woods, constantly harassing the Germans, attacking them and thwarting their plans when they could. Migdilowitz remained with the partisans until 1944. He left the woods only once, to see what had happened in Lenino. He found that all the Jewish homes were destroyed.

When the Soviet Army returned to the area, chasing the retreating Germans westward, Migdilowitz joined them. He was wounded fighting at Vroclaw and sent to a hospital. For a while, it looked as if he might lose his arm, but after six months his wounds healed. He left the hospital on May 9, 1945, the very day that Germany surrendered.

Migdilowitz was free at last, but he had no home and no family. Wandering from one Jewish village to another, he saw nothing but destruction. Then he heard that a few Jews had returned to Pinsk, which is now part of Russia, and he made his way there. The Jews in Pinsk reported that other Jews were returning from further east, where they had fled from the advancing German Army, and were settling in the nearby villages. One of those who returned was a young woman named Sima. Migdilowitz was already thirty-five years old, and like so many survivors who had lost families, he was anxious to begin a new one. He went to visit Sima to propose carrying a precious gift for her and her family: a pound of butter. On June 5, 1945, the couple married.

Because of his war wound, Migdilowitz was no longer able to work as a carpenter. He found work collecting raw hides and furs and selling them to businesses that processed them. Although his plan was to leave Russia for Israel as soon as possible, Sima was reluctant to go. Her entire family lived in the area, and she did not want to leave them. In deference to his wife's wishes, Migdilowitz decided that they would remain in Pinsk. Their daughter, Zofia, was born there in 1946.

It was not until December 1958, the deadline for Polish nationals to repatri-ate to Poland, that the Migdilowitz family finally decided to leave. It was a difficult decision and one reached only after much debate and family discus-sion. By then, even twelve-year-old Zofia was urging them to move. She was bothered by the persistent antisemitism in Russia and wanted to live in a Jewish state. The family left Russia in March and took a train to Poland.

It took them three more years to arrange for passports. They arrived in Israel in February 1962.

In Israel, Migdilowitz first found work in the construction trades, but with the help of the Jewish Agency, an organization that helps new immigrants, he was able to purchase a grocery store. Since he had grown up in an observant home and had studied briefly in a Jewish school in Lenino, he knew some Hebrew and was able to apply it in this new situation. Sima learned Hebrew in an *ulpan*, a special language school for new immigrants. She then studied for a certificate in bookkeeping so she could add to the family income.

Mordecai Migdilowitz and his family at the wedding of his daughter Zofia to Akiva Berkner in Israel in 1971. Courtesy of Zofia Migdilowitz Berkner.

Migdilowitz worked in his grocery until 1999, two years before his death at the age of ninety-two. Zofia married in Israel and later moved with her husband to New York. Migdilowitz was able to enjoy his three grandchildren before he died.

References

Lazewnik, Grainom. *Personal Miracles: The Guiding Hand of Providence*. Translated by Baruch M. Lazewnik. Brooklyn, NY: Tova Press, 1993.
Berkner, Zofia Migdilowitz. Interview by the author. November 2005. Great Neck, New York.

Moser family

The Moser family of Haslach, Germany, was able to buy steamship tickets to leave Germany just before the war broke out. Arriving in Cuba, they discovered that their visas were not valid, and along with several hundred other Jewish refugees, they were forced to return to Europe.

Alfred Moser (1885–1943) was a businessman dealing in animal hides and horsehair products. His wife, Martha (1892–1978), was an educated woman who had studied in the United States. Once married, she remained at home, caring for their two sons, Eugene (b. 1926) and Helmut (b. 1928). They lived in Haslach, Germany, a small town in the Black Forest region, not far from the French border. Their home, formerly an inn, was large and had many rooms. Behind their house was the warehouse where Alfred kept his inventory and supplies. They were one of only two Jewish families in town, and they owned the only car in Haslach, which was driven by a chauffeur. The family had a housekeeper and employed many workers in the business.

When Hitler came to power in Germany, life changed for the Mosers. By 1935, with the advent of the Nuremberg Laws, Jews were no longer allowed to employ Christian workers or to own businesses. Moser was forced to sell his home and business to local government officials, and the family moved into the nearby city of Freiburg, where Alfred owned a small apartment house. His sons went to school; Eugene, aged twelve, was sent to a school for gifted children and an afternoon Hebrew school, and Helmut (later called Harvey), then ten years old, to a Hebrew day school. The boys experienced little overt antisemitism, although Eugene and Harvey were witnesses to a daily parade of Hitler Youth marching along the street singing. They remembered the threatening words to one song: "When Jewish blood spurts from our knives, then everything will be all right again."

In 1938 conditions for Germany's Jews became worse. The Nazis had annexed all of Austria and the Sudetenland (part of Czechoslovakia), and wherever they were in control, Jews were persecuted. *Kristallnacht* occurred on November 9, 1938, and marked the first pogrom carried out against Jews with the government's sanction. During that night, Jewish shops were destroyed, synagogues were burned, and thousands of Jewish men were arrested. Alfred Moser was among them.

Alfred was sent to Dachau concentration camp, but he managed to bribe his way out and return to his family. Their greatest fear, however, was that the Nazis would arrest children, and Alfred and Martha arranged to smuggle their sons across the border into France, only thirty-five miles away.

A woman came for the boys in the middle of the night. She had a French passport that listed two children. The photos of Eugene and Harvey were substituted for those of the children on the document, and they crossed the border with the woman. She left them, and they never saw her again. The boys were taken to relatives near Strasbourg, a city in eastern France, where they waited for their parents to join them.

Six months later, Alfred and Martha were able to obtain visas for Cuba and steamship tickets to sail on the *S.S. St. Louis*. They boarded the ship in Hamburg on May 13, 1939. Eugene and Harvey were taken by their French cousins to the port in Le Havre, where they boarded the same ship, and the Moser family was reunited—at least for a while.

The voyage on the *S.S. St. Louis* was pleasant and carefree. Captain Schröder gave strict orders that the Jewish passengers were to be treated "like everyone else," and even the SS troops who were on board left them alone for the seven days of the trip. When the ship docked in the Havana harbor, however, the Mosers, along with most of the other passengers, discovered that the Cuban visas they had purchased in Germany were not valid and they would not be allowed to disembark. Valid visas could be purchased for five hundred dollars each. Since most of the refugees had not been permitted to take any money out of Germany, a payment of that amount was impossible.

The Moser family outside their home in Germany, 1935. Courtesy of Harvey Moser.

An American-Jewish relief organization, the Joint Distribution Committee (JOINT), undertook to collect the money required for the visas, and the Cuban president agreed to wait forty-eight hours. The JOINT did return with most of the money, but the forty-eight-hour deadline had passed, and the Cuban president refused to let the Jews in.

Desperate to find a place of refuge where they would be safe from the Nazi threat, the passengers formed a committee to find a country that would accept them. With the cooperation of Captain Schröder, they began sending telegrams to one country after another. Their first appeal was to President Roosevelt of the United States. With the ship sailing up the coast of Florida, in sight of America's shores, the refugees waited for an answer to their request. It came within a short time. The President refused to accept the four hundred refugees, explaining that because of the depression in America, there were no jobs.

Other responses had also arrived, but most were negative. The Dominican Republic was ready to accept them but demanded a large sum of money from each applicant. The committee, totally unfamiliar with that land, held out for some other place. Shanghai was also granting visas, but that would entail a return to Europe and passage on another ship. Most of the refugees had no money left for that.

As the *S.S. St. Louis* turned eastward, they received the news that the stateless passengers could be divided up; Holland, Belgium, France, and England each agreed to accept one quarter of the refugees. Less than a month after it had sailed for Cuba, the ship was back in Antwerp, Belgium.

The Mosers were among those sent to France. As soon as they landed, they were loaded onto an open boat to cross the English Channel and be transported to Paris. Eugene and Harvey were taken to a Jewish orphanage outside the city, while Alfred and Martha went to a refugee center near Lyons. They were penniless.

In September 1939, as soon as Germany invaded Poland, the French declared war on Germany. Air raid warnings and drills were instituted, and in the orphanage where the Moser boys were living, all the children were taken to shelters during the night.

Countries of Refuge for Jews, 1933–1943		
Country	Number Admitted (in Thousands)	Percentage of Refugees Taken In
United States	190	23.5
Palestine	120	14.8
England	65	8.1
France	55	6.8
Belgium	30	3.7
Holland	35	4.3
Switzerland	16	1.9
Spain	12	4.6
Other European countries	70	8.8
Argentina	50	6.2
Brazil	25	3.1
Uruguay	7	0.8
Bolivia	12	1.4
Chile	14	1.7
Other Latin American countries	20	2.4
China	25	3.1
South Africa	8	1.0
Australia	9	1.1
Canada	8	1.0
Other countries	40	4.9
Total:	*811*	*100.0*

—Martin Gilbert. *The Holocaust: Maps and Photographs.* New York: ADL and Braun Center for Holocaust Studies, 1992, pp. 27–28, map 12.

Harvey remembered those times as particularly frightening. He began to wet his bed at night, and this added another tension to the fear of the planes flying overhead. But despite the onset of war, Eugene and Harvey learned French and attended school. They heard almost nothing from their parents, and the brothers grew apart at that time. Eugene, two years older, was involved in sports and had a set of friends, while Harvey was teased and disliked by the other boys because of his bedwetting, and he felt isolated.

Then in the spring of 1940 the Nazis invaded France. The Moser parents understood that their temporary haven was no longer safe. Martha was able to get in touch with her cousin, René Weil, who lived in the United States. Weil sent an affidavit guaranteeing that the Moser family would be cared for and would not become wards of the state. The affidavit arrived just days before France fell, and once again, the Mosers managed to obtain steamship tickets, this time on the *S.S. Champlain*, the last ship to leave France. The Moser boys were taken by their Parisian cousin to the port. On the way, they passed hundreds of refugees at the train stations, who were trying to make their way south, into the free zone.

This time, the transatlantic voyage was not so pleasant. The ocean was full of German U-boats, and there were lifeboat drills every day. The day the *S.S. Champlain* docked in New York harbor, June 22, 1940, Hitler's troops were marching down the Champs Elysées in Paris. The Mosers were safe in New York. Later they learned that their ship was sunk by German U-boats on its way back to Europe.

Like most refugees from the Holocaust, Alfred began working almost immediately, selling pencils and then office supplies. Martha worked with him while the boys went to school. She continued the business alone after Albert died in 1943.

As soon as Eugene turned eighteen, he was drafted into the U.S. Army and sent to Europe, where he fought in the Battle of the Bulge. After a bout in a military hospital being treated for frostbite, he returned to Germany as part of the American Army of Occupation. After three years in the army and several years at college, he married his wife, Phyllis, and they adopted two children. Eugene recently retired from a long career at IBM in Poughkeepsie, New York.

Harvey studied at New York University and then New York Medical School. He graduated and immediately went into the U.S. Army, where he served as a doctor at an army base in Nuremberg from 1956 to 1958. After his army service, he specialized in dermatology and married his wife, Harriet. Harvey and Harriet Moser had two children and then three grandchildren.

References

Thomas, Gordon, and Max Morgan Witts. *Voyage of the Damned*. New York: Stein & Day, 1974.
Moser, Harvey. Interview by the author. December 2005. Great Neck, New York.

Munic, Sara (1926–)

While still a teenager, Sara Levenberg Munic of Liepāja, Latvia, was arrested and taken to work as a slave laborer. Dragged from one camp to another by the retreating Nazis, she and her younger sister, Henie, although starved and sick, were the only survivors in her family.

Munic's parents, Yitzhak and Raule Levenberg, had lived in Latvia their entire lives. They had three daughters, Sara, who was the oldest, Ella (b. 1928), and Henie (b. 1929). They lived in a roomy apartment in a mixed neighborhood of Jews and gentiles, and despite a considerable amount of antisemitism, they lived a comfortable life. The girls went to a Yiddish-language school, and their social life was centered on the Jewish Sports Club and the Zionist Youth Movement.

Munic was fifteen years old when the Soviet Union annexed Latvia to Russia, but that political situation did not last for much more than a year. On June 24, 1941, the Germans decided to ignore the Molotov-Ribbentrop Pact, the non-aggression treaty they had made with Russia in August 1938. They bombed Liepāja, the second largest city in Latvia and an important port on the Baltic Sea, and burned down its harbor area and granary storage facilities. Then they took over the town.

The Nazi occupiers quickly turned their attention to the Jews. They comman-deered all their valuables, including not only jewelry and gold, but radios, bicycles, and even copper pots and pans. Then they began taking Jewish men away in trucks for slave labor. The remaining Jews later learned that some of the men were transported to the forests and shot by German and Latvian soldiers.

Slowly, most of the men disappeared from the city. Those who remained, both men and women, had to wear a yellow patch in the shape of a Star of David on their clothing. They were no longer permitted to walk on the sidewalks.

In December 1941, the Germans began to implement the "final solution." All Jews were ordered to stay in their homes so they could be found easily. The Nazis went from house to house collecting Jews, took them into the nearby forest, and shot them. Yitzhak's family and much of Raule's family were killed in this first roundup, but the Levenbergs were allowed to remain in Liepāja. Because Yitzhak was working for the German Army, he had a special permit issued by the SS that excused him and his family from deportation.

By 1942, however, time was running out. There was only a small number of Jews remaining in the city, and now those Jews were forced into a ghetto. Food became scarcer, and for a while the Levenbergs depended on a gentile woman who had once been the girls' nanny. She sold articles of their clothing in the marketplace for food and sneaked it into the ghetto for the family. Soon even this became impossible, and the extra food rations ceased.

All the girls worked, even Henie, the youngest; this was the only way to survive. After September 1943, when the entire ghetto was liquidated and all remaining Jews were taken to Kaiserwald concentration camp, the Levenbergs were among the first to volunteer for work. It was, they understood, a ticket to life. In the camp, near Riga, Yitzhak continued working for the German Army, Raule became a housekeeper for a German officer, and Munic and her sisters learned how to repair parts for damaged trains and engines. They worked ten hours a day and were given a single meal of soup and bread. Every night, the prisoners lay in their bunks and talked of food, but besides the relentless hunger, there was no deliberate cruelty there. Prisoners were not beaten or killed for minor infractions.

This relative leniency changed on July 27, 1943. On that day, all the prisoners were assembled. A selection was made, and the Levenberg parents, along with many who were old or too sick to work, were sent to Auschwitz, where they were murdered in the gas chambers.

Now only Munic, Ella, Henie, and their aunt Mary, their mother's youngest sister, remained. They were taken with the other workers to have their heads shaved. Then they were given uniforms, and sent back to work for another few weeks. Munic could hear the Russian guns as the Soviet Army approached their camp, and she hoped that liberation would come soon. The Germans loaded all the prisoners onto boats and crossed the Baltic Sea to Danzig, once a free port but now a German city. From Danzig they were taken by barge and then on foot to nearby Stutthof.

Stutthof was a concentration camp. It did not have a gas chamber, but it did have a crematorium and a sadistic German commandant named Max. Max wore boots and a leather coat. He carried a whip, which he used freely, and was always accompanied by two large dogs. The Levenberg sisters remained here for only a month before they were sent with a large group to Stolp, another labor camp. In Stolp they worked from September 1944 to March 1945.

The three sisters became progressively weaker. Each time the Russian Army drew closer, the prisoners were forced to leave once again. After several intermediate stops, they were delivered back to Stutthof in April 1945. From there, they were piled onto barges with a group of Norwegian prisoners of war, and under unbelievably crowded conditions and with almost no food, they roamed the sea.

One morning, they discovered that the German guards had disappeared. Suspicious, the Norwegian soldiers discovered that the barge had been wired with explosives and was set to be blown up. The Norwegians disarmed the charge, maneuvered the boat to shore, and helped the prisoners off. But the SS soon returned. They began shooting at the starving and weakened prisoners, herded them together, and brought them to an open field, where they awaited the arrival of another boat. As they watched, that boat was blown up by British war planes. All those on board—mostly Jewish prisoners—were killed.

On May 3, when the British arrived and liberated them, most of the prisoners were too sick to celebrate their freedom. Munic's sister Ella died in a hospital one week after liberation. Sixteen-year-old Henie was also seriously ill but managed to survive. After recuperating in a hospital in Neustadt, Germany, Munic and her sister were sent by the United Nations Relief and Rehabilitation Administration to Sweden where Henie spent some time in a sanatorium.

While Henie recovered, Munic found a job caring for a sick woman. In Sweden, she met her husband, Abe Munic, a survivor from Poland, and the couple soon married. Their first son, Chaim Yitzhak, was born in Sweden,

> *The whole experience is not something one can forget. I'm on Prozac now. It helps a little but now that I live alone, it's even harder. When I was working and had a husband and children at home, I was so busy with day-to-day living that I didn't think much about it. But in bed at night, I'd wake up in a sweat because everything came back. . . . But I am still a believer.*
>
> —Sara Levenberg Munic

and the Munic family remained there until 1951. That year, with papers from Abe Munic's relatives, they arrived in Hartford, Connecticut. Three other children were born in the United States. In 1954, Munic sent for Henie, who was married with a daughter of her own. Henie and her family settled in New York.

After her children were grown, Munic took a job in an insurance company. She worked her way up from file clerk to retire twenty-one years later as a supervisor in the accounting department. Munic had seven grandchildren. Abe died in 1987.

Reference

Glassner, Martin Ira, and Robert Krell, eds. *And Life Is Changed Forever: Holocaust Childhoods Remembered.* Detroit: Wayne State University Press, 2006.

Muzylowski, Sara Lusia (1922–)

Sara Lusia Gruber Muzylowski was a young married woman living in Lvov, Poland, when war broke out. She and her husband, Roman Gruber, were rescued by a Christian friend who risked his life first to save Muzylowski and Roman and then to save Muzylowski and her baby. With her friend's help, Muzylowski escaped many times from the Nazis as well as from the threats of hostile neighbors, finally building a new life with her rescuer. But she could never overcome the horrors of the war.

Muzylowski grew up in the city of Lvov in a large family. The household consisted of her parents, Nathan and Jetti Gruber, her maternal grandfather, Aron Korensztajn, three brothers, and three sisters. The family began to fall victim to the Nazis within the first days of occupation, in 1941, when Muzylowski's mother and grandfather were taken away and killed.

Fearing the worst, Muzylowski's husband, Roman Gruber (he and Muzylowski had had the same last name when they married) asked a gentile friend, Roman Muzylowski, to save them by taking them to Toporow in Radzechow county, where Roman Muzylowski and his father lived. He agreed, and they walked the eighty kilometers to his home at night and hid in cornfields during daylight so they would not be discovered by the Nazis. When they arrived in Toporow it was September 1942.

After a short time in hiding, Roman Gruber secretly returned to Lvov to make sure his family was safe, but as soon as he showed himself in town, he was recognized and arrested. Roman Gruber never returned to Toporow or to his wife, who was now pregnant.

Muzylowski remained in hiding in her friend's home, but soon the neighbors discovered her and began blackmailing her to maintain their silence. At first she paid, but they kept demanding more money, and Roman Muzylowski, realizing the danger, took Muzylowski to a shelter in the woods. Alone in this hiding place, at the end of 1942, she gave birth to her son. Because the Germans were everywhere in the woods, no one dared to help her. Finally, Roman Muzylowski arrived. He took the infant to the home of a peasant family. The peasant woman washed the little boy and returned him to his mother. Remaining alone in the woods, the new mother nursed her child and waited for the war to be over.

Many of the Poles in the neighborhood remained hostile to her, however. A man named Senderski said to the woman who had washed Muzylowski's infant in those first days after his birth, "[Roman] Muzylowski is hiding a Jewish woman and child." Although the peasant defended the Jews' right to live, the blackmailer would not give up. He demanded more money from Muzylowski. If he got what he asked, he promised to leave the town and forget about her.

Once again, Roman Muzylowski came to her rescue. He signed over his house to Senderski in return for his promise not to bother or threaten her. Still, Roman Muzylowski was not content that he had done enough. He asked his priest to get false birth certificates from Lvov for Muzylowski and her infant son. The priest was afraid, but he finally agreed to purchase the appropriate papers for them. In exchange for these papers, Muzylowski had to swear that she would never tell anyone where she got them.

Muzylowski and her baby lived as Christians for a while, but eventually, the fear and tension became too much for her. In February 1943, they returned to Roman Muzylowski's home, where he prepared an underground hiding place for mother and child. From the underground dampness, poor diet, and lack of air, the baby became sick. He developed rickets and then pneumonia, and he was plagued with sores. Although Muzylowski had continued to nurse him, her own diet was meager. Sometimes she had only grass to eat.

While Muzylowski hid, Roman Muzylowski tried to keep in contact with her remaining family in Lvov. He would sneak into the ghetto whenever he could and bring food for her father and her one surviving brother. One day, the Germans noticed him lingering outside the ghetto, carrying food. They beat him so severely on his head that the pain and symptoms persisted long afterward.

In Toporow, the Nazis had taken over Roman Muzylowski's house and allowed him only one room in which to live. This added to Muzylowski's fears, and she almost never emerged from her underground shelter except at night. She was well aware that even if she managed to evade the Gestapo, their neighbors might very well deliver her to the Germans in exchange for two liters of vodka or a few yards of fabric. In order to avoid suspicion, Roman Muzylowski made a hole in a tree near Muzylowski's hiding place and left food there to retrieve during the night. Only once in a while did she have the luxury of emerging from her hole and being able to wash herself and her baby in Muzylowski's tiny room.

By 1944, the Soviet Army was approaching and by the fall of that year, liberation had come to Toporow. Muzylowski later wrote, "I didn't know, should I rejoice or cry." She soon realized that it was too early to rejoice. Bands of men calling themselves the Bandera after their founder, a Ukrainian Fascist and antisemite, now began to roam the forests murdering Jews and Poles. Despite the danger, Roman Muzylowski led Muzylowski through the woods toward Lvov. Stopping in the nearby town of Buski, Roman Muzylowski remained with the baby while Muzylowski went to look for her family. She found no one and returned to Buski and to Roman Muzylowski and her baby son. They were now her only family.

In 1945, Sara and Roman Muzylowski were married and had put their names on a list of those wanting to settle in "regained territories," the areas that had been taken back from Germany. They were given permission to settle in Glubczyce, in Silesia.

In December 1945, Muzylowski returned once again to Lvov searching for family. She met two men who were looking for her. One of them told her that he had been with her first husband, Roman Gruber, in Mauthausen and could confirm that he had survived the war and returned to Lvov to look for his family. After three days in the city, he died of weakness and starvation. His friend gave her the certificate ascertaining that Roman Gruber had been in Mauthausen from 1942 until May 1945 and had still been alive when she and Roman Muzylowski were married.

After everything she had gone through, this last bit of news seemed to be the final blow for Muzylowski. From that time on she lost much of her strength and health and could not work. Her new husband, too, was forced to go on a pension as a result of the injuries he had sustained when the Nazis beat him. The Muzylowskis and their son remained in Silesia, living under Communist control. There is no record of their deaths or of the fate of their son.

Reference

Muzylowski, Sara Gruber. Survivors testimony. Record Group #104, Series 3 at YIVO Archives, 15 West 16th St. New York, NY.

N

Narotzky, Fanny (née Lehrer) (1937–), and Eva Lehrer Kawalek (1914–)

Fanny and Eva Lehrer, originally from Borszczow, Poland, were among the relatively few Jewish survivors who immigrated to Germany rather than away from it. Living in the wreckage of postwar Europe, Eva and Fanny were able to thrive and lead successful lives.

Borszczow, where the Lehrers lived, was a small town in Galicia, a region of Poland. In 1939, when the Nazis invaded Poland, Galicia came under Russian rule. Two years later, the Molotov-Ribbentrop Pact was broken, and German soldiers began to take over the lands that had belonged to the Soviet Union. Russia, now in a defensive war, mobilized its troops, and Narotzky's father was drafted.

One of Narotzky's first memories was saying goodbye to her father when he left with the Soviet Army. It was 1941, and she was four years old. Narotzky kissed him goodbye, and he promised to return very soon. He did try to return. Hearing that the Germans had occupied the town, he left the Russian Army and began making his way back home, but he was captured by the Nazis and killed.

No sooner had the Russians left Borszczow, the Germans came. Narotzky and her mother, Kawalek, were living with her maternal grandmother and an uncle. Kawalek's family, the Hessings, was large and respected, and Kawalek was an only daughter with seven brothers, who looked after her and her child. One of the Hessing brothers, Simon, whose work as a photographer took him to many different towns, soon found out what was happening to the Jews in other areas. He knew it was only a matter of time before all the Jews in Borszczow would be rounded up and killed, too, so he took steps to prepare to save his family.

Simon offered Mr. Blaszkow, a gentile farmer who lived nearby, gold coins and jewelry in exchange for a safe hiding place. Blaszkow agreed, and together, he and Simon dug a large hole under Blaszkow's barn, with an entrance underneath the outhouse, and then built a secure bunker where the family could hide. They both understood very well the danger in which they placed themselves. It was illegal to hide a Jew, and if Blaszkow were discovered, he would pay with his life, so the work was done only at night. Once completed, Simon found a way to bring electricity into the bunker by connecting with the main line. This enabled them to have some light, a radio, and a hot plate to cook meals.

Once their hiding place was completed, the Lehrers and the Hessings had to decide when to enter it. They understood that once they went down, they would not be able to come up until the war was over, so they waited. During that time, five-year-old Narotzky witnessed instances of violence and cruelty that continued to haunt her into her adult years. One day, she saw two Nazis on a motorcycle chasing a woman carrying a baby in her arms. She watched as they shot the woman. At that moment, her grandmother pulled her away from the window so that she would not see them throw the baby against the wall to kill him.

Kawalek and Narotzky were almost murdered themselves. Another Hessing brother, hearing that there might be a roundup of Jews that night, advised his sister to stay with a relative who had her own bunker under her house. They followed his advice. The following morning they heard shooting in the street, and both families, twelve people in all, rushed down into the bunker. From underneath the floor, they heard the German soldiers enter and begin to shout for the "Jewish pigs" to come out. Trembling, afraid to breathe, they listened as the soldiers beat and then shot their dogs and trashed the house. Only after they were sure that the Nazis had left did they came out of hiding.

It was becoming more and more dangerous to be a Jew in Borszczow. Most had already been deported to work camps in the east, and the family realized that it

Fanny Lehrer (later Narotzky) just before her family descended into the bunker. Courtesy of Fanny and Alfie Narotzky.

was time for them to disappear. Narotzky was carried from the house by an uncle. The night was dark. Kawalek walked by her side, and they entered their bunker. Other family members were hidden in other bunkers. When the last roundup of Jews was finished, neither the Hessings nor the Lehrers were found.

Living underground was primitive and difficult. There was a pail for a toilet and a large barrel of water that was filled once a week by Blaszkow, who also brought them food. Narotzky spent her time learning to read and write and tell time. She also listened to the BBC, the English radio station, on their secret radio, but she suffered terribly from hunger.

"One of my jobs was to peel the potatoes," Narotzky later wrote. During the war, potatoes were very scarce, and she became skilled at removing the skin so carefully that not even a tiny bit was wasted. When she did a particularly good job, she would receive a little extra food that night.

The Lehrers and the Hessings spent eighteen months together in the bunker, always in fear of their lives. There were several narrow escapes when Simon Hessing left the bunker to find out what was happening. One night he and his brother Leo left their respective bunkers to meet and exchange news, but they were discovered by the Ukrainian police. Leo was killed in this encounter, but Simon managed to escape and return safely.

In May 1944 when the Russians reoccupied their town, Narotzky, now seven years old, was carried out of the bunker. She was so weak by then that she could not walk, and it took her several months to regain her strength. Since their old house had been destroyed, Kawalek found a new place to live and waited until the war was over in the West before leaving Russian-occupied territory.

From Galicia, they traveled first into Silesia, a part of Poland already under Communist rule. Here, in 1946, Kawalek met and married Leon Kawalek, a survivor from Borszczow who had lost his own family. In 1947, Eva and Leon Kawalek gave birth to another daughter, Narotzky's half-sister, Cara, and Leon officially adopted Narotzky as well. From Silesia the new family continued westward to Prague, where officials from the Joint Distribution Committee, a Jewish charity, took them to Munich, where they joined Kawalek's older brother. From Munich they moved to Berlin. Their original intention was to go to the United States, but the immigration papers were slow in coming. In the meantime, Leon needed to make a living. He started a business in Berlin with his only surviving relative. Three years later, when the immigration papers arrived, things were going well and the Kawaleks chose to remain in Berlin.

To keep her daughter from what she regarded as the "bad influence and poor morality" of the German girls, Kawalek sent Narotzky to boarding school in Switzerland when she was thirteen. She was the only Jew in the school, and although she hated being away from her parents, she spent three years there. She returned to Berlin to finish her baccalaureate degree (the equivalent of two years of college) and began studying at the University of Berlin. In 1961, after three semesters, she left her studies to marry.

Fanny met her husband, Alfred Narotzky, on a ski vacation. Alfred, an American Jew who was working in Berlin, lived with Narotzky in Germany for many years. In 1979, the Narotzkys and their three children, Philip, Clarissa, and Nadia, moved to the United States but continued to spend a great deal of time in Germany visiting Kawalek and other relatives.

Kawalek, who has been a widow for many years, was still living comfortably in Berlin in 2006. Of her seven brothers, two were killed in the war, and five survived. Simon, now deceased, also settled in Berlin but moved to Israel after his children had completed their high school educations.

References

Narotzky, Fanny. "Living Through Darkness: Life in a Bunker." *The New Light* 47 (winter 2004): p. 19.
Narotzky, Fanny Lehrer. Interview by the author. October 2005. Manhasset, New York.

Nathan family

Raymonde and Jacques Nathan and their daughter Muriel were all native Parisians, and so they felt certain that Nazi roundups and threats did not apply to them. Then in 1941, Raymonde's cousin went to Gestapo headquarters and never returned. For the first time, the Nathans feared for their lives. They fled south to the free zone and from there to Algeria.

Jacques was a respected professor at the Sorbonne in Paris, and his wife Raymonde was from an old and respected French Jewish family. They were surrounded by family and friends, both Jewish and gentile, and knew no Jewish immigrants. Jacques believed that the right thing to do was to simply ask the Germans to allow them to go into the free zone, the part of France not yet occupied by the Nazis. He assumed the answer would be yes. Then Raymonde's cousin's husband, the proprietor of an antique store where the Nazis often did business, did exactly what Jacques had suggested. He dressed in his best clothes, took with him an antique walking stick to use as a bribe, entered police headquarters, and was never seen again.

Suddenly, the Nathans realized the seriousness of the threat, and their first action was to send their daughter, five-year-old Muriel, to safety. They arranged for Muriel to be taken south by their housekeeper. Although this was a risk, they felt confident that the plan would succeed. Muriel was a blonde child with blue eyes. When a German soldier came through the car asking for identity papers, the housekeeper handed over her identity card and said Muriel was her daughter. There were no questions asked, and they were safe in the free zone.

The next step was for Jacques and Raymonde to follow them, and this was more dangerous. However, there were many French people who would smuggle refugees to the free zone, sometimes for money and sometimes for idealistic reasons. The Nathans made the necessary arrangements and traveled to the border town to meet their contact at a farm. They waited at the farm until dark. Just before they were ready to leave, two German soldiers arrived on bicycles. Raymonde, who was always conscious of looking "very Jewish," was more frightened than she had ever been in her life. She and Jacques sat quietly, their hearts pounding, without saying a word. But the soldiers were not interested in them; they had only come to buy eggs from the farmer. As soon as the Germans left, the farmer's son took the Nathans down a little path into the woods. They crossed over with no problems and were reunited with Muriel.

In 1942, just months after their arrival in the south, the German Army occupied the free zone and began arresting Jews there as well, but the Nathans

Raymonde Nathan was still living independently in her Paris apartment at the age of 95. Courtesy of Sylvie Weil.

kept one step ahead of them. They were able to book passage on a ship across the Mediterranean to Algeria. There Jacques found a teaching job at a Jewish *lycée* (high school) in the city of Algiers, and the family remained there until World War II was over. When they returned to Paris, Jacques resumed his position at the Sorbonne, and Raymonde became an innovative psychologist and had an active practice. Muriel resumed her schooling.

In 1958 Muriel was in a car accident. She was seriously injured and became paralyzed. She never married and eventually died of cancer when she was sixty-five. Jacques had predeceased Muriel, but Raymonde lived into her nineties. She continued practicing as a psychologist until she was ninety-one. After Muriel's death in 2001, she retired. She still remembers those difficult days and often tells stories of their experiences during the war.

Reference

Weil, Sylvie (Raymonde Weil Nathan's niece). Interviews by the author. December 2005 and May 2006. New York, New York.

Newfield family

Although the Newfield family of Vienna had ties to America, they were unable to leave Europe in time to avoid deportation to the concentration camps. They were found after the war by an American brother-in-law serving

Alice and Armin Newfield with their three sons, Bernhard, Marcel, and Arnold (center) shortly after the war. Courtesy of Jill Newfield Joseph.

in the U.S. Army and brought to America, but the years of degradation and suffering took a toll even on the youngest in the family.

Lisl Hofbauer Newfield (1912–1992) and her husband Armin Newfield (1903–1990) lived in Vienna before the war with their three sons, Bernhard (b. 1934), Eric (1936–1936), who died in infancy, and Marcel (1938–1996). Armin had been educated as a rabbi but chose to go into business and was a successful grain merchant.

The Newfields lived a comfortable, middle-class life until the Nazis annexed Austria and began putting the Nuremberg Laws into effect. After *Kristallnacht* and the destruction of synagogues and Jewish shops throughout Germany and Austria, the Newfields fled to Westerbork in Holland, where a refugee camp had been set up by the Dutch. Less than a year after the war officially began, Germany invaded Holland, and once more the family was faced with Nazi antisemitism and terror. The Nazis took over Westerbork and using the existing infrastructure, turned it into a transit camp. Lisl became pregnant in Westerbork and a son, Arnold, was born there in February 1942. In March 1944 the Newfields were shipped off. Lisl and the three boys were taken to Ravensbrück, and Armin to Buchenwald.

Ravensbrück was a women's concentration camp that housed both Jews and gentiles. In addition to the work assigned to prisoners, Lisl organized the women into a special squad to dispose of the bodies of those who died each night in order to prevent more disease. Her children, along with other youngsters, were left to their own devices during the day and spent most of their time foraging for food. One evening Bernhard encountered a German soldier, who handed him a container of potato salad that he did not want. For nine-year-old Bernhard, always hungry, this was a feast. Marcel, only five or six years old, went to the camp's bakery every day to collect crusts of bread from the Roma and Sinti who ran the bakery.

Lisl and her sons remained in Ravensbrück for approximately a year. In March 1945 they were transported to Bergen-Belsen, which was considered the worst of the camps. Newfield had the forethought to be one of the first on the train so she could stake out a place in the corner for her family. Nevertheless, the three-day journey from Ravensbrück to Bergen-Belsen was horrifying. Remembering that terrible journey to the camp, Lisl later wrote, "To die was easy."

"We were about forty people," she described in her short memoir, "and the doors were never opened. We had hardly any room to sit. And we didn't get any sleep. We had to relieve ourselves in that train. You can't imagine the smell."

When the train stopped, the prisoners were all exhausted, but they were told there was a three-mile walk to the camp. With her youngest child, Arnold, only three years old, Lisl knew that it would be impossible to carry him all the way. She was told that she could put Arnold on the truck, but she hesitated, worrying whether she would lose him forever. Finally, she decided to chance it. She placed him on the truck and began walking with her other two sons. But Marcel, who was six and a half, became exhausted and said he could no longer walk. Lisl's narrative continued, "It just so happened that a woman, she gave up . . . so a soldier came and shot her to death. So I said to the kid, 'You see if you can't walk what will happen?' So he started to walk."

When they arrived at the camp, Lisl and another mother went to look for the children that had been placed on the truck. It took them a while to find the building where they had been taken. When the two women opened the door, a female SS officer asked what they wanted. Newfield was careful not to ask permission to take the children. Instead, she said, "I came to pick up the children." Other German soldiers answered, "No. You can't take them; they go to the slaughter," but the German woman whispered, "I will give them to you but . . . they will shoot." Newfield answered, "If you have to shoot, go ahead and do it." She and the other mother took their children and left without turning back. The Germans started shooting into the air. The women kept walking. "Again," wrote Lisl, "luck was on my side."

The Newfields were in Bergen-Belsen when the British Army liberated the camp on April 15, 1945. During those last days they suffered most from hunger and thirst. The Allied bombings had destroyed their source of bread and water, and everyone went hungry, even the Germans. When the British soldiers came in, they brought water and food, but Lisl understood that eating too much could be fatal in their condition. She forbade her children to eat anything, and they all survived.

Even after the war, however, disease remained a serious threat to all the occupants of the camp. Lisl and Arnold contracted typhus and were taken to hospitals. Bernhard and Marcel remained alone in the camp. Then Lisl contracted spinal meningitis. There was no medicine available, but somehow, she survived.

During Lisl's recovery, an American soldier attached to the British Army showed her a photo and asked her if she recognized the woman in the picture. It was Lisl's half-sister, Edith, born to her mother and her second husband.

Lisl's mother had remarried and gone to live in the United States before the war. This soldier was Edith's husband, Fred, who had been looking for the family. One by one, he found all the boys and brought them together in the displaced-persons camp at Bergen-Belsen, but Armin's whereabouts were still unknown.

Finally they found him. In January 1945, Armin had escaped from a German transport out of Buchenwald when the Germans evacuated the camp ahead of the advancing Russian front. He returned to Holland, and eventually the family was reunited in Amsterdam. They were taken in by a gentile family named Singer and lived in a room behind the Singers' bookbinding factory.

The entire Newfield family arrived in America in June, 1947 and a fifth son, William, was born in March 1948. The Newfields first lived in lower Manhattan, and the children went to an Orthodox Jewish school, where their experiences with antisemitism continued. Marcel remembered being beaten up by neighborhood children as he walked to school wearing his *yarmulke*.

The Newfield parents worked hard in their adopted country. Armin first found work selling brushes and brooms from door to door. Later, he became a travel agent. Lisl (now called Alice) worked a machine in a knitting factory. Together they supported their four sons, who all married and had children of their own. But it was their mother, Alice, who wrote down their story for her grandchildren. She titled her article "So That You May Hear and Remember."

References

Newfield, Alice. "So That You May Hear and Remember." Unpublished manuscript.
Joseph, Jill Newfield. Interview by the author. December 2005. Great Neck, New York.
   Special thanks to Arnold Newfield.

Niemöller, Martin (1892–1984)

Martin Niemöller was a Lutheran pastor in Germany and a leader in the Resistance. Although he had given antisemitic sermons during the early years of Hitler's rule, as soon as it became clear that Nazi policy was against all religion, Niemöller organized the Pastors' Emergency League in direct opposition to Hitler's policies. As a result, he was imprisoned for eight years, most of them in Sachsenhausen and Dachau concentration camps. Even in prison, his principles and his courage served to strengthen German opposition to Nazism.

Niemöller was born in Lippstadt, Westphalia, the son of a pastor. During World War I he was a naval lieutenant and served as a submarine commander. Not until after the war did he study for the ministry. He was ordained in 1924 and in 1931 became pastor in a church in Dahlen, a fashionable suburb of Berlin. Although Niemöller initially supported the Nazis, perhaps because of their stand against Communism, he soon broke with their policies. In 1933, right after Hitler took power, Niemöller preached against the National Socialist Party's interference in the church and founded the Pastors' Emergency League. The league was designed to help individual pastors who were in danger from the Nazis, but the organization took an early stand against discrimination of converts from Judaism and spoke out against the sterilization law, which demanded that those the Nazis considered unfit would be sterilized.

Niemöller was a principal founder of the Confessional Church, established in order to counteract the German Christian Faith Movement with its slogan "One People, One Reich, One Faith." Hitler demanded that every pastor take an oath of loyalty to the state and agree that anything in Christianity that contradicted government policy would be set aside. In the face of such an antireligious policy, it is shocking that only three thousand pastors joined the opposition. Another three thousand signed on to support the new Nazi religion, and the rest remained silent.

> *First they came for the Communists,*
> *and I didn't speak up,*
> *because I wasn't a Communist.*
> *Then they came for the Jews,*
> *and I didn't speak up,*
> *because I wasn't a Jew.*
> *Then they came for the Catholics,*
> *and I didn't speak up,*
> *because I was a Protestant.*
> *Then they came for me,*
> *and by that time there was no one*
> *left to speak up for me.*
>
> —Martin Niemöller

In face of this overwhelming passivity, Niemöller continued to speak out. He preached all over Germany, criticizing every policy of the Third Reich. He even joined the underground to help formulate a plan to assassinate Hitler. He knew it was only a matter of time before he would be arrested. On March 1, 1938, he preached his last sermon before being taken to jail. He was found guilty of crimes against the state but given a suspended sentence, mostly in deference to the foreign press, who had been following Niemöller's activities.

Immediately after his release, Niemöller was rearrested on Hitler's orders and sent directly to Sachsenhausen concentration camp, where he was put in "protective custody." Later he was transferred to Dachau, where he remained until the end of the war.

After the war, Niemöller continued his activism. Insisting that the German nation as a whole was responsible for the atrocities of World War II, he was instrumental in producing the "Stuttgart Confession of Guilt," in which the German Protestant churches formally accepted guilt for their complicity in allowing the suffering that Hitler's reign had caused. In 1961, he was elected as one of the six presidents of the World Council of Churches, the ecumenical body of the Protestant faiths. He preached to audiences all over the world, including Communist Russia in the 1950s and Vietnam in the 1960s. Later in his life he became an active pacifist, preaching against all war.

Niemöller won several awards, including the Lenin Peace Prize in 1967, and the West German Grand Cross of Merit in 1971, but he is perhaps most famous for his poem, written in 1945, just after his liberation. The poem described the succession of events and the conspiracy of silence that made the Holocaust possible.

Niemöller died in Wiesbaden on March 6, 1984, at the age of ninety-two, but his name remains "a towering symbol of the Church's struggle" against Nazism.

References

Encyclopedia Britannica. s.v. "Niemöller, Martin." 1969 edition.
http://www.hoboes.com/html/FireBlade/politics/niemoller/shtml.
http://www.forerunner.com/champion/X0006_5._Martin_Niemller.html.

Nir, Yehudah (1930–)

Yehudah Nir of Lvov, Poland, born Julius Gruenberg, spent his childhood years hiding among the Nazis. The evidence of his circumcision, the mark of the Jewish male, placed him in constant danger of discovery. Through a combination of quick thinking and luck, he succeeded in avoiding capture and lived to see the end of the war.

The Gruenberg family, parents and two children, lived in Lvov, where Nir's father owned a prosperous carpet-manufacturing business. Nir and his older sister, Lala, were raised with a nanny to care for them and servants to cook and clean. But that life ended in 1939, when the Germans invaded western Poland. According to a secret agreement between Germany and the Soviet Union, the eastern parts of Poland, including Lvov, were occupied by Russia.

The effects of Communist policy were felt immediately by the Gruenberg family. They were forced to move into a smaller apartment and take in a Russian soldier as a boarder. Almost all their possessions were confiscated. This, however, was just a prelude to what would happen under the Nazis. When the Germans broke their pact with the Soviet Union in 1941 and drove the Russian Army out, new antisemitic policies put all Jews at risk. Nir began to hear about the deaths of family members and friends. Even young children were gunned down, and the Nazis made it clear that no one was exempt. Later that year the German police came to get Nir's father. Nir followed him to the police station but was turned back by the guards. He never saw his father again.

After moving into the Lvov ghetto, the family was determined to avoid capture and deportation. They arranged for false papers that gave them new Polish names. Nir, now twelve years old, Lala, then an attractive teenager, and their mother had to memorize all the details of their new identities. Armed with their Aryan documents, they left Lvov for Krakow, traveling separately by train in order to avoid suspicion.

The Gruenberg women were blonde and looked more like Poles, while Nir had dark hair and looked Jewish. In addition, Nir, like all Jewish boys, had been circumcised as an infant. Since Poles were never circumcised in those years, this physical mark added a distinct risk for Jewish males. His hair might be bleached, but once he was undressed, his true identity would be revealed. Friends even tried to camouflage his circumcised penis by attaching a foreskin with dental glue, but the attempt was unsuccessful, and Nir had to take his chances. In the course of hiding, first with one family and then with another, he had many close calls. Luck and quick thinking somehow protected him and he was never discovered.

From Krakow the Gruenbergs moved to Warsaw. Here Nir's mother found a job keeping house for a German civilian industrialist. Lala worked for a dentist and arranged for a job as a messenger for Nir with another dentist, who gave him a room in her office where he could sleep. The dentist wore her Nazi uniform to work and had a picture of Hitler on her wall. It was a constant risk for Nir, but he managed to avoid suspicion, and his boss eventually trusted him and taught him some dental skills. It was during those days that Nir discovered the pleasures of women and had his first sexual experience. There were many encounters with antisemitism, too, and a few close calls. Nir acknowledged that some Germans and Poles may have guessed his true identity, but they did not turn him in. He later commented, "We were living in times when one had to be grateful to another human being for not exercising his option to kill."

Nir came to Warsaw in the spring of 1943, shortly after the Warsaw ghetto uprising had begun. After this all-Jewish rebellion was put down, there were no Jews left in Warsaw except for those passing as gentiles. As the Germans began to contemplate that they might lose the war, attacks on Poles became more frequent. German soldiers rounded them up and shot them down in the streets. Nir now had to confront the fact that his life was in danger not as a Jew but as a Polish male.

Then, late in 1944, with the Germans experiencing defeat on the Russian front and the Russian Army close to Warsaw, the Polish partisans finally attempted to drive out the Germans. By that time, Nir was fourteen years old, just old enough to join the army. His dentist was leaving, moving back to Germany, and Nir wanted to participate in the liberation. He became a courier for the partisans. This was one of the more dangerous assignments, as it involved carrying messages through underground tunnels from one military post to another. Even there, he still could not admit that he was a Jew because of the rampant antisemitism that was so common among Poles.

In spite of many individual incidents of courage by the Polish fighters, they were defeated by the Germans. Nir joined a group of partisans attempting to escape through the sewer system, but their attempt failed. Nir rejoined his mother and sister, and, still using their Christian identity cards, they were taken to Germany with other Polish prisoners of war to be used as slave labor. They were finally liberated by the Russians and allowed to return home.

After the war, Julius Gruenberg changed his name to Yehudah Nir and immigrated to Israel. Like so many survivors, he put his painful past behind him. He became a physician and then a psychiatrist before moving to the United States. In America, Nir married Bonnie Maslin and raised a family. He worked as a professor of psychiatry at Cornell Medical College in New York.

Nir did not write about his war experience until the 1980s. In his book, *The Lost Childhood*, he acknowledged his sister, who, he claimed, was "the true hero in this story." He credited "her quick wit, audacity, intelligence, and above all her courage" as the reasons he survived to bear witness. The book was acclaimed by one reviewer as "an unforgettable memoir of a resilient family."

Reference

Nir, Yehudah. *The Lost Childhood: A Memoir*. New York: Harcourt Brace Jovanovich, 1989.

Nussbaum, Sam (1920-)

Sam (originally called Shmuel or Samek) Nussbaum lived an ordinary life in Przemysl, Poland, but one thing made him stand out: he was a skilled plumber. Nussbaum believes that plumbing saved his life.

Nussbaum was first educated in a Polish public school. In addition, he began learning in a Jewish school (a *heder*) when he was three years old. By the age of eight, he was enrolled in an afternoon yeshivah, a Jewish secondary school. He also attended synagogue regularly with his family and joined a Zionist Youth Group. But his father, Laibish Nussbaum, did not want him to be a scholar. He believed that his son needed to learn a trade.

Even before the Germans came, antisemitism was widespread in Poland. Laibish thought that life would be better for his son in Palestine. Jews were building a Jewish state and plumbing, he thought, would be an ideal trade because his training would be in demand there. Nussbaum left the yeshivah, and by the time he was fifteen years old, he had learned to be a plumber and had installed the town's first indoor toilet in his family's apartment.

When the Nazis came to Przemysl, the first thing they did was to gather up five hundred Jewish children. They took them to a nearby cemetery and shot them all. Soon after, that part of Poland was turned over to the Russians in conformity with the Molotov-Ribbentrop Pact. The Nazis honored that treaty until 1941 and then invaded Russia.

By the time the Germans returned, Nussbaum was an experienced plumber and was conscripted to work for the Nazis in a labor camp. "We were slaves," he later told an interviewer. Hunger, beatings, killings. . . . People died from hunger."

Nussbaum tried to escape by volunteering for a transport, believing the lie that those on the transports would be taken to work in Germany, but a Gestapo agent pulled him off the truck. The eight thousand other Jews were transported to the gas chambers without Nussbaum, who continued to serve the German Army, first in the Przemysl camp in Poland and then in a labor camp in Austria. He was liberated by the Jewish Brigade, a group of Palestinian-Jewish soldiers who fought under the British flag. They took him to a displaced-persons camp in Italy, where he began the search for other surviving relatives. There were none. His entire family had been murdered.

In the refugee camp, Sam Nussbaum managed the camp kitchen for three hundred people and sold used clothing to earn extra money. On November 25, 1945, barely six months after liberation, he met and married Elizabeth, a young girl of seventeen whose family had also been killed during the war. Together, they waited for space on an illegal ship that would smuggle them into Palestine.

But before long, Elizabeth was pregnant, and after the birth of their first son Larry, the Nussbaums felt that illegal immigration to Israel was too dangerous. Instead, they obtained a visa for the United States. In 1948, the Nussbaums sailed across the Atlantic Ocean to New York and were immediately sent to Kansas City because "there were already too many new immigrants in New York."

Through the help of Jewish communal organizations, Sam and Elizabeth Nussbaum met a rabbi who helped them find an apartment. Now Nussbaum needed a job so he could support his family. With hardly any knowledge of English, he walked into a plumbing shop and was hired immediately. He did well in the plumbing trade, and soon the Nussbaums had three more children, David, Mel, and Bonnie.

The Nussbaums never realized their dream of living in Israel, but in 1973, they bought an apartment there. "I'm waiting for one child to go to Israel," Nussbaum said, adding that if only one of their children is there, "I won't be here ten minutes."

Sam and Elizabeth had put their past behind them and hardly spoke about their war experiences until 1992. During that year, Sam went to Stuttgart, Germany, where he testified as a witness against Nazi Josef Schwammberger, known as one of the cruelest camp commanders. Then memories came flooding back. Survivors related how Schwammberger set his German shepherd on camp inmates and personally shot Holocaust victims for being pregnant, stealing bread, or hoarding their valuables. Despite those reminders of a painful past, Nussbaum insisted, "It was worth surviving for my children." As of 2005, the Nussbaums' four children had produced nineteen grandchildren.

Because the Nussbaums never knew where their family members were buried, they decided to purchase ten thousand trees and build a monument in their memory. That monument still stands in a Jerusalem forest.

Reference

Dodd, Monroe, ed. *From the Heart: Life Before and After the Holocaust—A Mosaic of Memories*. Kansas City: Kansas City Star Books and the Midwest Center for Holocaust Education, 2001.

O

Ovitz family

The Ovitz family of Rozavlea, Transylvania, included ten siblings, some with spouses, and was one of the very few who survived Auschwitz together. They were saved because of the Nazi interest in biological abnormalities; seven of the Ovitz siblings were dwarfs.

The Ovitz children were all the offspring of Shimshon Aizik Ovitz, a dwarf. He was well educated in Jewish law, married a woman of normal size, and fathered two daughters, Rozika (b. 1886) and Franziska (b. 1889), both dwarfs. When his first wife died, he married another woman, also of normal size. Together they had eight more children. Avram (b. 1903), Frieda (b. 1905), Micki (b. 1909), Elizabeth (b. 1914), and Perla (b. 1921) inherited their father's disability and were less than three feet tall. Sarah (b. 1907), Leah (b. 1911), and Arie (b. 1917) grew tall.

Shimshon Aizik, who made a good living as an itinerant rabbi and healer and also as an emcee at weddings, died long before his wife, Batia Ovitz. Batia continued caring for all the children. Before she died, she urged them all to stay together. They held to their mother's advice and were convinced that it saved their lives.

The Ovitz children were musically talented, outgoing, and friendly. They organized themselves into a musical theater group and, calling themselves the Lilliput Troupe, traveled throughout Eastern Europe, entertaining in Yiddish as well as other languages. The group was popular and had bookings in all the major cities. To help them get in and out of trains and maneuver all the large-size conveniences of modern life, the dwarfs depended on their normal-sized siblings and spouses as well as a neighbor, Simon Slomowitz, who lifted them in and out of wagons and drove them wherever they needed to go. The Ovitzes, involved in their careers, paid little heed to the storm that was brewing throughout Europe. Although they were observant Jews, they felt that

The Ovitz family in 1949. All of them survived Auschwitz. Courtesy of the U.S. Holocaust Memorial Museum Photo Archives.

Germany was far away and events in that country did not affect them. Even when war broke out and Poland was invaded, they were not overly concerned.

The first event that forced the Ovitzes to think about the war occurred in 1940, when Transylvania, a part of Romania since World War I, was annexed by Hungary. At that time, Hungary had an antisemitic government. Every Jew was expected to have his identity stamped on his papers, and Jews were severely restricted in travel and other activities. Most important for them, Jewish entertainers were not allowed to appear before non-Jewish audiences. But when the family went to Budapest to obtain new identity cards as Hungarians, their appearance caused so much curiosity, and such a commotion, that the official never asked them if they were Jewish. They received cards for non-Jewish Hungarian citizens. This made it possible for them to continue traveling and entertaining for much longer than would ordinarily have been allowed. Involved with their own physical, day-to-day problems, the Ovitzes were still unaware that hundreds of thousands of Jews had already been murdered.

Nevertheless, the antisemitic laws could not be ignored for long. In Rozavlea, Transylvania, the Ovitzes were known, and their Jewish identity could not be denied. In 1943, when the Germans finally invaded Transylvania, a prelude to the occupation of all of Hungary, the Ovitzes were forced to wear the Star of David on their clothing just like everyone else and hand over their valuables to the Nazis. By this time, the Ovitz family was famous and well off. Before they were forcibly transferred to a ghetto, they hid their gold and jewelry in a box and buried it underneath their motorcar, the only car in the entire town. Then they joined the other Jews in their march to Dragomiresti, where a ghetto had been established. Because the Ovitz dwarfs were unable to walk for any distance, Slomowitz, their driver, was allowed to wheel them in a cart. Their taller sisters walked along beside them.

From Dragomiresti, the next stop was Auschwitz-Birkenau, the infamous death camp in Poland. Told they were simply being relocated with all the other Jews of the area, the Ovitzes packed all their belongings and their musical instruments, made to order for their small size. In May 1944 they were lifted into the boxcars, the doors were locked, and they proceeded to Auschwitz. The small stature and physical disabilities that went along with dwarfism made it impossible for the seven smaller members of the Ovitz family to do any hard labor, so their transfer to a camp meant almost certain death. However, the family got a reprieve thanks to Mengele, the German doctor and researcher who was present at the arrival of every train and ran a laboratory in the camp.

As the Ovitz family arrived, exhausted and barely able to stand, the German soldiers at the station immediately summoned Dr. Mengele. When he saw the Ovitzes, he took charge of the entire family, including the taller members and baby Shimshon, the child of Elizabeth Ovitz and her normal-sized husband. Shimshon was then eighteen months old. Also claiming to be a part of the family was their wagon driver and helper Simon Slomowitz and his wife and children, whose lives were saved because of their connection to the dwarfs. All their other relatives and neighbors were herded to their deaths.

For nine months, the Ovitz family remained in Auschwitz, separated from the regular inmates and protected from the brutal work protocol. They were given a bit more food than the other prisoners, although it was still not enough, and they were used in an array of medical experiments to enable Mengele to understand dwarfism. Many of the experiments were painful and dangerous. Sometimes blood was taken from them daily and sent to laboratories for a variety of tests. Other times, they were measured. The women were given painful internal examinations. More than once, they were transported to other places and forced to line up and take off their clothes so that others could view them while Mengele lectured.

In spite of all this pain and humiliation, the Ovitz siblings regarded Mengele as their savior. They knew that without him they would all have been sent to the crematorium. The experiments continued even as the Russian Army was approaching, but finally the camp was evacuated. Mengele collected his important papers and test results and fled. All prisoners who were still capable of walking were forced to leave and were marched westward to other work camps. Those who could not keep up were simply shot.

The Ovitz dwarfs could not possibly manage a march of twenty-five miles to the train station over snow-covered roads. They resigned themselves to death. However, the Russian Army arrived a few days later, and at liberation they were all alive.

The long road home began. Their own physical limitations combined with Russian bureaucracy and postwar confusion prolonged the journey for several months. When they finally arrived in Rozavlea, they discovered their treasure intact, exactly where they had buried it, but their home was in ruins. They tried to fix it up but were unable to. Nor did they feel welcome there any more. Most of their family and friends were dead and the Christians did not want Jews there. They moved to Sighet, Romania, and from there to Belgium, where they tried to resume their old life. But without knowing the language, they could not get any bookings.

In 1948, the family got two interesting offers. One was for an extended tour in the United States. Another was an invitation from the new state of Israel. The Ovitzes chose Israel. They felt that they would be among their own people and that they could entertain in Yiddish, their primary language. They sailed to Israel in 1949, celebrating the country's first Independence Day on the ship.

Although life in the new and still-developing country was difficult, the Ovitz family eventually succeeded and came to be known as "the seven dwarfs of Auschwitz." They not only played their instruments and sang in Yiddish, they learned Hebrew and produced skits and plays in their new language.

As they got older, they could no longer support the rigorous schedule of performances. The Lilliput Troupe officially retired in 1955, and one by one, the Ovitzes died. In 2000, the only surviving Ovitz dwarf was Perla, the youngest. She was interviewed for a book, *In Our Hearts We Were Giants*, which tells the story of the family and its survival. Perla died peacefully in Haifa in September 2001.

Reference

Koren, Yehuda, and Eilat Negev. *In Our Hearts We Were Giants: The Remarkable Story of the Lilliput Troupe—A Dwarf Family's Survival of the Holocaust*. New York: Carroll and Graf Publishers, 2004.

P

Pagis, Dan (1930–1986)

Dan Pagis, born in Radautz, Bukovina, which was then part of Romania, was orphaned at a young age but managed to survive three years alone in Transnistria, a literal no-man's land where Romanian Jews were transported during the war and left to die. After the war, he emigrated to Israel and became a professor and a renowned Hebrew poet.

Pagis, an only child, was four when his father left for Palestine in 1934. That same year, his mother died, and for the next seven years, Pagis was raised by his grandparents. His grandfather was in the sugar business, and his grandmother stayed at home and filled the role of mother for him.

When World War II erupted, the province of Bukovina was first occupied by the Russians. A little over a year later, the Germans broke the nonaggression pact they had made with the Soviet Union and marched in. Now the residents of Bukovina faced the same antisemitic regimen as those areas previously occupied by Germany. Late in 1941 deportations began, and the Jews from all the Romanian provinces were sent to Transnistria, a barren wasteland in what is now the Ukraine. Pagis and his grandparents left together on one of those transports. Many years later, his haunting poem, "Written in Pencil in the Sealed Railway-Car," is a memory of that experience.

Pagis's grandfather died in Transnistria, and he and his grandmother were left to cope with the misery and deprivations with which all the Jewish deportees lived. In an interview many years later, Pagis described the camp where he spent three years, "It was not a death camp," he explained. "It was a camp in the Ukraine under German occupation, managed mainly by Romanian troops but with German commanders. . . . It was not the most terrible thing directly. Many people lived through more terrible things. But still the impact was very, very great."

For Romania, the war ended in 1944, when the Germans were driven back by the Russians. Within two years, Pagis, at sixteen, was able to leave for

> *Written in Pencil in the Sealed Railway-Car*
>   *here in this carload*
>   *i am eve*
>   *with abel my son*
>   *if you see my other son*
>   *cain son of man*
>   *tell him that i*
>   —Dan Pagis (translated by Stephen Mitchell)

Palestine, where he joined his father, who was working in Jerusalem as a chemist.

Educated in an Israeli high school, Pagis learned Hebrew quickly and published his first Hebrew poems by the age of nineteen. He continued his education at the Hebrew University in Jerusalem, eventually earning a PhD in Medieval Hebrew Literature. Pagis wrote many books in his field and became a highly respected professor, teaching at various universities in Israel and the United States. He married and had two children.

It was many years before Pagis was able to write about the war. Even then, his writings took the form of poetry, and like **Aharon Appelfeld** he avoided writing about his own personal experiences. Nevertheless, his collections of poems resonate with the tragedies and sorrows of World War II, and before his death at the age of fifty-six, he was considered "one of the most vibrant voices in modern Israeli poetry" and "a major world poet of his generation." He was survived by his wife and his twin son and daughter, whom he once described as "really the best thing that ever happened to me."

References

Langer, Lawrence, ed. *Art from the Ashes: A Holocaust Anthology*. New York: Oxford University Press, 1995.

http://www.aish.com/holocaust/People/Pagis_Gebhard_he61n06.asp.

http://www.bukovinajewsworldunion.org/English/88People/Pagis.totul.html.

Papiernik, Charles (1919–)

Already an orphan before World War II, Charles (born Yisrael) Papiernik, originally from Poland, was used to fending for himself. However, nothing could have prepared him for the challenges and cruelty he faced as a prisoner in Auschwitz and Sachsenhausen concentration camps. A series of narrow escapes and near-miracles kept him alive when most of those around him were killed. After the war, he picked up the pieces of his life and started again on a new continent.

Papiernik was the youngest of seven brothers, all born in Przysucha, a small town in Poland. He also had one sister, who was the oldest of all eight children. His mother died when he was ten, and two years later, his father died and Papiernik, now an orphan, had to make his way alone. Except for Feival, the brother nearest to him in age, all his older brothers were married and living in Warsaw. His sister had emigrated to Uruguay. Although his siblings did their best to help him, they were far away.

At first, Papiernik continued in the yeshivah where he was studying when his father died. With no home, he slept on a bench in the house of study and depended mostly on charity for food.

After two years of life as a poor student, he became interested in secular and political issues. He left the yeshivah, apprenticed as a tailor, and joined the

Socialist Bund Youth Group. Still, his living conditions were challenging. He was not paid for his work as an apprentice and often went hungry. When he became ill, physicians warned that he would get tuberculosis if he did not have a better diet, so his brothers each sent money and brought him to be with them in Warsaw where he worked in the clothing factory of one brother and regained his health.

From Warsaw, he followed his brothers to Paris, where life was better and antisemitism much less obvious than in Poland. At seventeen, Papiernik quickly learned French, joined the Paris branch of the Socialist Bund, and began to earn money. He slept in the home of one brother, ate his meals with another, and worked with a third. He felt well cared for. Then World War II erupted.

Even in 1938, France was filled with talk of a possible attack by Nazi Germany. There were those in France who insisted that the country must remain neutral. Others urged a pre-emptive attack on Germany, and a third faction was pro-Nazi and agreed that Jews should be singled out for harsh treatment. Those with anti-Jewish feelings became more outspoken, and when Germany did attack Poland, they justified Nazi actions against the Jews.

In 1940, when the Germans marched into France, their first agenda was to deport the Jews who were originally from Germany and Poland, and Papiernik and his brothers, totally unsuspecting, appeared at the police station as ordered. They did not expect to be jailed and deported, but all seven of them were. Papiernik and two of his brothers were sent to Pithiviers, a French transit camp, in May 1941. A year later, they were deported to Auschwitz-Birkenau.

Because he was under twenty-five, Papiernik was chosen as one of several hundred young men to go to the "construction school" at Birkenau. Ostensibly to learn the construction trades, they were assigned to hard labor and grossly mistreated by sadistic guards who were actually convicted criminals from Poland. The young men were beaten with whips and iron pipes, forced to do exercises in the freezing cold, deprived of food, and exposed daily to the stench and smoke from the crematoria that were located at Birkenau.

It was almost a relief when Papiernik, along with others from the so-called construction school, was transferred to Auschwitz, just a short distance away. Although the abuse in Auschwitz was constant and the food was minimal, Papiernik found it more bearable and discovered that here, a few of those in charge were not as cruel. Nevertheless, death was something that all the prisoners expected—and some longed for.

In the fall of 1944, when Papiernik was chosen as one of the young men to go along with a group of Jewish teenagers, he assumed that he had been selected for the gas chambers. The next morning, following the guards, he marched off in the direction of Birkenau. The boys had already confided in him that they had assembled some weapons: razor blades and a few knives and rods. They were determined to die fighting. At the last second, however, the group was turned around and led to the trains. There had been

> *Hitler did not defeat us, not with his soldiers, SS agents, and all the others. Hitler could kill, but he did not succeed with what he had proposed to do with the Jewish people. The Jewish people continue living. Judaism, secular as well as religious, continues.*
>
> —Charles Papiernik, *Unbroken: From Auschwitz to Buenos Aires.* Translated by Stephen A. Sadow. Albuquerque: University of New Mexico Press, 2004. p. 134.

a new shipment of prisoners and the gas chamber and crematoria could not handle any more bodies. Instead they were shipped off to Sachsenhausen-Oranienbourg and put to work in an aircraft factory.

Papiernik thought nothing could be worse than Auschwitz, but he found conditions equally horrifying at the new camp, where they worked from 6:00 a.m. to 8:00 p.m. every day. He later wrote, "Auschwitz was the camp of brutal, rapid, massive death. Sachsenhausen was the camp of the slow death."

Papiernik remained in Sachsenhausen throughout the winter of 1944. As the Allied bombings became more frequent, the prisoners were encouraged, and with defeat imminent, conditions in the camp improved slightly. Then they heard that the Germans planned to single out the Jews and kill them before the Allied armies arrived. Once again Papiernik prepared to die, and once again he got a reprieve. That night, a bomb destroyed the records office of the SS, and now no one knew for sure who was Jewish and who was not. The prisoners all agreed to deny being Jewish.

In the final days, no attempt was made to find the Jews. Jews and gentiles alike were marched out of the camp with neither food nor water and were urged on by the SS guards. Anyone who could not continue was executed by a bullet. Anyone who tried to grab some food that he found along the way was also shot. After nine days, Papiernik could not stand up. He was helped by a French comrade, who carried him on his back for two kilometers, thus saving his life.

On May 1, 1945, the exhausted prisoners met a convoy of Red Cross trucks and received some food, but the Germans still urged them on. They learned that the Russian troops were ten kilometers to the rear and American troops were eight kilometers in front of them. The prisoners refused to move. The next day, they were liberated by the Americans. Of the fifty thousand deportees who had left Sachsenhausen ten days before, only two thousand remained alive.

Back in Paris, Papiernik discovered that all his family but his oldest brother had been murdered. The new French government was sympathetic and helpful to those who returned from the camps, but it was difficult for Papiernik to pick up the pieces of his old life. He had met a young woman, Micheline, the surviving daughter of someone he had met in Auschwitz, but was not ready to marry. He took the opportunity to take a young niece and nephew to Uruguay, where his older sister was living. She greeted him warmly and lovingly, and he welcomed her care but understood that he would have to become independent.

Papiernik sent for Micheline. She came to Montevideo, Uruguay, where they married and started a family. Papiernik, following the family tradition, opened a factory for ladies' clothing, joined the small community of Holocaust survivors there, and helped Micheline raise their two daughters, Elana and Francis. Papiernik's sister and her family left for Israel after 1948, but Charles and Micheline remained in Uruguay for twenty-five years. In 1974 they moved to Buenos Aires, Argentina, where there was a larger Jewish community and more economic opportunity. In response to his daughters' question, "Why don't we have any grandparents or relatives?" Papiernik began telling them about his life. Eventually, he wrote the stories down and had them published under the title *Una Vida* [*A Life*]. His book was later translated into English as *Unbroken: From Auschwitz to Buenos Aires*.

The Papierniks' older daughter, Elana, remained in Montevideo and had her own children and grandchildren. Francis, the younger daughter, settled with her family in Israel. Papiernik had the satisfaction of knowing that despite his plan to eliminate all the Jews, Hitler had not succeeded.

In Buenos Aires, Papiernik had one last brush with death. On July 18, 1994, he cancelled an appointment at the Jewish Community Center in order to visit Elana. That very morning, a bomb blew up the center, and eighty-five people were killed.

Reference

Papiernik, Charles. *Unbroken: From Auschwitz to Buenos Aires*. Translated by Stephen A. Sadow. Albuquerque: University of New Mexico Press, 2004.

Pechersky, Alexander (1909–)

Alexander (Sasha) Pechersky, a musician and actor in Russia before the outbreak of World War II, planned and led the only successful rebellion by concentration camp inmates at the Sobibor concentration camp.

Pechersky was born in Kremenchug in Soviet Russia but moved with his family to Rostov-on-the-Don in 1915. Although he was Jewish, he attended a general school for seven years and went on to music school. By 1941, when the Germans attacked the Russian Army, he was already married with a young daughter. He worked for the Soviet government and was active in dramatic and literary circles. On the first day of the German-Russian war, Pechersky was mobilized as a junior commander. He quickly made his way up the ranks until his capture by the Germans in October 1941.

Pechersky remained with other Russian prisoners for a year, until he tried to escape. He was caught and sent to a punitive detachment, ending up at a labor camp in Minsk with other Jews. When the Nazis liquidated the Minsk ghetto in September 1943, Pechersky and several thousand others were transported to Sobibor. In a memoir written immediately after the war, Pechersky reported on the conditions of transport: "Men, women and children were herded together, seventy to a car," he wrote. "Even when standing up one felt crushed from all sides. The doors were bolted, the windows blocked with barbed wire. We were not given any food, not even a drink of water." After traveling in this way for four days, they arrived at Sobibor.

Sobibor was a death camp from which there were hardly any survivors, but the Nazis did keep a detachment of workers, both male and female, to help run the camp, dispose of the bodies in the crematorium after they had been gassed, and sort the clothing and possessions of the dead prisoners. Pechersky was chosen as part of a carpentry squad and was allowed to live. In exchange for a meager amount of food, the prisoners did backbreaking work and risked being whipped for the smallest infraction. Almost daily, they could hear the screams and cries of those being led to the gas chambers, and they knew that soon their turn would come.

Once Pechersky realized what was happening at Sobibor, he immediately began thinking of escape. He did not want to go alone, however, nor in a small group. He knew that if one person tried to run, many more would be killed in retaliation. Plotting with a small group of trustworthy prisoners, he became the acknowledged leader of a plan to bring all the prisoners out of the camp. Enlisting the aid of the *kapos* (Jews who had the authority of camp police) and those in charge of the various workshops, the group arranged to collect knives and axes and to kill all of the camp's officers simultaneously. At the same time, someone would cut the phone lines. Once that was accomplished, and weapons and ammunition were collected, the Russian soldiers would storm the guardhouse while others led the rest of the prisoners out in an orderly way. The day chosen for the revolt was October 14, 1943.

Everything went according to plan until the frightened prisoners, realizing that there was a chance for escape, began to run and overtake the soldiers planning an attack on the guardhouse. Confusion ensued, and the Nazi guards shot many people. Others were killed by land mines that had been laid around the periphery of the camp or were shot before they could get into the woods.

Pechersky and other Russian Jews, both soldiers and civilians, ran eastward, toward Russia. Those from Poland turned west. Each group wanted to find people who spoke their own language. The Dutch, French, and German prisoners had a more difficult time, but a few did manage to find help and survive. The goal of all was to join the partisans and continue fighting the Germans. "We must not perish," Pechersky had told one of his friends before the insurrection, "because we must take revenge." A small group of Russians did succeed in joining a partisan group. In 1944, with the Germans in full retreat, Pechersky rejoined the Russian Army and was wounded fighting.

Pechersky lived to return to his family. In 1963, he attended a twentieth-anniversary reunion of the revolt at Sobibor. Two years later, a trial was held in West Germany for twelve of the SS men who had worked at the camp. The court, reporting on that revolt, claimed that the camp had been responsible for the deaths of 250,000 Jews and was destroyed by the Germans after they "crushed" the revolt.

Indignant at these misstatements, Pechersky, presenting himself as the leader of the Sobibor revolt, wrote a public reply that appeared in the Yiddish press. He stated that over half a million Jews had been murdered at Sobibor, that the revolt had indeed been successful, and as a result, Sobibor had been completely destroyed by the Germans according to secret orders sent from Berlin.

References

Pechersky, Alexander, "A Public Reply," *Sovietish Heimland* (April, 1966).

Suhl, Yuri, ed. *They Fought Back: The Story of the Jewish Resistance in Nazi Europe.* New York: Schocken Books, 1967.

Pechman, Maurice (1928–)

Maurice Pechman, the fifth of six Polish siblings, was a mischievous child who often played tricks on his teachers and got into trouble at school. He felt that it was this trait that allowed him to escape death time and time again during the war years.

The Pechman family was poor and often hungry. In Jaworow they lived together in a one-room house with no electricity. Just before World War II, the family moved to Krakow and they were in that city when the war began. Fleeing from the German advance, they took refuge in a small town, believing they would be safer, but the refuge proved a false one. The Nazis assembled all the Jews in the town and took them on wagons to the fields. They were ordered to stand in front of a giant pit. As each one was shot in the head, he or she fell into the pit, one on top of the other. Many of those who fell were not yet dead, and the fourteen-year-old Pechman, still waiting his turn, could hear their terrible moaning.

Pechman ran as fast as he could toward the woods. Although the Germans did not catch him then, the rest of his family was murdered there and buried in that pit.

Pechman first ran to Tarnow, where one of his older brothers lived. When he arrived, he learned that this brother, too, had been killed by the Nazis, shot for not wearing his identifying armband with the Star of David. Alone and at a loss, Pechman managed to connect with the Jewish Underground and obtained false papers. Armed with his new identity as Jan Zachwala, a Polish Christian, Pechman approached the train station and was promptly stopped by the Gestapo. Although he wanted to escape, Pechman was trapped there with fifty others who, like him, had been told to wait for further investigation. While they waited, a young boy standing nearby asked him to carry a valise for him. He assured Pechman that it contained only food, and promised to share it with him later. But when Pechman's turn came to be checked by the Gestapo, and he was told to open the suitcase, it was filled with anti-Nazi propaganda.

When the Gestapo discovered this contraband, they beat Pechman, arrested him, and sent him to Auschwitz but not to the gas chambers. He was strong enough to work, and did so even on starvation rations. At one point Pechman weighed only seventy-five pounds.

In 1944 Pechman and others were transferred to Sachsenhausen-Oranienburg, a concentration camp in Germany. With the Soviet Army approaching, however, the prisoners at Sachsenhausen were forced on what was later called a death march, driven by their German captors who were fleeing the Russians. Many prisoners died along the way, but Pechman escaped once again and succeeded in hiding in the woods. After three days, he was liberated by the Russians. He discovered that one of his older brothers had survived Auschwitz and was still alive. Everyone else he knew was dead.

Pechman waited for four years before he was finally able to leave for the United States. When he arrived, he was twenty-one years old, completely alone, with no money. He was not afraid, however, and many years later explained to an interviewer, "After all I'd been through, I wasn't afraid of anything."

He began his working life as a Fuller Brush salesman. Then he sold other products, but soon settled on the ceramics business. For many years, Maurice Ceramics manufactured household ceramic ware. Pechman's successful company was located in California. Today, Pechman's ceramic products have become collectors' items and are sold at auction for high prices. His business empire has given Pechman the opportunity to become philanthropic, and he has donated large amounts of money to a variety of causes.

Reference

Del Calzo, Nick. "Maurice Pechman." *The Triumphant Spirit: Portraits and Stories of Holocaust Survivors,* p. 123. Denver, CO: Triumphant Spirit Publishing, 1997.

Penraat, Jaap (1918–2006)

Jaap Penraat, a nonpracticing Christian from Amsterdam, became a hero of the Holocaust by becoming an expert forger. His skills in forging documents saved many Jews from the hands of the Nazis. Many years after World War II was over, he was named Righteous Among the Nations and awarded a medal by Yad Vashem, Israel's museum of the Holocaust. He rescued 406 Dutch Jews.

Penraat grew up with Jews in Amsterdam and as a youngster he worked as a *Shabbos goy,* a gentile who turns lights on and off for observant Jews on the Sabbath. After continuing his basic education he studied architectural design and when the Nazis invaded Holland in 1940, he was already working as an architect and draftsman.

As soon as the Germans instituted restrictive laws for the Jews, a secret resistance was organized to help them escape. Penraat was part of this underground resistance. At first, he only designed fake identity cards, copying official stamps and models from papers smuggled out to him by a friend who was married to a German. He was discovered, imprisoned and tortured by the Nazi police, but did not divulge anything and after a few months, was released.

Penraat not only continued his forging, he also helped devise a plan to disguise Jews as construction workers and help them cross the border into France (ostensibly to help the Germans build a wall along France's Atlantic coast). When they arrived in France, they would meet with the French Underground who helped them cross the border into neutral Spain.

Penraat himself accompanied the Jewish workers on these dangerous trips. He brought approximately twenty Jews at a time to safety and made the trip about twenty times. In a later interview, he explained that if the papers presented to the officials were discovered to be forgeries, "they would shoot you right then and there, so other people could see what happens when you do anything against the German army." But Penraat was never caught; his documents always passed inspection.

By 1944, it became too dangerous to continue the trips. Penraat went into hiding in a small Dutch village and waited for the defeat of the Nazis. In spring of 1945, when the war was over, he immediately resumed his work as an architect and became a well-respected designer in Amsterdam. He continued this work in the United States where he moved in 1958 with his wife Jettie Jon-

> *You do these things because in your mind there is no other way of doing it.*
>
> —Jaap Penraat, in an interview with *The Pittsburgh Post-Gazette*, 2000.

gejans (died 2003). Among his better-known designs in America was the Dutch Mill Café, built for the 1964 New York World's Fair.

Penraat rarely spoke about his wartime experiences until pressed by his three grown daughters who wanted their children to learn about his heroism. As a result of their urging, he began to speak to school groups and grant interviews. Penraat died in 2006 in his home in Catskill, New York.

Reference

Martin, Douglas. "Jaap Penraat Dies at 88: Saved Hundreds in Holocaust." *New York Times,* July 2, 2006. p. 30.

Perkal-Jacubowitch, Betty (1925–2000)

Betty Perkal-Jacubowitch was born in Antwerp, Belgium. As a teenager, she organized an escape route to lead Jews from Nazi-occupied Belgium to neutral Switzerland. She was able to rescue fifty-four Jews, although she could not save her parents.

When the Nazis invaded and occupied Belgium in May 1940, Perkal was fifteen years old and an active member of B'nai Akiva, a religious Zionist Youth Movement. She watched for two years as the Jews of Belgium were denied work and education, forced to wear the Star of David on their clothing, and threatened with arrest. However, most felt they could survive the antisemitic laws imposed by the Germans.

In 1942, the situation worsened and mass arrests of all Jews began. Helped by large numbers of sympathetic Belgians, the Jews searched for ways to hide. Perkal's parents found refuge in Wallonia, a small, rural village, and assumed that their two daughters would remain with them. But Perkal-Jacubowitch was restless. She wanted to leave Belgium and go to Switzerland, a neutral country where there was no fighting and no antisemitic laws. She left for Brussels and began planning her escape.

In Brussels, she met a friend, Tilly Kirschenbaum, and together they set out. With the help of their Youth Movement, they obtained false identity papers and some money. Then they bleached their hair blond so they would not look Jewish.

The young women spoke fluent French and this helped them pass the German checkpoints that had been set up at every train station and border crossing. At the French border, they met some members of the resistance who helped them. After waiting in a small border town where they lived in the home of a sympathetic priest, they crossed into Switzerland. It was September 1942.

Once in Switzerland, they were sent to an internment camp. Here, Perkal-Jacubowitch made contact with the Swiss branch of B'nai Akiva and became involved with helping the many refugees who managed to cross the border. But she wanted to bring her parents and her sister to safety as well as others. To do that, she needed money.

Perkal-Jacubowitch approached the Swiss Jewish community and asked for funds. Many of the Jewish leaders were reluctant, fearing her plan would not work. Others worried that bringing too many Jews into Switzerland would endanger their own safety. She did raise some money, though, and in September 1943, exactly one year after her arrival, she crossed back, first into France, then to Belgium. She made arrangements with the French Resistance and searched out safe hiding places.

Back in Brussels, the challenge was finding the Jews she knew. Almost all were in hiding but she did contact some people and visited her family. She even appealed to the Queen Mother, Elizabeth, and through her, obtained food and clothing for the refugees. She still needed money, however, to purchase false identity cards and pay for travel expenses for those attempting to cross. Finally, through the efforts of Chaim Perelman, a member of the Jewish Resistance, she received the amount she needed and was ready to make the journey again, this time with four others.

At eighteen, Perkal-Jacubowitch was indefatigable. She persuaded border guards, smoothed the way with local police, and found food and places to stay for her small group. When she saw them safely over the border, she went back for the next group.

Perkal-Jacubowitch's final group included her parents as well as two counselors from the Wezembeek Children's Home outside Brussels, run by **Marie Blum-Albert**. But this final group, fleeing in January 1944, ran into difficulties and all those from this and the previous group were denounced, arrested, and deported to concentration camps. Only three of the twelve survived. Perkal-Jacubowitch's parents perished in the camps.

After the war, Betty Perkal married an American and had two children, a son and a daughter, before she was divorced. After her marriage ended, Perkal-Jacubowitch moved to Israel. She died there at the age of seventy-five.

Reference

Brachfeld, Sylvain. "Jews Who Rescued Jews." *Hidden Child* 14 (2006): p. 10.

Perl, Gisella (1910–)

Gisella Perl was a practicing obstetrician/gynecologist in Transylvania (Romania) before World War II. She used her skills in the ghetto and then in Auschwitz and continued to help women after the war, first in the displaced-persons camps of Europe and then in America.

The invasion of Poland that began World War II was worrisome for the Perls but had little effect on their lives. In 1940, however, Transylvania, then part of Romania, was annexed to Hungary, an ally of Germany, and Jews were herded into ghettos. Despite the lack of food and medical supplies, Perl continued practicing medicine. When the transports to the concentration camps began in 1944, she, her son, her husband Frederick, and her parents were loaded onto a boxcar with no food or water and brought to Auschwitz/Birkenau. Her parents were immediately sent off to be killed. She was chosen for work in Auschwitz and was separated from her husband and son. Gisella never saw them again.

Even though Auschwitz was considered a death camp, there was a hospital there and Perl, now prisoner 25404, worked as a doctor, often ordered to heal those who had been used for medical experimentation. Dr. Perl eventually became famous for performing hundreds of abortions on prisoners. She did it without instruments, drugs, or even clean bandages, "on a dirty floor, using only my dirty hands." Although she felt terrible destroying all those unborn children, she knew she had to do it. "If I had not," she later wrote, "both mother and child would have been cruelly murdered."

The prisoners loved Perl and referred to her as "Gisi doctor," but no doctor's efforts could prevent thousands of women from dying. She recalled that when she came to Auschwitz, she was one of thirty-two thousand women from Poland and Hungary. Six months later, by September 1944, only ten thousand of those women were still alive.

Gisella Perl spent almost a full year in Auschwitz concentration camp before being transferred to a prison hospital for slave laborers in Hamburg, Germany. Here she treated prisoners who had been wounded in the allied bombing raids against the Nazis. Although conditions were still terrible, she later described them as "heaven compared to Auschwitz."

As the war neared its end in late winter of 1945, Perl, along with other prisoners, was evacuated by truck from the burning city of Hamburg and taken to Bergen-Belsen, another concentration camp. There, among heaps of corpses, she found the bodies of her brother and sister-in-law.

Although she was surrounded by the dead and dying, Perl was dedicated to saving lives, and continued to do so. On April 15, 1945, as the British troops marched into the camp, she delivered "the first free child" born in the maternity ward at Bergen-Belsen. She remained at the camp for a while, treating the recovering prisoners and delivering babies. While there, she heard that just before the war ended, both her husband and son had been killed. This news so devastated Perl that she attempted suicide. Found in time, she was saved from death and in a convent outside Paris, was able to rest and regain her health. It took many more years for her spiritual wounds to heal.

For Perl, part of the healing process was being able to speak about—and justify to herself—what she had done during the war. She felt guilty not only because of the abortions she had performed but because she had remained alive when her loved ones had been murdered. Calling herself the "ambassador for the six million," Perl traveled throughout America speaking to doctors and other groups about her experiences. One day she met Eleanor Roosevelt, then widow of President Franklin D. Roosevelt. "Stop torturing yourself," Mrs. Roosevelt told Perl. "Become a doctor again."

Perl took that advice, and with the help of American friends, she was granted U.S. citizenship and set up a practice in New York City. She became an expert in fertility and helped many women to become pregnant. Just before her seventieth birthday, she moved to Israel. In 1982, Perl was honored by the National Women's Division of *Shaare Zedek* hospital in Jerusalem where she was still working and healing, donating her time to the gynecological clinic. In 2003, a TV film, *Out of the Ashes*, was based on her life.

References

Fisher, Bob. "Out of the Ashes—A Story to Remember, Rendered by Donald M. Morgan, ASC." International Cinematographers Guild. http://www.cameraguild

.com/interviews/chat_morgan/morgan_outofashes.htm (accessed October 10, 2005).

Perl, Gisella. *I Was a Doctor in Auschwitz*. New York: International Universities Press, 1948.

Perlasca, Giorgio (1910–1992)

Giorgio Perlasca is one of the least known of the righteous gentiles. He was an Italian who refused to ally himself with Italy's antisemitic policies. He posed as a Spanish diplomat after Spain had abandoned its embassy in Budapest, and saved over 5,000 Hungarian Jews, risking his reputation and his life to do so.

Perlasca was born in Como, Italy, and grew up in Masera in the province of Padua. From his youth, he sympathized with the Fascist policy of Italian nationalism and even went to Spain to fight in the Spanish Civil War in support of General Franco and the Fascists. However, when he returned from that war, his political opinions had changed, mainly because of his country's alliance with Nazi Germany and the antisemitic policies it was now sanctioning.

After World War II began in 1939, Perlasca was already back in Italy. He was given the title of Diplomat and sent east to purchase meat for the Italian Army. When Mussolini's government fell in July 1943, he was still abroad, in Hungary, also an ally of the Nazis, and Germany had occupied northern Italy. At that time, all Italians were requested to return home but Perlasca refused. He would not return to what he considered "a German-ruled Italian puppet state." Explaining his political views at that time, Perlasca said, "I was neither a fascist nor an antifascist, but I was anti-Nazi."

Because of his refusal to return to Italy, Perlasca was taken into custody by the Hungarians on October 13, 1944, but he was able to escape and reach the Spanish Embassy in Budapest. Because Perlasca had fought in General Franco's Army, he asked for and received Spanish citizenship, adopted the Spanish version of his first name (Jorge), and was given a job in the Embassy by Angel Sanz-Briz, the Spanish envoy to Budapest.

Spain, officially neutral in World War II, tended to be sympathetic with the Nazis but had, nevertheless, been issuing protective passes to the Jews of Budapest beginning in the spring of 1944 when the Germans invaded Hungary. Spain also kept several safe houses, officially extensions of the Embassy and thus under the protection of the Spanish government, where Jews could find safety, ostensibly until their papers came through for travel to Spain. This technique was similar to that used by **Raoul Wallenberg** of neutral Sweden and soon Perlasca was collaborating with Sanz-Briz, issuing safe conduct passes to Hungarian Jews.

Barely two months after Perlasca's initial employment at the Spanish Embassy, the puppet government of Hungary, in place after the Germans officially occupied the country in March 1944, asked that the Spanish Diplomatic offices be moved out of Budapest to Sopron, near the border with Austria. In protest, Sanz-Briz left his post and left Hungary, leaving no one in charge. When Hungary's Ministry of Internal Affairs heard of Sanz-Briz's absence and proceeded to take over the Embassy's safe houses and arrest the inhabitants, Perlasca stepped in. Claiming that Sanz-Briz had merely gone to Switzerland temporarily and that he had been put in charge during his absence, Hungarian officials aborted the roundup of Jews. To prove the truth of his claim, Perlasca quickly created a document, using official Embassy stamps, that indicated that in the absence of Sanz-Briz, he was the Spanish Ambassador.

From that day at the end of November until the war was over, Perlasca maintained that deception. He spent those months protecting and feeding the thousands of Hungarian Jews that were crowded into Spanish safe houses. He also went with Wallenberg to the train station as the Jews were being deported and handed out "safe-conduct" passes. These passes stated, "Spanish relatives have requested your presence in Spain; until communications are restored and the journey is possible, you will remain here under the protection of the Spanish government." Perlasca—and Sanz-Briz before him—was able to do that because of a Spanish Law effective from 1924, recognizing that all Jews whose ancestors had originated in Spain before the expulsion of Jews in 1492, were entitled to Spanish citizenship. Through this legal ruse, as well as his personal courage, Perlasca was able to save 5,218 Jews from death at the hands of the Nazis.

When the Soviet Army marched into Budapest and liberated Hungary, Perlasca, like Wallenberg, was also arrested, but he was quickly released and he returned to Italy. Back in his native land, he lived a quiet life, never discussing his exploits during the war, even with his own children. Not until the 1980s were his righteous actions revealed by a few Hungarian Jewish women. They had been children during the Holocaust and had been saved by him. Through a local Jewish community newspaper, they initiated a search for the Spanish diplomat who had helped them survive and traced him to his home in Italy.

Once his story was out and testimonies collected from other survivors, Perlasca began to talk about his experience with school groups "so that no such madness is ever repeated." He was awarded citations for courage by the Hungarian, Italian, and Israeli governments and was written up in newspapers and books. Perlasca died in 1992, and at his own request, his tombstone contains the words (in Hebrew), "righteous among the nations." In 2005, Italian filmmakers produced a film about his life, which was shown briefly in theatres in the United States.

References

http://www.giorgioperlasca.it/ingles/vita2.html (accessed April 2006).
Szymanski, Tekla. "Italian Wallenberg." *World Press Review* 48, no. 1 (January 2001).
http://www.worldpress.org/Europa/1236.cfm (accessed April 2006).

Pessah family

Leon and Gracia Pessah, husband and wife, were both born in Salonika, the largest Jewish community in Greece. They spent most of the war in hiding with the partisans, and Leon risked his life many times to help other Jews. Most of their extended family was murdered in Auschwitz, but the Pessahs and their infant son survived.

Leon (whose Hebrew name was Yehudah) was raised in a traditional home. An only child, his father, Joseph Pessah, died when he was five and he was raised by his mother, Mazal Tov, and his maternal grandfather, Rabbi Joseph Matalon. His grandfather was a religious man and strict, insisting that his young

Rabbi Leon Pessah in the United States with his wife Mazal. Courtesy of Marius Pessah.

grandson attend morning *minyan* (the daily prayer service) each day. Leon was given a religious education, and just as World War II began, he graduated from the rabbinical seminary as a rabbi and a *shokhet* (ritual meat slaughterer).

Gracia Pessah was the daughter of Joseph and Mazal Tov Masliah, and one of five children. Her father had a prosperous business manufacturing burlap bags and his children were all well educated. In addition to having a fine education, Gracia was a skilled seamstress who later supported herself by sewing clothes. She married Leon Pessah in 1940.

In 1941, after serving in the Greek Army, Leon became rabbi to a community of five hundred Jews in Trikala, a town in western Thessaly. Trikala was in a mountainous region south of Salonika, where Jews had lived for hundreds of years. Leon and Gracia were respected there. They lived near the schoolhouse and in addition to his duties as rabbi, Leon taught French to the local children. Included among his pupils were the children of the chief of police and the children of the prelate of the Greek Orthodox Church.

The Pessahs' first son, Joseph, was born in 1942. That same year the Nazis came to Trikala and began their attacks on the Jews. These would be followed by roundups and deportations; their goal was the complete destruction of all the Jews of Greece.

With the help of their Greek neighbors, the Pessah family, along with many other Jewish families, was able to flee to the mountains. The townsfolk even saved the old synagogue by camouflaging it to look like a warehouse.

Once safe from Nazi roundups, Rabbi Pessah joined the partisans, many of whom were Jewish men. They kept the Germans out of the area by ambushing them as they came through the narrow mountain passes. Because of his relationship with these paramilitary groups, Pessah was able to warn Jews who were hiding nearby to move to safer locations. He also gave substantial moral support to his scattered community, providing them with spiritual comfort and serving their religious communal needs. He risked his life by sneaking into Salonika to retrieve his *shokhet*'s knife so that he could supply Jews with kosher meat if an animal became available. He also smuggled out his religious books and the astronomical material that helped him to ascertain when the Jewish holidays were to be celebrated.

Leon's language skills made him a valuable asset to the partisans, who used him to relay messages between different partisan groups. He spoke French, Italian, and Greek as well as several local dialects and, disguised as

The Fate of the Jews of Greece

City	Number of Deportees	Number Killed Immediately
Athens	800	800
Corfu	1,800	1,600
Janina	1,860	1,860
Rhodes	1,700	1,000
Salonika	45,000	37,000
Trikala	50	50
Volos	130	130

Total Population of Greek Jews in 1939: 75,000
Total Amount Murdered: 60,000 (80%)
Total Number of Jews in Greece in 1944: 10,000

a farmer, he went on many dangerous missions. Once, he was stopped by a German patrol while carrying a suitcase full of Jewish books. He insisted that he was "a simple farmer delivering bags." He did not know what was in the satchel, he claimed. The Germans believed him, and he was released. At another time, Leon was forced to hide with a Greek family for several days while Nazi soldiers searched for him.

During the time that Leon was working with the partisans, Gracia remained hidden in a mountain village with her infant son. In order to support the family, she sewed shirts for the villagers in exchange for food. Faced with a shortage of buttons for the new clothing, she used her ingenuity. She collected the buttons from the bottom part of all Leon's shirts and used them for the new ones.

Later in the war, Allied units infiltrated into Greece to help the partisans, and together they were able to drive out the Germans. German forces left Greece in September 1944 and Leon and Gracia with their two-year-old son, Joseph, returned to Trikala. They found that only fifty of Trikala's Jews had been deported by the Nazis, but Salonika had not fared so well. Of the fifty-six thousand Jews living there in 1941, forty-eight thousand had been deported. Of those, thirty-seven thousand had been gassed and burned immediately on arrival at Auschwitz. With them were most of Leon and Gracia's extended families. Gracia's only sister, Anna, and Marius, one of her three brothers, were both murdered. (Her oldest brother had immigrated to Palestine in 1930.) Only one brother, Isaac, survived Auschwitz and the subsequent death march. He had been one of the Jews responsible for helping to bomb one of the crematoria at Auschwitz-Birkenau in 1944.

Once the final peace treaty was signed in 1945, the Pessahs were determined to leave Europe for the United States. While they waited for a visa, a second son, Marius, was born in 1946 and a third son, Yehoshua (Jerry), in 1948. A year later, the family arrived in New York, where Rabbi Pessah became one of the spiritual leaders of the *Kehillah Kedoshah* (holy community) of Janina, Greece, a synagogue located on the lower east side of Manhattan, and one of the few Greek synagogues in the United States. After several years, he moved to the Bronx and became an assistant rabbi of a small, Sephardic community (Jews originating from Spain). From there, he moved to a larger synagogue, the Sephardic Jewish Center, and remained there until his retirement.

The Pessah's three sons were educated in the United States at a traditional yeshivah. After high school, they all continued on to college and professional careers. Joseph became an educator and eventually a school principal, Marius became a physician, and Jerry an electrical engineer. Rabbi Leon Pessah died in New York at the age of eighty-one but Gracia Pessah lived for another fourteen years. Her later years were spent in a nursing home in Great Neck, New York, near her son, Marius. She remained a devout woman and continued to read her religious books and study the Torah portion for each week until her death.

References

To Life: 36 Stories of Memory and Hope. Preface and historical essay by David G. Marwell. Foreword by Robert M. Morgenthau. New York: Bulfinch Press, 2002.

Pessah, Marius. Interview by the author, June 2005, Great Neck, New York.

Pessah, Moissis (d. 1955)

Moissis (whose Hebrew name was Moshe) Pessah of Greece was the chief rabbi of Volos and played a major role in Greek Resistance during World War II. Working with other Greek clergymen and political leaders, he led the mostly-Jewish partisan unit in the areas of Volos, Larissa, and Trikala, Greece, and was able to rescue many Jews.

Rabbi Pessah, a distant relative of Rabbi Leon Pessah, was the son of Symeon Pessah, who had been Chief Rabbi of "Old Greece," before the annexation of additional territories after the Balkan War of 1912–1913. His son Moissis first taught at the small rabbinical seminary that had been established in the town of Volos and served in that capacity from 1895–1902. He later became chief rabbi of Volos and eventually held the title of Grand Chief Rabbi. Rabbi Pessah was active in founding charitable associations. He was known among Jews and Christians for his social, religious, and patriotic activities and maintained good relationships with community and religious leaders.

By the time World War II began, the Jewish population of Greece was 77,000 but the number of Jews in Volos was decreasing and had gone from 2000 in 1920 to 872 in 1940. That year, the Greeks were attacked by the Italian Army and by 1941 most of Greece was occupied by German or Italian troops. The Volos synagogue was burned and destroyed in March 1943.

After the surrender of Italy to the Allied Forces in September 1943 and the complete German takeover of Greece, antisemitic measures were quickly initiated in Thessaly, the area where Volos was located, and the threat to Jews increased considerably. In Volos, the mayor and the Metropolitan Bishop of Demetrias took action to protect Rabbi Pessah. Pessah went into hiding on Mt. Pelion and from that re-

---

Excerpts from an Exchange of Letters between M. Pessah, Chief Rabbi of Volos, and His Beatitude Spyridon, Archbishop of Athens and All Greece

Your Beatitude:

. . . We take this opportunity of stressing to Your Beatitude that the Jews of Greece do not forget the beneficent efforts on the part of the local ecclesiastical authorities, dictated to them by the religious spirit of love towards their suffering fellow human beings, for their salvation, as far as it was possible during their implacable persecution by the Bulgarians and the Germans. We do not forget either the strenuous efforts for the same purpose of the late Archbishop Damaskinos, nor the daring action taken by Your Beatitude for the protection of the Jews of Ioannina, who, together with their co-religionists all over Greece, were exterminated by the above enemy forces. We shall always remember that Your Beatitude took under your safekeeping at the Holy Metropolis of Ioannina the scrolls of our Sacred Bible and other articles of the Holy Synagogue there, which after liberation, Your Beatitude returned to the few Jews who had survived. For all these deeds we thank you with all our heart . . .

—M. Pessah

Your Reverence:

. . . Your letter reminded us of our common struggles and perils during the dark years of the enemy occupation and made us recall with deep sadness the terrible martyrdom undergone by our brother Greek Jewish element when the conquerors started with unwavering determination to turn against it and our Greek homeland. Whatever we did in defiance during those tragic times, either ourselves or the Reverend Bishops everywhere and the Greek Church in general, was simply a duty imposed not only by a sense of the need to help our suffering fellow human beings but mainly inspired by sincere love towards our imperiled brethren, dear children of the same Mother Greece, forming an inseparable part of its people.

—His Beatitude Spyridon, Archbishop of Athens

fuge, succeeded in saving many Jewish lives. Although the Germans attempted to liquidate the Jewish community in Volos as they did in other parts of Greece, coordinated efforts of the resistance and the religious leaders prevented it. Only 155 Jews from the area of Volos were deported. All were killed.

Rabbi Pessah took responsibility for most of the members of his small community, hiding them in mountain villages. He also aided hundreds of other Jews as well as helping to smuggle a number of Greeks and Allied officers out of Greece to the safety of the Middle East. Pessah personally took charge of the predominantly Jewish Resistance troops that operated in Thessaly and was described as "an aged rabbi . . . who roamed the mountains with a rifle in his hands."

Greece was liberated in the fall of 1944 and the Jews, mostly destitute by this time, returned to their homes. In recognition of his service to Greece, Rabbi Moissis Pessah was awarded the Gold Cross of the Phoenix. In 1945, the Allied Forces awarded him the Scroll of Honor for helping Allied soldiers escape from the Germans.

Although many Greek Jews left for Israel as soon as the government granted them permission to leave, Rabbi Pessah remained in Greece. He died there on November 13, 1955 and was buried in Volos. In 1977, however, his remains were taken to Israel and buried on the Hill of the Wise.

References

Constantopoulou, Photini, and Thanos Veremis, editors and researchers. *Documents on the History of the Greek Jews: Records from the Historical Archives of the Ministry of Foreign Affairs.* Athens: Kasloniotes Press, 1999.
Encyclopedia Judaica. Vol. 7, s.v. "Greece: Holocaust Period," col. 880.

Pinkus, Oscar (ca. 1925–)

Oscar Pinkus, a high school student in Miedzyrzec, a town in eastern Poland, was scheduled to take his yearly exam on September 1, 1939, the day the Germans bombed Warsaw. His education ended abruptly and he and his family spent most of the war hiding, first from the Germans and then from the Polish Partisans. Those years in hiding became a test for Pinkus's endurance and leadership.

Pinkus was born in the town of Losice, the middle child and only son of the family. Like most of the Jews there, his parents were poor and could not afford to send him to the Gymnasium in nearby Miedzyrzec. Instead, he studied on his own, taking an exam each year. When World War II began, Pinkus did not believe it would affect him or his family, but he quickly learned the truth.

As occurred in most of eastern Poland, Losice was occupied at first by the Soviet Union. This was in accordance with the treaty between that country and Germany to divide Poland. But in Losice, the Russian occupation lasted less than a week before the realization that the new border was farther to the East. The Russians pulled out and the Germans replaced them.

The Jews of Losice were well aware of the Nazi policy of antisemitism in Germany and many left with the Soviet troops, crossing the river into what was now Russian territory. But Oscar and many others remained. They were confident that Germany would lose the war and decided to stick it out. The Pinkuses soon regretted that decision.

Almost immediately, the Germans initiated a series of rulings. All schooling was outlawed, Jews were forbidden to travel by train and could not use the sidewalks; they had to tip their hats to all Germans. Ignoring these laws resulted in punishments such as beatings and imprisonment. In addition, Jewish shops were routinely looted and Jews were impressed for slave labor. Assuming that women and children would be safe, Oscar and his father now attempted to cross into Soviet territory with the help of peasants, but their attempts failed and they were forced to return. Oscar was conscripted to do heavy construction work to help build Nazi facilities.

During the winter of 1941, a ghetto was established in Losice and Jews from neighboring towns were transported there, creating even more of a burden on the community's resources. When Oscar was transported temporarily to a nearby labor camp, he was actually relieved not to have to witness the suffering and the daily deaths from starvation.

Next followed a series of roundups in which Jews were taken from their houses with only short notice, ostensibly for deportation. Only a few escaped from those transports. Those who did manage to return reported to the others about Treblinka, a death camp with its own crematorium. The Pinkus family, in an effort to avoid their pending deportation, prepared a hiding place in their attic, with Oscar's uncles, aunts, and cousins who lived on the lower floors of the same house.

Hidden in that tiny space under the eaves, Pinkus, his parents, and his sisters, Manya and Belcia, survived a roundup that resulted in the deportation of almost the entire population of Losice to Treblinka and death. But they could not stay in that tiny hole for long. For the next two years, from 1942 to 1944, their lives consisted of moving from one hiding place to another. For the last one and a half years, they were hidden in an underground bunker with barely enough room for the eleven family members to sleep. The bunker was a hole dug under the floor of a shed and camouflaged with manure. It was on a farm owned by a Pole named Karbicki, their reluctant savior.

Karbicki's poverty was the main motivation for his good deeds. He took as much money from the family as he could and begrudged them anything extra, but as Oscar Pinkus later affirmed in his moving book *The House of Ashes*, he saved their lives at the risk of his own, and kept the German police away from their hiding place. Only his older sister, Manya, did not survive the war. She had obtained false papers and attempted to live as a Christian, but was eventually caught and sent to Auschwitz. She was killed there just before the German retreat.

Rumors of a Soviet victory were everywhere during the winter and spring of 1944, but each time there was new hope, it was followed by disappointment. As he matured, Pinkus took a leadership role within his extended family. He began to leave their bunker regularly, making contact with other Jews who were hidden and bringing back news. Twice he returned to Losice, under cover of darkness, to retrieve money that his uncle had hidden under the steps of their old home. That money was used to pay Karbicki whose good will allowed them to be fed daily and provided a safe haven for them.

Gradually, the Germans, feeling the pressure of the Russian offensive, stayed away from the forests and Pinkus spent more time out of the bunker, contacting other Jews who were in hiding there, as well as helpful Poles and escaped Russian prisoners of war. With some of his uncle's extra money, he began to go to a nearby farm and buy extra provisions for the family.

As the German presence lessened, however, the Polish Underground Army, the *Armia Krajowa*, began to make its presence felt. At first, the Jews assumed that this "Home Army" was on their side. They quickly discovered that their orders, like the Nazis, were to kill all the Jews. Those hidden in the groves and woods were particularly vulnerable. Several were shot by the *Armia Krajowa* and Pinkus retreated back to the bunker. The family wondered how much longer they would have to wait.

At last, the long-awaited moment came. German soldiers, now on the run, passed through Karbicki's farm but now they were no longer giving orders. They were begging for water and some help in their retreat. Pinkus watched the Germans from the tiny hole in their bunker. He watched them leave and shortly after, saw the lights of the Russian tanks enter the farm. It was July 30, 1944. They had been liberated.

The Pinkus family—with the exception of Manya—was among only thirty Jews who survived and returned to Losice. The bulk of the population of seven thousand had all been murdered by the Nazis or their collaborators, or died of hunger. A few more were killed by the *Armia Krajowa* in Losice after the war. The remnants of the Polish Underground tried to murder Pinkus several times. This new danger, plus the desolation of their old home, led them to relocate to a displaced-persons camp in Germany. They waited there, trying to decide where to go.

Oscar's uncle and his family, who had shared their bunker for two long years, left for the United States after a three-year wait. His sister Belcia married another survivor and eventually emigrated to the United States. Oscar and his parents moved to Lodz, where he completed high school in four months. Then he left Poland, traveling south to Italy and the Mediterranean to wait for passage to Palestine, still not an independent Jewish state. After two more years of waiting, Pinkus decided he could wait no longer. He sailed for America and settled in New Mexico. In addition to his book *The House of Ashes*, based on the diaries he kept during the war, he has written several other books about his war experiences including *Son of Zelman*, *Friends and Lovers*, *A Choice of Masks*, and *Victor*. His most recent book is a history of the war, called *The War Aims and Strategies of Adolf Hitler*. In addition, Pinkus, a mechanical engineer, has published several technical works in his chosen profession including his latest, *Thermal Aspects of Fluid Film Tribology*.

Once settled in the United States, both Pinkus and his wife continued to keep in touch with Karbicki, the farmer who had saved them. They sent him goods and money and never forgot that they owed their lives to him.

Reference

Pinkus, Oscar. *The House of Ashes*. Schenectady, NY: Union College Press, 1990.

Polanski, Roman (1933–)

A young child in Krakow, Poland, when World War II began, Roman Polanski's early years were mostly unsupervised. Shifted from one reluctant gentile family to another, he found refuge in the cinema and this eventually became his passion and his life's work.

Polanski was born in Paris, the only child of an assimilated Polish father and a half-Jewish Russian émigré mother. When he was three years old, his parents moved to Krakow, Poland, and were there when Germany invaded that country in 1939. His family first fled to Warsaw, thinking it would be safer, but after Warsaw was heavily bombed, they returned to their home in Krakow. Within a short time, the Polanskis, including Roman's half-sister, Annette (from his mother's previous marriage), had to leave their apartment for another lodging within the designated ghetto.

As a child of seven, Polanski watched the Germans build the wall around the ghetto and realized for the first time that they were being locked in. Although his early experiences were not terrifying, and sneaking out of the ghetto seemed like an adventure at first, life became increasingly difficult. Food was scarce and constant roundups of Jews left many children without parents and quickly reduced the Jewish population.

Polanski's father, understanding the risks to his family, made financial arrangements for his son to leave the ghetto and hide with a gentile family. The Wilks, friends of his father from before the war, had been given a large sum of money. They were responsible for finding a home for him outside the ghetto walls. Each time there was a rumor of another roundup in the Krakow ghetto, Polanski's mother or father would sneak him out and bring him to the Wilks's. When the roundup was over, he would be picked up and brought back home. One day, when his father came, he told Roman, "They took your mother."

With the ghetto emptying out, the Polanskis were transferred to another section and it was from there that his father and half-sister were taken away. Polanski had been sent once again to the Wilks's but when he found no one home, he returned by himself to the ghetto. On the street, he saw his father being marched to the railroad station with hundreds of other Jews. He tried to catch up with him, but his father signaled him to go away. With no place else to turn, Polanski went back to the Wilks's.

The young Roman Polanski spent the remainder of the war being shifted from one family to another. Mostly unsupervised, he wandered around the city alone. With no papers, he could not attend school and he spent much of his time visiting the movie houses, a refuge from the harsh reality of his life. When the Puteks, the Krakow family where he was boarding, became angry with him, they found another place for him in the country. His new guardians, the Buchalas, had three children of their own. They were poor and uneducated, but were kind to him and mostly left him to his own devices. He shared the work on the farm and although he had no access there to the cinema, he enjoyed the beauty of the countryside. Living on a farm also meant that there was more food available, at least in the summertime.

Polanski remained with the Buchalas until August 1944, when that area of Poland was attacked by the Russians. The German Army came in and prepared for a major battle, and Polanski, now eleven years old, was sent back to Krakow and the Putek's home.

"The German occupation of Poland ended for me as it had begun, in an air-raid shelter," wrote Polanski many years later in his autobiography. Except this time, he was with the Puteks in Krakow and his family had disappeared from his life. After the Russian Army liberated the city, Polanski remained with the Puteks, who gave him room and board and largely ignored him. He became a child of the streets, moving around with a gang of young boys who spent their time collecting explosive material and detonating it for their amusement.

On the street, Polanski was discovered by his Uncle Stephan, his father's younger brother, who had survived the war in hiding. Stephan Polanski took him back to his home but his nephew was now used to unsupervised living. Stephan found his behavior intolerable, and sent him to his Uncle David. David and Teofila Polanski shared a flat with the **Rosner brothers**, their sister, **Regina Horowitz**, and her son **Ryszard**. It was here that Polanski had his first experience living with a family who observed Jewish tradition, but he hated living with his uncle and still hoped for his parents' return.

Many months after the war was over, Polanski's father appeared at his uncle's home in Krakow. He had survived the camps and been nursed back to health by the American soldiers. Polanski's half-sister, Annette, had survived Auschwitz and was living in Paris. His mother had been murdered just a few days after being captured by the Nazis.

The young Polanski now hoped to be able to leave his uncle's home and live with his father, but that never happened. His father left Krakow, ostensibly on business, and returned with a new wife, Wanda. Although Wanda Polanski resented Roman in those first years, their relationship eventually improved. When Polanski turned fourteen, however, the tension in the family was so bad that his father found separate rooms for his son in a boarding house. Polanski senior always supported him financially but disapproved of most of his activities.

Catching up on his education was difficult, but somehow Polanski managed it, simultaneously becoming involved in theater and cinema in postwar Poland. He acted in his first play in Krakow, got to know the actors, and found his way to an art school, where he almost completed a high school equivalency degree, and then to the first Polish film school in Lodz. Committed to his new profession, he simultaneously worked as actor, director, scriptwriter, and film editor, gaining a reputation while treading carefully around the Communist system of censorship. He graduated from the Lodz film school in 1957, made his first full-length movie in 1962 with a film called *Knife in the Water*, and a short time later, moved to France and then to England.

By 1968, Polanski had made his Hollywood debut with *Rosemary's Baby*, followed by other, controversial and innovative films including *Macbeth*, and *Chinatown*. A growing success in his professional life, Polanski's personal life was plagued with problems and tragedies. He was married several times and had relationships with many other women. In 1969, his American wife, Sharon Tate, then eight months pregnant, was tragically murdered by the Charles Manson family in a horrifying series of murders that shocked the nation.

Years later Polanski was accused of having sex with a thirteen-year-old girl. In order to avoid standing trial for the charges, he fled the country and established a residence in France. Here he made the movie *Tess*, based on the classic novel *Tess of the D'Urbervilles*. This was his last box-office success for many years until his film *The Pianist*, the movie about the Jewish Holocaust survivor, **Wladyslaw Szpilman**. In 1984, Polanski published the story of his life, an autobiography called simply *Roman*.

References

Polanski, Roman. *Roman.* New York: William Morrow & Co., 1984.
"Roman Polanski." *New York Times.* http://movies2.nytimes.com/gst/movies.
"Roman Polanski." *American Movie Classics.* http://www.amctv.com/person/detail?
   CID=5314-1-EST.

Popielatz, Rika (1891–1985), and Evelyn Pike Rubin (née Popielatz) (1930–)

Evelyn Rubin, the daughter of Rika and Benno Popielatz, was born in Breslau, Germany, into a comfortable, middle-class family. The Popielatz family thought their life was secure and that the social democratic government instituted by Adolf Hitler would not last. Less than ten years later, they were living in a slum in faraway China, far from family and from the country they had loved.

Beginning in 1932, when the Nazis first took power in Germany, the restrictions against Jews steadily expanded, causing increasing hardship for the Jews of Breslau. For Evelyn, much too young to understand what was going on, it meant no more ice skating lessons and no swimming at the pool because Jews were barred from these places. It also meant no more excursions into the country on Sundays, since Jews were prohibited from using automobiles. Then Evelyn's nanny had to leave them since German women under forty-five years of age were not allowed to work for Jews.

All around them, their friends and family were leaving Germany, going to any country that would take them in. The Popielatz family contacted Rika's sister Rosa in America and asked for her help, but Rosa refused to help them. She was concerned that she would have to support her sister's family. Although Rika was disappointed, Benno still felt that the Jews were overreacting. We just have to wait it out, he insisted, and everything will go back to normal. But conditions only worsened.

As a result of all the anti-Jewish laws, Jews had to give up their jobs and close their stores. Rika, who had her own twine and paper goods business long before she married, was no longer able to earn enough to support the family. Benno had worked with her in the business since their marriage and now he, too, was earning nothing. Then a new order came: all Jews were to deliver their valuables to a government office. The family's fine silver, their jewelry, and precious heirlooms were all handed over to German officials. There was no payment and no recourse. By 1937, the family was forced to move out of their spacious apartment into a small furnished room. On their last day in the empty apartment, Evelyn sadly celebrated her eighth birthday.

Benno and Rika Popielatz now began the serious business of looking for a country that would take them in. There were very few choices. Palestine was still closed to most Jews. Without sponsorship from family in America, the quota in the United States meant years of waiting. England had agreed to accept only children, and the surrounding countries of Europe were all in danger of invasion by the Nazis. Then they heard of one place that had no quota: Shanghai. It was certainly not where they wanted to go; it would be their last resort.

The Popielatz family was still trying other possibilities for emigration when Ernst Vom Rath, a German diplomat stationed in Paris, was assassinated by a young Jewish student. This triggered a massive pogrom throughout Germany on November 8, 1938. Jewish shops were destroyed, synagogues burned, and thirty thousand Jews were arrested. Benno Popielatz was one of them.

Most of the Jews arrested that day were taken to Buchenwald, a concentration camp in the eastern part of Germany that had been operating since 1937. Because Benno Popielatz had been the recipient of the Iron Cross for service in World War I, he was released after a few months on condition that he must leave Germany immediately. This time, he did not hesitate. His experiences of cruelty and deprivation at Buchenwald convinced him that his family must flee. He took a course in typewriter repair and maintenance, an occupation that would serve him well wherever they went, and the family purchased steamship tickets on a Japanese ship sailing for Shanghai, China.

The month spent on the ship was pleasant for all three of the Popielatzes, but when they arrived in March, 1939, the reality was harsh. The climate was oppressively hot, sanitation was poor, and housing was scarce. Still, they were free. Benno set himself up in business as a typewriter repairman, solicited all the European businesses in Shanghai, and soon was making a nice living. They were able to find an apartment in the French part of the city and to send for Benno's mother. Evelyn was enrolled in a fine Jewish school, where she learned English and later Japanese, and for a few years, life seemed normal. In 1941, however, their lives took several turns for the worse.

First, Benno Popielatz died suddenly of an unexplained illness, and his wife Rika, with no technical background, had to take on the repair business he had established. The family income was now reduced considerably. Next came December 8, 1941, the day after the Japanese attacked Pearl Harbor, when America declared war on Japan. Suddenly, the war had spread into their safe haven. Foreign nationals from all the allied powers, including France, England, and Holland, were interned in camps and the Japanese, only a minimal presence when Rika Popielatz and her daughter had first arrived in Shanghai, took over the administration of the city. They were strict overseers and soon all the refugees were feeling the pinch as food was rationed and movement was limited. On February 18, 1943, all stateless refugees were ordered to relocate to a small section of Shanghai, the poorest part of the city, and stay there unless they got permission to go to other areas. This meant that Evelyn had to request a pass to continue going to the Jewish school, and Rika had to beg for permission to move about the city to pursue her business.

Life grew harsher and both mother and daughter became undernourished. When Rika had had an exceptionally bad week, they were forced to resort to the soup kitchen. On Passover, they begged for matzah from the Yeshivah.

Proclamation Concerning Restrictions of Residence and Business of Stateless Refugees:

I. Due to military necessity, places of residence and business of the stateless refugees in the Shanghai area shall hereafter be restricted to the undermentioned area in the International Settlement: east of the line connecting Chaoufoong Rd . . . and south of the boundary of the International Settlement.

II. The stateless refugees at present residing and/or carrying on business in the district other than the above area shall remove their place of residence and/or business into the area designated above by May 18, 1943.

III. Persons other than the stateless refugees shall not remove into the area mentioned in Article I without the permission of the Japanese authorities.

IV. Persons who will have violated this proclamation or obstructed its reinforcement shall be liable to severe punishment.

—Commander-in-Chief of the Imperial Japanese Navy in the Shanghai area, February 18, 1943.

Somehow, they managed to survive until 1945, when American air force planes began to bomb Shanghai. Although all the refugees hoped that the United States would be successful, they were living in a Japanese-controlled city and did not want to be killed by bombs. To compound their problem, there were no underground shelters in Shanghai because most of the city was built on water.

Many of the Jewish refugees were killed by bombs in those last days of the war but Rika and Evelyn were lucky enough to survive. They heard about the atomic bombs that had fallen in Japan. Soon the Japanese soldiers disappeared from the streets and the Shanghai ghetto was open. On September 3, 1945, Rika and her daughter were among the refugees that remained when the American soldiers came to the city. Although Evelyn was sick with jaundice, she heard about the parties that were organized and the victory parades. Along with happiness at war's end, however, was sadness at the news coming out of Europe. They heard for the first time that six million European Jews had been murdered. One after another, they heard the news of brothers and sisters, aunts, uncles, and cousins who had been killed and they realized that in spite of all the hardships, Shanghai had saved their lives.

Their next step was to try once more to come to America. They finally succeeded, with the help of friends whose family in Lakewood, New Jersey, agreed to sponsor them. They arrived in San Francisco on March 20, 1947, eight years after they had come to Shanghai. Evelyn was now seventeen years old. She had completed her schooling in Shanghai and she and her mother were ready to work and build a new life.

It did not take long for Evelyn and Rika to find their way to New York and settle in. Within a few years, Rika had a steady job, they had found an apartment in Queens, New York, and Evelyn had fallen in love with Harold Pike. Within a few months, they married and Evelyn worked to support her American husband while he went to medical school in Switzerland. When they returned to the United States, they already had a baby daughter. Subsequently, Harold and Evelyn Pike settled down in Jericho, New York, a town on Long Island, and had a son and two more daughters. But by the time her four children had grown, Evelyn and her husband had separated. Those were difficult years, but Evelyn had learned resiliency and determination from her mother. She weathered the storm and married Leonard Rubin in 1984. One year later, Evelyn's mother died, just six months before her ninety-fourth birthday.

Evelyn Popielatz Pike Rubin remained in Jericho, New York. She became active in Jewish causes and was committed to sharing her Holocaust experiences, helping to teach the next generation. She told her audiences: "When everything seemed hopeless, there was an open door. I don't want anyone to forget where that door was. . . . Soon there won't be anyone around to remember how we survived against all odds."

Reference

Rubin, Evelyn Pike. *Ghetto Shanghai.* Forward by Jud Newborn. New York: Shengold Publishers, 1993.

Pressel family

Joseph and Miriam Schwerner Pressel and their son Philip were living in Brussels when World War II began. After Germany invaded Belgium in 1940, they fled to France and kept one step ahead of the Nazis throughout the war. Sixty years later, Philip Pressel wrote that although he had no tattoos on his arm as the concentration camp survivors did, "There is a tattoo in my memory."

Both the Pressel and the Schwerner family had their roots in Poland but had lived in Belgium for many years. Joseph Pressel was born in Belgium and Miriam Schwerner was educated there. The two met at the Macabi Center, a sports club for young Jews, and were married in 1930. Joseph Pressel had an administrative position with the Ford Motor Company in Brussels and looked forward to a promising career. He spoke many languages and was an expert in methods of stenography, which he used to copy entire speeches, especially those by Zionist leaders.

Their son Philip was born in 1937 and by then, Joseph Presser had moved from one job to another, often as a translator and transcriber. Miriam worked as a dressmaker and those skills served her well throughout the war and long after. Despite the fact that both Philip and his father were born in Belgium, they were registered as Polish citizens.

When German planes crossed into Belgium on May 10, 1940, and bombed Brussels, the Pressel family joined many others fleeing south into France. There, Joseph, still a Polish citizen, enlisted in the Polish army and sent his wife and son further south. Within months, however, the Germans had overtaken France. The French army surrendered and Pressel's Polish unit was dissolved.

Joseph Pressel joined his wife and son and found lodgings in Marseilles, a southern city where Nazi troops had not yet penetrated. Because the Pressels had left Belgium before the antisemitic rulings of the Nazis were in place, their identification papers were not stamped with a "J" indicating that they were Jewish. However, as Polish citizens, they were subject to deportation and thus were in constant danger.

In Marseilles, Joseph was not able to find employment and Miriam now supported the family on her wages as a dressmaker. They lived in the poorest part of town and barely had enough to eat. The Pressels desperately tried to get visas to leave for the United States where they had many relatives, but were not successful. Attempts to sail to Great Britain via Spain or to arrange for visas to Cuba proved equally fruitless.

By June 1942, the Pressels were frantic with worry as they began to hear rumors of the wholesale murder of women and children by the Nazis in Poland. Faced with constant roundups by the German and French police in Marseilles, the Pressels moved to Lyon. Here, Joseph Pressel found work for a large French firm that provided an apartment for him and his family. Philip began school and life took on a semblance of normalcy, but not for long. The Pressels heard through a neighbor that someone thought they were Jews and had sent the French police to investigate. The Pressels fled again and stayed temporarily with relatives who were hiding in Argenton sur Creuse. When the danger had passed, they returned to Lyon.

But when the Allies began bombing France, Lyon became a dangerous place and in March 1944, the Municipal Government ordered all children to be evacuated for their own safety. Miriam met one of Philip's teachers who agreed to take him in until the war was over. Philip was taken to Vourles, a small village about seven miles from Lyon, and settled in with the Sabathier family, parents and a son Jean.

The Sabathier were kind and caring but Philip missed his parents desperately. In addition, Vourles was a center of resistance activity. The underground was active and the area was regularly bombed by the Germans. Once, a bullet flew in through the window and just missed Philip's head. Another time, when the Pressels were visiting in Vourles, a call came through from the German army threatening that if they attacked German troops as they passed through the town, they would return and destroy the entire village. Since Joseph Pressel was the only person there who understood German, he was summoned to take the call and translated the German demands. The French Underground desisted from any violence and the village was saved.

In the summer of 1944, after the Allied landing in Normandy (referred to as D-Day), Philip returned to his parents in Lyon. But the danger had not passed completely. News trickled in about Jewish orphans in Paris still being arrested and deported. Then the police called the Pressels to their headquarters to report that their papers—the false ones that they had obtained from the underground—had not checked out. Miriam Pressel, using her own brand of charm, plus a dose of bravado, managed to convince the officials to look further as their records from the north of France must have been destroyed. Then, with the help of an acquaintance, their suspicious documents were burned.

Without any identity papers, the Pressel family waited tensely for the war to be over. On September 3, 1944, Lyon was liberated by American troops coming up from North Africa.

It took more than six months before the war was finally at an end and the Germans had accepted defeat. By then, the Pressels were back in Paris, in time to see the famous victory parade with General Charles de Gaulle marching down the Champs Elysées.

The German defeat brought happiness but also sadness as the Pressels took stock of their family and discovered who had perished in Auschwitz and who had been saved. With peace, they were free to travel back to Belgium and see

Miriam's parents, who had remained safe in Antwerp. Their old apartment, however, was emptied of all its belongings.

The family decided to resume their attempts to get to America. With the United Nations newly formed in New York, Joseph obtained a position there as translator and sent for his family. They arrived in November 1946 and settled near U.N. headquarters in Great Neck, New York.

> When I ask myself, "Why did you survive?" my answer is that I did so because of the courage and love Papa and Ma had for me and for life itself. Other than that, I believe it was just plain luck.
>
> —Philip Pressel, *They Are Still Alive: A Family's Survival in France during World War II* (p. 176).

All through the war, Philip, still very young, was never told that he was a Jew for fear he would inadvertently give himself away. Once the war was over and Philip was almost eight years old, he learned that he was Jewish. In the United States, his parents, although not very religious, were anxious for him to learn about Judaism. They joined a synagogue and Philip went to a Hebrew school and became a bar mitzvah.

Joseph Pressel continued working at the U.N., but his life was cut short by a fatal heart attack in 1952. Miriam Pressel now returned to work in New York City, finding jobs with famous couturiers. After remaining a widow for many years, she married Harvey Groner. His death in 2001 left her a widow for the second time, but in 2004, at the age of ninety-eight, she was still enjoying life.

Philip Pressel received his education in the public schools and then studied engineering at New York University. He graduated, found a good job in his field, and married Marion Levy. They had three sons (one of whom died in a tragic accident) and a daughter. Philip was instrumental in helping to design and build the famous Hubble telescope.

In 1980, after his children were grown, Philip divorced and later married Patricia Trudel. Together, they made a pilgrimage back to Vourles and Philip was reunited with the Sabathiers. As of 2005, Pressel and his wife were retired and living in San Diego, California.

Reference

Pressel, Philip. *They Are Still Alive: A Family's Survival in France during World War II*. Pittsburgh, PA: Dorrance Publishing, 2004.

Preston, Halina (1922–)

During the war, Halina Wind Preston (originally Fayga Wind), from Turka, Poland, obtained false papers and tried to live as a Christian outside the walls of the Lvov ghetto. She was betrayed by her Polish landlady and arrested. Escaping from prison, she returned to the ghetto and went into hiding in the sewers of Lvov until the war was over.

Preston was the only daughter of Joshua and Hannah Wind. The family, including a younger brother, Leon, lived in Turka, a Polish town in the Carpathian Mountains. Although her father was a religious man, he made the decision to educate both his daughter and his son equally in a private secular school in Turka. Leon also spent a year in college in Poland, but the antisemitism there was so troubling to him that he left for the United States. He wrote to his sister urging her to follow him. Preston applied and was admitted to the Teachers College of the Jewish Theological Seminary for the fall term of 1939. On September 1 of that same year, war broke out and Halina was not able to leave.

Turka was in the part of Poland that was first taken over by the Russians, but Joshua Wind, a simple watchmaker who owned no property, was not threatened by the Soviet policy of confiscation. It was not until June 1941, when the Nazis drove the Russians out and occupied that area, that their lives were threatened. Gradually, the Germans eliminated all the Jews of Turka, either by outright murder or by sending them on to concentration camps. By the end of 1942, the Winds were one of only three Jewish families remaining in the town.

Joshua and Hannah Wind knew they would not survive, but they thought their daughter had a chance. She was well educated and spoke perfect Polish with no Yiddish accent. She also knew the Catholic prayers from her school days. She was given false papers, identifying her as Halina Naskiewicz, her mother hung a Catholic medal around her neck, and she was sent out into a hostile world. Her father's last words to her were: "Survive . . . and tell the world what happened."

Preston, then twenty years old, took a train to Lvov and found a room in the home of a Christian family. Pretending to be a Catholic, she had to be silent when her landlady made antisemitic comments about the Jews. It was difficult, but she managed to keep her secret until Christmas. When a priest came to the house to celebrate Christmas mass with the family, Preston made a crucial mistake: instead of waiting for the priest to place the communion wafer in her mouth, she reached for it with her hand. No Polish Catholic would ever have done that and her landlady, realizing that she must be Jewish, immediately sent her from the house, giving her the address of another room she might rent. When she arrived there, the Ukrainian police were waiting for her.

Preston was brought to jail and beaten with clubs and then with whips, but she would not confess that she was Jewish, insisting that her name was Halina Naskiewicz. Not believing her, the Nazi police threw her in jail inside the ghetto with a group of others who had tried to pass as Christians. The next morning, the guards ordered her to empty the pail the prisoners used as a toilet. Bruised and battered, she grabbed the pail and headed toward an open door. No one was there to stop her. Preston put the pail down and continued walking.

Pressed against Lvov's ghetto walls, she could hear the alarm sounding in the prison and the police dogs barking. Terrified and still in pain from the beating, she did not know where to turn. Then she heard a voice telling her to come in. At first she was afraid, but when she heard the voice of a woman coming from inside, and realized she was speaking Yiddish, she entered. The Jews in that room, the Weiss family and a few others, made a place for her and found her another identity (Jewish, this time) so she would be able to work in the ghetto. Having a job was the only way a Jew could survive the selections and transports.

Preston lived with the Weiss family for a year, working with all the other Jews as a slave laborer, until the Nazis decided to liquidate the ghetto completely. They began a mass slaughter of all the Jews remaining in Lvov from which only a few survived. A small number, including the Weiss and **Chiger families**, had prepared a hiding place underground in the sewer pipes of Lvov. Although ultimately Weiss's wife and children refused to go with him, and Weiss himself was later killed, Preston did descend into the sewer and remained there for thirteen months, until the Russians came and liberated the ten Jews who had managed to survive underground. Their savior was a Polish sewer inspector, **Leopold Socha**, who discovered the men while they were building their hideout, agreed to help them, and brought them food and news of the war on a regular basis.

Liberated in July 1944, the entire group of ten survivors stayed with Socha for a while, then moved to Krakow and waited for the war to end in the rest of Europe. After peace was established in May 1945, Halina Wind Preston emigrated to the United States and joined her brother. She married an engineer and had two children. Settled in Delaware, Preston contributed toward the erection of a monument in honor of Catholic Poles and other Christians who helped Jews during the Holocaust.

References

Marshall, Robert. *In the Sewers of Lvov: A Heroic Story of Survival from the Holocaust.* New York: Scribner's, 1991.
Wells, Leon W. *The Death Brigade.* New York: Holocaust Library, 1963.

R

Radasky, Solomon (1910–2002)

During World War II, Solomon Radasky of Warsaw survived labor battalions, several concentration camps, numerous train rides under inhuman conditions, forced marches, overwork, and starvation. But he was committed to staying alive. He emerged from the hell of the Holocaust to build a new family and start again.

A native of Warsaw, Radasky was a furrier. He was twenty-nine years old when the war began. His parents, Jacob and Toby Radasky, and their family of three sons and three daughters were quickly swept up in the Nazi campaign first to isolate and then to eliminate Jews. In 1941, Toby Radasky and her oldest daughter were murdered by the police when they denied having any jewelry or furs in their possession. At that time, Radasky was working in a labor gang that maintained the railroads and came back to discover the deaths of his mother and sister. A year later, his father was shot in the back when he bought a loaf of bread that had been smuggled into the ghetto. Then, in July 1942, his remaining two sisters and two brothers were sent on a transport to Treblinka and killed there. He was working as a furrier at the time, sewing warm coats for the German soldiers, and was therefore exempt from the transport.

On April 19, 1943, the Warsaw ghetto uprising began, initiated by young Zionists in a desperate attempt to die fighting. Radasky was caught up in the fight and shot in the ankle by a German soldier. Although only a flesh wound, it prevented him from escaping and he was rounded up with twenty thousand other Jews from the ghetto and brought to the central station for deportation to Treblinka, the nearest extermination camp. At the station, one of many strokes of luck intervened in Radasky's favor. Because Treblinka

> There were 375,000 Jews living in Warsaw before the war. I doubt that there are 5,000 living there today. That is why it is so important for me to tell my story.
>
> —Solomon Radasky

could accommodate only ten thousand people per day in their killing routine, his half of the train was detoured and sent to Majdanek, another concentration camp in Poland.

At Majdanek, Radasky met a Jewish doctor who operated on his bullet wound with a small pocketknife he had managed to keep with him. There were no bandages or medicine and the doctor advised him to clean the wound with his own urine. The wound healed and Radasky was able to hide his pain and walk past the camp guards without limping so he would not be pulled out of line. Whoever was not able to work was killed.

Radasky described his work in Majdanek only as "dirty field work." Many men died on the job and the others would have to carry the bodies back to the camp at the end of the day. "If one thousand went out to work," he later explained, "all one thousand had to come back."

Radasky had several other narrow escapes. Once, selected to be hanged as part of a general punishment, he was saved at the last minute when a German soldier indicated that he was on a list of workers to be transferred to another camp. The noose was removed from his neck and along with 749 others he was put on a train. He had been in Majdanek for nine weeks. During that time, he had never been able to change his clothes or take a bath. Most of the men were eaten up with lice and swollen from hunger.

His next stop was Auschwitz. Radasky expected to be sent straight to the gas chambers, but instead he was selected for work, tattooed with a number, and transferred to Buna, an auxiliary work camp. Radasky's number, 128232, added up to eighteen. In Jewish tradition, the number eighteen is considered a lucky number, since it is equivalent to the Hebrew word *hai*, meaning "life," and Radasky took some comfort in this.

After several months in Buna, Radasky collapsed at work and could not get up. He was pulled out and thrown into a hospital barracks. Again, he expected to be killed, but managed to escape his death sentence. With the help of other prisoners who bribed a guard, he was assigned instead to the sand mines. The men in this work detail dug sand all day and transferred it to the area behind the Auschwitz-Birkenau crematoria where they deposited the remains of those who were gassed and burned. The sand was used to cover up the ashes.

Working there for over a year, Radasky witnessed many of the worst of Nazi atrocities. Every few days, he saw another group of prisoners brought in to be gassed and burned. Once, he watched while the SS guards threw living children into the crematorium. He was still alive when the Germans, with the Russian Army at their heels, evacuated Auschwitz in January 1945. Taken on a forced march in the dead of winter, he walked to Gröss Rosen, another concentration camp that Radasky described simply as "brutal." From there, they were transported by train to Dachau, in Germany. With bombs falling all around them, Radasky and a few others were pulled off yet another train and chosen for work detail. Now he believed that he would surely be killed but he survived this, too. Back on the train his small group saw some soldiers. They thought they were Russians, but they had encountered the U.S. Army. The American soldiers arrested the Germans and told the Jewish prisoners that they were free. It was May 1, 1945.

With the help of the Americans, Solomon Radasky gradually recovered his strength. He went to Feldafing, a German displaced-persons camp where they had lists of survivors from all over Europe. Not a single member of Radasky's family had survived, but he did meet some friends from Warsaw and through them, Frieda, the woman who became his wife. They were married on November 11, 1946, and settled temporarily in Landsberg, Germany. Their first son was born on May 13, 1948, just one day before the new state of Israel declared its independence. In 1949, the Radaskys came to the United States and settled in New Orleans, Louisiana.

Radasky could not speak English when he arrived, but managed to convince his first boss that he was a skilled furrier. He was hired at fifty cents an hour. He worked his way up from there and eventually became foreman of Haspel Brothers, a large store that manufactured their own furs.

Solomon and Frieda Radasky raised their two children in New Orleans and worked hard. They did not take a vacation until 1978. Their first trip was to Israel.

Reference

Interview with Solomon Radasky. http://www.holocaustsurvivors.org/.

Raisglid, George (1919–)

George Raisglid's family was separated during World War II. His father, Wladek Raisglid, on a business trip to the United States, was stranded there after war broke out. His mother, Fela Raisglid, remained at home in Warsaw, and George went farther and farther east, fleeing from the Nazis.

Raisglid was an only child. His father, an engineer, owned an industrial hardware shop and after weathering the depression of 1929, earned a good living. Although threats from Germany were worrisome, the Raisglids, along with many other Polish Jews, were confident that Great Britain and France would not allow Germany to invade Poland. George took his matriculation exams and was accepted to study engineering at the university in Nancy, a city in eastern France. By the time they realized that war was inevitable, George had completed one year at the university, and Wladek was on his way home from a commercial fair in New York City. His boat never arrived in Poland. It was held in England for several months, and then sailed back to the United States where he remained for the entire war.

During his time in England, Wladek Raisglid tried desperately to find a way to rescue his wife and son, but none of his attempts was successful. He continued his efforts from New York but by this time, Germany had full control of Poland and no one was allowed to leave. Raisglid and his mother Fela remained in Warsaw, hoping for a quick end to the war.

At first, George felt secure that the Nazis would not bother him, but he quickly learned how dangerous they were. They first closed the Raisglids' store and confiscated all their goods. Then they came to search their apartment and helped themselves to whatever they wanted. When Raisglid went to Gestapo headquarters to complain, they threatened to throw him out of the window to his death. "That day I lost my innocence," George later wrote. He made up his mind to flee Warsaw and cross the river to the Russian side. Assuming that only the men were in danger of being deported to labor camps, he felt certain that his mother would be safe in their home. Once again the assumption proved false. After a year in the Warsaw ghetto, Fela Raisglid was deported to Treblinka and murdered in the gas chambers.

Raisglid was able to smuggle himself across the border posing as a Christian. There were several close calls. Once, a German officer demanded that he recite the Lord's Prayer to prove he was not a Jew. Raisglid had gone to a Polish school and knew the prayer by heart. He was aware that German officials could, at any time, ask him to undress to check whether or not he was circumcised but they never did.

First Raisglid settled in Bialystok, then part of Russian-occupied Poland, where he had a few acquaintances. He was able to find a job and a place to stay and began to feel at home in this new city. But soon he had to make another move.

The Russians passed a law declaring that all Polish citizens living in what was now Russia must either accept Russian citizenship or be returned to Poland. It was a difficult decision to make. If he became a Russian, he feared he would never be able to leave and rejoin his mother. If he did not, he would have to go back and live under Nazi rule. He knew what that meant. He had already heard too many stories about deportations and killings. Reluctantly, he accepted Russian citizenship.

After the paperwork was done, Raisglid was granted only permanent resident status. That meant he could not live in a large city like Bialystok, but was sent east to Slonim, where he found a job helping to construct a canal. It was not as comfortable as his old job, but he adjusted to this, too. George made friends among his co-workers and during the first year, corresponded with his mother. In 1941, however, Germany declared war on Russia and all communication between Russia and Poland was cut off.

As the German Army advanced eastward, Raisglid kept one step ahead of them. He went from Slonim to Baranovichi, then, running from German bombs and tanks, he settled in Tambov, where he found work as an ambulance driver. A breakthrough came in the winter of 1943 when Raisglid learned that Stalingrad had been retaken by the Soviet Army and the Germans had surrendered. In quick succession, the Russians regained control of Leningrad, Smolensk, and Kiev. The tide of war had turned.

With Russia now fighting with the Allies, mail was again accepted from the United States and George received telegrams and packages from his father along with instructions and the papers necessary for him to come to America. It was merely the beginning of a long process.

The Nazis were no longer a threat to Russia, but the war was still being fought on Polish soil, and after a tremendous loss of Soviet troops, replacements were needed. George Raisglid was drafted in October 1944 and became a Russian soldier. He never served on the front, but shared the glory when he returned home as part of a victorious Russian Army.

With the war finally at an end, Raisglid began his journey westward. Arriving in Warsaw, he found nothing but destruction and memories. From his father's old store manager, a Polish Christian, he learned about his mother's deportation and subsequent death. His next stop was Sweden, where friends of his father were able to receive him and help him find a job. Once again, he made new friends, found a place to live, and waited there for his visa number to come up. He was number 1158. That meant he would not be able to leave before 1950.

Wladek had another idea. He began writing to colleges throughout the United States, trying to find a place that would accept his son. William and Mary College in Virginia was ready to accept him and in August 1948 George left Sweden with a student visa. Five days later, after nine years of separation, he was reunited with his father in New York.

George Raisglid attended William and Mary College and Columbia University. He settled on Long Island and worked for the Department of Labor for many years. George married Rebecca and the Raisglids had two children. His family encouraged him to write and his memoir, *Uprooted*, was published in 1996. It is dedicated to his mother.

Reference

Raisglid, George A. *Uprooted*. East Setauket, NY: George Raisglid, with the help of SUNY Stonybrook, 1996.

Rakowski, Marie-Claire (1943–)

Marie-Claire Rakowski of Belgium was an infant when she was given to a Catholic couple for safekeeping during World War II. She did not meet her mother until many years after the war. For a long time, she struggled to overcome the trauma of her childhood, but not until the 1990s was she able to acknowledge her suffering. "I feel it's important to share our stories with the

Marie-Claire before the war with her parents in Brussels. Courtesy of the U.S. Holocaust Memorial Museum Photo Archives.

world," she told an interviewer. "If we don't speak up, there will be nothing to stop people from denying what happened."

Marie-Claire Rakowski, born in Belgium in the middle of World War II, was the younger of two sisters. Faced with the possibility of her children's death at the hands of the Nazis, her mother arranged to hide both her daughters. Marie-Claire, only two months old, was placed with a childless Catholic couple, her four-year-old sister was sent to a convent. Shortly after finding safe havens for their children, the Rakowski parents were captured by the Germans and transported to Auschwitz.

While Marie-Claire's older sister had a difficult time during the last two years of the war, Marie-Claire recalled that her early childhood was "very rich." She remembered loving her Catholic parents—the only parents she had known—and was with them for four happy years. Her own personal suffering did not begin until the war had ended. One day, with no warning, she was kidnapped by a Jewish organization and taken to Switzerland. "They probably had very idealistic intentions," said Rakowski, "but it ruined my life. . . . My whole life went into complete chaos from the age of four."

In Switzerland, Marie-Claire was united with her older sister, who was a complete stranger to her. Her sister had been sick with typhus during the war, and had lost most of her hair. She was also very angry. Only eight years old

Marie-Claire and Doro Rakowski arriving in the United States shortly after the war. Courtesy of the U.S. Holocaust Memorial Museum Photo Archives.

herself, she took out her pain and frustration on her younger sister, often physically attacking her and making her life generally miserable. The girls were placed in foster care together and went from one home to another. Marie-Claire admitted that there were blocks of time during this early postwar period that "are just blind." Each day, she anticipated that the foster parents that she loved would come and get her and her life would go back to normal but it never did.

The Rakowski girls spent two years in Switzerland before being brought to the United States. Here, they were presented to American Jews as symbols of the Jewish children who had survived the Holocaust. Once again, they went from one foster home to another; sometimes they were treated kindly and other times abused. Marie-Claire remembered one home where the man of the house sexually abused her. After some years, the two sisters were reunited with their mother, but for Marie-Claire, this woman was a total stranger. "I was her daughter," she acknowledged, "and she was, I guess, very happy to see me, but to me, she wasn't anyone I liked or loved. . . . She wasn't what I had in mind for a mother."

It was not until she was much older that Marie-Claire Rakowski learned that her father was killed at Auschwitz. Her mother, who survived the camp, had undergone a series of medical experiments. She came out sick and half-starved, weighing only seventy or eighty pounds. This knowledge made Marie-Claire feel guilty, but she was never able to establish a good relationship with her mother. When she was sixteen, her mother was not able to cope with her and sent her to a home for girls.

Some fifty years after the war, Rakowski became a successful career woman. She earned an M.B.A. in finance and international business and managed a company. Still, she counted her first four years with her Catholic parents as the only happy years of her life. That memory, plus her twenty years of therapy, "pretty much saved me," she admitted in a later interview. But she continued to have serious problems maintaining relationships, and was never able to decorate her home and settle in. "Perhaps it's because I still half expect to be taken away or moved or kidnapped," she confessed. "It's like I don't dare get too comfortable."

The emotional wounds of Rakowski's childhood slowly healed, however, and she began to think more and more about her past. In her later years she wanted to be sure that other people understood how traumatic it was for children to be wrenched from their homes and their parents as so many were during World War II. She didn't want anyone to say, "Those children were so young then, and it was so long ago, how could it matter anymore?" Marie-Claire Rakowski knows that it matters very much.

Reference

Marks, Jane. "The Hidden Children." *New York Magazine* (February 25, 1991): pp. 44-45.

Reger, Christian (1905–1985)

Christian Reger was a Lutheran Pastor in Stegelitz, Germany, and one of many Christians who were imprisoned by the Nazis. When Hitler came to power,

Reger spoke out against policies that made the church subservient to the State. He spent four years in Dachau concentration camp, but his faith in God remained intact. Reger survived the war and continued serving the church in Communist East Berlin.

Pastor Christian Reger and his wife Mina lived in Stegelitz, a small city near Leipzig, Germany, where he led a Protestant congregation. At first, Reger admits, he was sympathetic to the new National Socialist Movement because it gave the people hope and pride. He even wore a party uniform himself to show his sympathies. But when the Nazi party came to power and began to insist that the church follow Nazi principles, Reger began to rethink his opinions and share his opposition with his congregants.

One night, shortly before Hitler came to power, Reger's home was attacked by pro-Nazi zealots who threw stones and shouted threats. Shocked and frightened, Reger and his wife nevertheless committed themselves to continue speaking out against Nazi policy. Reger joined a new organization called the Confessional Church, organized by Pastor **Martin Niemöller** as an opposition group to the Nazi-supported German Christian Faith Movement. Although Reger was under constant pressure to cast his lot with the government, he resisted and continued preaching against the Nazis throughout 1933, 1934, and 1935.

Late in 1935, after a passionate sermon, he was arrested and put into prison along with seven hundred other clergymen of all faiths. The German people were indignant; they protested in the streets and the government relented and released them, but Reger could not remain quiet. After *Kristallnacht*, the nationwide pogrom against the Jews of Germany on November 8, 1938, he again spoke out, insisting that "all men are equal in the sight of the Lord." Once again he was taken into custody and held for a short time.

In 1940, Reger was reported to the Gestapo by his own church organist and arrested a third time. He was sent to Dachau, the concentration camp near Munich where the government sent rebellious clergy. Upon arriving in Dachau, he was shocked to be treated like a criminal, chained to other prisoners, and given a number. His head was shaved, he was often beaten for no apparent reason, and called a traitor. But Reger was not alone; he was assigned to the prison block where clergy from many denominations lived together. The men helped and encouraged each other as best they could but no one was protected from the constant hunger, the random brutality, and the risk of falling sick and being condemned to death.

Christian Reger lived through four years at Dachau working with other pastors and priests at forced labor, constantly smelling the burning flesh of those who were killed and sent to the crematorium. Even though many died, the barracks became more and more crowded as others were arrested and crammed into the plank beds that lined the walls. At first, Reger questioned the existence of God, but his faith was reaffirmed by a seeming coincidence.

While still in prison, before being sent to Dachau, he had received a letter from his wife that contained a verse from the Christian Bible, Acts 4:6-30. It read: "Grant unto Thy Servants to speak Thy Word with all boldness." Several years later, already in Dachau, he was called into the authorities to be questioned. He was in despair, fearing torture or worse if he did not report on others. Just as he was about to enter the office, another prisoner slipped him a matchbox. He had no time to look at it then. He entered and passed the interrogation without problems. When he returned to the barracks, covered with sweat, he opened the tiny box and found written on a slip of paper the very same Biblical quotation that his wife had sent him years before. Somehow, this caused Reger to be sure that God was there with him in Dachau. After that, he never stopped believing.

Catholic, Protestant, and Greek Orthodox clergy built a makeshift chapel in the pastors' barracks at Dachau and prayed together regularly on Sundays and holidays. Reger remembered it as his only solace during those difficult years. On Christmas Eve 1944, knowing that the Russians were already outside the city of Warsaw and were advancing on Germany, Reger prayed that they would remain alive until the war was over. During the years of his incarceration, his weight had dropped from 198 pounds to 98 pounds; he was at the end of his strength.

Every day, the sounds of the guns grew closer. Then on April 2, 1945, a policeman entered their barracks with a list. "Some of you will be released," he announced, and began reading the numbers. Christian Reger's number was on that list. He was released and went home to Mina and his church. A month later, the war was over.

After the war, Reger was reassigned to a new parish in East Berlin. Because of his arrest and imprisonment in Dachau, he was one of the few pastors that the Communist authorities felt they could trust. In addition to his pastoral work, Reger volunteered as a tour guide at the Dachau concentration camp, sharing some of the horrors of the Nazi era with young people from all over the world. Mina Reger died in 1970; Christian Reger died fifteen years later, at the age of eighty.

References

Friedman, Ina R. "Pastor Christian Reger: Barracks 26." In *The Other Victims: First-Person Stories of Non-Jews Persecuted by the Nazis*, pp. 31–46. Boston: Houghton Mifflin, 1990.

Yancey, Philip. *Where Is God When it Hurts?* Grand Rapids, MI: Zondervan, 1997.

Rey, Hans A. (1898–1977), and Margret Rey (1906–1996)

Born in Germany, living in France, and protected by Brazilian citizenship, the Reys managed to escape from Paris in 1940. They bicycled south, fleeing the German bombardment of the city and survived, becoming the authors of the children's book series *Curious George*.

H. A. Rey, as he later became known, was born Hans Auguste Reyersbach in Hamburg, Germany. His family was well educated and Hans grew up in a good neighborhood, near the famous Hamburg zoo. As a child, he spent many hours at the zoo, watching the animals, imitating their sounds, and drawing pictures of them. After serving in the German Army in World War I, he painted circus posters for a time. In the mid-1920s, following two years in German universities, Hans Reyersbach traveled to Brazil and found a job selling bathtubs in the Amazon.

The Reys brought their drawings and ideas about a curious monkey with them when they fled from France. In the United States, that monkey became Curious George and made the Reys famous. Courtesy of the de Grummond Children's Literature Collection, McCain Library and Archives, University of Southern Mississippi.

Margarete Waldstein, eight years younger than Hans, was also a German Jew and a native of Hamburg. In fact, Waldstein and Reyersbach had known each other as children but had lost touch. In the 1930s, after Hitler came to power, life became increasingly difficult for the Jews. In order to escape the growing antisemitism in Germany, Margarete Waldstein moved to England where she worked as a photographer. After a short time, she, too, decided to emigrate to Brazil. It was in Brazil that Margarete and Hans met once again. They married in 1935.

Their initial plan was to start their own advertising agency in Rio de Janeiro. Margarete now changed the spelling of her name to Margret and Hans Reyersbach decided to shorten his last name to Rey, since it would be easier for the Brazilians to pronounce. The Reys became Brazilian citizens, a decision that was instrumental in saving their lives.

Although they were free from persecution in Brazil, the Reys decided to return to Europe. They settled in Paris, a city that seemed safe from German influence and was less affected by antisemitism. Living in Montmartre, the artists' section of the city, they began writing and illustrating children's books. Their first effort was called *Raffy and the Nine Monkeys*. Hans did the illustrations and Margret and Hans wrote the story together. This book did not become a best seller, but the youngest of the nine monkeys in the story became a popular character. In 1939, the Reys decided to write another book just about this little monkey, whose name was Fifi and who was constantly getting into trouble. They began the work but were soon interrupted by the spread of World War II.

After the invasion and takeover of Poland, the Nazis turned west. They conquered Holland and Belgium in 1940 and then marched toward Paris. Realizing that it was time to leave, Hans built two bicycles out of spare parts while Margret gathered up their important possessions: Hans's artwork and their half-finished manuscripts. They bicycled south, joining thousands of others who were fleeing from the German bombs and tanks. The only money they had was a small advance that their French publisher had given them for their next book.

Each night, when they stopped to rest, they had to search for a safe place. Once they found shelter in a farmhouse, another night in a stable. Finally, they were able to board a train to take them farther south and ended up on the French-Spanish border. Thousands of people, both Jews and non-Jews, were trying to get visas for other countries. Most did not succeed, but the Reys were citizens of Brazil and this saved their lives. They obtained transit visas for both Spain and Portugal and from Lisbon they were able to book passage to Rio de Janeiro. But this time, they did not stay in Brazil; they continued on to the United States.

In the United States, the Reys's book about Fifi the monkey was finally published, but not before Fifi's name was changed to "Curious George." Their publisher, Houghton Mifflin, felt that Fifi was not a suitable name for a male monkey. A total of eight books were published in New York relating the adventures of Curious George and his owner, "The Man in the Yellow Hat."

In addition to their "Curious George" books, Hans and Margret Rey wrote an astronomy book called *The Stars: A New Way to See Them*. Their book charts the stars in a way that makes it easier to see and recognize the constellations. In 1989, nine years after Hans's death, Margret established the Curious George Foundation to help creative children and to prevent cruelty to animals.

References

Borden, Louise. *The Journey That Saved Curious George: The True Wartime Escape of Margret and H.A. Rey*. New York: Houghton Mifflin, 2005.
Smith, Dinitia. "How Curious George Escaped the Nazis." *The New York Times*. September 13, 2005. p. E3.
http://www.absoluteastronomy.com/encyclopedia/h/h/h._a._reyhtm.

Reynders, Henri (Dom Bruno) (1903–1981)

Henri Reynders of Ixelles, Belgium, was a Catholic priest. At the risk of his own life, he spent most of World War II saving Jewish children, personally escorting many to gentile homes and Catholic institutions. After the war he tried his best to reunite them with their relatives.

Reynders was the fifth of eight children of Joseph and Marie Reynders, both devout Catholics. By the age of seventeen, he had committed himself to a

Father Bruno poses with five of the many Jewish children he helped save from Hitler. Courtesy of the U.S. Holocaust Memorial Museum Photo Archives.

religious life and from 1920 to 1922 he was a postulant at the Benedictine Abbey of Mont-César in Louvain, Belgium. After completing his novitiate, he was given the name Dom Bruno. Although committed to a monastic life, Reynders spent several years studying in Louvain and in Rome. He was ordained as a priest in 1928 and received a doctor of theology degree in 1931.

Recognized as a nonconformist within the Catholic Church, Reynders spent several years teaching and lecturing under the supervision of his abbot at the Mont-César Abbey. One lecture brought him to Germany, where he met with German Catholics and witnessed German antisemitism for the first time. In writing about that experience many years later, he called it "shocking, revolting and nauseating."

When World War II began, Reynders became a chaplain in the Belgian Army. He sustained a leg injury during the German invasion of Belgium and spent six months in a German prisoner-of-war camp. After being released, he resumed his teaching activities, but also made contact with the local resistance. At first, he helped to rescue British paratroopers who had been shot down over Belgium, but in 1942, when the Nazis actively began to deport Belgium's Jews, Reynders became involved in that cause as well.

Assigned to minister to a home for the blind, he became aware that many Jews were hidden there. After that refuge became unsafe, it was closed and the occupants sent to other places. Soon, Reynders, known to many only as Dom Bruno, or Father Bruno, devoted himself entirely to saving Jews. He built a network of independent rescuers and resistance groups and kept track of all of them. He worked to find individual families or Catholic institutions such as boarding schools and orphanages that were willing to hide Jews, especially Jewish children, brought them to their assigned places, and transported them to other places when the Germans became too suspicious. Often he picked them up in the middle of the night, hid them in the back of his truck, and drove them through Nazi checkpoints to newly found safe havens. Although those who hid Jews were always at risk if discovered, Reynders appealed to their faith as good Catholics and convinced them to save lives. By war's end he had rescued three hundred Jewish children.

Reynders himself was often the only link between children and their parents, visiting the children and bringing news of their families. He made sure that each of his Jewish charges had false papers identifying him or her as a Christian, and appropriate ration cards, all forged through his underground connections.

In 1944, the Gestapo, the Nazi police, heard about Father Bruno and went to Abbey Mont-César to arrest him. He was away at the time, but the raid forced him to go into hiding. He took off his priest's hassock but did not give up his work. Wearing civilian clothes, he continued helping Jews until the Germans were driven out of Belgium in September 1944.

After the occupation was over, Reynders committed himself to reuniting the children with their families. In many cases, there was no remaining family and he found himself acting as intermediary between the Catholic foster parents who wanted to adopt these children and raise them as Catholics, and Jewish organizations who wanted to take them back and place them in a Jewish environment. Reynders had opposed converting the children while their families were still alive. But with so many of the parents now dead, a new problem arose. Often, very young children had no memory of their birth parents and wanted to remain and embrace the religion of the only parents they knew. Reynders now insisted that each case should be judged on its own merits and that each child's best interests should be considered.

Eventually, Reynders returned to his regular duties as teacher and pastor. In 1964, the state of Israel declared Dom Bruno Reynders to be a righteous gentile. He was invited to Jerusalem for a special ceremony and a tree was planted in his honor on the Avenue of the Righteous at Yad Vashem, Israel's museum of the Holocaust.

Reynders eventually succumbed to Parkinson's disease and died in a nursing home in 1981.

References

Gilbert, Martin. *The Righteous*. New York: Doubleday, 2002.
Michman, Dan, ed. *Belgium and the Holocaust*. Jerusalem: Yad VaShem, 1998.
Résistance: Père Bruno Reynders, Juste des Nations. Paris: Les Carrefours de la Cité, 1993.

Rochman, Leyb (1918–1978), and Esther Rochman (1920–)

Esther and Leyb Rochman of Minsk-Mazowiecki, Poland, were married during the war in the ghetto. Less than a year later, they escaped a vicious massacre in their town and, together with Esther's younger sister Zipporah and two friends, went into hiding for almost two years. They were the only members of their families to survive, and were liberated by Russian troops in the summer of 1944.

Leyb Rochman, one of five siblings, was already a journalist for the Yiddish press when the war began. Minsk-Mazowiecki, a town about twenty-five miles from Warsaw, was occupied on September 13, 1939, and a year later all the Jews were forced into a ghetto. In 1941 Leyb and Esther married, with both their mothers present, a fact that took on great meaning after they learned that their parents had been killed by the Nazis.

The Rochmans were still in the ghetto when rumors began to circulate that there would be a general roundup of all the Jews. Still, the suddenness of the German onslaught was unexpected. German soldiers came in trucks and on motorcycles, shooting at any Jew who tried to run. The ghetto and the surrounding streets were strewn with corpses and the bodies of the dying. Those who submitted were marched to the railroad station for deportation or lined up outside of town, shot, and buried in mass graves.

Leyb and Esther and their families tried to run to the home of a Christian friend, but Leyb's mother and younger sister could not run fast enough. They were caught and taken to the railway station and murdered. His two other sisters and one brother were also killed as were Esther's mother and her brother Shmuel. Leyb, Esther, and Esther's younger sister, Zipporah, were able to hide in the furrows of a field and evade their pursuers, but the Christian family begged them to leave. If they were caught hiding Jews, they, too, would be killed.

They found another hiding place that night in a nearby farm, where they hid inside a haystack, barely able to breathe. After a Nazi police dog sniffed them out, they quickly leaped into another stack of hay before the German could return with his gun. Leyb then decided he would have to find another safe place for them. He made his way to Kopernik, the nearby work camp where many Jews were employed, and searched for a way to smuggle his wife and sister-in-law in. After three days, he found a German guard who agreed to take him to that farm and bring Esther and Zipporah back. In return, he promised the guard Esther's gold wedding ring. Miraculously, the two women were still alive. For a short while, they were safe in Kopernik.

Within a few days, however, the Germans began to empty out the camp. The Rochmans and Zipporah were chosen as part of a group to be marched to the cemetery and shot, but a temporary reprieve brought them back to camp. When they learned that all the women at the camp would be deported the following day, Leyb again took action. He sneaked out of camp and tried to find a gentile among his acquaintances who would agree to put them up just for that night. All refused until he stumbled into the apartment of a strange woman, an ex-prostitute, living alone. She was sympathetic and agreed to take them in. Because of her help, they escaped the deportation.

Leyb began talking with her about a more permanent hideout and the woman, known to them only as "Auntie," said her brother Felek had a farm in a nearby village. She promised to arrange with him to let them stay in his house. Within days, they were hiding in Felek's home, set up with a secret compartment behind a false wall in their cottage where they stood motionless and silent whenever guests came to visit.

Auntie was their savior at first. She even returned to the surrounding labor camps to rescue their friends. She brought Ephraim, Zipporah's fiancé, in broad daylight, dressed like a peasant girl, and Leyb's friend, Froiman, who was the only survivor when his original hiding place was bombed. The Rochmans gave Felek money to buy food for them. From time to time they sent for fabrics that they had placed with Christian friends for safekeeping and Esther sewed clothing for their hosts. Later, she also knitted for Felek, his wife, and Auntie.

The neighbors became suspicious many times and on several occasions, the Germans searched the house but never found their hiding place. Only once they were discovered by a group of Polish partisans who beat them up and took their clothes but otherwise did not reveal their secret. After this incident, they prepared a new hideout in the attic. When this, too, aroused suspicion, they moved to the barn.

In the course of a year in hiding, Felek, who added to his meager income by stealing from the neighboring farms, was killed by the Nazis. A terrible feud then erupted between Felek's wife and Auntie, which made the Rochmans' lives more precarious and eventually drove them to a new hiding place in the barn of Felek's brother, Janek. The family feuds continued, however, and eventually forced them to find another refuge.

In May 1944, with the help of an itinerant Jewish beggar who called himself Kanyak, they arranged to stay with another peasant family, the Szubes. Although the Szubes shared the secret with many of their family members, they assured Rochman that he would be safe. They prepared a pit beneath their granary but were able to spend much time above ground because the Szube family's dog always barked at the approach of strangers.

As the summer came and news of the Allied landing in France reached them, hiding became increasingly difficult. They waited impatiently for the Russian offensive. When German and Russian troops finally engaged, the battle took place in the village right next to the Szube farm. Both the Szubes and the Jews they were hiding were convinced they would not live to see the war's end. But they did. The only casualty was the dog who had always warned them of approaching danger.

Cowering in their underground bunker, they heard the noise of the cannons and the staccato of machine guns above their heads. Then silence. When Mrs. Szube came to uncover the top of their bunker, she told them that the Russians had arrived. As the soldiers entered the granary, Leyb leaped out of the hole shouting in Russian: "Comrades! We are Jews!" The Russian officer, moved by this discovery, kept repeating, "You are free. You are free."

Leyb Rochman dedicated his book "To the Sacred Memory of My Unforgettable Ones."

After listing the names and dates of death of all his relatives and all his wife Esther's relatives, he finished the dedication with the following words:

and all my relatives, comrades, and friends—who starved to death in the Warsaw ghetto, or were shot to death, tortured to death, choked to death, gassed to death, burned to death, or otherwise hideously removed from this world, and the whole community of men, women and children of my home city, Minsk-Mazowiecki, who perished in Treblinka—

MAY GOD AVENGE THEIR BLOOD!

The Rochmans with Zipporah, Ephraim, Froiman, and the young beggar Kanyak, hugged and thanked the Szubes, then left to find the Russian Army and perhaps, some other Jewish survivors. Leyb carried with him the diary he had kept during their two years in hiding.

Leyb Rochman completed his account of their war years while in Switzerland, where they went immediately after the war. His book was published in Yiddish by a French publisher under the title *In Your Blood Shall You Live*, and in 1949, it won a prize from the World Congress for Jewish Culture. It was translated into English and published in New York in 1983, as *The Pit and the Trap*.

After Israel's independence, Esther and Leyb Rochman settled in Jerusalem and had a daughter, Rivka Miriam, named after his mother and little sister, and a son, Joshua. Their tiny, three-room apartment became a center of Jewish language and culture, attracting both Yiddish and Hebrew writers. **Aharon Appelfeld**, the acclaimed Israeli novelist, was one of his protégés and wrote the forward to the English edition of Leyb's book.

Esther's sister Zipporah also moved to Israel as did Ephraim and Kanyak (whose real name was Isaac Rosenberg). Rosenberg was killed fighting in the Israeli Army. Leyb's friend, Froiman, came to the United States. Rivka Miriam Rochman became a famous artist and Hebrew poet in Israel. Joshua was a concert violinist.

Reference

Rochman, Leyb. *The Pit and the Trap: A Chronicle of Survival.* New York: Holocaust Library, 1983.

Rose, Rose (née Kfar) (1927–)

Rose Kfar Rose of Lvov, Poland, lived through the worst of World War II in hiding. When the fighting was over, she was seventeen years old and utterly alone in the world. Then she received a letter from America and found a new branch of the family.

Rose, or Roza, was the only daughter of Benchik and Tinka Kfar. She was born in Lvov, a city in eastern Poland that was initially occupied by the Russians in 1939. It was only in 1941, after the Germans broke their earlier pact with the Soviet Union, that Nazi troops marched into the city and began to systematically destroy this community of 135,000 Jews.

As in every other city the Germans occupied, they quickly instituted anti-Jewish regulations. A ghetto was established, all Jews were required to identify themselves with armbands displaying the Star of David, and the population was forced to work at hard labor with no wages. Rose, then fourteen years old, was sent to work in a factory.

By August 1942, the Kfar family realized they had to take drastic measures to save themselves. They explained to Rose that sixty thousand Jews had been deported during the last three weeks alone. They would not be able to escape the same fate if they remained in the ghetto. Although Rose did not want to leave her parents, she allowed herself to be persuaded. Her father had purchased false papers for her from a Christian girl and had arranged for her stay in a small village at the home of a schoolteacher named Krystyna Moskalik. Benchik and Tinka Kfar promised that they, too, would make arrangements to hide and they would all reunite after the war.

Rose Kfar remained with her Christian host for almost three years. During that time, she pretended to be a Catholic and continued her education as best she could under the guidance of Polish teachers. Once, neighbors threatened Krystyna Moskalik that they would report her to the Nazis for hiding a Jew unless she gave them money. Moskalik was able to deflect the threats by reminding them of their own illegal acts. There were several other close calls as well, before the Russians finally liberated the area in January 1945. During those years, Kfar never saw or heard from her parents. Moskalik told her that her father had joined the partisans and her mother was hiding in a village near Lvov. Now she encouraged Kfar to move to Krakow to attend a real high school and complete her education. She would be able to live there with Moskalik's friends.

Even though the war was over and the Nazis were thoroughly defeated, Kfar was still afraid of antisemitism and retained her Catholic identity. However, she did register with the Jewish Committee under her real name and continually checked to see if anyone in her family had survived. Her parents' names never appeared on any of the lists, but in the spring of 1945 she met an old friend of the family. He told her that her mother had been deported to Belzec concentration camp. She had escaped from the train but died in February 1943 from typhus. Her father had escaped from Janowska, a labor camp in Lvov, but also succumbed to typhus, just a month after her mother.

Kfar was devastated. She later wrote, "I remember feeling all alone in the world. I could not forget all my dead relatives. I had nightmares of the atrocities I had witnessed in the ghetto: people shot on the street, young girls jumping to their death to avoid arrest, starving children and adults begging for food; unidentified bodies on the street every morning."

But even in the depths of despair, Kfar remembered how important it was to her parents that she should survive. She realized that for them, she had to get an education and build a new life.

Her chance came on August 27, 1945. A letter from an uncle in New York, searching for her, was sent to the Jewish Committee in Krakow. Just two months before, she had discovered that her Aunt Friedka Herzer had survived Auschwitz. When Kfar sent a telegram back to her uncle Charles, she wrote, "Roza Kfar, Benchik's daughter, and her mother's sister, Friedka Herzer, survived."

A series of letters followed and the American branch of the Kfar family tried to arrange a visa for Rose to come to the United States. There was a long waiting list, however, and it would be years before her turn would come. Because the Polish government would not agree to give any of their citizens passports unless they already had a visa granting them permission to emigrate, Rose's uncles thought of another way. They obtained a visitor's visa for her issued by Cuba. With this visa and her passport, she could try to obtain a transit visa to pass through the United States.

The plan worked, and when Kfar's plane landed in New York, her uncles were there to greet her. She was taken almost immediately to see her great uncle, Sanya Greenstein. Uncle Sanya was on his deathbed and was clinging to life in order to see his only relative who had survived the Holocaust. Rose arrived in time; Sanya Greenstein died that same night.

Kfar remembered the funeral of her great uncle the following day as one of intense emotion. "It was not only Uncle Sanya's burial that I attended," she wrote. "It felt as if I were witnessing the burial of all my dear relatives and friends who had perished in Europe. I . . . found relief in being able to cry at last."

After the funeral, Kfar left for Havana, Cuba, and remained there from September 1946 until January 1948, when she was finally allowed to enter the United States. She completed her education with a Ph.D. in chemistry, married, and became a professor in New York City at Kingsborough Community College. By 2001, she had retired and had been named Professor Emeritus.

Reference

Rose, Rose Kfar. "Reuniting With My Family (1945–1948)." *The Hidden Child* 10, no. 1 (summer 2001): p. 9.

Rosensaft, Hadassah (1912–1997)

Hadassah Bimko Rosensaft of Sosnowiec, Poland, was a practicing dentist when World War II began. Sent to Auschwitz and then Bergen-Belsen, she saved hundreds of Jews, many of them children, while she herself was a prisoner. Rosensaft was one of the prime witnesses testifying against Nazi atrocities after the war and was one of the founders of the U.S. Holocaust Memorial Museum in Washington, DC.

Born Ada Bimko in Sosnowiec, Poland, Rosensaft, was already an adult in 1939. The oldest daughter of a Hasidic family of jewelry makers, she studied medicine at the University of Nancy in eastern France and earned a Ph.D. in dental surgery in 1935. She was married to Josef Preserowicz and the couple had a son, Benjamin. Her life was successful and untroubled until the Germans invaded in 1939.

Rosensaft was still a practicing dentist in the ghetto of Sosnowiec when she and her family were deported to Auschwitz concentration camp in 1943. Her husband and son, then only five years old, were immediately sent to the gas chambers. Her parents and her sister also died there. Because of her medical training, Rosensaft was assigned to work in the Jewish infirmary at Auschwitz. During the fifteen months she remained at that camp, she saved hundreds of women, performing minor surgeries when necessary and then sneaking her patients out of the hospital barracks before they could be selected for the gas chambers.

In November 1944, with Russia on the attack and the German Army in

> *It is difficult for me to describe all that we inmates experienced here in the camps. As a small, very small example I can relate that we inmates were thrown onto the earth of a filthy, lice-filled camp, without blankets, without bags of hay, without beds. We were given a twelfth of a piece of bread daily and one liter of turnip soup so that almost seventy-five percent of the inmates were swollen from hunger. A severe typhus epidemic broke out, and the hunger and the typhus devoured us.*
>
> —Dr. Hadassah Rosensaft, speaking for a British Newsreel Agency in April, 1945.

retreat, Rosensaft, along with hundreds of other prisoners, was marched out of Auschwitz and taken west to Bergen-Belsen, another notorious death camp, this one in Germany. In Bergen-Belsen, aided by seven other women prisoners, she set up a makeshift hospital where she treated the camp's orphaned children suffering from typhus and other diseases. She went from one prison block to another searching for children and escaping with them to her own barracks where she fed and washed them and treated their illnesses as best she could. She was still there—and still working as a doctor—in April 1945 when the British Army arrived to liberate the camp.

Now Bergen-Belsen became a displaced-persons camp and Brigadier H. L. Glyn-Hughes, Director of Medical Services of the British Army, asked Rosensaft to supervise the hospital there. She treated hundreds of people in the Bergen-Belsen displaced-persons camp who were not only physically ill, but depressed and in despair. With a staff of 28 doctors and 620 other volunteers, mostly untrained, she tried to nurse them back to health. A total of 13,944 Jews died in the first two months after the war. For a month, the death toll was over one hundred people a day. On May 11, it fell below one hundred a day for the first time. Rosensaft later wrote about that time,

Hadassah and Josef Rosensaft with a young Jewish refugee at Bergen-Belsen in April 1946. Courtesy of the U.S. Holocaust Memorial Museum Photo Archives.

that for many of the Jews, "liberation had come too late. We had lost all our families," she explained, "we had no place to go. We were liberated from death, from the fear of death, but the fear of life started."

Rosensaft had also lost everyone during the war. At the camp, she met **Josef Rosensaft**, another survivor. He had become one of the leaders of the displaced-persons community, organizing social, cultural, and political activities in the camp. He was later elected chair of the Central Jewish Committee in the British zone. Josef Rosensaft and Hadassah Bimko were married in 1946 and in less than a year, she became pregnant. The Rosensafts' son, Menachem, was one of the first of two thousand children born free at Bergen-Belsen between the years 1946 and 1950. He is now a practicing attorney in New York and was founding chairman of the International Network of Children of Jewish Holocaust survivors.

Hadassah Rosensaft was a principal witness, testifying for the prosecution of Nazi war criminals before a military court in Luneburg, Germany. After that, she and Josef continued their work with Jewish refugees until 1948. When the camp at Bergen-Belsen was closed in 1950, they left for Switzerland, and eight years later for the United States. Rosensaft remained an active leader of Holocaust survivors in America and in 1978, President Jimmy Carter appointed her a member of the President's Commission on the Holocaust. Two years later, she was appointed a member of the U.S. Holocaust Memorial Council. In this role, she was one of the founders of the U.S. Holocaust Memorial Museum in Washington, DC, with **Elie Wiesel** and other prominent survivors in the United States. She participated in the initial groundbreaking for the museum in 1985 and was there when it was officially opened in 1993. In addition to her work with the Holocaust museum, Rosensaft was also an honorary alumna of the Hebrew Union College and honorary president of Survivors of Bergen-Belsen.

In 1997, her memoir, *Yesterday: My Story*, was written and she was able to see the completed work before she died, on October 17, 1997. Her death at the age of eighty-five was attributed to hepatitis, contracted during her months in concentration camps. She was survived by her son, her daughter-in-law, and a granddaughter.

References

Jacobs, Susan. "Another Life Cut Tragically Short by the Nazis." *Jewish Telegraphic Agency* (October 17, 1997).
http://www.historiography.project.com/nonsense/1997/1017rosensaft.
Rosensaft, Hadassah. *Yesterday: My Story*. Washington, DC: U.S. Holocaust Memorial Museum, 2004.
Rosensaft, Menachem. "Encounter with My Mother, Eight Years after Her Death." *Moment* (August 2006): p. 34.
———, with comments by the editors. "The Woman Who Shaped the U.S. Holocaust Memorial Museum." *Lilith* 29, no. 1 (spring 2004): pp. 12–14.

Rosensaft, Josef (1911–1975)

Josef Rosensaft of Bedzin, Poland, was the youngest of five children, and one of the few who was able to escape from a train to Auschwitz. He was recaptured and escaped once more. By the time World War II had ended, he had lost his family, but had become a leader of the Jews.

The Rosensaft family was part of a Hasidic community based in Bedzin, a Polish town near the German border, and Josef's father, Menachem Mendel, was a prominent and respected member of that community. He owned a scrap metal business and he and his wife Devorah Szpiro Rosensaft had five children: Leah, Rachel, Mari-Mindl, Itzhak, and Josef. Josef was the youngest and by the time he was eight or nine years old, had lost his mother in a flu epidemic.

As a youngster and then a young man, Josef was active in the labor Zionist movement. When he had completed his schooling, he went to work in his father's scrap metal company and continued there until the Germans came to Bedzin on September 4, 1939. Almost immediately, they burned the synagogue and several streets of Jewish homes. Following that, the Nazi officials enacted a series of antisemitic rulings, confiscating Jewish businesses and depriving Jews of access to education.

The Zionist Youth movements played a role in organizing schools for the children and set up a training farm in preparation for emigration to what was then Palestine, but these measures could do little to save Jews besides warning them not to report voluntarily to the transports.

Transports from Bedzin, with the promise of "resettlement," did not begin until July 1942, and a ghetto was not set up there until the spring of 1943, when the Jews of Bedzin and of Sosnowiec were relocated into a single area. Josef Rosensaft was able to avoid the transports until June 22, 1943, when he was placed on a deportation train to Auschwitz.

Fully understanding the intention of these transports, Rosensaft dove out of a small opening in the train as it was passing the Vistula River. The guards shot at him as he jumped but he fell into the river and escaped. Wounded, he made his way back to Bedzin and remained there for a few weeks. He was there to witness the death of his father of natural causes—that was considered a "good death" in those days—before the final liquidation of the ghetto.

> ## To The Bergen-Belsen Survivors
>
> *With your visible and invisible*
> *Innumerable scars,*
> *You are a greater miracle*
> *Than the one in Ezekiel's valley.*
> *What sort of Jewish strength is there in your*
>   *risen bones?*
> *Not only skin to skin, bone to bone,*
> *And flesh to flesh,*
> *But person to person, husband to wife,*
> *Through joy and mourning,*
> *Through sorrow risked.*
> *Lively winds murmur around your new house-*
>   *holds*
> *Your newly-built homes.*
>
> —Jacob Gladstein (translated by Barnett Zumoff)

In order to avoid capture, Rosensaft fled to the nearby town of Zawierce, but soon the Nazis had given the order to round up all the Jews there as well. Once again, he was back on a train to Auschwitz. He spent five months there before being transferred to work in Lagisza Cmentarna, one of Auschwitz's satellite camps. Once again he escaped and returned to Bedzin, now empty of Jews, and was hidden by a Polish Christian friend for six weeks. He was recaptured in April 1944 and sent back to Auschwitz, where he was tortured and placed in the punishment barracks. With the Auschwitz number on his arm, it was easy to recognize him as an escaped prisoner.

Rosensaft remained in the punishment barracks for seven months before his transfer first to one of Buchenwald's subcamps and then to another. In early April 1945, with the war almost over and the Germans in full retreat, he was sent to Bergen-Belsen. The camp at Bergen-Belsen was liberated by the British on April 15, 1945, and Rosensaft was now free.

Bergen-Belsen concentration camp was among the worst of all the German camps and the condition of its inmates was appalling. Filth, starvation, and disease were everywhere and most of the prisoners were too weak to walk. Within days, however, they had organized a governing committee to address the needs of the survivors at the camp and Josef Rosensaft was chosen as the chairman. That September, after a general meeting of Jewish survivors in the British zone of Germany (called the First Congress of Liberated Jews), he was also elected chair of the Central Jewish Committee for the British Zone. He held both posts until the Bergen-Belsen Refugee Center was closed in 1950. During his years as leader of what were now referred to as displaced persons, Rosensaft organized cultural and educational events and consistently fought for the rights of the Jewish survivors to move around Germany freely and to be recognized as a separate category of refugees. He insisted that the British keep the survivors of

Bergen-Belsen together rather than move them to other camps. He was also outspoken in his criticism of the British policy of barring Jews from emigrating to Palestine, then still under British mandate, and actively assisted the groups that were trying to smuggle Jews out of Europe into what would soon become Israel.

Rosensaft had met Dr. Hadassah (Ada) Bimko (see **Hadassah Rosensaft**) shortly after the liberation of Bergen-Belsen, when she was asked to take charge of the medical needs of the Nazi victims. The two, both natural leaders, and both with no family remaining, had much in common. They were married in August 1946 and continued working for the Jewish displaced persons. Their son Menachem was born in Bergen-Belsen in 1948.

With all the refugees settled, Great Britain closed the displaced-persons camp at Bergen-Belsen and the Rosensafts moved to Montreux, Switzerland, where they lived for eight years before emigrating to the United States. Josef Rosensaft became a businessman but continued to be active in Jewish causes. Until his death in 1975, Rosensaft served as president of the World Federation of Bergen-Belsen Survivors.

Reference

http://www.ushmm.org/uia_doc/query/27uf=uia_BrBaPL.

Roslawowski, Bronia (1926–)

Bronia Roslawowski was one of only a handful of Jews from Turek, Poland, who survived the Holocaust. Almost all of her family was murdered but she was a strong young woman and lived through five different concentration camps and a death march.

Roslawowski was one of five children born to Tzvi Eliezer Kibel and Bluma Bajrach. Her parents owned a prosperous business, where they both worked. The children attended school and Hebrew school, took music lessons, and did their homework.

When World War II began, schools were closed to all Jewish children, Jewish businesses were confiscated, and Jews were continually threatened. But even after the ghetto was established, the Kibel family could not believe that such a thing as the Holocaust would happen.

By 1941, the Nazis began assembling the Jews of Turek for deportation. When Roslawowski's older but weaker sister was chosen for transport to the camps, she insisted on taking her place, saying, "I am not afraid of the Germans. I am strong like iron." She did go, but could not save her sister or any other members of her family from eventual deportation and death at the hands of the Nazis. Only one brother survived the war.

Roslawowski was taken first to Hohensaltz, a transit camp. Here, the women were made to walk and then run while the Gestapo whipped them. From there, they were transferred to a labor camp. Roslawowski worked with other women draining the swamps. Their feet were immersed in the water all day and they were constantly bitten by leeches. Almost three years later, with the Russian Army driving the Germans back to the west, the Jewish prisoners were marched to the train station, crammed into a boxcar already filled with people, and shipped to Auschwitz. It was late in 1943.

As soon as she descended from the train, Roslawowski was chosen for death. She later described that experience to an interviewer. The women had all been stripped of their clothing. Completely naked, they were loaded onto a truck. Two German soldiers in the front were singing, seemingly happy that they were taking two hundred people to their deaths. But they were too drunk to guard the convoy efficiently and Roslawowski took the opportunity to jump off. She found a hollow place beside the road, laid down inside, and covered her body with snow. The guards did not see her. After all the trucks were out of sight, Roslawowski found her way to block seventeen and asked the prisoner in charge of the block, Gisi Moscowitz, to help her. Moskowitz agreed, but insisted she must go and tell the official at the camp that she had escaped from the transport to the gas chambers. Roslawowski approached the notorious Adolf Eichmann and confessed that she had jumped off the transport. He agreed to let her live but not before he knocked her down with a slap and stomped on her.

Roslawowski was nursed by the other women in the block and her wounds healed. She was assigned to work cleaning the latrines, considered a good job because it was indoors and more protected from the elements.

Early in 1944, when the first convoys of Hungarian Jews began arriving in Auschwitz, Roslawowski watched a well-dressed German man inspecting the women and pulling some out of line. She suspected that they were being chosen for a work detail and thought that she might try to be part of it. She approached the man and, in her best German, asked him to take her, too. He agreed and Roslawowski was among a group of nineteen young women taken to Reichenbach to work in a factory making lighting equipment for aircraft. Conditions there were much better than they had been in Auschwitz, but it was not long before the nineteen women were being driven in an endless march through the cold. They walked for what seemed like months, were shouted at by the guards, beaten, and threatened. They slept in barns at night. "We were just like animals," said Roslowowski. Exhausted, the women trudged from one camp to another, but all were too crowded and they were not allowed in. Finally, the workers from Reichenbach were allowed into a camp that housed mostly prisoners of war. Of the approximately eight thousand women who began that march, only eight hundred remained alive at the end of the war.

Roslawowski was finally liberated by the Americans in the spring of 1945. When she was freed, she told the soldiers, "You are my father, my mother, my brothers, my sister."

In January 1946, while still in Germany, Roslawowski met and married Willie Jaks, a survivor from Berlin who had enlisted in the American Army. Roslawowski quickly became pregnant. But she was adamant that this child not be born on German soil. In order to get to the United States before her due date, she signed a paper releasing the ship from any responsibility for her health. Roslawowski's first daughter, Beverly, was born in America, followed by two more daughters, Alice and Judy.

Shortly after her arrival, Roslawowski settled in Kansas City, Missouri. Jaks joined her there after serving in the U.S. Army, but he wanted to return to his native Germany. Roslawowski refused to live in Germany where "my next door neighbor may have been the one who killed my mother," and the couple divorced.

Alone with three young children, Roslawowski borrowed $450 from the Jewish Family Service and took a course in nursing in order to support her family. Then in 1962, she married Mendel Roslawowski, a widower, and together they opened up the M&M bakery. The shop was named by her daughters and stood for "Mommy" and "Mendel." Roslawowski worked in the bakery and raised her three girls and her stepson Walter.

Always conscious of the absence of any extended family—she didn't have a single photograph of her parents and her one surviving brother lived in Israel—Bronia Roslawowski found substitute grandparents for her children from among her neighbors. She invited them for dinner and they joined the family for board games and other activities.

Roslawowski was one of the first of the Holocaust survivors in her area to speak about her experiences. She insisted, however, that she never hated the Germans. "You cannot condemn a nation," she said.

References

Dodd, Monroe. *From the Heart: Life Before and After the Holocaust—A Mosaic of Memories*. Kansas City: Kansas City Star Books and the Midwest Center for Holocaust Education, 2001.
Roslawowski, Bronia. Telephone interview by the author, April 2006.

Rosner family

The Rosners, a family of musicians, was well known in Krakow and their prestige even carried over to the camps. Used as entertainers for the Nazi commandant in the Plaszow labor camp, they were able to survive because of their musical talents.

The Rosner parents, Henry and Francesca, had nine children—five sons and four daughters. Henry and Francesca were transported to an unknown destination and shot by the Nazis in 1942. Two of the Rosner sisters and one brother were also killed in the Holocaust and another brother, George, had gone to America before the war. The remaining three brothers, Hermann, Leopold, and Wilhelm and one sister, Regina, remained together and survived.

The oldest Rosner son, Hermann (b. 1905) (he later changed his name to Henry), was a violinist. Leopold played the accordion and Wilhelm played several instruments including the bugle. They were popular musicians in Krakow, entertaining in the most fashionable restaurants and cafés in the city and even traveling abroad. While performing in Vienna, Hermann met and married Manci Robitcshek (b. 1910). After their son, Alexander (Olek) was born in 1935, they settled in Warsaw while Hermann continued traveling.

When the Germans attacked Poland, on September 1, 1939, Hermann first fled to the Russian-occupied zone. His plan was to settle there and send for his wife and son, but with no means of communication between the Russian and German sectors of Poland, Hermann returned to his family early in 1940 and they reunited with the whole Rosner family who had fled to a small village outside of Krakow. When the order came for all Jews to be transferred to the Krakow ghetto, the family was still together.

Manci Rosner (middle), wife of Hermann Rosner, with Oscar Schindler (left) at a reunion of Schindler's Jews in Munich in 1946. Courtesy of the U.S. Holocaust Memorial Museum Photo Archives.

Crammed into one six-room apartment with many other families, including **Regina Rosner Horowitz**, her husband, and two children, life was still bearable. The Rosner brothers found work as entertainers in a café. When the café closed down, they began playing for the German pilots at the local airbase. Because the German officers enjoyed his music so much, Hermann was given an easy job in the ghetto so his fingers would not be injured. Once, when a roundup of Jewish children was scheduled, the German barman at the airbase came to warn him and even hid their son, Alexander, in his own home for five days until the danger was passed.

When the Krakow ghetto was liquidated, those who were not sent to Auschwitz were transferred to Plaszow, the labor camp located just outside the city. Most of the Jews in Plaszow were either worked to death or fell victim to random violence perpetrated by the camp's commander, Amon Goeth. But Goeth loved music and he made sure that the Rosners and their family were safe so he could continue to enjoy his regular concerts. Manci Rosner was put in charge of one of the women's blocks in the prison, a job that gave her a bed of her own and a small amount of extra food, and Manci and Hermann's son, Alexander, was also protected by the Germans. Alexander later explained that his father had an explicit agreement with Goeth: if his son was not protected, he would stop playing. "The minute he dies or is taken away," Hermann Rosner warned, "it doesn't matter any more what you do to me."

The Rosners also had another protector: **Oskar Schindler**. Schindler used many of the Plaszow prisoners as workers in his enamelware factory, where they were treated more humanely. As the war progressed and Germany lost more and more territory, Commander Goeth was faced with the necessity of closing his camp and Schindler suggested that they move those working in his factory into another facility in Brinnlitz, then in German-controlled Czechoslovakia. A list of approximately three hundred workers was compiled and Schindler promised the Rosners that they would all be on it.

When the Plaszow camp was evacuated, the men and women were divided and sent to different places; the men went to Gröss Rosen concentration camp and the women to Auschwitz. The understanding was that those on the list would then be shipped to Brinnlitz to work in Schindler's factory. The men, including the three Rosner brothers and Hermann's son Alexander, arrived in Brinnlitz first, but while Schindler was out of the camp, guards came and rounded up the youngest boys and their fathers, transferring them to Auschwitz. They were singled out for use in the infamous Dr. Mengele's medical experiments. At Auschwitz, all those young boys were separated from their fathers and most died in the camp. Alexander remained alive. He was spared because he and his father had performed the night before for the guards.

From Auschwitz, Hermann and Alexander were shipped to Dachau, a concentration camp near Munich, Germany. It was from Dachau that Hermann and Alexander Rosner were liberated and moved to a displaced-persons camp in Munich. Meanwhile, Manci Rosner and her sister-in-law Regina had been liberated from Brinnlitz and returned to Krakow hoping to meet their husbands. It was not until the autumn of 1945 that Manci saw her husband's and son's names on a list in a Polish newspaper. She immediately went to Munich and the family was reunited. Later, Wilhelm and his new bride, Erna, joined them.

After the family had spent a year in Munich, George Rosner, the brother who had gone to the United States before the war, sent for them, a few at a time, and they all settled in Queens, New York. Hermann changed his name to Henry, in memory of his father, and quickly found jobs as a violinist in New York's finest restaurants. His brother Leopold often played with him. Manci Rosner worked for a furrier that she had known, sewing linings into fur coats. Alexander, only eleven years old when World War II ended, had never been to school and had spent most of his life in concentration camps. He learned English, finished school, went on to college, and opened a business as a sound technician. He has two sons, Benjamin and Gregory.

The youngest Rosner brother, Wilhelm (now called Bill), continued to play instruments and sometimes performed in the hotels in the Catskill Mountains, but he made his living as a piano tuner for Steinway Pianos. Regina Rosner Horowitz was reunited with her family and remained in Poland. Her son **Ryszard Horowitz** moved to the United States in 1959.

The Rosner brothers kept in touch with Oskar Schindler, who had saved their lives. Schindler visited them in Munich right after the war and again in New York in the 1970s. When the movie *Schindler's List* was filmed in 1993, the Rosners went to Israel to participate in the filming.

Reference

Brecher, Elinor J. *Schindler's Legacy: True Stories of the List Survivors*. New York: Dutton, 1994.

Roth, Joseph, and Ilonka Roth, and Irving Roth (1929–)

The Roth parents of Czechoslovakia and then Hungary were separated from both of their children during World War II. Their older son never returned, but they and their younger son were reunited at war's end.

Joseph and Ilonka Roth lived in Udavske, a small town near the Lubarec River close to the city of Humenne in what was then Czechoslovakia. They owned a successful lumber business with Ilonka's parents. The Roth's sons Irving and his older brother Bondi were raised by a nanny, a Hungarian Catholic woman who supervised their daily lives, disciplined, comforted, and loved them. Then, in 1939, Czechoslovakia was taken over by Germany and the Nuremburg laws were imposed. Jews could no longer own businesses or employ non-Jews. Their nanny was sent away and Irving, just ten years old, was barred from the public school he had been attending.

To avoid losing the business entirely, Joseph Roth and his father-in-law agreed to nominally hand it over to a loyal, non-Jewish employee. The lumberyard would be in his name, but it was understood that the Roths would still get the profit. Gradually, however, the new owner changed the arrangement and, ignoring their agreement and their friendship, took most of the profits for himself, paying Roth a small salary.

Ilonka Roth and her older son, Bondi, before World War II. Courtesy of Irving Roth.

In quick succession, the rights of the Jews of Czechoslovakia were taken away. In 1942, the Jews were gathered up and most of them were deported. The Roths and a handful of other families who were considered vital to the business of the town were allowed to stay. But they knew their days were numbered and searched for another country that would take them in. They settled on Hungary. Because Joseph had been born in a town that was annexed to Hungary, he could claim citizenship there. Most importantly, the German army had not occupied Hungary and they thought they would be safe. Ilonka's parents, however, were not included in Joseph's citizenship, so the family had to cross the border illegally by means of bribes to the stationmaster.

Once safely in Hungary, the family settled first in Zdana, Joseph's birthplace. From there, Irving and Bondi went to a Jewish boarding school while their parents went to Budapest to find work. This reprieve lasted about a year and then the Nazis moved into Hungary. By March of 1944, all the Jews had to wear yellow Stars of David. That spring a new order was issued: the Jews were to be transported to ghettos. Joseph and Ilonka Roth, believing it would be safer for their sons, withdrew Irving and Bondi from the boarding school and sent them back to the family in Zdana while they remained in Budapest.

Irving decided to follow his Uncle Moritz, his aunt, and cousins, who were going into hiding. Moritz believed that some of the peasants he knew would help them until the war was over. Bondi and other relatives opted to stay in Zdana, hoping that the Nazis would lose the war before the relocation went into effect. None of their plans was successful and all were brought to the trains and transported to a ghetto in Czechoslovakia. From there, they were brought to Auschwitz in May 1944.

On arriving at the platform in Auschwitz, Irving, Bondi, and their cousin Gabi, were sent to the left by the guards. Their grandfather, uncle, aunt, and younger cousins were sent to the right. The Roth brothers never saw them again. The next day, when numbers were tattooed on his arm, Irving realized that he was chosen for work and not for death. "Workers got numbers," he thought to himself, "not people who go up the chimneys."

Work was grueling. It consisted of piling gravel into carts, pulling it up the hill, and unloading it. They did this all day with no food except a drink of weak coffee in the morning and some bread and thin soup at night. But Irving and Bondi knew someone from their town who ran the camp hospital. Through his intervention, they managed to get less taxing work in the camp stables, cleaning the stalls and exercising the horses. They remained alive and somehow avoided the repeated selections that condemned the weaker prisoners to death. They were there when Jewish prisoners blew up one of the four crematoria at the camp and, even though all the perpetrators were caught and executed, Irving rejoiced at the destruction.

The war was coming to an end. Russian troops were closing in and the Germans were planning to destroy Auschwitz and the evidence of the mass murder that occurred there. They forced the remaining prisoners to march westward, toward Germany; and Bondi and Irving joined the line of retreating prisoners. Knowing that if they stopped walking they would be shot, the brothers continued through the icy cold, snow-covered countryside. In order to keep awake and not succumb to fatigue, they recited psalms together. After two days of marching, they were shoved into open boxcars and brought to another concentration camp: Buchenwald.

Irving Roth, director of the Holocaust museum at Shelter Rock Jewish Center in Manhasset, New York. Courtesy of Joan Mandel.

In Buchenwald, the two brothers were separated. Irving, alone and vulnerable, tried to hide when people began to be evacuated, but ultimately, the camp guards found him. At the last minute, as allied bombs fell on Buchenwald, that final evacuation was aborted. The following day, April 11, 1945, the camp was liberated. Then came the work of finding others from his family.

With free transportation provided by the American army, Irving went back to his hometown in Czechoslovakia and, miraculously, found both his parents alive. They had been hidden in Budapest by their Christian landlady, Mrs. Farkash, a Seventh Day Adventist, who took them into her own tiny apartment and shared her food with them. In this way, Joseph and Ilonka Roth survived the German occupation and the bombing raids by the Russians. From the time of their liberation, the Roths began sending food packages and money to Mrs. Farkash. They continued helping her after they moved to the United States and even after she died, they sent packages to her family.

Bondi never returned. After months of searching, they were told that he had been taken to Bergen-Belsen. Beyond that fact, there was no other record. The Roths waited for three more months, then, with the help of relatives, they left for America in 1947.

Once there, the Roth family's new life began. Settled in Brooklyn, New York, Joseph Roth found work, while Irving finished his schooling at Midwood High School, served in the U.S. Army at Ft. Knox, and became a citizen. When he completed his army service, he returned to New York and enrolled in Brooklyn's Polytechnic Institute to study engineering. Roth married Addie, a young woman he had met when he first joined a Zionist Youth organization. The couple raised two sons.

Irving Roth enjoyed a successful career as an electrical engineer at the Sperry Rand Corporation on Long Island. Eventually, he became director of research there. After retiring, Roth devoted his time to establishing and directing an independent Holocaust museum at the Shelter Rock Jewish Center, a synagogue in Manhasset, New York. The museum is dedicated to keeping the facts of the Holocaust alive and recording survivors' stories. In 2004, he wrote his memoir, recounting his childhood and his family's war experiences. Called *Bondi's Brother*, the book is dedicated to his lost brother, and to the one and a half million children who perished with him in the Holocaust.

Reference

Roth, Irving, and Edward Roth. *Bondi's Brother: A Story of Love, Betrayal, Loss and Survival.* Williston Park, NY: Shoah Educational Enterprise, 2004.

Roth-Hano, Renée (1932–)

Renée Roth-Hano, a child when the Nazis invaded Alsace, France, where she and her family lived, was hardly aware of her Jewish identity until then. She was ultimately saved by The Little Sisters of the Poor, a Catholic convent in Normandy.

Roth-Hano, the oldest of three daughters, was born in Alsace, a province in eastern France on the border with Germany. Alsace had been under German control before World War I, but it reverted to France in 1919, after Germany lost World War I. A few months after World War II erupted, Germany annexed Alsace once again, and by June 1940, most of France was under Nazi occupation.

> I had gone to bed one evening an ordinary, innocent eight-year-old, barely knowledgeable about her Jewish faith, and I woke up the next day, forced to flee my home.
>
> —Renée Roth-Hano

Roth-Hano's parents, originally from Poland, had already lived in Hungary before coming to Alsace. Now they moved again, this time to Paris. Although the southern regions of France were technically still free, Roth-Hano's father felt he had a better chance of finding work in a large city.

The entire family, including the parents, their three girls, and their blind grandmother arrived in Paris, then under the rule of a pro-Nazi regime led by General Pétain. Their new apartment was not as nice or spacious as the one they had left behind, but they adjusted to the change. It seemed safe and gradually Roth-Hano began to feel less homesick. Then late in 1940, Pétain's government, following the advice of a German "expert" on Jewish affairs, began to issue ordinances and restrictions against Jews. There were special curfews, synagogues were burned, and Jewish men were rounded up and sent to labor camps. But the one ruling that Roth-Hano hated the most was the requirement of wearing a Star of David on her clothing. By then, she was already ten years old and it made her feel ashamed and shy.

By 1942, more and more Jews were being arrested and deported to concentration camps by the Nazis, and Roth-Hano's father realized that he had to make plans to protect his family. Acting on a tip from Christian friends, the Roth parents and grandmother found "a secret maid's room" where they could hide from the police. Roth-Hano and her sisters were sent to a convent in Normandy.

Now eleven years old, Renée Roth-Hanau understood that hers was "a different kind of hiding." They were in plain sight, but were hiding their Jewishness. They lived with all the other children as Catholics, and although the nuns were considerate of their differences, they learned the prayers along with all the Christian children. Being the oldest, Roth-Hano understood why she had to do it but she was filled with fear and guilt for turning away from her own religion.

In 1944, the Americans arrived in Normandy and the Germans launched a counter-attack. To be sure they would be safe and with their parents' permission, the nuns baptized the girls and gave them first communion. For Roth-Hano, this felt like a total betrayal. She thought that things would never be the same again. Her guilt was compounded by the fact that she liked Catholicism. She dreamed of "flying up to Heaven without my parents," and the constant anxiety caused her to sleepwalk and to suffer from all kinds of illnesses. Nevertheless, she and her sisters prayed to the Catholic God and the saints; they prayed for an end to the war and for protection of the Jews. "I did not really believe in them," wrote Roth-Hano many years later, "but that's all I had." She knew very little about Jewish history and felt abandoned by her parents.

When their village and the convent were bombed continuously for three days, Roth-Hano made a vow that if she remained alive, she would become a nun. Although she never did, she was haunted by that private commitment for five years. Even after the war was over and she was back with her family, Roth-Hano, then a teenager, felt alienated from her roots. She was fearful and ashamed to tell anyone she was Jewish, and would often sneak away to attend Sunday mass. When her father discovered this, he was very angry and scolded her, shouting, "You are not going to church. You are a Jew for God's sake!" He died a few days after that incident and she never went again.

Growing up in France after the war, Roth-Hano was still afraid to admit she was Jewish. It was not until 1951, at the age of nineteen, when she came to the United States as a governess, that she began to feel safe. The realization that being a Jew was acceptable came when she was shopping in Macy's in New York City and heard two women casually and openly discussing their Passover seder. "I felt like something inside me was breaking free," she told an interviewer.

Roth-Hano remained in the United States. She continued her education and became a psychiatric social worker. In 1968 she married John Hano. Twenty years later, she wrote *Touch Wood,* a children's book about her experiences during the war, which enjoyed critical acclaim. In the 1990s she became involved in the Hidden Child Foundation. Here, she finally found a group of Jews with whom she could identify completely. This identity allowed her to admit her Jewishness "without choking or blushing." But she is also grateful for her "dual experience," explaining that it has made her "more tolerant of differences."

References

Marks, Jane. "The Hidden Children." *New York Magazine* (February 25, 1991): p. 39.
Roth-Hano, Renée. *Touch Wood: A Girlhood in Occupied France*. New York: Four Winds/Macmillan, 1988.
———. "A Girlhood in Occupied France: A Dual Experience." *The Hidden Child* 7, no. 1 (fall/winter 1997): p. 1.

Rozen, Richard (1935–)

Richard Rozen, originally of Radom, Poland, spent the war years first hiding in a closet, then in a ghetto, and then with the partisans in the forest. When the war ended, he was ten years old and had seen more death and destruction than most people do in a lifetime.

In September 1939, when Germany attacked Poland and World War II officially began, Richard Rozen was a four-year-old boy, the only child of his parents. They lived in Radom, where his father was a doctor and the head of a large hospital. When the Nazis occupied Radom, the Rozens escaped to Luboml, a town in what was then Russian-occupied eastern Poland. However, by the summer of 1941, ignoring their earlier pact with the Soviet Union, the Nazis invaded eastern Poland as well. When they reached Luboml, the Rozens went into hiding at the home of a farmer.

The Rozen parents and their son stayed in a closet in the basement of the farmer's house for thirteen months. Although Richard was able to stand upright, his parents could not. They never left their hiding place and were totally dependent on the farmer for all of their basic needs. He was paid with gold coins, but after a year they ran out of money to pay for their room and board and the farmer insisted they leave.

Outside in the light, Rozen was delighted with the bright colors he saw, but his pleasure was quickly overshadowed when they were captured by two Ukrainian guards. The guards took them to a German officer. The Rozens tried to pass as Christians, but the Germans had one infallible test. He asked Richard and his father to lower their pants. As soon as he saw that they were circumcised, lying was useless. At that time in Poland only Jewish boys were circumcised. They were taken to the ghetto in Lublin.

In the ghetto, food was scarce and death was everywhere. Each morning, Rozen could see dead bodies being taken away in a cart. It was just a matter of time before the family would be sent to Treblinka to be killed. Rozen knew that his parents were very worried and did not want to go.

Then a new opportunity arose for Rozen's father. He heard that the Polish partisans desperately needed a doctor. If he could prove he was a competent physician, they would take him and his family out of the ghetto so they would not be killed in Treblinka. Dr. Rozen passed the test and while he worked in a nearby hospital, Richard and his mother lived in a small town with the family of one of the partisans. There was one difficulty, though. In order to avoid suspicion that he was a Jew, Rozen had to pretend to be a girl.

This ruse was difficult, but it worked for about four months. Then suspicions were aroused in town and it simply became too dangerous. Rozen was taken to join his father.

After the war, Richard Rozen and his mother sailed on the *S.S. Cyrenia* to Australia to start a new life. Gift of Richard Rozen. Collection of the Museum of Jewish Heritage—A Living Memorial to the Holocaust, New York.

Rozen did not remain with his father, who lived at the field hospital partially under ground. He stayed with the partisans in a nearby wood and wandered around with them. Food was scarce and the one meal they had each day was made up of produce stolen during the night by one of their members. Discipline was strict and when two partisans came home from a nighttime search for food drunk and with no provisions, they were tied to a tree and their throats were cut. Although Rozen, still only nine years old, had seen many dead bodies, this was the first murder he actually witnessed. He was shocked at the violence, but even more difficult was the hunger. They had had no food for forty-eight hours.

A few months after joining the partisan band, the commander decided to make Rozen "a full-fledged partisan," and gave him an official job as feather boy. This job entailed holding a feather to the nose of each German soldier who had been attacked and stabbed by the partisans, and counting to a hundred. If the feather didn't move, that meant the soldier was no longer breathing. If it moved, the partisans would finish him off. Often the soldiers were not yet dead. One pleaded with Rozen to let him live, indicating that he had a wife and children, but Rozen was a good feather boy. He never killed any of the Germans himself, but he didn't allow himself to feel any pity for them.

The Nazis sometimes bombed the area where the partisans stayed in order to eliminate them, since they posed a continual danger to German troops and troop movements. After a while, Rozen got used to that, too, and stayed up in a tree while the bombs fell around him. He was never hit. One night in 1944, an unusually cold winter, there was a massive bombing raid and when it was over, the woods were littered with dead bodies and body parts. Rozen looked down and saw a human leg. He decided to take it to his father at the hospital; perhaps he could use it for a partisan who had lost his own leg. He found his father and showed him what he had brought, but to his surprise his father started crying. Not until many years later did Rozen understand "that perhaps this was not the way he'd hoped that his nine-year-old son would be spending a winter's morning."

That was Rozen's last memory of his father. A short while later, the hospital was attacked. He searched for his father in the ruins, but then learned that he had been taken away by the Germans.

When the Russians came and liberated eastern Poland, the war was over for Rozen. His mother came to find him and they returned to Radom, but now they were no longer affluent and respected; they were penniless and homeless. Rozen wore rags and was barefoot. When his mother went to visit the wives of the Christian doctors who had once been their friends they slammed their doors in her face.

Rozen spent a few months in a children's home in Otwock, recuperating from tuberculosis. There, for the first time, he made friends with boys his own age and played games. When he had recovered, they went to a displaced-persons camp in Stuttgart, Germany, where Rozen went to school for the first time. While there, they made contact with French relatives and were brought to Paris.

Their first meal together was very elaborate and plentiful and Rozen, conditioned by years of starvation, "stole" some slices of roast beef and hid them in his shirt. His French relatives were horrified at his behavior and he was shipped off to a Jewish orphanage, while his mother struggled to earn a living and learn French. Rozen stayed at the orphanage until 1951, when he and his mother sailed for Australia. He completed his studies, married, and raised two sons in Melbourne, where he became a successful real estate investor. He also served as a volunteer at the Melbourne Holocaust center and began discussing his war experiences. His mother, who ended her days in a nursing home in Melbourne, had never discussed the war. But Rozen could not forget that he was one of only thirty-five child survivors from the twenty-five thousand Jewish children of Radom, and that he had lost twenty-three members of his own family, murdered by the Nazis. He admitted to an interviewer that he was successful in his life but still not sure whether he was happy.

References

Appel, Allan. *To Life: 36 Stories of Memory and Hope*. New York: Bullfinch Press, 2002.

Marks, Jane. *The Hidden Children: The Secret Survivors of the Holocaust.* New York: Fawcett Columbine, 1993.

Rubel, Ruth (1928–2001)

Ruth Bonyhadi Rubel of Vienna, Austria, survived the Nazi ghetto and the camps. She was able to stay with her mother throughout the war, only to lose her to typhus and malnutrition just days after liberation.

Rubel, an only child, was cared for by her loving parents Ludwig and Gertrude Bonyhadi. Ludwig, a Jew of Hungarian background, was successful in sales and insurance and the family lived well until 1938. In March of that year, the Germans, under their new National Socialist (Nazi) rule, invaded and annexed Austria. Suddenly, Jews were deprived of their rights. They were not allowed to own their own businesses or to participate in the cultural life of the city. On the streets, Austrian and German Nazis singled out Jews for beatings, humiliations, and arrests. By 1939, Ludwig Bonyhadi, too, was arrested and sent to a labor camp. The family received one post card from him from Lvov, but Rubel never saw him again. Then Rubel's grandmother, Ottilia G. Loewit, was deported to Theresienstadt. She disappeared and no one knew how she died.

Rubel, then eleven years old, remained with her mother in Vienna until 1941, when they were deported to the Lodz ghetto in Poland. In order to insure her survival, Rubel lied about her age and was put to work sewing and mending German uniforms. Her mother was placed in a factory making straw boots. This vital work kept them alive and out of the camps for another two years.

In Lodz, as in all the Nazi-established ghettos, food was scarce and hunger was widespread. Rubel and her mother worked ten hours a day and lived in a single room with two other families. Despite these conditions, however, Rubel secretly studied in the evenings and learned English. They attempted to celebrate the Jewish festivals and holidays as best they could. At Purim, a happy, carnival holiday when children customarily dress in costumes, Rubel and a young boy from another family decided to switch clothing so they would feel dressed up for the holiday. Their parents heartily disapproved, however, when they appeared with their "costumes."

By August 1944, even those small pleasures ended. The Lodz ghetto was liquidated and Rubel and her mother joined thousands of others on the trains. They traveled in unbearably overcrowded conditions, with no sanitary facilities and no food, for three nights and four days. When the train stopped, they were in Auschwitz.

By the time Rubel and her mother were brought to Auschwitz, the war was going badly for Germany and the camps were

Ruth Bonyhadi married Herbert Rubel in the United States in 1948. Courtesy of Joan Rubel.

less organized. Within a short time, they were transferred—again on the terrible cattle cars. They arrived at Bergen-Belsen, a camp in Germany, where they remained for nine months.

Bergen-Belsen was a place of terrible deprivation. By the time they got there, food was scarce throughout Germany, and at the camps there were hardly enough rations to stay alive. Hundreds died every day and their bodies lay unburied. With no medicine or care, diseases were rampant. When liberation finally came in April 1945, Bonyhadi was too weak from starvation to fight off typhus. She died just two weeks after the British Army had arrived and begun giving the prisoners food and medical care.

Devastated by her mother's death, Rubel remembered nothing of those first few weeks. In Bergen-Belsen, she had begun to keep a diary, inscribed on scraps of paper, and continued the practice for a time after liberation. It details the journey to recover her health and rebuild her life.

Later, Rubel could remember being in Stuttgart, Germany, in a displaced-persons camp. She had been tracked down by an American cousin, Ernest Bonyhadi, who was serving in the U.S. Army. He brought her from Bergen-Belsen to Stuttgart to the Degerloch displaced-persons camp where she lived with a Jewish couple. Through his help and an affidavit from an aunt and uncle in the Bonyhadi family, she was able to leave Germany for the United States, departing on the first civilian transport out of Europe. She lived with relatives in San Francisco for a short time and attended a public high school. But she found nothing in common with her American classmates, whose experiences and concerns were very different from hers. She dropped out of school and took a job as a key-punch operator. She was urged to forget her experiences and begin a new life.

While working in San Francisco, Ruth met Herbert J. Rubel, then serving in the U.S. Army. By 1948, at the age of twenty, she and Herbert were married and living in New York. Herbert became an aircraft engineer who worked for Pratt and Whitney and then for Lockheed and earned a good living. The Rubels raised three daughters and later had four grandchildren.

Rubel devoted her life to creating a home for her family; she was an accomplished seamstress, knitter, and cook. After her husband's death in 1991, she created the Herbert J. Rubel Holocaust Education Fund in Richmond, Virginia. Though she struggled with the painful memories of her past, she dedicated her remaining years to speaking about her experiences. Her goal was to educate others about the Holocaust.

Throughout the remainder of her life, Ruth Bonyhadi Rubel's greatest pride and pleasure continued to be her daughters and their families. She died in 2001 from the complications of emphysema.

Reference

Rubel, Joan G. Interview by the author, June 2006, Northampton, Massachusetts.

Rubin, Tibor (1930–)

Tibor Rubin of Paszto, Hungary, faced death in two prison camps. The first was in World War II, when he survived Mauthausen in Austria. The second was when he survived thirty months in an army prison camp in Korea while fighting in the U.S. Army.

Rubin, one of six children, was born in Paszto, a small Hungarian town of 120 Jewish families. His father was a shoemaker and his mother cared for the family. Like many Hungarian Jews, they thought there was a good chance that World War II would be over before it got to Hungary, but in 1944, the Nazis came and evacuated all the Jews in his town. Rubin's father was taken to Buchenwald concentration camp, where he died. His mother and ten-year-old sister were gassed in Auschwitz, and Tibor, then thirteen years old, was transported to Mauthausen, a work camp in Austria. Rubin recalls one of the first things the guards told them when they entered the camp: "None of you Jews will ever make it out alive." But Tibor Rubin was one of the few who defied that prediction.

"Every day so many people were killed," Rubin later told reporters. "Bodies [were] piled up God knows how high. We had nothing to look forward to but dying." Nevertheless, Rubin found ways to survive. He was still alive on May 5, 1945, when the U.S. Army marched into Mauthausen and Rubin was immediately impressed by their kindness and compassion. When they discovered the prisoners, filthy and sick, explained Rubin, "they picked us up and brought us back to life." He had been in prison for almost two years when he was freed by the Americans and he made a vow that he would go to the United States one day and become a soldier in the U.S. Army to express his thanks.

Tibor Rubin fulfilled that vow. Although he was still a minor after the war, he was lucky enough to find other members of his family who had survived and with them, emigrated to the United States in 1948. He first worked in New York as a shoemaker and then as a butcher, biding his time until his English was good enough so he could enlist in the army. Finally, in 1950, he passed the language test and was inducted. Almost immediately, he was shipped off to Korea.

Fighting in the Korean War, Ted Rubin, as he was called by his army buddies, had many opportunities to use the survival skills he had learned at Mauthausen. His First Sgt. Artice Watson, was antisemitic and always chose Rubin for dangerous assignments. Once he commanded him to hold a strategically critical hill all by himself so his battalion could withdraw. For twenty-four hours, Rubin, then a private, fought wave after wave of North Korean soldiers. He "ran around to fire from different directions and rolled hand grenades down so the enemy would think there were many soldiers to face in the battle." But when his commanding officers told Sgt. Watson to prepare the paperwork and submit Rubin's name for a medal of honor, he ignored them. Several other acts of bravery won Rubin recommendations for the Medal of Honor, the Distinguished Service Cross, and the Silver Star, but each time his Sergeant refused to follow through.

Toward the end of October 1950, massive Chinese troop concentrations crossed the border into North Korea and attacked the Americans. Most of his regiment was wiped out, and Rubin, severely wounded, was captured. Along with over one hundred men from his company, he spent the next thirty months in a prisoner-of-war camp.

While most of the men gave up, Rubin had experience in surviving death camps. He encouraged the other soldiers, stole food from the North Korean supply depots, and helped care for those who were wounded or sick. James Bourgeois, a fellow prisoner, remembered that Rubin would boil a helmet full of snow every day to clean his bandages and tend to a large open wound on his shoulder. When the wound became infected, Rubin foraged for maggots and placed them in the gash to eat away the infection, saving Bourgeois' arm.

Another soldier, Leo Cormier, testified that Rubin "was a godsend. . . . Tibor saved my life, as well as many other guys. . . . He also took care of us, nursed us, carried us to the latrine. . . . He did many good deeds, which he told us were *mitzvahs* in the Jewish tradition. . . . He was a very religious Jew, and helping his fellow men was the most important thing to him."

Sgt. Carl McClendon, a POW also saved by Rubin, wrote, "He had more courage, guts and fellowship than I ever knew anyone had. He is the most outstanding man I ever met, with a heart of gold. Tibor Rubin committed everyday bravery that boggles the mind. How he ever came home alive is a mystery to me."

For the second time Rubin had survived. In 1953, he became a U.S. citizen and after his discharge, lived quietly in a small house in Garden Grove, California, with his wife Yvonne, a Dutch Holocaust survivor. The couple had two children, Frank, now an Air Force veteran, and Rosalyn.

It wasn't until the 1980s that Rubin's old army buddies started protesting. They were angry at the army's inaction in recognizing the man who had saved so many of their lives. In 1988, Sen. John McCain (R-Ariz.) introduced a special bill on Rubin's behalf. Others added their voices, demanding that Rubin be given the recognition he deserved for his war service. Still nothing happened. Then in the 1990s, the U.S. Army began reviewing its old policies, which often passed over soldiers from minority groups in awarding medals. First it was the turn of the U.S. soldiers in World War II. Then the Kravitz Bill was introduced to review the files of Jewish soldiers. Tibor Rubin's was the thickest of all the files.

Finally, on September 23, 2005, almost fifty-five years after his military service was over, Tibor Rubin was invited to the White House and the Medal of Honor, the nation's highest award for gallantry in combat, was hung around his neck by President George W. Bush. Rubin, then seventy-six years old, smiled and told reporters, "It would have been nice if they had given me the medal when I was a young, handsome man. It would have opened a lot of doors." Then in a more serious vein, he said, "I want this recognition for my Jewish brothers and sisters." Tibor Rubin was the fifteenth Jewish recipient to be awarded the Medal of Honor since it was first instituted by Congress during the Civil War.

References

Proft, R. J. "United States of America's Congressional Medal of Honor Recipients: And Their Official Citations." *Blogcritics Magazine*. http://blogcritics.org/archives/2005/10/19/043202.php (accessed October 25, 2005).

Tugend, Tom. "Behind the Headlines: After long campaign, Jewish veteran will finally be honored by U.S. military." *Jewish Telegraph Agency* (September 14, 2005).

White, Josh. "President Honors a Hero of the Korean War." *Washington Post,* (September 24, 2005): p. A3.

Rufeisen, Oswald (Father Daniel) (1922–)

Born a Jew in Krakow, Poland, Oswald Rufeisen posed as a German and risked his life to save the Jews of Mir, Poland. But he emerged from World War II as a devout Catholic who took vows as a Carmelite monk and spent his later years in Israel.

Rufeisen grew up in western Poland, near the German border. His father had earned a medal for bravery while serving in the Austro-German army during World War I. The family was culturally close to Germany and Rufeisen was fluent in both the German and Polish languages. He never spoke Yiddish, the *lingua franca* of most Polish Jews, but he did join a nonreligious Zionist Youth organization. He had hoped to live in Israel, but his plans were thwarted by the war.

When the Germans invaded Poland on September 1, 1939, Rufeisen and his parents, like hundreds of other Jews, fled to the east. He stayed for a while in Vilna, where he finished his education and also learned shoemaking skills. When the Nazis marched into Vilna in the summer of 1941, he was arrested and worked in a labor camp but managed to escape. His parents were killed and Rufeisen ended up in Mir, a small Polish town near the Russian border that was famous for its yeshivah (academy) for advanced Jewish learning. In Mir, he was not known. He posed as a citizen of German and Polish ancestry and was not suspected of being a Jew.

Attracted by this well-spoken young man, the German troops stationed in the area offered Rufeisen a position as an officer in the German police force where he could put his language skills to good use. Although he hated to work for the Germans, he reasoned that it would enable him to save Jews and he accepted the offer. He eventually became personal secretary to the Commandant, Meister Reinhold Hein.

In early 1942, Rufeisen made his first secret contact with the Jews. He met Dov Resnick, a young man he had known in Vilna, in the Zionist Youth Movement. They met secretly and Rufeisen indicated to Resnick that he could help the Jews smuggle arms into the ghetto at Mir, located in an abandoned castle just outside the town. Arrangements were made and weapons were brought in a few at a time by the Jewish workers. Most of the supplies were hidden in cracks and holes in the crumbling castle walls and then pulled in from the inside, so the workers would not risk being searched by Nazi guards at the gate. About forty young men were involved in the plans for this insurrection, but only a handful knew that Rufeisen, the German policeman, was really a Jew.

When the Jews had accumulated enough weapons, the men decided that rather than fight the Germans while confined inside the castle walls—a battle they could not possibly win—they would escape with their arms and join other partisans who were fighting in the forests around Mir.

Rufeisen was again in a position to help the Jews of Mir. He had learned that the Germans planned to liquidate the ghetto on August 13, 1943, and

> *My religion is Catholic but my ethnic origin is and always will be Jewish. I have no other nationality. . . . If I am not a Jew what am I? I did not accept Christianity to leave my people. It added to my Judaism. I feel as a Jew.*
>
> —Father Daniel (Oswald Rufeisen)

advised his contacts in the ghetto to plan their escape before that day. He would then divert the police with false reports of a partisan attack in another area of the forest, giving the Jews a chance to get away undetected. Subsequently, Rufeisen also expected to lead the Nazis' search for the runaways, carefully keeping the men away from certain safe areas that had been previously designated. Then he would lead them into a trap where partisans would be waiting to attack and kill the Germans.

But now, the forty Jews planning the insurrection faced a moral dilemma. They felt obligated to tell the other Jewish residents about the planned liquidation so that they, too, could escape and try to save themselves. However, if they told them the source of their information, they would put Rufeisen at risk of being discovered, since he and his commanding officer were the only two who knew of the date of the liquidation. Finally, they decided to inform the *Judenrat* (the Jewish committee in the ghetto), advising them to plan their escapes for August 9 or 10, several days before the planned liquidation. They also told the committee that Rufeisen was a Jew. This news spread quickly through the ghetto and ultimately Rufeisen was betrayed by a Jew who hoped that this information would save his own life.

The betrayal tied Rufeisen's hands. He could no longer help the escaping Jews or lead the search party, but he was never arrested or killed. Meister Reinhold Hein was extremely fond of Rufeisen. Even after he learned of his protégé's crimes, Hein refused to take immediate action. Instead, he invited Rufeisen to join the other officers for dinner while he considered his fate. During the dinner, Rufeisen found an opportunity to slip away. He hid in a wheat field for several days and the German search parties never found him. When he felt sure they had stopped searching, Rufeisen took refuge in a Catholic convent in Mir itself, right next to the German police station where he had worked for two years.

During the remaining months of the war, Rufeisen served with the Russian partisans, but also learned about Catholicism and eventually converted. Many of the Jews from the Mir ghetto did manage a successful escape (see **Julius and Jack Sutin**). The original group of insurgents left the ghetto on August 9 and was able to live undetected in the forest. The following day, others escaped. A total of three hundred Jews were saved by Rufeisen's efforts.

After the war, Oswald Rufeisen took vows as a Carmelite monk, was ordained as a priest, and adopted the name Father Daniel. In 1962, he moved to Israel and requested citizenship as a Jew. This request aroused a great deal of controversy among the Jewish citizens of Israel as well as in the press and the courts. Father Daniel claimed to be an ethnic Jew but a Catholic by religion. The separation of these two categories and the questions they engendered had never before been dealt with in Jewish law and there were no precedents. Ultimately, the Supreme Court of Israel ruled that Father Daniel was welcome to apply for citizenship as a gentile but not as a Jew. They amended the law of return to stipulate that a person practicing another religion cannot be considered a Jew.

Rufeisen became well known in Israel as Father Daniel. He settled in Jerusalem and was the head of the Jewish-Christian Church there. His acclaimed goal was to improve Jewish-Christian relations in his adopted country and he continued his old friendships with the Jews of the Mir ghetto, many of whom also settled in Israel.

References

Tec, Nehama. *In the Lion's Den: The Life of Oswald Rufeisen*. New York: Oxford University Press, 1990.

http://www.literacyconnections.com/cgi-bin/apf4/amazon_products_feed.cgi?Operation=ItemLookup&ItemId=019503905X.

Weiner, Rebecca. "Who Is a Jew?" Jewish Virtual Library, A Division of the American Israeli Cooperative Enterprise. http://www.jewishvirtuallibrary.org/jsource/Judaism/whojew1.html.

S

Salton, George Lucius (1928–)

George Lucius Salton of Tyczyn, Poland, was barely in his teens when the war began. He survived numerous concentration camps, abuse, and beatings by the Nazis. Separated from his parents early in the war, then from his older brother, he willed himself to survive and fulfill his promise to his parents: grow up to be a *mentsch* (a good man).

Salton was born Lucek Salzman, in the small Polish town of Tyczyn. His father, Henry, was a lawyer. His brother, Manek, was six years older and already applying to a university when World War II erupted. Almost immediately the area around Tyczyn was occupied by the Germans and conditions for Jews changed. Henry Salzman was no longer allowed to practice law. All Jews over the age of twelve had to wear identifying armbands showing that they were Jews, and received identification papers of a different color from non-Jews. Jews were subjected to random beatings and humiliations by Nazi soldiers, and often the Poles stood by and laughed. Salton was shocked to see that even the Polish boys who were his friends from school sometimes joined in the antisemitic activities or stood by and did nothing. Several times, Salton was caught by individual SS men and beaten for no reason.

When Salton's father, Henry, was arrested by the Gestapo, he got his first taste of what it might mean to be separated from his family. With Henry Salzman in prison in the neighboring town of Rzeszow, his mother left to try and arrange for his release, which took many months. Finally Henry Salzman returned, but he was a broken man, sick and weak. He never talked about his experiences in prison, but spent a good deal of time in bed and

> *Take care of yourself and live. . . . And if it should happen that you will have to grow up without us, remember that we want you to grow up and become a good person, that we want you to become a mensch.*
>
> —Salton's mother, before being transported to Belzec concentration camp.

never fully recuperated. Food was in short supply and the family began to sell or trade its possessions for food.

Because Jewish children were barred from attending school, work not only kept them busy, but also kept them safe, at least for a while. Salton, only thirteen years old, found a job as a locksmith's apprentice. His brother set up his own shop for bicycle repairs. When the locksmith closed his business and the winter season meant that few people rode bicycles, the boys needed to find other work quickly.

As the months passed, the situation for Jews became worse. First, all the Jews of Tzycyn were forced to move into the ghetto of Rzeszow. Then, deportations to the east began and only those with work cards, showing that they had jobs, were allowed to stay. The Salzman boys were lucky enough to be assigned to work in a metal shop making parts for German airplanes. They worked twelve hours a day with one short break for food, but they were grateful to be excluded from the regular deportations that began in the winter of 1942.

Salton was fourteen when an order came that all those with no work cards would be deported and he realized that he would be separated from his parents. He wanted to go with them and be "relocated" in the Ukraine, as the Nazis had promised. But his parents, perhaps sensing that the relocation was a lie, refused to let him go. They left him in the care of his older brother, Manek. Manek would take care of him and after the war, they would be reunited. Salton's mother gave each of her sons the name and address of her sister Pauline in New York. If they got separated, they must contact Aunt Pauline; she would be the central point for information. As Salton wept, his mother made him promise to take care of himself and stay alive.

Within a short time, Salton was transferred out of the ghetto into a work camp. One day, as he was walking to his workstation, the German in front of him dropped an envelope. Salton ran after him and returned it. It was the payroll envelope for the German workers. Because of this almost automatic good deed, the German rewarded him with a sandwich. Months later, when he was on a truck being deported because of work-related injuries, that same German saved him from death. It was one of George's many narrow escapes.

Although the brothers were separated from each other, they managed to stay in contact through clandestine meetings at the factory. When Manek was deported and escaped from the trains, he somehow found ways to send messages to Salton through the Polish Underground. The last message Lucek received from Manek told him that he was going on a mission and would no longer be able to write. He promised that they would find each other after the war.

As the Russians advanced further, counterattacking the Germans from the east, the front line gradually moved westward and the camps and their prisoners moved as well. Salton was shipped to another camp and then another. Each time, conditions got worse. There was less food, more brutality, and harder work assignments. Salton pushed himself to go on, constantly searching for less strenuous work that might give him even a short respite from the brutal conditions. Occasionally, he was able to obtain a few more spoonfuls of soup or another piece of bread to keep him alive for one more day. As the

Allied bombs began to fall on the German factories, prisoners were put to work cleaning up the debris in the freezing cold. They had no gloves, no socks, and no clothing except their thin uniforms. Several times, Salton was ready to give up, lie down in the snow, and wait for death. Each time, something or someone roused him and he survived.

When the war was finally over and Salton's camp was liberated by the Americans, he was overjoyed. Although weak from hunger and barely able to stand, they ran to the soldiers, touching them to make sure they were real. The Americans cared for the starving prisoners and transferred them to a displaced-persons camp. After five years of persecution and fear, Salton was astonished to discover that Jews were serving in the American and British Armies and were carrying weapons for their countries. At the same time, the Jewish soldiers were amazed and overjoyed that some Jews still remained in Europe. "We thought the Germans had killed them all," they said.

Although Salton had lost the scrap of paper with his aunt's address long ago, he remembered the name and the city. After many attempts, his relatives received his letter and contacted him. They had not heard from anyone else. Salton's parents had been gassed in Belzec and Manek had simply disappeared without a trace.

In 1947, Lucek Salzberg came to America and changed his name to George Lucius Salton. Beginning with a menial job and night-school classes, he learned English and became a television and radio repairman. He was drafted into the Army in 1950 and was able to improve his English and learn other skills. He became an American citizen in 1953.

During his years in the army, Salton met and married Ruth, also a Polish-Jewish refugee. With her encouragement, Salton continued his education, earning a B.S. degree in physics and then a master's in electrical engineering. He worked for the Pentagon for eighteen years, overseeing the development of satellite systems. The Saltons had two sons, Henry and Alan, and a daughter, Anna.

Originally, Salton had decided to leave the Holocaust behind and raise his children without the terrible knowledge of what he had gone through. However, when they were grown, they wanted to know about his family. In 1998, the Saltons took their children back to Poland to see the town of Tzycyn where he was born, and the places that he remembered from his childhood. They went to the Belzec camp and recited the *Kaddish* (the prayer for the dead) for his parents. Encouraged by his children, Salton wrote a book recounting his experiences during the war. In it, he confessed that even though his life was happy and fulfilled and he felt that he had kept his promise to his parents, "the pain and trauma of the ghetto and camps" remained with him.

Reference

Salton, George Lucius. *The 23rd Psalm: A Holocaust Memoir*. Madison, WI: University of Wisconsin Press, 2002.

Saltzberg, Walter (1931–)

Walter Saltzberg of Warsaw was one of many hidden children who survived the war. During the last days before Warsaw was liberated, he was injured when the building in which he was hiding was bombed by German planes. His leg injury went untreated and resulted in a permanent handicap, an ever-present reminder of those years of terror.

Saltzberg was born in Warsaw, Poland. His original name was Wacek Zalcberg, but he remembered almost nothing of the war years and little of his parents. He did know that when the Nazis began the liquidation of the ghetto in 1942, his parents arranged to hide him with a family friend, a Polish gentile doctor named Wenckowski. Saltzberg remained with the Wenckowski family until the fall of 1944, when the Polish uprising began.

Walter Saltzberg is not sure why, but he knows that at the start of the uprising he had to leave the Wenckowskis' home. By then thirteen years old, he was placed in another building with a number of Jews who had been hiding there. During the course of the fighting between the Polish Underground and the Nazis, this building was bombed and Saltzberg was buried in the rubble with his leg severely broken.

In serious pain and unable to move, Walter Saltzberg was rescued by a young Jew named Peter Jablonski, who carried Saltzberg to a new hiding place, where he remained with three other Jews. The five young men stayed in a sub-basement for about five months. During that time, they had almost nothing to eat except a sack of onions. Only after the Germans put down the Polish uprising did the Russian Army march in and liberate Warsaw. Peter Jablonski cared for his young charge throughout the time of the fighting and for two months after. In 1945 he brought him to a refugee center and from there Saltzberg went to a Jewish orphanage in Otwock, outside of Warsaw. His leg had healed by then, but it was a full fourteen inches shorter than the other leg, and Saltzberg had considerable difficulty walking.

Seeing that Saltzberg's injury caused a serious handicap, the Russians sent him to a military hospital, the first time he had received any medical attention for his fracture. The operation did not succeed, though, and Saltzberg's movement remained severely limited: he could not play ball or run with the other children. His overriding memory of that first year after liberation was waiting for his parents to come for him. Each day his hopes were dashed when they failed to show up. Finally, he began to understand that they were among the millions who were murdered by the Nazis.

His parents, however, had friends who had left Poland and gone to the United States. They were able to track him down, the only surviving member of the Saltzberg family, and they began the long process of procuring papers for him to join them in the United States. While he waited, he was selected by a Swedish Red Cross mission to go to Sweden for another operation on his leg. This one was more successful. Now his leg was only three inches shorter than the other one and he began to learn how to walk properly. He even was able to ride a bicycle.

Walter Saltzberg lived in Sweden for approximately two years while his American friends tried to arrange for his visa. When they realized that this would not be possible for many more years, they contacted some distant relatives living in Winnipeg, a city in Manitoba, Canada. With their help, Saltzberg was able to emigrate to Canada.

Arriving in Winnipeg on November 30, 1947, Saltzberg was not quite seventeen years old, but he had only a second grade education. He had not attended school during the war, and after the war, had spent most of his time in hospitals or recuperating. Now he would have to begin again, first to learn a new language and then to catch up to his peers. "On January 2, 1948, I started in the second half of the ninth grade," he wrote, "and continued my education with some interruptions for the purpose of making money."

Saltzberg did catch up, and in 1957, graduated from the University of Manitoba with a Bachelor of Science degree. He was twenty-seven years old. His first job was with the Department of Highways and Transportation for the Province of Manitoba. He worked his way up and by 1995 he was Director of Bridges and Structures in his adopted country.

Reference

Saltzberg, Walter. "Fifty Years After Otwock." *The Hidden Child* 5, no. 1 (spring 1995): p. 4.

Schiff, Liliane (1932–)

Liliane Mendrowski Schiff was born in Belgium to assimilated parents. She never thought of herself as Jewish until the German invasion. Hidden with a Christian family, then spirited away to a convent, she and her sister survived the war. She promised never to forget those who saved her and she never did. Even though memories of her childhood remained painful, Schiff knew that she was "fortunate to have met many kind and caring people, righteous people who saved my life and my sister's life."

"I didn't ask questions," recalled Lili Schiff, relating the story of her childhood under the Nazis. Only eight years old when the German occupation of Belgium began, she was nevertheless old enough to wear a yellow Star of David. Her father, Benjamin Leib Mendrowski, a silversmith, lost his work, and even at that young age she knew "that horrible things were happening to the Jews." When her parents told her and her sister Frida that they would be going to live with strangers, she did not ask why.

In 1940, Lili and Frida Mendrowski were placed with François and Josephine Donnay, a middle-aged couple in Liège who had recently lost their own daughter. Donnay was a coal miner and the couple was uneducated and illiterate, but they were loving foster parents and kept the girls for two years. Then one night, the Gestapo came searching for Bernard, the Donnay's son and a member of the Belgian Underground. Suddenly, their home for the last two years was no longer safe and they were quickly placed in a truck and hidden underneath a load of coal and tree logs. There was no time for goodbyes or explanations. When the truck stopped, they were at a convent. They remained there from 1943 until the war ended in the spring of 1945. Although not known to them at the time, the driver of the truck that brought them there was **Henri Reynders (Dom Bruno),** a Benedictine monk who was active in saving several hundred Jewish children.

The Donnays survived the war and so did Lili's parents, Benjamin and Paula Mendrowski, who were able to pose as gentiles. They worked at the Wezembeek orphanage as janitor and cook until the end of the war. The Wezembeek Children's Home, run by **Marie Blum-Albert**, succeeded in saving many Belgian Jewish children from deportation and death. Lili and Frida Mendrowski's older brother, Isy, was caught by the Nazis in 1943, transported to Auschwitz, and killed in the gas chambers when he was fourteen. The rest of the Mendrowski's extended family, in both Belgium and Poland, were also murdered in the camps.

The Mendrowski family remained in Belgium, and when Liliane completed her education, she worked for the Belgium National Broadcasting System as an interviewer. She spoke English well, and when offered a position in the United States, she accepted. Mendrowski became an interpreter for the United Nations in New York and worked at the U.N. for six years. In New York, she met Edward Schiff, married him, and remained in America. The Schiffs have three children.

When the Schiff family moved to California, Lili Schiff returned to school and earned an M.A. in urban sociology. She then worked in the courts as a family relations mediator for a while and then for Project Food Chain, an organization that prepares meals for homebound AIDS patients.

Schiff was always reluctant to talk about her war experiences, but now, she said, "my conscience compels me." Liliane Schiff's story was part of a joint exhibit on Holocaust survivors presented in 2003 by the University of California at Santa Barbara and the Santa Barbara Jewish Federation. At the opening, she said, "I haven't the dimmest notion of what wars are really about, but I know we must overcome again and again and again for our children's sake and for humanity's sake."

Reference

"Lili Schiff née Mendrowski." Imagetext: Portraits and Biographies. http://www.imagetext.ca/portraits/lili2.html.

Schiller, Hugo (1930–)

Hugo Schiller of Grunsfeld, Germany, was a child of the Holocaust. Deported to Gurs, a holding camp in France, while the Nazis constructed Auschwitz, he and his family lived in almost unbearable conditions until he was taken out by a relief worker and placed in a children's home in Aspet, France. He credits this relief worker, **Alice Resch Synnestvedt**, with saving his life.

Schiller first began to feel the effects of Nazi antisemitism in the 1930s, when he was still quite young. His parents, Oscar and Selma Schiller, were forced to give up their clothing business, and in 1938, after *Kristallnacht* (the Night of Broken Glass), his father was arrested briefly. That same year, Schiller had to leave the school he was attending and go to a special Jewish school in Offenbach. Only nine years old at the time, he stayed with an aunt and uncle.

Once the actual war began, conditions became worse for Germany's Jews and many were banished to concentration camps. In October 1940, shortly after the Germans invaded France, the ten-year-old Schiller and his family were deported to Gurs, a transit camp located just outside a small village in the foothills of the Pyrenées Mountains.

The camp at Gurs has been described as a sea of mud surrounded by barbed wire. It was overcrowded, there was inadequate sanitation, hardly enough food, and disease was rampant. Added to this was the fear and depression of the inmates who did not know what would happen to them, how long they would remain in the camp, and where they would go next. Hugo Schiller was among many children lingering in these miserable conditions, dirty and hungry, with no education or recreation available to them. More than sixty years later, he described his memories of the camp to an interviewer. "I would talk to people one morning," he said, "and a day later, I saw them being carried out. They were dead mostly from dysentery and typhus."

Alice Resch Synnestvedt, a nurse and worker in a Quaker Relief Agency, was determined to help the children of Gurs. Early in 1941, she arranged to bring forty-eight of them to La Maison des Pupilles de la Nation, a children's home near Toulouse. It was difficult for Schiller, already ten years old, to part from his parents, but he understood it was for the best. The younger children were even more traumatized by the separation. Many did not understand the situation and simply assumed their parents no longer wanted them. Nighttime was the most difficult time for the children who slept together in two large rooms. Schiller, who had a nice voice, would sing to the other little boys, to help them fall asleep.

Synnestvedt remained at La Maison des Pupilles for six weeks to help the children become acclimated to the new place. She assisted the youngest children to get washed and dressed, she comforted them all, and set up a routine for them to follow. Most important, she made sure the children got enough to eat. Since the director of the home spoke no German and the children spoke no French, there was a great deal of organizing and explaining to do. Within months, however, most of the children had become fluent in French, and Schiller, along with all the boys between the ages of eight and fifteen, were able to attend the local school beginning in the fall of 1941.

By 1942, the Vichy government had begun to actively round up Jews for deportation, including children. Because all the children's identity cards were stamped with the word *Juif,* they were in danger of being sent east. To avoid that possibility, Synnestvedt found new places for each of them and continued to keep in touch, bringing them small gifts whenever she could.

Schiller remained in the south of France only a short while longer. He was among eight children, all with relatives in the United States, that the relief agency had chosen to take to America.

Schiller had an uncle, his father's brother, who was ready to take him in. He was secretly spirited away with the other seven children and kept hidden in an old house in Marseilles. Then they were put on a ship bound for Baltimore, Maryland, early in June 1942, placed far below decks so no one would notice them.

The day before his departure, Schiller's parents came to see him and say goodbye. They were being watched and were very careful to do nothing suspicious that might endanger their son's departure from Europe. It was the last time Schiller saw them. Shortly after he left for America, they were sent to Auschwitz and murdered.

Upon arrival in Baltimore, the eight children were cleaned up and sent on to their separate destinations. Schiller, then eleven years old, was brought to New York City and joined his new family, his uncle and aunt and their two

Hugo Schiller and his wife at their home in Myrtle Beach, South Carolina. Courtesy of the Schillers.

older sons, Schiller's cousins. For the first time in many years, he was able to sleep at night and feel safe.

Hugo Schiller attended elementary school and high school in New York and set out to find a job to earn money for college, but the Korean War intervened and he was drafted. After that war, he applied to college on the GI Bill and earned a degree in industrial management from the Fashion Institute of Technology in New York City.

When Schiller moved to Baltimore for work, he met his wife, Elinor Cohan, at a synagogue dance. They married and had a daughter and a son. In 1967, Schiller was invited to Myrtle Beach, South Carolina as a consultant for the Aberdeen Manufacturing Company, specializing in home furnishings. He liked the area so much that the family settled there. In time he was made vice president of manufacturing of Aberdeen, retiring at the age of seventy-one. By then, both his children were successful professionals. As of 2006, three grandsons had been added to the family.

More than sixty years after coming to the United States, Hugo Schiller had not forgotten Alice Synnestvedt. For her ninetieth birthday, he invited her to visit him. Several others who had been part of the forty-eight Gur children joined them in Myrtle Beach for their first reunion in fifty-seven years. Schiller greeted Synnestvedt at the airport with a bouquet of flowers and took her to his synagogue where she once again heard him singing, this time leading the service and ceremony in her honor.

References

Schiller, Hugo. Telephone interview by the author, July 2006.
Synnestvedt, Alice Resch. *Over the Highest Mountains: A Memoir of Unexpected Heroism in France during World War II*. Pasadena, CA: International Productions, 2005.

Schindler, Emilie (1907–2001)

Emilie Pelzl Schindler, the wife of **Oskar Schindler**, has often been overshadowed by the more dramatic personality of her husband; however, she was a humanitarian and a righteous gentile in her own right. She was also a constant and loving wife in spite of her husband's many indiscretions and ultimate abandonment.

Emilie Pelzl was born in 1907 in a village in the Sudetenland, then part of Czechoslovakia. As a child, she was friendly with a young Jewish girl named Rita Reif and recalled that the local pastor advised her against that friendship.

Emilie defied the pastor and the young women remained friends. Reif was later murdered by the Nazis in front of her father's store in 1942.

Emilie first met "the tall, handsome, and outgoing Oskar Schindler" when he came to the door of her father's farmhouse in early 1928 selling electric motors. After a brief courtship, they were married on March 6, 1928, in Zwittau, Schindler's hometown. According to the custom in those years, Emilie's father had given his new son-in-law a dowry of 100,000 Czech crowns. Schindler used it to buy a luxury car and squandered the rest on trips and other amusements.

In Schindler's book, *A Memoir Where Light and Shadow Meet*, she wrote about how she struggled to understand and accept her husband's difficult and complicated personality, but acknowledged that, in spite of his flaws, her husband had a big heart. He was always ready to help whoever was in need. He was "affable, kind, extremely generous and charitable, but at the same time, not mature at all." Throughout the war years and after, Schindler constantly lied to and deceived his wife and later returned feeling sorry.

When they moved to Poland in hopes of making a better living, the couple benefited considerably from Oskar's Nazi contacts. Oskar opened a factory and, using Jewish slave labor, began to make large profits. As the war progressed, however, the Schindlers became attached to their 1,300 Jewish workers and ultimately decided to risk everything in desperate attempts to save them from certain death. They were able to accomplish this by means of massive bribery and Oskar's influential Nazi connections. Not a single one of their workers was killed.

Schindler was an active partner in this rescue. Until the spring of 1945, when the war was over, the Schindlers used all means at their disposal to ensure the safety of their Jewish workers. They spent all their own money and, when their funds ran out, Schindler sold her jewels to buy food, clothes, and medicine for their charges. Schindler's personal domain was the secret sanatorium set up in a back room of the factory, which contained medical equipment purchased on the black market. Here, she looked after the sick and nursed the starving Jews back to health. She saw to it that those who did not survive were given a traditional Jewish burial in a hidden graveyard established and paid for by the Schindlers.

One night, during the last weeks of the war, Oskar was away when Schindler heard of a freight train containing Jewish prisoners that was stranded on the railroad tracks. Acting alone, she went to the location and was horrified at what she saw. Inside the crowded boxcars were 250 Jews. They were on the way from Golechau to a death camp when the trains got stuck. In her book, Schindler wrote, "We found the railroad car bolts frozen solid." After prying them open, "the spectacle I saw was a nightmare almost beyond imagination. It was impossible to distinguish the men from the women: they were all so emaciated. Weighing under seventy pounds most of them, they looked like skeletons. Their eyes were shining like glowing coals in the dark."

Schindler succeeded in persuading the Gestapo to let her take the Jews to their factory camp so they could be added to those workers already helping the continuing war production. None of them was able to walk. Schindler described how each one "had to be carried out like a carcass of frozen beef." Thirteen were already dead, but the rest were still breathing and so throughout the night—and for many nights afterward—Schindler worked nonstop on the frozen and starved skeletons. One large room in the factory was emptied for use as a hospital. And although three more men died, with care, medicine, and lots of warm milk, the others gradually rallied.

After the war, survivors told about Schindler's unforgettable heroism, not only in nursing the frozen and starved prisoners back to life but in many other acts of kindness. The Jews on Oskar's list of prisoners recalled how she worked tirelessly to find food for them on the black market, and managed to provide the sick with extra nourishment and apples. Lew Feigenbaum remembered that when he broke his eyeglasses, Schindler arranged for a prescription for the eyeglasses to be picked up in Krakow and delivered to her in Brunnlitz. Another Jew on Oskar's list, Feiwel (today Franciso) Wichter, wrote, "As long as I live, I will always have a sincere and eternal gratitude for dear Emilie. I think she triumphed over danger because of her courage, intelligence and determination to do the right and humane thing. She had immense energy and she was like a mother."

After May 1945, when the war ended, the Schindlers said goodbye to the Jews they had cared for and a few years later, left for Buenos Aires in Argentina. With them were Oskar's mistress and a dozen of his Jewish workers who were planning to build a new life there. In 1949, while being supported financially by JOINT, a Jewish charitable organization, the Schindlers tried their hand at farming. They were also helped financially by the Jews from the list, who never forgot their gratitude to the Schindlers. But Oskar became bankrupt and disillusioned and returned to Germany, leaving his wife in Argentina alone. Schindler did not see her husband for the next seventeen years. He died in poverty in 1974.

Schindler remained in Argentina, supporting herself modestly with small pensions from Israel and Germany. She had no family except for a niece who lived in Bavaria. But she was not forgotten. Jewish organizations honored her several times for her efforts during the war. In May 1994, with Miep Gies (who hid Anne Frank's family in the Netherlands and preserved her diary), Schindler received the Righteous Among the Nations award. In 1995, Argentina decorated her with the Order of May, the highest honor given to foreigners who are not heads of state. In 1998, the government of Argentina granted her a pension of $1,000 a month and later named her an Illustrious Citizen.

In July 2001, Schindler visited Berlin and donated some of her husband's documents to a museum. By that time, she was frail and confined to a wheelchair. She told reporters that she had become increasingly homesick and wished to spend her final years in Germany. Three months later, on October 5, 2001, Schindler died in a Berlin hospital.

Those who knew Emilie Schindler spoke of her bitterness at the way her husband had treated her, remembering that she called him "a drunk and a womanizer," but had no doubt that she continued to love him. Describing her thoughts after visiting his grave in Israel, she wrote, "I do not know why you abandoned me. . . . I have forgiven you everything."

References

Schindler, Emilie. *A Memoir Where Light and Shadow Meet*. New York: W.W. Norton, 1997.

"Oskar Schindler: His List of Life." http://www.oskarschindler.com/10.htm.

Schindler, Oskar (1908–1974)

Oskar Schindler saved 1,300 Jews during the Holocaust by pulling them out of the death camps and employing them in his factory, and is counted among the many righteous gentiles. But he was also a war profiteer, a drinker, and a womanizer, who ended up penniless and despised after the war. Historians are still questioning his motives and trying to understand this complicated man.

Schindler was born in Svitavy, a town in the Sudetenland, a part of Czechoslovakia. As a child he lived next door to a Jewish family and played with their children. He met his wife, Emilie Pelzl (see **Emilie Schindler**), while working as a door-to-door salesman selling electric motors, and in 1928 they married. Probably in hopes of better business opportunities during the depression, Schindler joined the Nazi party, and when the Sudetenland was taken back by Germany in 1938, he was in a position to profit.

Following the German Army into Poland in 1939, Schindler and his wife settled in Krakow. Here, his outgoing personality and his charm worked to his advantage and his growing connections with Nazi officials enabled him to take over two enamel and kitchenware factories that had been confiscated from Jews. With these businesses as a beginning, he expanded and established his own enamel works in Zablovir, just outside Krakow.

Oskar Schindler (top row, second from right) in 1946, at a reunion with some of the Jews he helped to rescue. Courtesy of the U.S. Holocaust Memorial Museum Photo Archives.

Most of the workers in Schindler's plants were Jewish and employment in his firms saved them from deportation. As more and more Jews were deported, Schindler insisted that he needed additional employees for the war effort. When he became concerned about their treatment in the nearby Plaszow camp, which was notorious for its poor treatment of Jews and its high death rate, Schindler found new ways to help "his Jews." He requested that a branch of the Plaszow camp be established in his factory so the nine hundred workers he employed would not need to walk there and back every day. His request was granted.

As the war continued, Schindler found other opportunities to save Jews. Not only did he smuggle in extra rations for them; he and his wife also supplied medical equipment and medicines, purchased mostly on the black market at his own expense. He allowed the Jews in his factory to celebrate Jewish holidays and if they died, to conduct a traditional Jewish burial. He often chose additional workers based on requests from his original employees, lying about their ages so all would appear to be fit for work even if they were not. Those who were sick were nursed and fed by Schindler's wife, Emilie.

In October 1944, the tide of war had turned and the Germans were retreating, pursued by the Soviet Army. Schindler managed to get permission from the authorities to move his factory along with all his workers back to the Sudetenland and transform it into an armaments production company. Insisting on his need for more and more workers, he saved seven hundred to eight hundred men from the Gröss Rosen camp and approximately three hundred women from Auschwitz. All the Jews were treated humanely, as were the one hundred additional Jewish men and women that his wife had rescued late in the war.

Although Oskar Schindler came under suspicion several times for his activities, and was even arrested and imprisoned twice, he was always able to use his connections to be promptly released. He drank regularly with his Nazi friends, spent large amounts of money entertaining them, and even larger sums on bribes.

Aware of his Jews' fear of being discovered and deported, Schindler stayed in his factory every night to make sure they were safe. He called them "his children" and ultimately spent all his money helping them to survive. Only when the war was over did he leave them. In an emotional farewell, he told the workers that they were now free but that he was a fugitive. "My children, you are saved," he said. "Germany has lost the war." Schindler had only one request of them. He asked that they not rob the neighboring houses as other released prisoners were doing. "Prove yourselves worthy of the millions of victims among you and refrain from any individual acts of revenge and terror," he urged. Finally, he gave each one three yards of fabric from his warehouse stores and a bottle of vodka, a commodity of high value on the black market. After the war, Schindler was considered a traitor by the Nazis and a Nazi by those who had stood against Hitler. Disillusioned, he took both Emilie and his mistress and moved to Argentina, where he tried his hand at farming, but without success.

In 1957, Schindler left his wife in Argentina and returned to Germany. Attempting and failing in one new business after another, Schindler became more and more dependent on Jewish charity. For their part, "his Jews" never forgot him and continued to support him and send him money for his new ventures.

In 1962, Schindler went to Israel to plant a tree bearing his name in the Garden of the Righteous at Yad Vashem in Jerusalem, the Israeli museum of the Holocaust. At the age of sixty-six, he died of liver failure and in accordance with his request, was buried in a Catholic cemetery in Israel "because that is where my children are," he said.

Eight years after his death, an American author wrote a book about Schindler's life and his humanitarian efforts on behalf of Jews. The book was picked up by Hollywood director Steven Spielberg and transformed into the famous movie, *Schindler's List*.

References

Keneally, Thomas. *Schindler's List.* New York: Penguin, 1982.

"Oskar Schindler: His List of Life." http://www.oskarschindler.com/1.htm, also /7.htm, and /6.htm.

Paldiel, Mordecai. *Encyclopedia of the Holocaust.* s.v. "Schindler, Oskar." New York: Macmillan Press, 1990.

Schoenbrun family, and Marguerite Markowski (née Reich) (1920–)

From the time that Marguerite Reich Markowski left her native Czechoslovakia for Belgium in 1937, her life was completely intertwined with the life of her cousin Suri Schoenbrun (1907–1986) and Suri's family. Together, they fled from the Nazis through Belgium, then to France and Italy and back to France, sometimes barely escaping with their lives.

Both Suri Schoenbrun and her cousin Marguerite Markowski were born in Czechoslovakia. Suri, her husband Josef HaCohen Schoenbrun, and their first child, Judy (b. 1930), settled in Antwerp, Belgium, in 1933. In Belgium they had two more children, Eli (b. 1938) and Abraham, later called Arnold (b. 1939).

Marguerite Markowski was thirteen years younger than Suri Schoenbrun. Although she had a job as a mother's helper when she left Uzhorod, Czechoslovakia, in 1937, it was cousin Suri who became her family in Belgium. She hoped to remain there and learn the diamond trade.

Two years after she left home, Czechoslovakia was taken over by Germany. Markowski, the oldest of seven children, wanted to return to be with her parents, Siegmund and Hannah Reich. Her father, already in a work camp, wrote to her telling her to stay in Belgium. That letter may have saved Markowski's life. By the end of the war, the Reich family—parents and siblings—had disappeared without a trace. By the beginning of 1940, letters from the family in Czechoslovakia had stopped. A few months later, the Nazis invaded Belgium.

The German occupation of Belgium drove both Jews and Christians out of the country fleeing south to what they believed was the safety of France. Markowski joined the Schoenbrun family, catching the last train out of Antwerp before all transports were discontinued. Their train ended up in Ghent, a city in southern Belgium. From there, the refugees were loaded onto trucks and crossed the French border into Tuys, a small town outside Dieppes. There was no food and no facilities for large numbers of refugees.

Marguerite Reich Markowski carried this photo of her family, taken in 1938, throughout the war. Courtesy of Elaine McKee.

As the Nazis continued advancing through Belgium and into France, the Schoenbruns and Markowski kept moving, always just one step ahead of the German troops. Their next stop brought them to Paris, where they camped outside the city with hundreds of other refugees. There, Josef Schoenbrun heard that a Czech army-in-exile was being organized and he immediately went to join.

Because he was part of the Czech Army, Josef's family was taken to the Czech colony, about sixty kilometers from Paris, and promised transportation and housing in the south of France, which was still relatively free of German occupiers. But they had to wait for the trucks to take them.

Suri Schoenbrun did not want to wait. She was anxious to leave for the south immediately, even if she had to walk. Schoenbrun discovered a truck that was leaving with a shipment of Czech gold. The drivers agreed to take only women with children, but Markowski managed to get on by posing as the mother of Suri's youngest child. They later learned that this had been the last truck to depart.

Markowski, Suri Schoenbrun, and Suri's children were delivered to the railroad station. The train took them to Bordeaux, and from there they settled in nearby Agde, a small French village that housed a military camp. Suri had hoped to find her husband, but he was not there. The Schoenbruns and Markowski stayed in Agde, and eventually Josef tracked them down and joined them. The Czech army had been dissolved.

By 1942, with no end to the war in sight, the Schoenbruns made the decision to send their oldest child, Judy, who was twelve years old, to a children's home and then to Josef's relatives in America. She was able to leave on one of the last ships sailing from France. Later that same year, Suri and Josef had another baby, a daughter, Feige, born in Agde.

The refugees were not allowed to work in southern France. They received an allowance of 70 francs per week, just enough for food. Most of the money was supplied by the Joint Distribution Committee (JOINT), a Jewish relief organization based in the United States. Later, the Organization for Rehabilitation and Training (ORT) set up a school near Agde for Jewish refugees to learn dressmaking and take French classes. Markowski attended the ORT school. The monotony of her days was broken by visits to the nearby beach, and in the fall by grape picking, the only paid work allowed to the refugees. She was able to earn some extra money in this way for two years, during the autumn of 1942 and 1943.

Late in 1943, the Germans caught up with them in Agde, too, and they were forced to flee again. This time, their way of life was too uncertain to accommodate young children. They left baby Feige in a children's home and ran first to Nice and then to St. Martin Vesubie, where they were allowed to remain for several months. Here, Markowski worked in the soup kitchen that had been set up for the refugees and the Schoenbruns reclaimed their baby daughter. Feige's unstable lifestyle and lack of proper nourishment had made her weak and sick. She was not yet able to walk and Suri nursed her back to health with eggs and milk that she bought on the black market.

In St. Martin Vesubie, the refugees lived under the Italians, allies of Germany, who occupied the southwestern section of France. The refugees were required to report two times a day to the Italian authorities, but otherwise they lived undisturbed. But by September 1943, the Italians had capitulated to the Americans in southern Italy. Within months they were forced to pull out of France as the Germans moved in. Faced with a choice of Italians or Germans, the Schoenbruns and Markowski opted to follow the Italian troops, walking through the mountains, carrying the children with them, and sleeping outdoors under the most primitive conditions. When they finally reached the town of Entrocque, Italy, they were crammed into a single room with no water. Schoenbrun broke off the icicles hanging from the eaves, put them in a baby bottle and waited for them to melt into drinking water for the baby.

Conditions gradually improved, but within five days of their arrival, the Germans appeared once again. The local priest warned the men to hide and avoid arrest. Although the Jewish men all rushed to comply, most were discovered. Josef Schoenbrun was among those taken away to Drancy, a French transit camp. From there, he was transported east to his death.

Markowski, Schoenbrun, and the children were also arrested, but they managed to delay until the transport to Drancy had left. Told by the Italian soldiers that they would now have to walk to their destination, they agreed.

We boarded the [ship] Anna Salen at Bremerhaven, Germany on June 26, 1951. My husband and I had both lost our families in the Holocaust. We were stateless, living in Paris and wishing to get as far away from Europe as we could. We had a baby of a year old at the time.

We joined the other refugees in third class. Many, like us, were Jewish and refugees of the Holocaust. Others were coming to fulfil contracts, to work in mines . . . [or] to join their husbands who were already in Canada on work contracts.

The men were all in a cargo hold room lined with bunk beds. The women with children had cabins. My friend also had a baby. He was a month younger than mine, but as hers was just under a year, she was assigned bottles and a crib. As we set sail, I quickly became very seasick and had a hard time caring for my child. I had to take her to the entrance of the men's quarters to wait for my husband so he would hold her giving me a chance to go to the washroom. I certainly couldn't face any food, so he would give my portion away. . . .

[Traveling by train from Halifax to Toronto] My husband would get off the train when it stopped, to purchase bread and milk. We had never before seen white, sliced bread and milk in cartons. After thirty-six hours on the train, we arrived at Union Station in Toronto, ready to start our new lives. We were met by my husband's friend and his Canadian girlfriend. She asked what the name of the baby was. I told her it was Eliane. She immediately said that it would be Elaine in Canada, and so it was, although I myself continued to call her Eliane for the first few years.

—Marguerite Reich Markowski

The arresting soldiers, much less zealous in rounding up Jews than the Germans, simply gave them instructions to get there and left. As soon as they had disappeared, the women and children ran toward the mountains, where they joined up with other escapees, but all were stranded with no idea where to go.

For Schoenbrun, this was the lowest point. Her husband was gone, she had three young children that she could barely care for, and there was no place to run. She was ready to surrender herself and the children and urged Markowski to leave without her and save herself. Just then they met a woman acting as a messenger for the underground. She scolded Schoenbrun, insisting that she must never surrender to the Germans. Her words gave the young mother the courage that she needed. She revived, and without a guide, the small group set out to find their way back to St. Martin Visubie, where they still had the key to the room that held their meager possessions.

Several French farmers helped them and one contacted the Jewish Committee while they waited in the mountains. The Committee sent couriers to take the children to safety. Eli and Abraham were given the false French names, Emil and Arnaud, and were placed with two separate families. Feige was brought to Switzerland by a refugee couple. Until the war was over, Schoenbrun did not know whether they had survived or whether they had been captured by the Nazis and "turned into soap."

Now alone, Schoenbrun and Markowski attempted to get their own new identity papers. Markowski succeeded and she became Marguerite Roland. Schoenbrun, however, could not get papers; she looked "too Jewish," the forgers said.

Schoenbrun spent the final year of the war living on a farm called La Pere with a handful of other refugees and worrying about her children. Markowski went to Grenoble, where she did kitchen work in a residential girls' school. After the war she went to find her cousin and together they made repeated trips to Limoges, where lists were kept and updated. First she found only Eli and Abraham and took them to Paris to join some friends while Markowski waited for news about Feige. Within a short time, Feige was brought from Switzerland. Markowski took the little girl and joined the family in Paris. The boys were enrolled in school for the first time and Schoenbrun began to get letters from Judy, safe in Cleveland, Ohio, and packages from the Red Cross.

The Schoenbrun family was reunited with Judy in Cleveland in 1951. By this time, Markowski was married and had a child of her own. Her husband, **Feibush (Fabian) Markowski**, was a Jewish refugee from Poland. Their daughter Eliane was born in 1950 and the Markowski family emigrated to Canada the following year. In 1957 their son Sidney Allen was born.

Although the Markowskis settled in Toronto and the Schoenbruns were in the United States, the families remained close. In 2006, Schoenbrun's daughter Judy was living in California.

Reference

McKee, Elaine Markowski. Telephone interview by the author, July 2006.

Sendler, Irena (1910–)

In Warsaw, Irena Sendler's efforts during World War II saved thousands of Jewish children, but her story remained relatively unknown until some American high school students rediscovered her.

Sendler was born in Otwock, a town near Warsaw, Poland, to Catholic parents. Her father, a doctor, died from typhus fever, the result of treating Jews during a typhus epidemic. Irena was only seven years old when he died, but the lesson she learned from her father's sacrifice was, "if a man is drowning, it is irrelevant what is his religion or nationality. One must help him. It is a need of the heart."

When the Nazis invaded Poland in 1939, Sendler was twenty-nine years old, a wife and mother, and a social worker in Warsaw's social welfare department. She saw how the German army forced 350,000 Jews into the ghetto. Once there, they were isolated, abused, and starved before ultimately being herded onto trains and transported to death camps. Sendler knew she could not stand by without trying to help. But in an occupied country, finding a way to help was difficult.

Sendler was already giving asylum to a small number of Jewish acquaintances when she was approached by Zegota late in the summer of 1942. Zegota, the code name for the Council for Aid to Jews in Occupied Poland, was an underground network organized to aid Jews. It was just being founded by a group of prominent scholars, religious leaders, and social activists from both Jewish and non-Jewish groups, including the prominent Jewish psychologist **Adolf Berman**. One of the things this organization did was to forge birth certificates, giving Jews safe Aryan/Christian identities so they could live outside the ghetto. Another of their goals was to smuggle Jewish children out of the ghetto so they might be saved. Sendler was asked to head this project and she accepted.

With false papers of her own allowing her to enter and leave the ghetto in the guise of a nurse and ten sympathetic helpers, Sendler (given the code name Jolanta) found ways to rescue 2,500 Jewish children. Babies and toddlers were covered and tucked in among potato sacks in merchants' carts; others were hidden in ambulances. One child escaped with the help of a sympathetic trolley driver who hid him under a back seat. Older children were taken out through the underground sewer system. Some children were even sedated and carried out in body bags, ostensibly to be buried. The Jewish children were taught some basic Christian prayers so they would fit in with their Catholic environment, either in foster homes, convents, or orphanages. Although most Jewish parents were reluctant to give up their children, Sendler convinced many that it was the only chance for their survival.

Sendler continued her work until her arrest by the Gestapo, the Nazi police force, in October 1943. She was beaten mercilessly in an effort to force her to give them the names of others who had worked with her. Although her legs and feet were broken, Sendler remained silent and did not divulge a single one of her accomplices. Sentenced to death, she was rescued at the last moment by means of a large bribe from Zegota and was hidden away in Poland. Sendler stayed out of sight until January 1945, when Warsaw was liberated by Russian soldiers.

Once the war was over, Sendler retrieved a list she had recorded and hidden under a tree in her friend's garden. On it were the original Jewish names and the new Christian names of every one of the children she had rescued, along with the names of their parents. She hoped that at least some of the families could be reunited, but that proved to be overly optimistic. Among the 2,500 children that she had saved, almost none of the parents or grandparents remained alive. In fact, only one percent of the Jewish population of Warsaw had survived.

After the war, Sendler returned to normal life. She raised her two children and continued working in the area of social welfare even though the beatings she received at the hands of the Nazis had left her partially disabled and made it difficult for her to walk. But living under communist Russian rule, she did not feel free to speak about her experiences during the war. Most of the Jews who had known of her efforts and her heroism were dead, the others had left Poland to begin new lives in other countries.

Sendler was recognized in 1966 with a Righteous Among the Nations award by Yad Vashem, a museum and center for Holocaust research in Jerusalem. After that, her deeds were mostly forgotten. Then, in 1999, three high school girls from Kansas, searching for a topic for a history project, discovered her name in a five-year-old news magazine. They wrote a play about her exploits and in March 2000 contacted her directly. Then ninety years old, she was living in a nursing home and confined to a wheelchair, but was happy to hear that her life story had been recovered. In 2003, mainly through the efforts of these young students, she was given a $10,000 humanitarian award from the American Center for Polish Culture in Washington, DC, as well as the Jan Karski Award for Valor and Bravery. That same year, Sendler was awarded Poland's highest distinction, the Order of White Eagle, in Warsaw. But Sendler remained humble about her exploits. "A hero is someone doing extraordinary things," she said. "What I did was not extraordinary. It was a normal thing to do."

References

Encyclopedia of the Holocaust. Vol. 4, s.v. "Sendler." New York: Macmillan Publishing Company, 1990.

Encyclopedia of the Holocaust. Vol. 4, s.v. "Zegota." New York: Macmillan Publishing Company, 1990.

"A Saintly Smuggler." *U.S. News and World Report,* October 21, 2003. http://www.usnews.com/usnews/news/article/031021/27sendler.peo.htm.

http://www.auschwitz.dk/sendler/htm.

Shapell, Nathan (1922-)

Nathan Shapell (born Schapelski) of Sosnowiec, Poland, managed to live through World War II by using his wits and offering the Germans a service that they needed. After the war, he began providing housing for those rendered homeless because of the war. He continued this work in the United States, where he became a major builder and a multimillionaire.

The youngest of five children, Nathan was left at home with his mother and sisters after his father and two older brothers fled the Nazis. Like so many Jews in those early days, they naively assumed that women and children would not be in danger.

Shapell, only seventeen when the war began, proved to be resourceful. He found a good job in the sanitation department of Sosnowiec and quickly learned how to make himself useful to the Germans by supplying them with scarce items like meat and fabric. His ability to satisfy his German employers kept him and his family from roundups and deportations for almost three years.

Then in the summer of 1942, a ghetto was established in Sosnowiec, and all the Jews were forced behind its gates with no access to food or other services. In an effort to rescue his mother, he told the Nazi officials that the ghetto area had major sanitation needs and he had to visit it daily. They agreed, and each day, wearing his official identifying armband, Shapell entered the ghetto with a crew of Jewish workers. He smuggled in food for his family and for others. Each time he came, he handed out a few armbands to Jewish men so they could slip out of the ghetto with the official crew.

The success of his rescue efforts emboldened him to attempt others. Soon he was smuggling out small children, hidden in the empty vats that had contained the daily soup ration. Once outside the ghetto, he told them to run and save their lives. When one little girl of five or six was told to run, she asked Shapell, "Where shall I go?" His answer: "Child, I don't know. Run, run!" Even fifty years later, when he related that incident to an interviewer, he wept from the frustration and sadness.

Shapell was not able to rescue his mother in that first week, but when the liquidation of the ghetto was scheduled, he did find a way to extricate her from the dragnet by carrying her out in a cart filled with dead bodies. But ultimately, all his efforts could not save his family or himself from deportation. Shapell was sent to Auschwitz-Birkenau in the summer of 1943. In Auschwitz, it was luck that saved him from the random shootings by the guards that took the lives of so many prisoners.

As the war was nearing its end, Shapell was taken on a forced march and brought to a camp in Waldenberg with hundreds of other prisoners. He was liberated from there on May 8, 1945.

Now Shapell was no longer a prisoner; he was a displaced person. Twenty-three years old and used to being active, he soon became a leader in helping to provide homeless Jews with homes. Instead of the institutional barracks of so many displaced-persons camps, Shapell turned the camp at Munchberg into a model displaced-persons community, with individual homes and one large house for children who were alone.

In Munchberg, Shapell was reunited with two of his siblings, David and Sala. His parents and two other siblings had been murdered. He married another Holocaust survivor in Munchberg, and immediately turned his efforts to making a living. He joined forces with his brother David and Sala's new husband Max Weisbrot, and started a textile business while waiting for visas to the United States. The business did well and when they arrived in America in the 1950s, they did not come penniless as so many other refugees did.

Shapell and his brother and sister settled in California and began a construction company in partnership with a young American builder. Shapell learned a great deal, and by 1955, was ready to be on his own. Counting from that year, Shapell Industries built sixty-four thousand housing units in the Los Angeles area and beyond and Nathan Shapell became C.E.O. of his own multimillion-dollar construction firm.

Shapell became involved with many community projects, including serving as the president of D.A.R.E. America, a drug abuse educational program, from 1987 to 1995. He also represented Holocaust Survivors Worldwide at a candle-lighting ceremony in the Vatican, commemorating the Holocaust in 1994, and in 2001 was one of fourteen people nominated by President Bill Clinton to be members of the Holocaust Memorial Council.

References

"Everything in History Was Against Them." *Fortune* (April 13, 1998). Inserted into the U.S. Congressional Record on April 22, 2001 by Rep. **Tom Lantos** (see http://thomas.loc.gov/cgi-bin/query/z?r105:E22AP8-187:).

White House Press Release, January 18, 2001. http://clinton5.nara.gov/library/hot_releases/January_18_2001_15.html.

Shapiro, Morris (1920–), and Dreyzl Zilberzweig (née Shapiro) (1918–1992)

Dreyzl and Morris were sister and brother, just two in a family of ten children originally from Goaz, Poland. They fled from a Nazi roundup and, with the help of many gentiles, remained hidden throughout the war. A combination of bravery, ingenuity, and luck helped them to escape the fate of their parents and eight other brothers and sisters.

The Shapiro family was originally from Goaj, a small town in Poland not far from Lublin. When World War II broke out in 1939, Morris was twenty-two years old and Dreyzl was twenty-four. Morris, a brilliant young man, was destined to be a rabbi like his father, Mendel Shapiro. Morris had been studying Jewish law from an early age and was a student in the respected Yeshivah Hokhmei Lublin (Academy of the Wisdom of Lublin). He lived in the rarified world of Jewish scholarship, was not involved with either commerce or politics, and spoke only the Yiddish language. Dreyzl was very different. She was a capable businesswoman who understood money matters, had contact with many gentiles, and spoke fluent Polish.

After the Germans invaded Poland, the Russians took over their area briefly, but within a month, they left, and the Germans entered the region. At first, the new rules concerning Jews did not seem so bad. Goaj was a small place, too small for a ghetto or for the Nazis to establish offices. Dreyzl continued her business, trading with the peasants and selling their wares in the towns. Morris continued his studies. Although there was a Nazi presence, and the threat of violence hovered over the small community of one hundred Jews, mass killings did not begin until 1942.

That year, on the second day of the holiday of Sukkot, fire broke out in the town of Goaj. The Shapiro home was burned along with half of the town. Now the Germans decided this would be the right time to evacuate Goaj and resettle all the Jews to nearby Frumpl. By then, Rabbi Mendel Shapiro had died of natural causes and Hinde, his wife, was alone with her younger children.

The Shapiros followed the order to evacuate Goaj and walked to Frumpl, carrying what little they had salvaged from the fire. On the way, Morris decided to visit his brother Shmuel in a nearby town. When he reached Frumpl the next day, the Jewish Council had already settled his family in an apartment with another family, and there was no room for him. Instead, they placed him with a shoemaker and his wife, a childless couple who already had staked out a place to hide, in the attic of a gentile acquaintance. They promised Morris that he could come with them into hiding, and even adopted him as their son. Morris agreed, but had one stipulation: his sister Dreyzl must be allowed to come, too. "Dreyzl had connections with many gentiles," Morris later explained, "and she was very capable of supporting us."

Dreyzl and Morris Shapiro were ready to go into hiding with the shoemaker and his wife. However, when the gentile saw Morris, he refused to accept this young man who looked too pious and might cause trouble because of his religious demands. It was November 22, 1942, the day when the Germans had decided to make Frumpl *judenrein*, free of Jews. A hiding place was now crucial, but still the gentile refused to accept Morris, so Dreyzl thought of another plan. She would ask for shelter from a Polish farmer that she knew. Leaving Morris alone in the woods, she went by herself to beg for his help. The farmer agreed to shelter them but only for two days. He feared German reprisals, he said, and they could stay only over the Sabbath.

Sunday morning, they left and turned toward the home of another gentile whom Dreyzl knew, hoping he would agree to help. As they walked through the woods they met a teenage boy on his way home from church. When Dreyzl stopped to ask directions, the boy showed them the way but added a warning: they should not be out during the daylight or they would surely be killed. He showed them where to hide in the woods and reminded them again not to move before dark.

Weeping in fear and desperation, Morris and Dreyzl were still there when the young boy, Leon Makshin, returned with his father. They offered them shelter in their home and promised to return after dark to get them. The Makshins were as good as their word and Morris and Dreyzl were able to stay with this family for almost a year. Only once, when Makshin heard that the Nazis would be coming to search his home, did he send them away. He brought them to a place in the woods where other Jews were hiding and advised them to remain there until the coast was clear. After three days, they were back at the Makshin farm.

Finally, in late 1943, Dreyzl ran out of money and the Makshins, with a family of eight children to feed, could not afford to keep them. They had to go back into the woods. Returning to the shelter where they had hidden earlier, they now found it empty. The Germans had discovered the hiding place and killed all the fugitives. Nevertheless, the Shapiro siblings settled in, reasoning that the Nazis would not be back. They no longer had any money, but once again a kind gentile, another friend of Dreyzl's, saved their lives. Tekla secretly brought them food every day and never asked for payment.

By 1944, the Russian Army had defeated the Germans and driven them westward. The war on the eastern front was over and by the Jewish New Year, September 1944, Dreyzl and Morris Shapiro were free. The remnants of the Jewish communities of eastern Poland began trickling back to the towns, looking for loved ones, and now it was Morris's turn to support his sister and himself. He became a rabbi in the newly organized synagogue in Khushnik. After a few months they went to Susneftza, a town with a larger Jewish community. From there, they moved on to Reichenbach and settled in.

There was no trace of the rest of the Shapiro family, and Morris and Dreyzl finally accepted the fact that they had all been killed. Like so many survivors of the Holocaust, they quickly found mates. In 1946, Morris, now the rabbi in Reichenbach, married Liebe, recently liberated from a concentration camp. Dreyzl's husband, Tzvi Hirsch Zilberzweig, was a Russian Jew who had also survived the war.

By 1948, with the help of Eliezer Silver, an American rabbi, Morris Shapiro was able to find a position as a rabbi in the United States and he and Liebe left for Cincinnati, Ohio. He quickly realized that the Yiddish language would not get him too far in his new country. While serving as a rabbi, he attended school at night and within two years had a high school diploma. In the early 1950s, another job offer brought him to Grand Forks, North Dakota. While serving as rabbi there, he and Liebe had three children and Morris was also able to complete B.A. and M.A. degrees in clinical psychology at the University of North Dakota. By 1957, the Shapiro family was in Waco, Texas, serving another congregation. After four years, they moved again, this time to Greenlawn, a small community in Long Island, and it was here, in 1964, that Shapiro's wife died. Within a few years, he had remarried and he and his new wife, Rachel, had two more children.

Dreyzl Shapiro Zilberzweig left Poland for France in 1948 and waited for an American visa for herself and her husband. Once settled in the United States she remained in Brooklyn, in an Orthodox Jewish community. She and Tzvi Hirsch had three children and lived to see them grown. Dreyzl Shapiro Zilberzweig died in 1992.

By 2005, Morris Shapiro had retired and had lost his second wife but continued to live independently, working part time as a teacher of Talmud. His five children all married and Shapiro had thirty-two grandchildren.

Reference

Shapiro, Morris. Interview by the author, December 2005, Great Neck, New York.

Sirota, Rosa (1933–)

Rosa Sirota from Lvov, Poland, lost most of her family during World War II. She and her mother did manage to survive, hiding with a poor Ukrainian widow and her daughter until they were liberated by the Russians. During those years, she learned how to be smart but act dumb and how to be silent and never trust anyone. It took her many years before she could unlearn those lessons.

Sirota was only six when the Nazis invaded Poland and began their attacks on the Jews. First, they took her grandmother, then her father was sent to a forced labor camp. She never saw either of them again.

In 1941, the Nazis decreed that all the Jews must live in a ghetto. As they began to pack, Janka, a Christian neighbor, offered to hide them in her home. She suggested that Sirota's mother pretend to be her sister. They agreed, packed as many of their belongings as they could, and moved in.

That very night, quite late, there was a loud banging on the door. They heard someone shouting: "Open up, you have Jews in there!" Sirota was terrified as she lay in bed and listened to the German voices. She heard Janka open the door and a male voice ordered her mother to come with him. One hour later, the German soldier had returned and Sirota heard Janka speaking with him. They were dividing up all her family's possessions. Sirota understood that it had all been a plot to steal from them. Desolate, she left the next morning for the ghetto, and Janka made no pretense of trying to help or hiding what she had taken. Sirota asked for only one thing: an old jacket that she wanted for her aunt. Her neighbor threw it at her and told her to go.

Sirota made her way to the ghetto and found her mother, her aunt, and a cousin. The tattered jacket that she had managed to rescue contained the family's jewelry, which Sirota's mother had sewed into the lining. With those jewels, they were able to buy false papers identifying them as Christians.

At that time, another Christian woman, Marysia, came forward to help them. Marysia had formerly worked as a maid for Sirota's aunt. Wanting to help save some Jews, she obtained the blessing of her priest who told her, "If you can save a few lives, do it." This attitude was not that common, Sirota explained to an interviewer fifty years later. In Poland, antisemitism "was perfectly okay and did not detract from a person's moral character."

Marysia first approached Sirota's aunt and offered to hide her and her young son, but her aunt refused. Because her son had been circumcised, she feared that they would not be able to hide as Christians. Sirota's mother suggested that she and her daughter go in their place and Marysia agreed.

Their new home was a one-room cottage in the Ukraine where Marysia's sister Nascia Puchal and her daughter Marynka lived. It was the poorest house in the village. Nascia did not know that her new boarders were Jewish. She was happy to have someone to help her make a living and the two mothers and daughters shared their earnings, cooked, and cleaned together. Sirota's mother hired out as a farm worker, harvesting grain and doing other chores and fieldwork and gave her salary to Nascia.

Sirota and her mother went to church, took communion, and celebrated Christian holidays with everyone else in the village. Sirota also had to pretend not to appear too intelligent. Nor could she say anything that might allude to their former life. Sirota made friends with some of the Ukrainian children but she was always careful never to trust anyone with her secret.

After six months with Nascia and Marynka, Sirota's mother found work in a German laundry. This was a better job than farm work but one day she failed to return home. The Germans had become suspicious and accused her of being a Jew. She was put into prison and held for four days.

Sirota was worried and frightened. Only she knew that they were Jews and could be killed at any time. Although she dared not tell Nascia, she begged her to try and find out what had happened. But Nascia felt certain there was nothing to worry about.

That Sunday, as they prepared for church, a car filled with Germans arrived at their house and began searching for evidence that they were Jews. They found nothing, but their suspicions persisted. They began asking Sirota about her mother, firing questions at her in German. Although she understood some

German, Sirota kept saying she did not and finally, the officials sent for an interpreter. They said, "We know you are Jewish. If you don't admit it, you'll never see your mother again." The nine-year-old Sirota insisted she was not a Jew and finally the Germans left.

But Sirota's mother still did not return. After begging Nascia for days, she agreed to go with Sirota to Gestapo headquarters and find her mother. They found that she had been released from prison but was under house arrest, forced to do the cooking and cleaning at the German Officers' Club and sleeping on the kitchen floor. When she saw her daughter she whispered to her, "Did you say anything?" "No," Sirota whispered back. Her mother smiled.

After those few weeks, Sirota's mother was permitted to live at home. She worked in the laundry again, but also had to continue cooking and cleaning for the German officers for another year. In 1944, the Russians reconquered the Ukraine. Sirota and her mother were penniless but they were free.

They first returned to Lvov to search for relatives. They found no one except for an uncle on her father's side. Her mother and her uncle soon married, and within a year, their son Albert was born. But even now, they did not settle down. They moved from Poland to Czechoslovakia, then to France. More than anything, they wanted to come to America but the waiting list was long and even though her uncle had family in the United States who sponsored them, they would have to wait for seven years.

Instead, they moved to Venezuela, South America. For the first time, they settled in and Sirota went to school. But still, she could not be a carefree schoolgirl. Her parents worked long hours and she was responsible for her baby brother.

In 1951, Sirota came to the United States alone on a student visa and lived at a boarding school. Here, for the first time in her life, she had fun. She learned how to swim, went to dances, and visited an aunt in New York City on weekends. She even made friends, but it took her many years before she was able to trust them and share confidences. It took many more years for her nightmares to stop plaguing her.

Sirota finished high school in the United States and continued on to college. She married Howard Sirota and they had a son and a daughter.

By the 1990s, the Sirotas were living in New Jersey and she was teaching high school Spanish. Her children were grown and successful professionals. She rarely thought about the war years and told an interviewer, "My husband and I are pretty fortunate." However, when friends spoke about family reunions, with aunts, uncles, and cousins, Sirota still felt "such a longing" for the large family she used to have and the sense of belonging she had lost as a hidden child.

Reference

Marks, Jane. *The Hidden Children: The Secret Survivors of the Holocaust.* New York: Fawcett Columbine, 1993.

Skier, Rose (1934–)

Rose Silberberg Skier of Jaworzno, Poland, survived most of the war hiding in a chicken coop behind the house of a Lithuanian woman. She remained there for almost two years, sometimes all alone. By the time liberation came, she had lost her parents and her little sister.

Moses and Felicia Silberberg and their daughters Rose and Mala were part of a large Hassidic family. The girls were cared for by a young woman who sometimes took them with her to church, but the family was a strong presence in their lives. Besides their parents, there was Felicia's sister, Aunt Sarah, and many uncles and cousins.

When Germany invaded Poland on September 1, 1939, their lives changed. First, the family fled their native Jaworzno for what they thought would be the safety of a larger town: Sosnovic. But the Germans arrived in Sosnovic within a few days, and by the end of that first week of occupation, the twenty-eight thousand Jewish residents were under attack. The synagogue was burned down, Jewish property was confiscated, and the Jews were subject to a variety of restrictions. Within months, the Jews were confined to a ghetto and were subject to conscription for hard labor in the coal and iron mines that were scattered throughout the region.

Slowly the Jewish population of Sosnovic was rounded up by the Nazis and sent to concentration camps or labor camps. By August 1942, about 11,500 people had disappeared from the ghetto, many sent to their deaths in Auschwitz-Birkenau. But the Silberbergs avoided all the transports. They had even managed to save their daughters from the children's selection, a roundup of all those under fourteen who were forcibly taken to their deaths.

Moses Silberberg knew that time was running out. He contacted Stanislawa Chicha, a Lutheran woman who lived near Sosnovic, and offered to pay her to hide his family. Chicha agreed and the Silberbergs snuck out of the ghetto into their new home: a chicken coop attached to the Chicha house.

Although it was very small, Skier's father built an underground bunker beneath the floor, and attached a trap door to create a hideout for them when strangers came. The four Silberbergs and an uncle hid there for many months.

Skier was already nine when they went into hiding but her little sister was quite a bit younger and it was difficult for her to keep still and not make any noise. The painful alternative was to send Mala to a Catholic family. The Silberbergs agreed that the family could adopt her and have her baptized, hoping this might save her life. The rest of the family remained in the dark chicken coop, but eventually the hunger was too great. Chicha simply could not get enough food to feed them all. It was agreed that only Skier would stay in the chicken coop and would be fed by Chicha. The adults would return to the ghetto.

Now the nine-year-old Skier was totally isolated for hours at a time in the dark. She saw only Chicha when she came to bring her food once or twice a day. Skier begged to be allowed to see her parents, and in spite of the risks they agreed. On one of the visits, during the summer of 1943, the final liquidation of the Sosnovic ghetto began. Aunt Sarah grabbed Skier and the two found a hiding place, but they were soon discovered and arrested. Offering the Jewish policeman a bribe, Aunt Sarah was able to arrange for Skier's escape and she ran back to the Chicha house and the safety of her bunker.

Within days, she was joined by other family members. Her parents, Aunt Sarah, an uncle, and some friends had all managed to avoid the roundup. Now sixteen people were crammed into the tiny chicken coop. And then, six months later, Skier's little sister Mala was returned as well. The family that had agreed to adopt her brought her back, claiming that the neighbors were suspicious.

By February 1944, the hideout was discovered. Chicha's house was surrounded by German police and all were forced out. As they were emerging, Skier's uncle pushed her and Aunt Sarah down into the bunker. They remained underground, unnoticed, while all the others, including Stanislawa Chicha, were arrested. Skier heard her little sister Mala screaming as the Nazis dragged her away. It was a memory that never left her.

An uncle who had managed to escape now returned and led Skier and her aunt out of the bunker. He helped them to obtain false identity papers so they could pass as Christians. With those papers, they were able to get work in Germany as food servers in a convent, but still they did not feel safe. The SS often stopped them and accused them of being Jewish. Once, a German officer pointed a gun at Skier's head and said, "If you tell me you're Jewish, I'll let you go." Skier refused to be tricked. Instead, she began to recite the Latin prayers she had leaned years before when her nursemaid had brought her to church. The officer was convinced and let her go.

Skier and her aunt were finally liberated in April 1945. They returned to Poland in hopes of finding other survivors from their family, but there were none. All had been murdered in Auschwitz. Only Stanislawa Chicha had survived.

Skier spent some time in an orphanage in Krakow, but in 1951 she and her Aunt Sarah emigrated to the United States. Skier married and had a family of her own, but she never forgot the woman who sheltered her during the war. Stanislawa Chicha was recognized as a righteous gentile by the Holocaust museum in Jerusalem.

Reference

Appel, Allan. *To Life: 36 Stories of Memory and Hope*. New York: Museum of Jewish Heritage and Bulfinch Press, 2002.

Slawin family

The Slawin family of Dunilowicze, Poland, was among many Jewish families who were hidden by righteous gentiles. Living under the eyes of the Nazis, Celina Anishkewitz did not give away their secret, even to other family members. The Slawins remained grateful for this sacrifice and never forgot her and her daughters.

Jeremiah and Sonia Slawin lived in Dunilowicze in the northeast section of Poland (now Belarus) with their two children, Leo (b. 1931) and his older sister Basia (b. 1929). Sonia's parents Aaron and Bayle-Geshe Taitz lived with them. The Slawins were proprietors of a general store in town, and the children were cared for by their grandparents.

Dunilowicze, a town of two thousand people in eastern Poland, was half Jewish and half gentile and the Slawins enjoyed good relations with everyone. Many of the Christian farmers knew Sonia Slawin and her parents and would often stay in their home when they came to the market.

Life was simple and pleasant until war broke out in 1939. When the Germans marched into western Poland, the Russian army occupied the eastern part of the country. This was in accordance with the nonaggression pact between Germany and the Soviet Union, signed on August 23, 1939. But by 1941, Germany repudiated that agreement and invaded the Soviet sector. That summer, about seventy Jews fled Dunilowicze with the Russian army, but the Slawins remained, with most of the Jews. Leo was eleven and his sister Basia was thirteen.

Several weeks after the Nazis arrived in Dunilowicze, all the Jews were ordered to leave their homes and move to one small street, which was enclosed in barbed wire. That was the ghetto. Life there was difficult. There was constant fear of the German police and Jews, forbidden to leave the ghetto, were dependent on the small amount of food brought in. They were always hungry, but they survived. Then in 1942, the residents of the Dunilowicze ghetto began to hear reports from the Polish farmers. They said that the Jews in neighboring towns had all been killed and the ghettos liquidated. Leo later wrote, in a brief memoir, "We knew our turn would come and the fear was unbearable."

Jeremiah Slawin decided to try and hide his family. In a small shack in their yard, he dug a hole in the earth, approximately five feet by ten feet. The entrance was covered with a box filled with sand. When they awoke one Saturday morning in November of 1942 to shots and screams, they knew the Germans had come for the Jews of Dunilowicze. The ghetto was surrounded by Nazi soldiers who were methodically murdering the entire Jewish population.

The Slawin parents grabbed their children and ran to the hole in the shack. But the grandparents refused to run. They were too old, they said, and would meet their fate.

All that Saturday the Slawins hid in the hole. They heard more screams and shots and finally, silence. Only much later, after the war was over, did they find out that the Germans had herded most of the Jews into a large barn. They were forced to run out, a few at a time, and the soldiers, stationed on a nearby hill, shot them one by one. The Slawins assumed that Aaron and Bayle-Geshe Taitz were also killed in that way.

The Slawin family remained hidden for two full days. Once there was silence, Sonia left the hole, crawled into the house and returned with bread and water. She reported that the ghetto was burning, and they waited for one more day. Finally, all four of them crawled out. It was a cold, windy night and few people were out. They managed to cross the river without being seen, and ran across a field. As they passed, they saw their old neighbor, Mrs. Prokopovitz, who began shouting, "Police! Jews are escaping!" Luckily, the strong howling of the wind carried her voice away and the guard standing at the bridge did not hear her.

It was getting dark, and the family was desperate to find shelter. They approached a farmer who lived outside the town. He answered their knock and reluctantly let them in, but he was very frightened. They all knew that anyone caught hiding or helping Jews would be executed. Nevertheless, he let them stay for two days.

The Slawin family walked toward the woods. Each night, they slept in small shacks along the way, and at daybreak they continued walking. They begged for food from the farmers that Sonia knew from business, but they were at great risk of being discovered, especially when the snow came and revealed their footprints.

One night, hungry and almost frozen, they knocked at the door of the Anishkewitz farm. Celina Anishkewitz opened the door. Recognizing them, she immediately let them in, urged them to warm up by the stove, and cooked a hot meal for them. She was outraged that the Nazis were killing even women and children. Anishkewitz told the Slawins that her husband had died from rabies after being bitten by a wolf and that she now lived alone with her two daughters, aged seventeen and fourteen. She gave them food and blankets and let them stay in her barn during the day. At night, they came inside and slept on the floor of the house. When it became too cold to remain in the barn, Anishkewitz and her daughters and her married son, Yuzik, helped dig a hole for them under the floor. From that time on, they stayed in the house, only hiding in the hole when strangers came near. "We had some close calls," said Leo in an interview sixty years later, remembering how frightened they were when the Germans approached the house, but they were never caught.

The Anishkewitz family was poor. They earned a meager living by knitting sweaters, socks, and mittens on a knitting machine and traded these items for either money or grain. The girls taught Leo and Basia how to knit as well and in this way, they helped earn their keep.

The Slawins stayed with the Anishkewitz family until the Spring of 1943, a total of six months. When the snow melted, they found leaflets reporting that 300,000 German soldiers had surrendered to the Russian Army in the battle of Stalingrad. Partisans had helped fight the Germans by blowing up railroad tracks and bridges to prevent reinforcements from getting to the front lines. The Germans and their Polish collaborators were now afraid to leave the cities and would not venture into the countryside. Heartened by this news, the Slawins went into the nearby woods and lived with a group of Jewish families. But they continued visiting the Anishkewitzs who fed them whenever they came.

During the winter of 1943, the last winter of the war, another farmer, Ivan Krivenki, and his wife Katia invited the Slawins and their small group, numbering about one dozen, to their one-room house. They kept everyone hidden there for the entire winter of 1943–1944, when the Russians drove the Germans out and the war was over in the east.

With the war over on the Russian front, the Slawins, still an intact family, returned to Dunilowicze, now part of Soviet Russia. They soon realized, however, that nothing remained there for them. They traveled through the ruins of Poland and west into a displaced-persons camp, first in Berlin, then in Bavaria. There, Leo and Basia went to night school to learn English and Jeremiah Slawin found work. They waited for their names to come up on the list that would allow them to enter the United States. While waiting, Basia, now nineteen, met and married Isaac Jesin, another survivor, and they emigrated to Canada. They settled in Toronto and had six children and twenty-three grandchildren.

Sonia, Jeremiah, and Leo arrived in the United States in 1949, when Leo was seventeen. Jeremiah Slawin found a job as caretaker of a synagogue and Sonia

The Slawin family in 1947. Courtesy of Leo Slawin.

kept house. Leo had missed several years of school and knew only a little English. Nevertheless, he completed his education at New Utrecht High School in Brooklyn, continued on to City College of New York, and then Columbia University Dental School. He married Gloria, a young woman from Toronto, in 1958, had three children and eight grandchildren, and at the age of seventy-five was still practicing dentistry in Brooklyn, New York.

Jeremiah died in the 1980s but Sonia lived on to see many grandchildren and great-grandchildren. She was one hundred years old when she died in 2004.

The Slawins never forgot the Anishkewitz family. During all the years that they lived behind the Iron Curtain, the Slawin family continually sent them food, clothing, and money. By the time Russia lifted its restrictions on travel, Celina Anishkewitz had died, but her daughter and granddaughter traveled to America and stayed with the Slawins. At that time, they were honored by the Jewish Foundation for the Righteous, a New York-based philanthropic organization that supports and honors those who saved Jews during the Holocaust. In 2006 Leo and Gloria Slawin and their children traveled to Dunilowicze and visited the descendents of Celina Anishkewitz and the Krivenkis.

References

Slawin, Leo. "My Holocaust Experience." Unpublished manuscript.
———. Interview by the author, October 2005, Valley Stream, New York.

Slotkin, René Guttmann, and Irene Hizme (née Guttmann Slotkin) (1937–)

The Guttmann twins, brother René and sister Renate, were from Czechoslovakia. Among the youngest twins to survive Dr. Josef Mengele's notorious experiments in Auschwitz, they were separated after the war but reunited in the United States when they were twelve years old.

René and Renate Guttmann were born in Czechoslovakia four years after Hitler came to power in Germany. Their parents had fled there from Dresden after the anti-Jewish laws were passed in Germany. They thought they would be safe in then-democratic Czechoslovakia. However, in 1938, their new country was taken over by the Nazis. When the twins were three years old, their father was arrested as a political prisoner and taken away. They never saw him again. Later, records show that he was executed in Auschwitz in December 1941.

In September 1942, the Guttmann twins and their mother were deported to Theresienstadt, a concentration camp in Czechoslovakia that was set up as a model ghetto to deceive the world about the Nazi's "final solution." Although there was certainly disease and hunger there, and many people were killed, there was no gas chamber and some families were able to stay together.

The twins and their mother remained in Theresienstadt for almost one year before being sent to Auschwitz in December 1943. There, they stayed in the Czech family *lager* (prison barracks) with their mother for three to four months before the entire group of 3,800 people was liquidated. The only ones saved from that mass murder were a few sets of twins.

Although only six years old at the time, both children remembered their mother's last scream as she was separated from them. Immediately after, they

The Slotkin twins and their mother, Ita Guttmann, right after their arrival in Theresienstadt in 1942. Courtesy of U.S. Holocaust Memorial Museum Photo Archives.

themselves were separated. René went to the men's camp and Renate was placed with the women. From then on, they only caught a glimpse of each other once through the barbed wire fence and knew "we belonged to each other," but both became part of an experimental program on twins that Dr. Mengele was conducting at Auschwitz.

The experiments themselves were life-threatening. Twins were injected regularly with drugs, measured, and examined, and sometimes operations were performed on one or both of them. But being chosen by Mengele also meant that they would not be killed immediately like most of the other children. Even for twins, however, life at Auschwitz was precarious and they were still subject to random selections.

Of the 3,000 individual twins that passed through that camp during the war, they were among only 160 that survived. (Usually, when one twin died, the other was also killed so autopsies could be performed on both.) But when Auschwitz was liberated, they lost track of each other completely. René was taken back to Czechoslovakia and cared for by a Jewish family. Renate was taken in by a Polish Christian woman who cared for her, renamed her Irenka (a more Polish-sounding name) and arranged for her to go to a church school. Although she knew she was Jewish, at the age of eight, Renate already understood that being Jewish was not good and she did not protest.

Within a short time, Renate (now Irene) was discovered by Jewish groups searching for survivors. She was removed from her Catholic foster mother and sent to a Jewish orphanage somewhere in France. A few years later, she was chosen, along with one other boy, to be taken to the United States by an organization called Rescue Children. The prominent leaders of this organization thought the children would be able to help raise money for the hundreds of thousands of orphans in Europe. Irene expected to be returned to France, but was eventually placed with the Slotkins.

Already several years after her liberation, Irene rarely spoke and did not feel that she could share her harrowing childhood experiences. She had never had a normal childhood, never played games, or gone to school. She barely remembered either of her parents. But in the United States, she found a loving home with the Slotkin family who legally adopted her. When she told them that she had a twin brother, they began to look for René, even hiring a person to go to Europe and search for him.

Another key factor in the twins' reunion was René's guardian, a doctor, whose threatened arrest by the Communists had caused him to flee to Israel. In Israel, he saw a photo of Irene in *Life* magazine (November 1947) with an article telling her story and giving her name. Based on what he knew about René (then being cared for by his sister in Czechoslovakia), he realized that his foster child was Irene's lost brother. From Israel, he made the necessary contacts and the process of getting René to America began.

It took three years before René Guttmann could leave Czechoslovakia, then behind the Iron Curtain, and come to America on a special immigration visa. Determined to unite Irene and her brother, the Slotkins spent a great deal of money in this effort and the twins were reunited on March 29, 1950, when they were twelve years old. From that time, they grew up together in Long Island, New York. They never discussed their war experiences, either with their family or between themselves. Irene, always the shyer of the two, went to Hunter College and pursued a career in biochemistry as a researcher. René went to Hofstra University and then went into business.

It was only after they had both grown and married and had children of their own (each married a twin, although their spouses are unrelated) that René and Irene began to open up and share their war experiences. The catalyst was a 1985 reunion of twins in Israel where a mock trial of Dr. Mengele was acted out. A few years later, while East Germany was still under Communist rule, Irene and a friend went back to Dresden. She contacted her father's relatives and was well received by the Christian branch of the family.

Irene, whose married name is Hizme, went to Dresden again in 2003, this time by invitation from the local government, to participate in the dedication of a rebuilt synagogue there. That same year, to commemorate *Yom HaShoah* (Holocaust Memorial Day), a film was made about their lives. It was shown on American television and later expanded to a full-length documentary. Called "René and I: From Auschwitz to America," the film recounted the memories of both of the twins but concentrated on Irene Hizme's present life.

After her retirement as a researcher, Hizme became an activist, dedicated to helping and educating others through a variety of Jewish organizations and by teaching and speaking about the Holocaust. Confined to a wheelchair due to multiple sclerosis, she never let her disability deter her. She visited the sick at her local hospital, taking the time to listen to the mostly elderly patients and befriending those in need of companionship. She is a member of the CAMERA e-mail team, an organization that supports Israel by correcting misleading images about the Jewish state that appear in the press. In her wheelchair, she even attended several demonstrations.

After his retirement, René Slotkin spent his days teaching physical education and coaching sports. Although not a joiner or a volunteer, he always was ready to help whenever he was asked.

Hizme had two daughters and Slotkin two daughters and two sons. Together they have many grandchildren and their growing families remain very close and supportive.

References

Angelone, Gina, Director. *Rene and I: From Auschwitz to America*. Produced by Leora Kahn and Zeva Oelbaum. 1 hour, 13 min. 2004.
Hizme, Irene. Telephone interview by the author, June 2006.

Socha, Leopold

Leopold Socha, a Polish Catholic from Lvov, began life as a petty criminal. The Holocaust turned him into a rescuer and a hero who saved eleven Polish Jews at the risk of his own and his family's lives.

Socha came from a poor background. There is no record of his parents or his date of birth. At a very young age he was on the streets on his own. He become a petty thief by the age of ten and was arrested many times throughout his childhood. His exploits became more daring as he matured and targeted banks and jewelry stores. For some of his crimes, he served time in prison. For others, he was never caught. But his career in crime taught him about loyalty and it was a lesson he applied later in his life.

By the time the war began, Socha had experienced a change of heart. He was married, had a family, and was a municipal worker in the sewer systems of Lvov. One day, while he was inspecting the underground pipes with two other workers, they encountered three Jewish men. When the workers asked where they came from, the Jews admitted that they were from the ghetto and were seeking a place to hide from the Nazis. Although the other two workers were reluctant to get involved, Socha was interested and seemed sympathetic. One of the Jews, **Ignacy Chiger**, felt Socha could be trusted. He agreed to show the workers their access to the sewers and asked for their help, offering them good faith money in advance.

For Socha, the decision to assist the Chiger family came when he was led up into their ghetto apartment and saw Chiger's wife, Pauline, and their two young children. He convinced his fellow workers to agree to the plan, and from that time on, he was committed. He saved not only the Chigers, but agreed to help the entire group of twenty-one Jews who had managed to attach themselves to the escape plan of a few. Eventually, the group became smaller; a number of them died trying to escape the sewers, and only eleven people remained, hiding in the filth and stench of the sewer pipes for fourteen months.

During those months, Socha did his best to make their unbearable lives bearable. He brought Sabbath candles and a prayer book. He brought textbooks for the Chiger's eight-year-old daughter, and regularly carried in food and reported on the war. Although there were tensions, the Jews were very well aware that Socha was the only one standing between them and a terrible death. They grew very close to him and he told them about his past. Ignacy Chiger believed that his extraordinary effort to save them was an attempt to make up for his past life, an effort for redemption. Socha was also touched by Chiger's complete trust in his honesty. When Chiger ran out of money to pay him, he told Socha where he had buried the family jewels and other valuables. He asked him to dig them up and bring them to him and he did. Chiger did not realize how tempted Socha was to take this treasure and disappear. Socha confessed to Jacob Berestycki, another man in Chiger's group, that he almost did just that, but that ultimately he could not bear to think of them alone in the sewers and at the last minute he forced himself to do the right thing.

When the Russians came to liberate Lvov, Socha was almost as happy and relieved as the Jews he had hidden and rescued. He himself was there to open the manhole cover and help lift the eleven survivors out into the light of day. As a crowd of onlookers stood around gaping at the filthy, ragged people, bent over and half-blind from their first exposure to light in over a year, Socha announced to the crowd: "This is my work. All my work. These are my Jews."

The group stayed with Leopold Socha for a few days and he helped find them places to live in an apartment house that had been abandoned by the Germans when they retreated. Slowly, each of his eleven Jews began

> *[There had been] a metamorphosis in [Socha's] soul, as he witnessed the tragedies that had befallen the people from the Julag (the ghetto). He believed it was a way of snatching his sins from his soul, just as he was snatching us from certain death.*
>
> —Ignacy Chiger

to recover from their ordeal and establish themselves. Although many left Poland, all of them kept in touch with Socha and, as soon as they could, they all contributed money to buy a small tavern for him, something that Socha had always wanted.

After the war, Socha and his family moved out of Lvov, a city that had become part of Russia, into the Polish city of Gliwice. On May 12, 1946, he and his daughter Stefcia were riding their bicycles down a steep hill, with Stefcia in front. Socha caught sight of a Russian Army truck coming toward them, seemingly out of control. Fearing that she would be hit by the truck, he pedaled ahead and was able to knock her to the side and out of the path of the oncoming vehicle. At the instant that he saved his daughter, the truck hit him and he was killed. Later, Ignacy Chiger wrote in his memoir, "He had fallen on a drain in the street and his blood flowed freely into the sewer."

All Leopold Socha's Jews attended his Catholic funeral, sharing the grief of other family and friends. But even here, the vestiges of antisemitism were still alive. One of the survivors heard someone say, "This is God's retribution. This is what comes of helping the Jews."

Reference

Marshall, Robert. *In the Sewers of Lvov: A Heroic Story of Survival from the Holocaust.* New York: Scribner's, 1991.

Solewics, David (1924–1994), and Helen Schenker (née Solewics) (1925–), and Rose Blauner (née Solewics) (1927–)

The Solewics siblings, David, Helen, and Rose of Kazimierz, Poland, were three of seven children. During World War II, they posed as Catholics and by using false identities were able to avoid the fate of so many other Jews. Of the nine members of their family, they were the only survivors.

Hannah and Samuel Solewics were cattle dealers in Kazimierz, Galicia, a province of southeastern Poland, and the Solewics were all living there when the war began. The lives of the Jews were quickly disrupted by antisemitic rulings and within a short time, most of the townspeople had been transferred to a ghetto and then murdered.

David, Helen, and Rose were able to save themselves by hiding with a Polish farmer and his family in Galicia, a few miles from their home. They remained there for more than five years, posing as Catholic Poles and working on the farm. David and Helen were both blonde and blue-eyed and were able to fit in with the neighbors more easily. Rose had dark hair and was less comfortable circulating in the community. Nevertheless, all three survived the war.

The four other Solewics children, Joseph, Zalman, Golda, and Koeppel, along with their parents, were first moved from Kazimierz to the ghetto in Grybov. From there, the Jewish population was rounded up by the Nazis and shot. With 386 other Jews, the Solewicses were buried in a mass grave.

When the fighting was over and a peace treaty had been signed, the remaining Solewics siblings moved to Breslau, Germany. Rose, the youngest sister, found work in a restaurant and met her future husband there. **Max Blauner** was a Jew who had escaped to Russia and then fought in the Russian Army. He made a favorable impression on Rose when she saw him dressed in his Russian Army uniform and carrying a machine gun. They were married within the year and remained in Breslau, where Blauner went into business with Wolf Schenker, Helen's future husband. They stayed there for seven years and their oldest son, Samuel, was born there in 1946.

Helen and David also lived in Breslau—a safer place than Poland for Jews after the war. Helen met and married Wolf Schenker, Max's business partner, and David married Edga, a widow. Edga had spent most of World War II in a Russian labor camp with her son Fishel, but had moved to Germany after the war.

All three young couples hoped to eventually get to the United States, but only Rose and Max Blauner succeeded, with the aid of HIAS (Hebrew Immigrant Aid Society). Because the United States, Canada, and Brazil were all accepting refugees, and each granted only a limited number of visas to those who had no sponsor, the choice was determined by alphabetical order. People whose names began with the first letters of the alphabet, therefore, had better choices. Because Max and Rose's last name was Blauner, they had the opportunity to choose before the supply of U.S. visas ran out. They came to America in 1952. Helen and David both had last names beginning with S, so by the time their turns came the quota for the United States was full. They had the choice of either Canada or Brazil and they chose Brazil.

David worked in the garment industry and became a successful businessman. Helen's husband Wolf Schenker also did well in the clothing business, establishing a large import/export firm. David and Edga Solewics had two more sons, Samuel and Ronaldo. The Schenkers had four children: Anita, Betchina, Janete, and Lilly. The Solewics, Schenkers, and Blauners had many grandchildren and their family continued growing.

Reference

Blauner, Sidney. Interview with Yaakov Taitz, July 2006, Riverdale, New York.

Sousa Mendes, Aristides de (1885–1954)

Aristides de Sousa Mendes was born in northern Portugal into a prosperous family. He pursued a diplomatic career and was Consul General in Bordeaux when World War II broke out. Although his country was officially neutral, and its policy was to refuse entry to refugees, Sousa Mendes made a different decision. "I would stand with God against man, rather than with man against God," he claimed. His insistence on this personal ideal destroyed his career and made him an outcast in his native land, but it saved countless numbers of Jews.

Sousa Mendes's family had a tradition of government service. His father was a judge and he and his twin brother, Cesar, studied law together. When Sousa Mendes decided to enter the diplomatic corps, there was never any question that his wife and family would be with him. They traveled together to several smaller countries outside the borders of Europe as well as to Great Britain and Spain, before Sousa Mendes was promoted to General Consul and assigned to Antwerp in 1929.

In Antwerp, Sousa Mendes's wife Angelina gave birth to two more children, making a total of fourteen. Not only was his family life a happy one, but the couple established a reputation for hospitality, and many important people were entertained in their home. Life was good for the Sousa Mendes family until the sudden death of one of the older sons in 1934, followed by the death of their youngest child. Sousa Mendes asked for a transfer, hoping that the change would alleviate the family's sadness. Although he requested a post in Asia, he was assigned to Bordeaux, putting him in a unique position to help the flood of refugees when war broke out.

The first thing Sousa Mendes did in 1939, when Germany attacked Poland, was to send his younger children back to the safety of Portugal. By spring of 1940, the German Army had launched a *blitzkrieg*, a series of "lightning strikes," and quickly succeeded in conquering Belgium and Holland. From there, they turned to France, and as the French Army fled south, thousands of refugees, both Jews and non-Jews, ran with them, escaping from the Nazis and their oppressive policies.

Bordeaux, a large city in southern France, was located near the border with Spain. Spanish policy was officially neutral, but the Fascist dictator there felt close to the Germans and refused to accept anyone escaping from German jurisdiction. Portugal had signed a treaty of friendship with Spain, but it was offset by a long and friendly relationship with England. However the Portuguese ruler, Antonio Salazar, was also a fascist dictator and wanted no problems either with Spain or with Germany. He issued a ruling that visas would be granted to refugees only on a case-by-case basis.

This Portuguese policy left little room for Aristides de Sousa Mendes to deal with emergencies, and emergencies were flooding into his consulate. Desperate refugees surrounded the building where he and his wife and two oldest sons lived, begging for visas. The refugees ranged from poor families with small children to well-known artists and academics. Even the Count of Hapsburg appealed for a visa to Portugal. However, most of the refugees were Jews who had first fled Poland, then Belgium, and now France. All were hoping to escape from Europe via the only country that still had an escape hatch: Portugal.

Sousa Mendes, was a compassionate man. He had been raised as a devout Catholic who took religious principles seriously. He opened his heart and his home to the refugees. Witnesses later reported that "all the rooms in the consulate building were full of people. They slept on chairs, on the floor, on the rugs. Even the consul's offices were crowded with dozens of refugees who had waited days and nights on the street, on the stairways, and finally in the offices."

Meanwhile Sousa Mendes sent telegrams to Lisbon pleading for directions in the face of this onslaught. He requested permission to issue hundreds of visas but got no response. Under tremendous strain, the Consul General became ill and was too sick to leave his bed. His son remembered that during those three days, his father's hair turned completely white. After his fever subsided, he had made a decision. With the help of Rabbi Chaim Kruger, a refugee who had become his friend, Sousa Mendes started an assembly line in the Consul offices. Transit visas were issued to everyone, requesting that they be given passage through Spain on their way to Portugal. First in Bordeaux and then in the city of Bayonne, Sousa Mendes took his stamp and, working day and night, issued thousands of visas. If the refugees had no official papers, he stamped blank pieces of paper for them. In total, thirty thousand people were saved by these visas; ten thousand of them were Jews.

When the Portuguese government learned about Aristides de Sousa Mendes's activities, they first reprimanded him and then recalled him. The Consul General ignored the reprimand and did not receive the recall, since he was in Bayonne at the time. As the Germans approached the city of Bordeaux, Sousa Mendes fled with the refugees to the border, supervising their exit into Spain and safety. But by the end of June 1940, he could no longer function. The Portugese government had sent an emissary to the border crossing, ordering the Spanish authorities not to honor any of his visas and declaring that their Consul General had "lost the use of his faculties."

In explaining his decision to his government, Aristides de Sousa Mendes wrote, "The imperatives of my conscience . . . never ceased to guide me in the performance of my duties, with perfect knowledge of my responsibilities." Nevertheless, Salazar would not forgive his disobedience. He was deprived of his job and his pension, was refused work of any kind; requests for a hearing, from him and other family members, were repeatedly denied. Sousa Mendes was spurned by his friends and colleagues and the family sank into poverty, being reduced to eat their meals at the soup kitchen with the refugees. Even Sousa Mendes's children could not earn a living in Portugal and were forced to emigrate. Angelina de Sousa Mendes died of a stroke and its lingering disabilities in 1949. She could not afford medical care. Six years later, Aristides de Sousa Mendes also died. The newspapers wrote no obituary for him.

Despite his personal rejection, however, Portugal's policy of accepting refugees—a policy forced by Sousa Mendes—was noted favorably by the Allies and Portugal quietly decided to continue allowing it. It is estimated that one million more refugees, both Jews and non-Jews, were saved by what was originally Aristides de Sousa Mendes's policy of compassion.

References

Bauer, Yehudah. *American Jewry and the Holocaust.* Detroit: Wayne State University Press 1981.

Cirurgiao, Maria Julia, and Michael D. Hull. "Aristides de Sousa Mendes." http://www .jewishvirtuallibrary.org/jsource/biography/Mendes.html.

Hogan, David J., ed. *The Holocaust Chronicle.* Lincolnwood, IL: Publications International, 2000.

Spett family

The Spett family of Tarnow, Poland, managed not only to live through World War II but to stay together. Throughout those terrible years, Sala clung to her American birth certificate, hoping that it would save her and her family. It eventually did, but that small piece of paper did not save them from the nightmare of Nazi rule and the terrible suffering shared by all the Jews of Poland.

Before the shadow of Nazi antisemitism fell on Europe, the Spett family had a life relatively free from prejudice; the children enjoyed a happy childhood and a warm extended family. Arthur Spett worked for the government of Poland in the finance department, and the Spetts lived in a government-owned apartment house. Sala cared for Martin and Roslyn (formerly Rozia) and maintained an observant Jewish home.

Even before the Nazi invasion, however, the Jews of Tarnow began to suffer from anti-Jewish laws. In 1937, a new policy banned Jews from government jobs and Arthur was laid off. Although he and Sala opened up their own business, running a food concession in a Jewish club, they had considerably less income than before. After the Germans invaded Poland and established themselves in Tarnow, by mid-September, 1939, that business was closed, too.

German policy was harsh and violent. In order to establish their authority, Nazi officers killed both Poles and Jews randomly and issued laws barring Jews from public life and preventing Christians from working for Jews. In order to maintain themselves, Arthur found work with a German-owned company building structures for high-tension electrical wires and Sala worked for a Jewish furrier. By 1940, twelve-year-old Martin also took a job as a helper in a tailor shop. Their employment saved them from the roundups that the Nazis initiated later that year—at least for a while—but they saw many relatives and friends killed. Others simply disappeared, most taken away to nearby death camps.

Martin Spett was thirteen in 1941, the age when Jewish boys celebrate a bar mitzvah, a coming-of-age ceremony. Despite the fact that their synagogue had been burned down two years before, Martin was sent to have lessons with Rabbi Wrubel to learn to read from the Torah scroll. One day, when he arrived for his lesson, he saw the rabbi standing in the courtyard, wrapped in his prayer shawl and surrounded by Nazi soldiers who were kicking and beating him. When Rabbi Wrubel caught sight of Martin he told him to run. On his way back home, Martin heard the shot and knew his rabbi had been killed. He did have a bar mitzvah, but without Rabbi Wrubel. It took place in the apartment in the ghetto that they shared with an uncle and his family. The windows were covered with blankets, since any Jewish religious ceremony was forbidden.

Throughout 1941 and 1942, pressure from the Germans increased. Roundups were continuous and anyone with no work was arrested and deported. The Spett family scrambled to find one job after another, as companies were closed or moved, or workers were arbitrarily removed from lists. At one point, Martin and his mother Sala worked in a civilian-owned factory, supervised by the Germans. Martin, one of the youngest workers, was conscious of the owner's attempts to help him, and at one point used this relationship to save his mother's job at the factory. In general, though, there was no relief from the fear, helplessness, and despair that all the Jews of the ghetto experienced.

Sala had been born in Newark, New Jersey, but returned to Poland with her family when she was a little girl. Still, she was certain that her birth certificate, which she always kept in her pocket, would save the family. A few times, it did save her from roundups, although Arthur Spett and his brother-in-law also prepared bunkers to hide in and often used them when they heard the Nazi soldiers coming.

Then, in May 1943, that birth certificate actually did save them. A Gestapo officer came to the ghetto calling for American citizens. Sala wondered at first if this was a Nazi trick, but decided to step forward. When the officer found that Sala had a family, they were all taken the next day and, with other Jews who had foreign papers, were sent to a prison in Krakow. Here, the family was separated: Sala and her daughter Roslyn went to the women's cells and Arthur and Martin to the men's. They were kept there for nine weeks without ever being told what was happening and then released, still with no explanation. Rumors circulated that they would be used in a prisoner exchange, but this did not stop the guards from abusing them and frightening them with threats of immanent death.

From Krakow, the Spett family, along with several hundred others, was taken to a train. After a journey to an unknown destination, they were loaded onto military trucks and ended up in Bergen-Belsen, a concentration camp in Germany. They were placed in a special *lager* (barracks) where the families stayed together and waited. They were treated relatively well, had decent food, access to some medical care and visits by the Red Cross, but conditions were still horrifying. In a memoir written over sixty years after the war, Martin Spett described that "special" *lager*, located near the "busy crematorium. Its smokestacks belched and glowed constantly. We were saturated with the stench of burning flesh, bones and hair."

The Spett family remained in Bergen-Belsen for more than a year, with conditions growing progressively worse for them and no indication of prisoner exchange. In the early spring of 1945, as the war was nearing an end, they were taken from that camp and loaded onto trains. They traveled for five days, on minimum rations, cold, hungry, and frightened. Then the train stopped. Bombs were falling all around and lines of defeated German soldiers were retreating. It was only a matter of days before Germany's final defeat. Yet, an order had been given to the captain in charge of this train: all the Jews were to be killed. Seven German soldiers were positioned with machine guns facing the train, but ultimately, they ran out of time. An American tank appeared over the horizon and the trainload of prisoners was liberated. The commander, an American Jew named Joseph Schwartz, told them that President Roosevelt had just died the day before.

The U.S. Army took the refugees to a displaced-persons camp. Martin was sent to a hospital to recover from pneumonia. Then the family moved from what had become the Russian zone of Germany. They tried to get into France, but that country was not taking any more refugees. They ended up in Belgium, where they were helped by the remnant of the Jewish community there along with some gentiles who had aided Jews during the war. They remained there until their visas for America came through. Finally, Sala could return to the country of her birth and join her sister and her family.

Because Sala's American passport was about to expire, the Spetts took the first ship to leave Europe and landed in New Orleans. From there, they made their way to New York, where Sala's sister lived, and settled in the Bronx, a borough of New York City. There, they opened their own delicatessen/restaurant.

Roslyn resumed her education in the United States, married, and had her own family. Martin, already eighteen years old, found work in a factory making ladies

> *Throughout this account . . . I recounted my mother's repeated comment "God will help." For a long time this view and the lack of any comprehensible response troubled me. As a young man, I asked for God's providence and despaired when it didn't come. Now with the benefit of a lifetime of experience, I realize that I was looking in the wrong place for consolation. Instead of asking where was God during the Holocaust, the question should properly be, where was man, or rather, where was humanity? It was humanity that abandoned the Jews and the other victims of Nazi brutality to their fate.*
>
> —Martin Spett (from *Reflections of the Soul*)

pocketbooks and later became a handbag designer. He also attended a school for cartoonists and illustrators, but was never able to work in that field. In 1960, Martin married Joan Wechsler and they had two children.

Martin had promised his father that he would not speak about the Holocaust and about their war experiences, but in 1980, he broke that promise and began writing poetry and illustrating his memories with a series of paintings called "Reflections of the Soul." One of these was purchased by the U.S. Holocaust Memorial Museum and another by Yad Vashem, The Holocaust Martyrs' and Heroes' Remembrance Authority. His memoirs were subsequently published with the help of the Holocaust Resource Center at Manhattan Community College.

Reference

Spett, Martin. *Reflections of the Soul: Martin Spett's Holocaust Experiences*. New York: Manhattan College Holocaust Resource Center, 2002.

Spiegel family

The Spiegel family, parents and two children, Rosa and Paul, lived in Westphalia, Germany. They fled to Belgium at the start of World War II, but the Nazis soon overtook that country as well. Although Rosa was captured and killed, Hugo, his wife, and their young son Paul survived. They were among the very few families that decided to return to their old home in Germany, the country that had persecuted them so mercilessly.

Up until the late 1930s, Hugo Spiegel was a prosperous merchant who bought and sold livestock. His family had lived in Germany for generations, following that same occupation, and the Spiegels lived in a comfortable little home in Warendorf, a small town in the German state of Westphalia. They enjoyed good relations with their Christian neighbors and business associates. But on *Kristallnacht* (The Night of Broken Glass), November 9, 1938, when Jewish homes and synagogues throughout Germany were destroyed, Hugo Spiegel was severely beaten. He realized that the country they loved had become too dangerous for Jews and they escaped to nearby Belgium.

Because of the danger to all Jews, who could not travel without a pass, the family split up. Paul, then two years old, went with his mother, and Rosa, age seven, with her father. They all arrived safely in Brussels, but this turned out to be a temporary respite, as the German Army overran neutral Belgium in the spring of 1940.

The Spiegels looked for separate hiding places but were only partially successful. Paul was taken in with a Belgian farm family who treated him well, and he remained there for most of the war. His mother also went into hiding and remained safe. Hugo, Paul's father, was betrayed by a pro-Nazi sympathizer and was deported to Buchenwald. Rosa was caught on the street and sent to Auschwitz, where she died.

When the war was over, Paul's mother took her son back and, believing that her daughter and her husband were dead, decided to emigrate to the United States. But Hugo was not dead. He had survived five years in German concentration camps, first in Buchenwald, then Auschwitz, and finally Dachau. When he was liberated, Hugo Spiegel returned to his village.

Back home, it was the Spiegels' gentile neighbor who, by his actions, convinced Hugo to stay in Germany. When Hugo first appeared in town, this neighbor invited him to dinner. When he arrived, his host invited him to the cellar, where he showed him stacks of Jewish prayer books and a Torah (a scroll of the first five books of the Bible) that he had saved from the Nazis as they were destroying the synagogue. Knowing that his neighbors had risked their own lives in order to save the sacred texts from the synagogue, Hugo was persuaded not to give up on Germany. He convinced his wife and son to return to their old home.

Hugo Spiegel immediately began rebuilding his cattle trading business and Paul returned to school. His was the first bar mitzvah to take place in that area of Germany after the war ended. When he completed his education, he became a journalist for the principal German-Jewish newspaper in the country, the *Allgemeine Jüdische Wochenzeitung*. Later, he was a representative for a banking group before setting up his own business as a theatrical and literary agent. In 1959, Paul met his future wife, Giselle, a French Jew. The couple was married and had two daughters.

In addition to his professional career, Paul Spiegel became a spokesman for the Jewish community of Germany and in the year 2000 was elected head of the Central Council of Jews in Germany, a post he held until his death in 2006. Late in his life, Paul Spiegel wrote *At Home Again?* a memoir of his life during and after World War II. In the book, he discussed his father's decision to return to Germany and examined the ties between Germans and Jews.

Paul Spiegel never regretted what was originally his father's decision to remain in Germany, but he was also cognizant of the problems the Jewish community faced there. One of his goals as leader of the community was "to make Jews feel at home again in Germany." Another goal was to work toward "the continuing reconciliation between Germans and Jews."

Hugo and Ruth Spiegel both died in Germany and never regretted their decision to return. Paul lived to see the German Jewish community flourishing. By the time he died of leukemia in April 2006, Jews numbered over 100,000 and were the third largest Jewish community in Europe, following France and England. In 2003, due partly to Paul Spiegel's efforts, the Central Council of Jews in Germany had been recognized by the government as having the same legal status as the country's main churches and was entitled to an annual stipend of $3.76 million a year from the German government.

References

"Germany Mourns Passing of Outspoken Jewish Leader." *Spiegel Magazine Online*.
  http://service.spiegel.de/cache/international/0,1518,413967,00.html.
"Paul Spiegel, 68, Leader of Jewish Council in Germany." *Reuters Know.Now*.
  http://go.reuters.com/newsArticle/.
Spiegel, Paul. *At Home Again?* (German). Munich: Ullstein Berlin, 2001.

Spies, Gerty (1897–1997)

Gerty Spies, a German Jew, spent three years during World War II in Theresienstadt, considered the "good" concentration camp. She found solace from the loneliness and suffering of those years by writing poetry and withdrawing into herself as much as possible, shutting out the awful conditions around her and turning her experiences into literature.

Gerty Gumprich Spies was born in Trier, Germany, the older of two children. Her father, a successful merchant, also wrote poetry and her mother was a nurse before she retired to raise her family. The Gumpriches had lived in Trier for many centuries and Gerty's brother Rudi was killed fighting for Germany in World War I. Although she was from a Jewish family, Gerty Gumprich was educated in German secular schools and in 1920, married Albert Spies, a non-Jew. The Spies had a daughter, Ruth, and a son, Wolfgang, but after seven years, the marriage ended in divorce.

When Hitler came to power in 1933, the laws directed against Jews did not immediately affect Spies because she had two children whose father was a non-Jew. Nevertheless, she identified herself with the Jewish community in Munich, where she lived, and volunteered in a Jewish children's home. Part of her job was preparing the young people for transports to concentration camps. It was not long, however, before she was also called up for deportation.

Spies's order of deportation came in July 1942, after a change in the Nuremberg race laws dealing with mixed marriages. By this time she was a mature woman of forty-five and her children were almost grown. Following a bout of spinal meningitis, Wolfgang had become brain damaged and was institutionalized. Ruth was completing high school and was allowed to finish. Because she was considered only half Jewish, she was never deported and lived out the war in Munich. Spies was sent to Theresienstadt, a camp in Czechoslovakia.

Theresienstadt was first conceived of in 1941 as a ghetto of sorts, a model camp where older Jewish people, as well as prominent Jews from Germany and Czechoslovakia, were to be interned. The plan was that they would gradually be deported from there to death camps. As the war progressed, however, and the "final solution" for exterminating all Jews became fully developed, many others were sent there from all over Europe. Just a few months after Spies arrived at Theresienstadt, the population was 53,004 people, crowded into an area of 125,770 square yards. From then on, in order to make room for new arrivals, and to eliminate the sick and unproductive, regular transports were sent to the gas chambers at Auschwitz and Treblinka.

In her memoir of that period, Spies described the hardships of the Theresienstadt ghetto: the lack of privacy, the poor sanitation, the continual, gnawing hunger, and the brutal work schedule. Spies was assigned to work in the mica factory, where the women sat for up to twelve hours a day splitting mica-slate into the thinnest slabs possible for use in the aircraft industry. It was this work, considered vital to the war effort, which saved her from selection for the transports to the east.

Because Theresienstadt was considered a model ghetto and was sometimes inspected by the Red Cross, the prisoners were given a certain amount of freedom. They were allowed to keep some of their own possessions, to receive mail and food packages from home, and, with the permission of the German authorities, could organize and participate in cultural activities. These activities were possible because many prominent and accomplished Jews were incarcerated in Theresienstadt. Spies described the concerts, lectures, and poetry readings that were held despite the constant hunger and fatigue of the presenters as well as the audience.

> *The Statistics of Theresienstadt, cold and numbing, each digit a human being:*
> *As of April 20, 1945, there arrived from Germany, Holland, Denmark, Poland, Luxembourg, Austria, Hungary, Czechoslovakia, and a few other places, a little over 141,000 Jews.*
>
> * *33,456 died in the ghetto [of Theresienstadt]*
> * *88,202 were transported to the death camps in the East.*
>
> *On May 9, 1945, there remained in Theresienstadt a total of 16,832 Jews.*
> *Of the 15,000 children deported from Theresienstadt to Auschwitz, 100 survived—none under the age of fourteen.*
> *Statistics.*
>
> *—I Never Saw Another Butterfly* (p. xx).

It was in Theresienstadt that Spies began to write poetry, tentatively at first, and then, with encouragement from other writers and respected prisoners, with growing assurance. There was no paper and no writing equipment permitted to the prisoners, and Spies often composed and memorized a poem during the night. She would repeat it to herself again and again until she had a chance to obtain a scrap of paper so she could commit it to writing. Fearing that her written work would be confiscated during one of the regular inspections, she carried her papers to the mica factory every day.

As the months passed, Spies watched those around her disappear; they either succumbed to disease or were transported to the death camps. As the war neared its end and Germany was being attacked from both sides, large groups of prisoners were sent to Theresienstadt from other concentration camps in the east and west. These men and women were far worse off than she was. They were desperate for food and fought for every bit of garbage they could find. They were also ridden with disease and caused new epidemics among the already weakened prisoners.

Despite rumors that the war would be over soon, the Germans kept running the transports and the death toll kept rising. Over the three years of Spies's incarceration, more than thirty thousand Jews died in Theresienstadt and eighty-eight thousand were sent to extermination camps and murdered. When the Russians came on May 8, 1945, and Theresienstadt was finally liberated, many rushed out to welcome the soldiers but others were too weak to enjoy the victory.

With liberation, conditions improved at Theresienstadt. Adequate food was provided, the factories closed down, and trucks began arriving from the different cities in Germany to bring their citizens back home. When Spies returned to Munich she was shocked to see the devastation of the city, but she found that her daughter was alive and well. She had married and Spies was now a grandmother.

Spies opted to remain in Germany and, while she could not forget what had happened to her, she found that she could forgive. Germany was her home and German was her language. She continued writing poetry and became a prominent and respected poet and writer. In 1987, the Gerty Spies Literary Award was established in Germany for students between the ages of thirteen and twenty. In her hundredth year, a celebration was launched in her honor. She died just a few months later in October 1997. That same year, her book, *My Years in Theresienstadt: How One Woman Survived the Holocaust* was translated into English and published in the United States.

References

Spies, Gerty. *My Years in Theresienstadt: How One Woman Survived the Holocaust.* Translated by Jutta R. Tragnitz. Amherst, NY: Prometheus Books, 1997. http://www.politische-bildung-rlp.de/angebot/download/d52005.pdf.

Stanké, Alain (1934–)

Alain Stanké, born Aloyzas-Vitas Stankevicius, was a Lithuanian Christian. He was only six years old when World War II began and eight when his family was conscripted for hard labor. Stanké, the youngest person at the camp, spent most of his childhood in the shadow of war.

Stanké was born in Kovno, Lithuania, into a prosperous family that employed servants and gardeners to work for them. His father ran the radio station and was an important person in town. Although Aloyzas was not a Jewish child, and therefore not automatically earmarked for death, he was nevertheless caught up in the war. Referring to the early occupation by the Russians, according to the secret Soviet-German pact of 1939, Stanké wrote, "On this day, June 15, 1940, war has entered my six-year-old world and I know that nothing will ever be the same again."

His first experience of war was with Russian soldiers who marched him, his brother, his aunt, and their chauffeur to a ditch and, with guns drawn, prepared to shoot them. A last minute reprieve saved their lives, but when Stanké was returned home he found that Russian soldiers had taken over their home and were carrying out all their valuables. He remembered running into his room and hiding his favorite toys so the soldiers would not take them.

Because Stanké's father was a wealthy businessman, he was considered an enemy of the Soviet state and was under constant threat of deportation to Siberia. But once again, at the last minute, there was a reprieve. This time, it was because the Germans had marched in and taken over the town from the Russians.

Now the Stankevicius family had to deal with German atrocities. Stanké's first realization of Nazi evil came when his best friend, Lazarius, was forced to go into hiding with his family. "Because we are Jews," explained Lazarius. Even though his family had converted to Christianity when he was born, and Lazarius himself was baptized, the Germans still considered them Jewish. After a short time in hiding, the family was arrested and disappeared. They became part of the six million Jews who were murdered in the Holocaust.

By the time the Germans marched into Kovno in the summer of 1941, Stanké had already seen innocent people arrested, beaten, and murdered. His family had been driven from their beautiful home to a tiny apartment in town and, because of the food shortage, their meals were now limited to bread and soup. Under the German occupation, even school children were forced to witness public executions and children were urged to spy on their parents. Then the Nazis arrested the entire Stankevicius family and brought them to a work camp. They were to work for the German Reich in exchange for food.

Although conditions were terrible, they were better for the gentile prisoners than they were for the Jews; Lithuanian Christians were not systematically killed. Still, Stanké was often hungry. As the youngest person in the camp, he did not have to work at first. But when he got older, he, too, was assigned a variety of jobs: sweeper, wood and stone carrier, general cleaner. Because of his age, Stanké was never required to do the heavy work that his older brother Lyudas, or his parents had to do.

When the bombing began, the Nazis moved the Stankevicius family, along with all the other prisoners, further west into Germany. They were housed just outside the city of Wurtzberg, in a stable, with each family or group assigned to a separate stall. The food was even worse than before and Stanké had a hacking cough. His new job was to cut wood, and when he didn't perform his work well enough, the two women in charge of the camp deprived him of a meal. One day, while working, he cut off a small round of wood to use as a boomerang. He threw it and it mistakenly hit one of those women. She beat him so mercilessly that he had to remain in bed for more than a week. He was ten years old.

In 1945, allied bombs began falling on this new location as well. Although Stanké understood that the bombs were meant for the enemy, the prisoners were also in danger and he had a few narrow escapes. Finally, on April 3, 1945, they were liberated by the United States Army. Stanké recalled this as a happy time in his life. The soldiers adopted him as their mascot. They provided him with extra milk and sweets and took him with them when they were on duty. A friendly American soldier of Lithuanian descent became especially close to them and when it came time for repatriation, arranged for them to go west to France rather than returning to Lithuania, ruled once again by Soviet Russia.

In France, Aloyzas Stankevicius became Alain Stanké and he resumed his studies and his childhood. Although learning French and fitting in to this new environment was challenging, he knew he was lucky. At the age of seventeen, Alain emigrated to Canada and settled in Quebec. There, he studied literature and translation at the University of Montreal and began a career in journalism. Stanké became known and admired as a radio and television broadcaster as well as a print journalist and hosted many popular television shows in Canada. He also worked for a publisher for a few years before establishing his own publishing house in 1975. In 1983 he received a prize from Toastmasters International for the best communicator of the year.

In addition to his many journalistic accomplishments, Alain Stanké has written a number of books. One of these, *So Much to Forget: A Child's Vision of*

Hell, recounts his war experiences from a child's point of view. The book is dedicated to his wife, Josette. In 2005, he was still active in the publishing and entertainment worlds, and was a highly respected citizen of Canada.

References

Stanké, Alain. *So Much to Forget: A Child's Vision of Hell*. Translated by Susan Altschul. Canada: Gage Publishing, 1977.
http://www.litterature.org/detailauteur.asp?numero=434.
http://mcml.canoe.com/fr/dossier/67html.

Stark family

The Stark family of Antwerp, Belgium, consisted of Anna and Paul and their two children, Edith (b. 1931) and Henry (b. 1938). The Starks hid, both together and separately, during World War II. Henry Stark was too young to understand much of what was happening to him; he only remembered being shuffled from one safe home to another, then from one school to another. The family was reunited after the war but their suffering did not end until years later.

Henry and Edith were born in Borgerhout, a district in Antwerp, Belgium, into a middle-class Jewish family. Their father, Paul, was a diamond cutter and their mother, Anna, cared for the two children. Edith was nine and Henry only two years old when the Nazis invaded Belgium and the Stark family tried to flee to France. They were turned back at the border.

Once again in Antwerp, they, along with thousands of other Belgian Jews, became victims of German antisemitic measures: loss of possessions, homes, and jobs, and fear of being rounded up and taken to labor camps. In 1942, when the Nazis began deporting Jews to the east, Anna and Paul realized that the transports meant death. They decided to go into hiding.

The Starks were able to take Edith, then eleven years old, with them. Edith was old enough to understand what it meant to be quiet and would not give away their hiding place. But Henry was small. He was often sick and he cried a great deal. His parents found a temporary home for him with a Christian family. At first, his mother would occasionally come to visit him at night. Many years later, Henry still remembered those visits. "I could not understand why she would not take me back with her when she left," he wrote. "Later, my mother told me that it broke her heart to have to 'reject' me when I so desperately reached for her arms."

Hiding a Jewish child was dangerous and any Christian caught doing so was risking his or her own life and the lives of the family. Henry was shuffled from one home to another and as he got older, he began to understand that he had to hide whenever the doorbell rang. He remembered one place especially. Whenever they heard someone coming, he would go down into a dark cellar and hide in the coal bin until he heard a whistle indicating that it was safe to come up.

As the war years continued, shortages became more acute and Nazi vigilance in rounding up Jews posed increasing danger. Henry was returned to his parents and joined them and Edith in a new hiding place in a small town. They lived in an attic room in a house surrounded by mud flats. There was no indoor plumbing and the family used a barrel for a toilet. At night one of his parents would sneak out to empty their waste into the mud surrounding the house.

Although the owner of the house was well paid by Henry's father to keep them and provide them with food, he eventually became too frightened and new arrangements had to be made. Edith's gentile piano teacher found a place for her in a convent. Paul, Anna, and Henry were hidden with a Flemish widow. They remained there until their part of Belgium was liberated, early in 1945. But the family's ordeal was not yet over.

Henry, now seven years old, had to be sent to school. Antwerp was still being bombed, however, so the Starks settled in a small farming village near Brussels where the only facility available was a Catholic school. The priests and Brothers (monks) who taught there complained to Henry that he did not go to church on Sunday. Henry begged his father to take him so the Brothers would not be angry.

When it was finally safe to return to Antwerp, he was transferred to another Catholic School. "Here," Henry wrote, "some really antisemitic teachers would find excuses to beat me and to refer to my Jewishness." Henry's next school was a yeshivah, a Jewish school. Henry felt that the teachers in the yeshivah were disappointed with him because his family was not planning to emigrate to Israel. When he asked his father about Israel, Paul informed him that they would be going to the United States to join his sister, Regina Lasher, in Chicago.

The family arrived in Chicago in December 1948, but here again, Henry felt like an outsider. His clothes were different and his cousin made fun of him. He had to learn English in an American public school where the other students were neither sympathetic nor interested in his wartime experiences. When the Starks moved to New York City, he was displaced again. This time, his parents enrolled him in an Orthodox yeshivah. He knew almost nothing about Jewish practices and was totally unfamiliar with the prayers. "I lived in terror that the teachers would call on me to recite the benedictions after lunch," he explained.

At home, the tensions caused by the individual adjustment of each family member created unbearable anxiety. Edith had violent outbursts and fought with her parents. She was also antagonistic toward her younger brother. Sometimes Henry worried that she would kill him in his sleep. Henry considered this period as even worse, in some ways, than the war years.

Despite the family's inner turmoil, the Starks did well outwardly. As a skilled diamond cutter, Paul was able to find work. Both Edith and Henry completed their educations in the United States. Henry attended the Bronx High School of Science and after graduation was accepted into City College of New York, where he studied electrical engineering and began a successful career. However, he still felt that he was "faking it." His years in hiding, and then as an outcast in many different situations caused constant insecurity. "I was terrified of becoming visible," he said.

Henry was married to Alice and they had two sons and then several grandchildren, but he almost never talked about his childhood until 1995, when he attended the Hidden Child Conference in Brussels. At that conference he met others who had lived through those times. Sharing common memories and fears, he was finally able to come to terms with his early life.

Reference

Stark, Henry. "Coming Out of Hiding." *The Hidden Child* 11, no. 1 (spring 2002): p. 15.

Starkopf family

Adam Starkopf (b. 1914) and his wife Pela were already married and living in Warsaw when the Germans invaded Poland and World War II began. They were among a small number of survivors who witnessed the unfolding of German policy in Warsaw, observing as the Nazis established a ghetto, systematically isolated all the Jews within its walls, and then began killing them. The Starkopfs were able to escape the ghetto walls and survived by posing as Polish Catholics.

Adam and Pela lived with Adam's parents, Miriam and Max Starkopf, in Warsaw, the city that housed the largest Jewish community in Poland. Only twenty-five when the war began, Adam Starkopf was immediately called into the Polish Army and, with all other eligible males, was ordered to report for duty. The German *blitzkrieg* was so sudden and effective, however, that he never arrived at the designated mustering spot. Bogged down in the flood of refugees clogging the roads, barely escaping the bombs that were falling all around him, he ended up in a small town that had been taken over by the Russian Army. A few weeks later, Adam was able to return to Warsaw, where his wife, her parents, Miriam and Aaron Miller, and his father Max were overjoyed to see him. But in those few weeks, everything had changed. Parts of the city were completely destroyed by German bombs and Adam's mother had died of heart failure.

In the early weeks of the war, with the occupation and the "War Against the Jews" just getting organized, the Starkopfs looked into moving to the Russian-occupied section of Poland. Their parents were reluctant, however, and ultimately convinced them to remain in Warsaw. Adam had worked as an office manager and chief accountant in a leather goods factory, but that business was destroyed in the bombing and he decided instead to set up a small toy business. He did well for a while and was able to help support his father and his in-laws, the Millers. Pela worked in the office of a cannery and contributed her salary as well.

Gradually, the noose tightened. Prominent Jews were arrested and others were picked up off the streets and ordered to clear rubble, shovel snow, and perform other menial jobs. Jewish businesses were confiscated, shops closed, and inventory simply removed by Nazi trucks with no compensation to the owners. When the trucks pulled up in front of the Starkopf toy store, Adam had no recourse. The family now began to sell off their furniture and other possessions in order to buy food.

Then on October 16, 1940, a full year after the war had begun, the ghetto was established in Warsaw, enclosed by brick walls and barbed wire. Rations were now closely supervised by Nazi officials and bread allowances sharply reduced. Families were forced to sneak out of the ghetto, buy food on the black market, and smuggle it back into the ghetto. This was, of course, illegal and anyone caught smuggling food was shot, even children.

Within a short time, people began dying from malnutrition, starvation, and diseases caused by lack of food and poor sanitation. Typhus was rampant. There was also a serious housing shortage as more and more Jews were deported from the nearby towns and crowded into Warsaw's ghetto. Whoever had a job working outside the ghetto walls was marched out under guard in the morning and returned under guard in the evening.

In the first year of the occupation, Adam was arrested for no apparent reason and released only because Pela was able to bribe an official. Arrested again in the winter of 1942, Pela was not successful in finding a way to release him and Adam remained in prison for many weeks, while those around him were selected at random to be killed. But when the Nazis emptied the entire prison for transfer to Treblinka, the newly established extermination camp near Warsaw, Adam Starkopf managed to escape and return home once again.

The Starkopfs knew they had to leave the ghetto or they would eventually join the other Jews who were being deported to concentration camps or extermination camps. A special incentive for Adam and Pela was their baby daughter, Jasia, born in January 1941. When she was a year and a half, with roundups of Jews ever more frequent and brutal, the Starkopfs conceived of an elaborate plan to obtain false papers, sneak out of the Warsaw ghetto, and establish themselves as Polish Christians in the countryside. Because they and the baby were all blonde, and they spoke perfect Polish with no trace of a Jewish accent, they felt they could avoid detection by both Poles and Germans.

On July 31, 1942, the plan was in place. Jasia was given a sedative by a doctor, placed inside a coffin, and brought in a wagon into the Jewish cemetery just outside the ghetto. With the help of a Jewish guard, they were smuggled over the cemetery wall into an adjacent, non-Jewish cemetery. From there, they made their way to the Aryan side and out of Warsaw. They had already arranged a place for their parents to hide and expected to return for them after they got settled, but when Adam returned to the ghetto just a few days later, it was too late. The Millers and Max Starkopf had been taken in one of the final roundups and were murdered in Treblinka.

The death of their parents was a terrible blow, but Pela and Adam were determined to survive for the sake of their daughter. Adam found a job in a lumberyard and the family rented a room in a small town an hour and a half from Warsaw by train. Although they always had to be on guard lest they give themselves away, they were able to support themselves and felt that most of the Poles accepted them. Nevertheless, the smallest remark or suspicion by a neighbor could trigger a crisis. Several times, they came under suspicion of being Jewish, but each time, either by bravado and quick thinking or by luck, they managed to neutralize the threat.

> *I want my grandchildren's generation to understand that mighty force which maintained in life so many of us who otherwise could have died or would have broken under the burden of subsisting for years as fugitives in perpetual flight and hiding: the love and devotion between husbands and wives, parents and children. We endeavored to survive not so much for our own sake as for the purpose of upholding one another.*
>
> —Adam Starkopf

The Starkopf family survived food shortages, visits by the SS, surprise round-ups by the Germans, Jasia's bout with tuberculosis, and Pela's surgery. Living near a railroad line, they often saw Jews trying to escape from the trains. Although they longed to help them, they knew that any gesture of kindness to a fugitive Jew would spell disaster for their family. Whenever Pela or Adam was in danger, they thought about their commitment to live because of their child and held back from doing anything foolhardy that might endanger their lives.

In January 1945, when the Russians finally marched back into Poland as a liberating army, the Starkopfs huddled in a shelter with all their neighbors while bombs fell all around. At one point, they doubted that they would survive this onslaught, but they did. When all was quiet the next morning, the group emerged and found that the Germans were defeated but the town had been leveled. With no home or shelter, the Starkopfs, holding Jasia between them, walked to the next town and found temporary refuge. When, a few weeks later, they learned that Lublin had been liberated, they moved into a Red Cross station there set up to accommodate homeless Jews from the camps.

Once the war was completely over, Adam and Pela wanted to emigrate to Palestine, where Adam's brother was living. With the help of a Jewish organization, they sneaked across the Polish border into Czechoslovakia and then Germany and waited for an illegal transport to Palestine. When a year had passed and they were still in a displaced-persons camp, they were given an opportunity to go to the United States and decided to accept. The family arrived in the U.S. in May 1946 and settled in Chicago. Jasia, whose name became Joanna, grew up there. Although her parents did not tell her that she was Jewish until she was almost five years old and the war was over, she was raised as a Jew in America.

Jasia/Joanna married Gary Brainin and they had two children, Ricky and Rohanna. Following her parents' example, Joanna Brainin became active in Jewish communal life. In 1981, Adam Starkopf wrote *There Is Always Time to Die*, recounting the experiences of his family during the war.

Reference

Starkopf, Adam. *There Is Always Time To Die*. Edited by Gertrude Hirschler. New York: Holocaust Library, 1981.

Steel, Judith (1938–)

Born in Berlin, Germany, Judith Koeppel Steel was caught up in World War II before she was old enough to know what was happening. Taken with her parents to Cuba by ship, they were refused entry and returned to Europe. In France, her mother and father handed her over to a children's welfare organization. They were killed but their daughter survived.

Joseph and Irmgard Koeppel of Berlin felt the cruelty and deprivation of antisemitism as soon as Hitler came to power in 1933. However, they were confident that they could weather these temporary difficulties and in 1938, Irmgard gave birth to Judith. Then, on November 9, 1938, they experienced

Kristallnacht (The Night of Broken Glass), a government-sanctioned pogrom that occurred simultaneously throughout Germany and Austria. When it was over, the Koeppels realized it was time to leave Germany.

It was not easy to find a country that was willing to take in Jewish refugees, but the Koeppels persisted, and found that Cuba was offering visas for $500 each. From there, they reasoned, they could try to reach America. They purchased visas and steamship tickets on a ship called the *SS St. Louis* and after fourteen days, arrived in Cuba. But now they found that their visas were not valid unless they had been purchased before May 6. Most of the 400 passengers were not allowed to disembark.

Captain Schroeder, the German captain of the *SS St. Louis*, tried to help the refugees, all fleeing from Germany. He began to telegraph to other countries seeking asylum for his passengers, but no one was willing to open their doors. He sailed his ship along the coast of Florida and appealed to the U.S. government to take in at least some of the people. There were stories in the American papers about the *SS St. Louis*, designed to elicit sympathy for the homeless refugees, but the president, Franklin Delano Roosevelt, refused the appeal. The United States was still suffering from a serious depression and there were not enough jobs, he said.

The *SS St. Louis* with all its passengers now sailed back toward Europe. While on their way, they heard that four European countries—England, Belgium, Holland, and France—had each agreed to take in one quarter of the refugees.

The Koeppels, with Judith still an infant, disembarked in Belgium and were sent to France. Just a short time later, September 1939, World War II broke out. Less than a year after that, Germany invaded France. The Koeppels, back under the hated Nazi dictatorship, managed to hide in the unoccupied zone of France with the Enard family. They lived there for more than two years with their young daughter and her grandfather. Steel's earliest memories are from the Enard home, of Mrs. Enard, whom she called "Mama Suzi," and the Enard's daughter, Elita.

Steel was four when the French police brought them to Gurs, in the south of France. Steel's grandfather was too sick to move. He lay in bed and wept as she said goodbye to him. Then the police took the Koeppels away and brought them to Gurs, a holding camp near the Pyrenees Mountains.

Joseph and Irmgard knew that it was only a matter of time before they would be deported from Gurs and sent to a concentration camp in the east. They made the difficult decision to save their daughter's life by handing her over to the French branch of the Jewish relief organization, Oeuvres de Secours aux Enfants (OSE).

Steel can still remember walking across the mud of the camp with her

> *[At Gurs] My mother was bouncing me on her knee, and we were having a wonderful time. And then, all of a sudden, she stopped bouncing me, and to this day I cannot forget the look in her eyes. She looked at me and she said, in German, something like "Judy, you may never see Mommy and Daddy again." And she said she just wished for me to grow up and be happy and have a good life. I didn't, of course, want to believe it. I just threw my arms around her and said: "Mommy, Mommy, don't be silly. Nothing's going to happen."*
>
> —Judith Steel, remembering her last words to her mother when she was four years old.

father. Suddenly he let go of her hand and a strange man took her, along with many other children, and brought her to a small room. The youngsters, separated from their parents with little or no warning, were all screaming. Finally, they fell asleep. The next morning, all the children were brought to Christian homes.

By prearrangement with the Koeppels, Steel was taken back to the Enard family, where her ailing grandfather was still living. She was treated well and taken to church regularly, but only for her own protection. The Enards never discussed religion with her nor suggested that she convert.

Steel remained safe with the Enards throughout the rest of the war. In 1943, her grandfather died of natural causes. In 1946, Steel was sent to New York to live with an uncle and aunt, one of sixty-eight Jewish war orphans that sailed on the *SS Athos II*. She was not quite eight years old and was raised like an American child. Later, she was told that her parents had been murdered in Auschwitz.

Steel grew up when folk music was popular in the United States and learned to sing and play the guitar. When she was older she wrote a song honoring her birth parents and went to Auschwitz to play it for them. "Most people have graveyards where they can go and be near their parents," she explained to an interviewer, "I have Auschwitz." Steel saw her song as a kind of prayer, a way of saying *Kaddish* (the Jewish prayer for the dead). She has few memories of her parents and almost nothing from those war years except for her photo identification and her ration card. Those items were the only remnants she had of her past life and her birth parents.

As of 2006, Steel was living in Queens, a borough of New York City, and serving as a cantor in her local synagogue. She was also a professional Reiki Master, an ancient method of healing by transferring positive energy. A few years before, she had donated her photo ID and her ration card to the Museum of Jewish Heritage in New York as part of an exhibit of wartime artifacts.

References

Appel, Allan. "Gerald Granston and Judith Steel: The Voyage of the *S.S. St. Louis*." In *To Life: 36 Stories of Memory and Hope*. New York: Bulfinch Press, 2002.

Ogilvie, Sarah A., and Scott Miller. *Refuge Denied: The* St. Louis *Passengers and the Holocaust*. Madison: University of Wisconsin Press, 2006.

Steinberger family

The Steinbergers, parents and five children, lived in Germany, but had their roots in Hungary. Although they suffered many hardships during World War II, their Hungarian passports helped save them from some of the worst excesses of the war.

Solomon Steinberger was a rabbi and cantor. Born in Hungary, he and his wife Regina Sicherman moved to Frankfort-am-Main, where there was an important German-Jewish community. Within a few years their family began expanding. Ruth, the oldest daughter, was born in 1911, Judith in 1913. Their only son Walter was born in 1915; then came Inez (b. 1916) and Brigitte (b. 1919). Rabbi Steinberger served as a cantor in a synagogue in Frankfort-am-Main and the children went to a Jewish school.

The Steinberger family at Walter's bar mitzvah in Germany. Courtesy of Inez Lewin.

Four of the five Steinberger children had already completed their schooling when Hitler came to power in Germany in 1933. Within the next few years, Judith and Ruth went to Hungary, where their grandfather, Aryeh Steinberger, still lived along with the Hungarian branch of the family. They both married and remained there. As the situation deteriorated in Germany, Walter also joined them in Hungary.

Inez had just completed her schooling in 1933 and got her first job as secretary in a Jewish company. Before long, however, her boss was forced to sell his business. He continued to employ Inez and ran the Belgian branch of his company for a while but the Jews were under continuing pressure. With the Nuremberg laws, they were increasingly shut out of Germany's political, cultural, and economic life.

On November 9, 1938, *Kristallnacht* (The Night of Broken Glass) occurred. It was a nationwide pogrom that marked a crucial change in the status of the Jews in Germany and Austria. That night, the beautiful Israelitische Religionsgesellschaft Synagogue in Frankfort-am Main was burned down and Solomon Steinberger was taken to the police station. But Steinberger had his Hungarian passport and it protected him from arrest by the Gestapo. Hundreds of German Jews were sent off to concentration camps, but because Hungary was officially an ally of Germany, he was allowed to return home. Their Hungarian papers also served to protect Regina and her daughters. Confronted by Nazi hooligans who wanted to destroy their home, the women showed their passports. "We are Hungarian" was enough to call off the destruction.

After the horrors of that night, many Jews searched for other countries that might agree to take them in. Regina Steinberger wrote to her cousin, Solomon Schoenfeld, a rabbi in London, asking for his help. Rabbi Schoenfeld was among those in charge of the *Kindertransport*, an organization set up to rescue Jewish children from Germany and other countries threatened by war, and bring them to England. He also had the names of Jewish families who were willing to sponsor a refugee and he was able to send two visas with sponsorship for Solomon and Regina Steinberger. But there were none for the two remaining children, Inez and Brigitte. Rabbi Steinberger went to the British Embassy to plead for two more visas for his daughters and, grudgingly, they were granted.

The four Steinbergers arrived in London in February 1939. They were destitute and spoke no English. Because Solomon and Regina had sponsorship, they were given a tiny room to live in and ration cards to purchase food, but Inez and Brigitte, now twenty-three and twenty years old, stayed in a hostel with children from the *Kindertransport* who had not been taken in by a family. They had no ration cards assigned to them and could not buy food. Their parents shared their rations with them and the result was that everyone was hungry. Inez later told an interviewer that she remembered having to walk a half-mile to their parents' room every morning to get something to eat. She was often so hungry that she could hardly stand.

When war broke out between Germany and Poland, England entered the fight on the side of Poland and the situation changed a little. Young men were drafted and the refugees were now permitted to work. Both Steinberger daughters found jobs in clothing factories and their father, Solomon, made a meager living selling Hebrew books that were sent to him from his family in Hungary. The four Steinbergers now lived together and began to adjust to the new country. Within a few months, Inez, with the help of a refugee organization, was able to go to school to learn secretarial skills and English and found a better job.

But Britain was not untouched by the war. By 1940, the nightly bombing of London by German warplanes, referred to as the Blitz, destroyed the city and killed many people. The Steinbergers had several narrow escapes. One night, while they were in the shelter in a nearby underground station, the house right next to theirs was bombed and destroyed. There was a general blackout in the city every night, and Inez and Brigitte had to make their way home from work in complete darkness. It was frightening and dangerous, but they always got home safely.

By 1942, Inez had met and married Daniel Lewin, an ordained rabbi originally from Berlin. He had come to England in 1937 and had studied at Jews College in London. The couple married in the midst of the Blitz, and while Rabbi Schoenfeld performed the wedding ceremony the bombs were falling around them.

Shortly after the Lewins married, Rabbi Lewin was offered a position with a small refugee community in Welwyn Garden City. It was outside of London and gave the couple a short respite from war. This job did not last long, however, and soon they were back in London and Rabbi Lewin was serving at the Clapton Synagogue, where he remained for over two years.

By 1944, when Brigitte married Joseph Bondi, also a refugee from Germany, the three older Steinberger children, Ruth, Judith, and Walter, were still in Hungary. With Germany retreating and Hungary considering a break with their German allies to make a separate peace with Russia, they thought the war would bypass them. However, the Germans invaded Hungary in March 1944 and began rounding up the Jews.

Walter had already received a notice calling him to the Hungarian Labor Brigades, special army units where Jewish men worked for the German and Hungarian Armies. Rather than allow himself to be drafted, he escaped by plane to Palestine and remained there for a while. Life was difficult in those early days, however, and with no work, Walter was forced to emigrate to Iran, where he became a translator for the post office. He stayed in Iran until the Shah was overthrown.

By spring of 1944, Ruth and Judith and their respective families were now the only Steinbergers who were in danger from Hitler's Army. Ruth was actually picked up in a roundup and taken to the train station for transport to Auschwitz. When her husband found out, he immediately went to her rescue. He bought a bottle of whiskey and offered it to the guard on duty. After the guard became drunk, Ruth's escape could pass unnoticed. The couple now sought refuge in a safe house run by the Swiss Embassy and survived the war. Judith, her husband, and two daughters aged two and six were also caught in a roundup. With no one to rescue them, they were pushed onto trains, taken to Auschwitz-Birkenau, and gassed. Other cousins were also killed that year, although some survived. The Steinbergers' grandfather Aryeh, died peacefully before the horrors of war came to Hungary. He was eighty-two.

When World War II was finally over in May 1945, Inez and Brigitte were settled in England and thinking about starting their families. Brigitte and Joseph Bondi chose to stay, but Inez and Daniel Lewin worried about the possibility of a third world war. They emigrated to Montreal, Canada, with one daughter, Eva, born in 1945. Four years later, Judy was born, named after the sister who had been murdered in Hungary.

By 1951, Inez sent her older sister a visa and Ruth, her husband, and five-year-old son joined the Lewins in Montreal. Only five years later, Hungary rebelled against Soviet rule, and for a short time Hungary's borders were opened up to the rest of the world. At that time, many of the Steinberger cousins escaped. They brought with them the precious *sukkah* canvas, a painting executed by their great-grandfather, Aryeh Steinberger, designed especially to decorate the family *sukkah* (a special hut required for the celebration of *Sukkot*, a Jewish harvest holiday). That canvas now hangs in the Museum of Jewish Heritage in New York City.

Inez Steinberg Lewin also came to New York. Her two daughters, Eva and Judy, had already left Montreal to attend college in New York City and remained there. When Daniel Lewin died in 1997, Inez came down to live near her daughters. She celebrated her ninetieth birthday in 2006.

Solomon and Regina Steinberger had died in England many years before. All Inez's other siblings had passed away except for Brigitte, who was still living in London, but she had seven grandchildren and eleven great-grandchildren who continued to visit.

References

Appel, Allen. *To Life: 36 Stories of Memory and Hope*. New York: Bulfinch Press, 2002.
Steinberger Lewin, Inez. Interview by the author, July 2006, Great Neck, New York.

Steiner, Ania (1922–), and Joseph Steiner (1934–)

Ania and her brother Joseph had the chance to leave their native Warsaw at the very beginning of World War II. Their mother, however, believing that the war would be over in a few months, did not want to abandon their home. When she realized her mistake, it was too late. She and one of her daughters were killed by the Nazis. Ania and her little brother Joseph had to spend three years in hiding.

Steiner's father had been so concerned of the dangers posed by the Nazis that he fled to Vilna as soon as the Germans took over Poland. Vilna was not yet occupied and was still safe. He arranged a place for his wife and family, his daughters Ania and Nusia, and his son Joseph. He even sent a car and driver to take them, but Steiner's wife refused to leave her beautiful home. She kept the children with her in Warsaw and their neighbors took their places in the car. The neighbors ended up in Australia and the Steiners lost their home.

By 1941, all 700,000 Jews in the city of Warsaw had to move into a designated area that was soon walled in and guarded. Within a year, the majority of those Jews had been deported, most to Treblinka and death. Children of five and under had almost all been rounded up and sent to the gas chambers, but Joseph was saved from that transport.

The Steiner children and their mother hid with a small group of Jews in a warehouse where rugs were collected and stored. Because the warehouse was so large, the Nazi soldiers who came to find Jews did not always discover those in hiding. There were many places to hide in the warehouse, but it was a filthy place. Joseph, now seven years old, was dirty and covered with lice. Just before Yom Kippur (the Jewish Day of Atonement) in a lull between round-ups, their mother suggested that Ania take her little brother for a bath.

Ania agreed to go and the two, along with two of Ania's friends, snuck into one of the vacated apartments in the ghetto, boiled water, bathed, and then went to sleep. They planned to wake up before it was light and return to their hiding place in the warehouse. But the young people slept too late. When they awoke, it was light, and they had to wait until dark to return. That day, hiding in the abandoned apartment, they heard the German and Polish police going by and Joseph wondered who they would find to arrest. Ania went to see and came back to report that their mother and middle sister Nusia had been taken.

Ania and Joseph were alone but were taken in by the family of Ania's fiancé, Wladek, who had run away to join the Russian army. They were able to spend the winter of 1942–1943 together. When spring came, there were reports that the Nazis would liquidate the entire ghetto and Wladeck's brother Ted found a place for them to hide. They left during the night, filing out through a small break in the fence. It was only hours before the first shots were fired and the Warsaw ghetto uprising began.

Their hiding place on the Aryan side was good only for a few days, then they had to find another. Being outside during the day was always dangerous, and, if they had to move, Ania, who was dark-haired and looked Jewish, always wore a black veil to cover her head and face so others would think she was in mourning. Joseph was blonde and could pass more easily. Even so, when they went from one hiding place to another, they never walked together. Joseph followed ten yards behind; if she was taken he would be spared.

Over the next three years, Ania and Joseph hid in twenty-two different places. Many of their rescuers were members of the Polish Resistance, and sometimes they used Joseph to deliver messages for them. The Steiner children had many narrow escapes. Their final hiding place was in the suburbs of Warsaw with a young Polish couple. They were able to remain there from the winter of 1943 until August 1944, when they were liberated by the Russians.

After the war ended in Warsaw, Ania tried her best to track down her fiancé, Wladeck. Finally, his father confessed that Wladeck had died—killed on his way east to Russia. He had not wanted to tell Ania that sad news until the war was over. Now she knew that both her parents and her fiancé were gone.

After May 1945, when the war was over in the west, Ania married someone else. With Joseph, they went to a displaced-persons camp in Germany to register for visas to America.

Joseph was only eleven years old in 1945, but was already involved in the black market "peddling, stealing, selling like everyone else." In 1948 at the age of fourteen, he came to the United States with his sister and her husband, attended high school, and graduated with honors in math. Then he went on to City College (CUNY) at night while working days. In the 1950s, Joseph joined the army and was sent back to Berlin as part of a military intelligence detachment. After his army service, he finished college, married, and had a son, divorced, and remarried. He and his second wife have an adopted daughter. Although he became a successful sales manager for a printing company, Steiner always felt as if he was looking for another hiding place. He was never secure; never felt as if he belonged. Even after his children were grown, he continued to have bad dreams in which he was always the outsider, the observer.

Joseph's sister Ania also raised a family in the United States. In 1949, their father, who had traveled east from Vilna, through Russia, and had survived the war in a Japanese concentration camp, arrived in America. Only their mother and sister had been killed.

Reference

Marks, Jane. *Hidden Children: The Secret Survivors of the Holocaust.* New York: Fawcett Columbine, 1993.

Stern, Frieda (1913-), and Edward Stern

Two of the lucky minority of people who were able to escape from Germany before World War II began, Frieda Mayer Stern and Edward Stern were driven from one place to another. They finally found temporary safety in Africa, but not until long after the war was over were the Sterns able to build a home and begin to feel secure.

Frieda Mayer Stern, the youngest of three children, was six years old when her father died of tuberculosis. From that time on, the education of the Mayer children was the responsibility of their wealthy grandfather who sent them off to Jewish boarding schools. During their time away, their mother remarried and Frieda, now thirteen years old, left school and rejoined the family. In her mother and stepfather's house, there were no Jewish traditions practiced; German culture was their high priority. Frieda worked from the age of fourteen to pay for her room and board at home and continued her education at night.

In 1933, the same year that Hitler took power in Germany, the family moved to Berlin but within a short time Frieda decided to live on her own. She found a room in the home of a Jewish woman in a small town near Heidelberg, and took care of the woman's son in exchange for room and board. That spring, the Nazis initiated the first boycott of Jewish stores. Those who refused to boycott and entered the stores were beaten and put on a special list. Young and unafraid, Frieda tried to enter one of the boycotted establishments and was struck by a policeman. Later, she was summoned to Nazi headquarters and again stood up to the officials. "Look," she told her interrogator, "my family is here for four hundred years. I'm just as German as you are." The officer's answer was, "Leave Germany as soon as possible."

Frieda understood that her individual defiance was no match for German policy. She was already aware that even in her little town, the Nazis had come in search of Jews. They would enter Jewish homes at 2:00 or 3:00 a.m., when everyone was sleeping and off guard, either killing the people or taking them away to concentration camps. But when she spoke to her stepfather about leaving Germany, he refused to consider it. "It will pass," he insisted. "Germany is a civilized country." Before the war was over, he and Stern's mother were killed.

At the age of nineteen, Frieda felt too young to travel all alone. Denied financial help from her stepfather, she found a Jewish family who also wanted to leave Germany. They hired her to care for their daughter and an expected new baby in exchange for room and board. The Wolner family needed to emigrate to a country that would accept them and where Dr. Wolner, a physician, would be able to practice. After many months, they were granted visas to Portugal and left for Lisbon in September 1933. Frieda came as their nanny.

Frieda lived in Lisbon with the Wolners for one and a half years. As the nanny to their two children, she received no pay and began to feel more and more dissatisfied. She turned to the small Jewish community in Lisbon, and with their help, found a room and set up a tutoring service, teaching German. She made a meager living but became fluent in Portuguese. She even made a few friends in her new environment. Nevertheless she felt alone and vulnerable.

At the end of 1938, after *Kristallnacht* (the Night of Broken Glass) and the realization that no Jew would be spared from the brutal, antisemitic policies of the Nazi regime, Lisbon became crowded with Jewish immigrants. One of those was Edward Stern, originally from Hungary. It was in Lisbon, at one of the soup kitchens set up by the Portuguese, in conjunction with the Jewish community, that Ed Stern met his future wife, Frieda Mayer.

As a fairly long-time resident who now knew the language, Frieda was in a position to help others. She was generous with her time, and later explained to an interviewer that although Portugal was ostensibly neutral, it was ruled by a Fascist dictator who was somewhat sympathetic toward Germany. Once the war began in September 1939, whenever Germany won a battle, the Portuguese police would be ordered to round up Jewish refugees and put them in jail. They would be released only if they promised to leave the country. Frieda often found herself in the position of intervening with the police to obtain the release of these prisoners. One day, she heard that Ed Stern had been arrested. Already "terribly in love with him," she rushed to the police station to help. By the time she got there, Ed had been transferred to another prison and was scheduled for deportation. Somehow, she charmed the police and managed to convince them to let him go. She knew, however, that he would have to leave the country and that she would go with him.

After being refused by many countries, Ed and Frieda heard that the Chinese embassy was granting visas to Shanghai and they made the necessary arrangements. With a visa in hand, refugees could buy a steamship ticket anywhere, with the understanding that they were on their way to a final destination that had agreed to accept them. Ed and Frieda, not yet married, sailed on a Dutch ship out of Portugal bound first to the Dutch West Indies and then to Mozambique, a Portuguese colony off the coast of Africa. With a transit visa, they were permitted to stay there temporarily.

In Mozambique, they met a Jewish businessman who helped them. Assuring the officials on their behalf that they would be leaving shortly for Shanghai, the man found an apartment for them. They hoped to wait out the war, but were soon arrested by the police and told that they would have to leave. Again their friend intervened, promising the Portuguese officials that their steamship tickets were due to arrive soon from South Africa.

During all these travels, Ed and Frieda were still not married. They decided that now was a good time and, with the help of the Portuguese consul, they were married in a civil ceremony. Almost immediately afterward, Ed Stern was ordered to leave the country. This time, it was Frieda who intervened for her husband. She requested an appointment with the Portuguese Governor of Mozambique and, in fluent Portuguese, explained to him what was happening in Europe and about the persecution and murder of the Jews. The Governor had known nothing about the events that sent the Sterns half way around the world. When she finished her explanation, he had changed his mind. The Sterns could stay as long as they wanted.

Granted temporary asylum, Frieda and Ed Stern started a small business repairing and making stockings. They supplemented their income by renting rooms in their apartment and helped other Jewish refugees coming through the port. After three and a half years in Mozambique, they had become part of a tiny Jewish community of about one hundred people, all of whom had found refuge there from World War II. They remained until 1944. Then, with the war winding down, they obtained British visas to go to Palestine as part of the South African quota.

The journey from Mozambique to Tel Aviv took thirty days. They sailed on a Greek freighter to Suez where they disembarked. The Jewish community then supplied them with a train ticket that took them to the border. From there, they walked across into what Frieda described as "a green garden." Finally, they felt at home. Although living conditions were difficult and they suffered from the heat and from poverty, they had found a place to live. Soon Frieda became pregnant, and their son was born a few years before Israel declared its independence.

When the War of Independence broke out between the new Jewish state and its surrounding Arab neighbors, the Sterns fled the shooting. With peace in Europe, they returned to Hungary, Ed's birthplace. Although greeted warmly by the surviving Jews who knew him, living conditions under communism were not to their liking and, with the British passports they had obtained when they first emigrated to Palestine, they were able to leave for Paris. Here, too, they were disappointed. The Jews of France had been murdered or scattered and Jewish community life had all but disappeared. After six and a half years of struggle, they obtained visas to the United States, settling in San Antonio, Texas, in 1955. Their son had his bar mitzvah in this southwestern city and the Sterns, after years of wandering from one continent to another, had found a safe haven where they could feel free.

Reference

Holocaust Survivors Project. William E. Wiener Oral History Library of the American Jewish Committee. #5, box 196. Interviewed by Louise Michelson, San Antonio, Texas, June 1975.

Sternberg family

Julius and Franceska Sternberg of Munkacs, Czechoslovakia, had ten children. Eight of them were able to survive World War II, in part because the Czech city in which they lived was annexed by Hungary in 1939. After the war, all the surviving siblings made their way to the United States where their family grew and prospered.

The city of Munkacs had originally been part of the Austro-Hungarian Empire. The Sternbergs lived there all their lives and their six daughters and four sons were born there. After World War I, the area around Munkacs was given to Czechoslovakia and its name changed to Munkacevo. By the time World War II began, Nazi Germany had already annexed part of Czechoslovakia and given another part to its ally, Hungary. The Czech Jews under German control were rounded up by 1941 and deported. Many of those who were not murdered outright died of starvation and disease before the war was over. But the Hungarian Jews were left alone at first. Hungary was pro-Nazi; its army was fighting with Germany so the Germans did not occupy the country until March 19, 1944, when they feared that their ally would make a separate peace with Russia.

By 1944, only the younger Sternberg children were still at home. Eugene, the oldest, was in England studying. Bill, Morris, and Marci had been conscripted by the Hungarians for forced labor, and Sari and Arenka, the oldest sisters, were married. That left Lili, Klári, Hanci, and Magda still at home.

When the Germans arrived in Munkacs, the first thing they did was to separate the Jews into a ghetto. The Sternberg family had to leave the home they had lived in all their lives and move in with relatives, taking with them only what they could carry. Once in the ghetto, they were forbidden to leave.

After only a few weeks of ghetto life, the four girls and their parents, with thousands of other Jews, were brought to a nearby brick factory to wait for a train. Their destination was unknown. Each of the girls had jewelry sewn into the hem of her skirt and tucked away in the lining of her jacket. They anticipated being able to exchange their valuables for food at some later date.

Loaded onto cattle cars and taken to Auschwitz, they tried to stay together, but as soon as the train pulled into the station their hopes were shattered. Julius and Franceska Sternberg and their oldest daughter Sári, with her little girl, were sent to one line; Lili, Klári, Hanci, and Magda were sent to another. The girls never saw their parents or sister again, and they never forgot the man who had separated them. It was the infamous Dr. Mengele, referred to by the prisoners as "the Angel of Death."

The four Sternberg sisters had been chosen for life, at least for a while. They were taken to the showers, their heads were shaved, and they were each tattooed with a number. Then they were issued new clothing and brought to a barracks where three tiers of planks were available for sleeping, ten women to each plank. Their hope of exchanging their jewelry for food was simply not a possibility; they had to undress and leave their clothing behind. It was collected by camp workers and all their possessions taken by the Germans.

The Sternberg sisters were in Auschwitz for just a few months before they were once again piled into cattle trains and taken to Tannenberg in northern Germany. By then, it was winter and the thin uniforms they wore did not protect them against the cold. When Magda, who was assigned to work outdoors, found an empty cement bag, she put it under her dress to keep her a bit warmer, but the female SS guard discovered it and beat her. In spite of this incident, however, Magda remembered Tannenberg as "an improvement over Auschwitz."

Lili Sternberg became the camp's nurse. She ran a small infirmary with Hanci as her assistant. Klári worked in the kitchen and Magda at the Krupp factory, breaking up stones to pave roads.

The war was coming to an end, however. Locked in their barracks at night, the girls could hear the Allied planes overhead, and bombs falling around them. The Nazi guards told them they would all be killed before the war was over but that did not happen. Instead, the SS guards and their dogs ran away one night and with the camp unattended, the Sternberg sisters escaped together. When they saw American soldiers, they knew they were free. It was April 15, 1945, barely one year since they had been rounded up by the Nazis.

The sisters remained in Germany for another year. During that time, Lili and Hanci found jobs with the United Nations Relief and Rehabilitation Administration (UNRRA). Klári became a social worker with the British Red Cross, and Magda worked for the British Red Cross as an interpreter. They never found any trace of their older sisters, Aranka and Sari, but they did have news of their brothers. Eugene was safe in England where he had been studying at

Cambridge. The forced labor brigade in which their three other brothers were working had been captured by the Russians. When the war was over, Bill, Morris, and Marci were released. The young men returned to Munkacs, now occupied by the Soviet Union, and found other people living in their home. They refused to return any of the Sternbergs' possessions except for the family's photos. The brothers left for Prague.

One by one, each of the surviving Sternberg siblings married and made his or her way to the United States. Magda came on an art scholarship and married in New York City. Klári remained in England and Lili in Belgium but they, too, eventually came to America with their families. In 2004, five of the Sternberg siblings were still alive and enjoying a large, extended family of grandchildren, nieces and nephews.

Reference

Bader, Magda. "Facing Mengele." In *Children Who Survived the Final Solution*. Edited by Peter Tarjan. New York: iUniverse, 2004.

Stock, Miriam (1929–)

Miriam Blass Stock of Pabianice, Poland, was one of five siblings. She lived through several bombings, near-starvation in the ghetto, and then three concentration camps. When she was liberated in May 1945, she learned that she was the only survivor from her entire family.

Stock was the oldest of the children of Itzhak and Hannah Zisler Blass. Enjoying a life of privilege, the Blass family lived in Pabianice, a small town in Poland outside the city of Lodz where Stock's father owned and ran a silk mill. Stock had a governess and the family even owned a telephone, a rarity in Poland before World War II. Although the family had Hasidic roots, the Blass children went to a state-run school just for Jews that taught secular and Jewish subjects and was closed on Saturdays. But on September 1, 1939, when German planes attacked Poland, school did not open and Stock never attended school again.

When the bombs began to fall, the entire population of Pabianice left to make their way to Warsaw. Warsaw would not fall, they believed; it would remain a safe city. Walking along the road, the German planes flew so low that the refugees could see the faces of the pilots and watch them shooting. By the time they arrived in Lodz, however, news came that Warsaw had fallen to the Nazis and everyone returned to Pabianice and waited.

Within months, the Blass family, along with many others, was evicted from their apartment and went to live in Lodz with their grandfather. In Lodz, conditions quickly deteriorated. Food shortages were acute and a 5:00 p.m. curfew prevented anyone from going out at night to find additional supplies. The youngest Blass child was only three and cried constantly, demanding bread, but no one had any to give him. Hannah Blass, pregnant with their fifth child, became increasingly weaker.

When the German officers came to count them, the family expected that they would soon be killed. Instead, they were taken the following day to the ghetto. There, they managed to find one room for their family of six, their grandparents, and a few others—ten people in all. Stock remembered that her mother gave birth to a baby boy, her fifth child, in that same room. She also remembered that he died from starvation within months, and shortly after, Hannah Blass also died. She had sustained a vicious beating by Nazi soldiers when she went out to search for milk for her infant son and never recovered.

Deportations began almost immediately after the ghetto was established, but Stock and her family were not picked up until August 1944. The journey to Auschwitz in cattle cars was "indescribable," Stock told an interviewer more than sixty years later. "There were 150 people, all standing in one freight car. Half were already dead when the train arrived at Auschwitz."

At fifteen, Stock was fit to work. Her younger siblings were not. They were sent immediately to their deaths and, she heard only later, were buried alive because the gas chambers and the crematoria at the camp were overloaded with bodies. Itzhak Blass was transferred to Buchenwald and died there.

In addition to being a death camp, Auschwitz was also a holding camp where people waited to be assigned to other camps or factories. A month after her arrival, Stock was transported to Bergen-Belsen, but there was no work there either, only more hunger and more beatings by the guards. Within a short time, there was another prisoner transfer; this time, Stock was taken to Magdeburg, a camp near Hanover. But the Germans were in retreat and rather than release their prisoners, they kept moving them away from the armies that were closing in on both sides. The prisoners at Magdeburg began a forced march to the Tyrol, a section in Austria, but they never reached there. On their arrival in Berlin, they were liberated by Russian troops. It was May 8, 1945.

From Berlin, Stock walked back to Poland, sleeping on the streets and finding food wherever she could. After several weeks, she arrived at Lodz and went to the Jewish Committee to try and find her family. They had all been murdered. Only one uncle, Barish Adler, had survived. He was living in eastern Poland when the war broke out and he and his family had been deported to Siberia by the Russians. Siberia saved their lives.

Stock and the Adler family found each other in Munich, Germany, and she and her cousin, Ari Adler, were married in Paris. From France, they continued on to Haifa, the port city in what was then still Palestine. Barish Adler was head of the Committee to Rescue Jewish Youth and had close ties with the Jewish community in Palestine. In 1947, the entire family, some with legitimate papers, others with false ones, immigrated and settled in Jerusalem.

Miriam and Ari Adler had two daughters, Naomi and Hava. They remained there even after Barish Adler moved to the United States and opened a business there. When Barish died in 1961, his son Ari came to New York to take over the business and the family resettled in Forest Hills, New York. In the United States, Miriam gave birth to two more children, Leora and Benny.

In addition to caring for her children and her home, Stock continued with her education and helped her husband in the business. Adler died in 1995 and by then, her children were grown and married. Three years later, she met and married Mark Stock, also a Holocaust survivor from Poland. By 2006, Miriam Stock had eighteen grandchildren. She and her new husband divide their time between a home in Brooklyn and another in Miami Beach.

Reference

Stock, Miriam Blass Adler. Interview by the author, February 2006, Miami Beach, Florida.

Stolowitzky, Michael (1936–), and Gertruda Babilinska (1901–1995)

Michael (Micki) Stolowitzky, born in Warsaw, was a toddler when World War II began. He survived the war in hiding with his Polish Catholic governess, Gertruda Babilinska. Babilinska had made a promise to Michael's mother before she died and kept her promise in the face of constant danger, bringing her charge to Israel and raising him there as a Jew.

Stolowitzky's parents, Yaakov and Lidia Stolowitzky of Warsaw, were ardent Zionists, always hoping that one day they would be able to go to an independent Jewish state. They were also among the richest people in Poland; they had servants and a chauffeur. When their son was born, they hired a young woman, Gertruda Babilinska, a devout Catholic, as his governess to care for him and as he got older, to educate him.

In September 1939, when Warsaw was bombed by the Germans at the outbreak of the war, Michael's father was in Paris and was unable to return. With thousands of other residents of Warsaw, both Jews and non-Jews, Lidia Stolowitzky decided to flee the war by going east to Vilna, then occupied by the Russians. She took her son and his governess with her, along with a considerable amount of luggage and valuables. On the way, the chauffeur stopped the car and refused to go on unless Lidia Stolowitzky gave him all her money and jewelry. Overcome with despair over this turn of events, Stolowitzky wept in the back seat of the car while Babilinska took over, negotiating with the chauffeur. "They are good people," she told him. The driver agreed to take only some of the jewelry and the car, after bringing them to Vilna.

Once in Vilna, it was Babilinska who took care of everything. She stood in line to obtain food, found them a place to live, negotiated their money, and cared for little Micki, whom she had grown to love. When the Germans attacked Vilna in 1941, Lidia had a stroke. She was cared for by Dr. Weinstock and his family, neighbors who had become good friends, but ultimately, the doctor could do nothing to help her. As Lidia lay dying, she begged Babilinska to protect her son as her own. The young governess assured her that she would. Lidia's next request was, "Only swear to me that he will remain a Jew and when the war is over you will bring him to Palestine." Babilinska promised again. Lidia died, and a few days later, the Jews of Vilna were forced into a ghetto and isolated from the rest of the population.

Babilinska, with her own valid papers, left the apartment in which they had been living and, taking Micki with her, rented a room in the home of a Polish woman, explaining that her husband was a German prisoner of war and that Micki was her son. She instructed the child, then only five years old, that he must forget his past and must call her *mamusha,* the Polish term for "mama." From now on, she was his *mamusha.* His real mother was still his "mama" but he must never talk about her to anyone.

Stolowitzky now lived as a Christian child. Babilinska took him with her to church every Sunday, while always reminding him that he was a Jew—but it must be a secret, she insisted. He went to school with the other Christian children. His *mamusha* began to work as a translator, translating German documents into Polish for her Polish neighbors, and made some money to support them. They lost sight of the Jews, who were now living behind the walls of the ghetto.

One night, Babilinska saw Aaron Weinstock, the son of their friend, Dr. Weinstock. His clothes were in rags and he looked starved. He had snuck out of the ghetto to find some food for his family. Babilinska offered to help, and from that time on, she regularly smuggled small amounts of food to the Weinstocks, hiding it in a hole in the ghetto wall every few days. The Weinstocks were extremely grateful for this help and were soon in a position to help her in return. When Stolowitzky became ill with scarlet fever, Babilinska was afraid to summon a Christian doctor, because he would then see that her child was circumcised. Instead, she sneaked into the ghetto and summoned Dr. Weinstock. He assured her that the child would survive.

Stolowitzky did survive, but the Weinstocks did not. They were taken by the Nazis into Ponary Woods, just outside Vilna, and shot to death with thousands of other Jews from the Vilna ghetto. Their son Aaron, an organizer of the Vilna ghetto uprising, was also killed by the Nazis.

With the ghetto liquidated and the Germans making an all-out search for Jews across the city, Babilinska was frantic, fearing that her foster son would be discovered. She went to her priest for advice and confessed her secret. The priest assured her that he would not betray her. He took Stolowitzky and baptized him, then made him an altar boy in the church. It was a perfect cover for a Jewish boy.

When the Russians returned to Vilna on July 13, 1944, Babilinska took Stolowitzky to the forest and they hid. Only after the Germans had fled and were completely out of the area did they come out of hiding. Now they began to find out what had happened to the Jews who had disappeared. Most had been slaughtered outside the town or had been killed in concentration camps. It was not until Stolowitzky was an adult that he discovered that after the Nazi invasion of France in 1940, his father had fled to Italy. Just weeks before the war ended in the east, he was caught by the Germans and sent to Auschwitz where he was murdered in the gas chambers.

Three years after their liberation, Babilinska was in a position to fulfill the rest of her promise to Stolowitzky's mother. In 1947, she and her foster son boarded the SS *Exodus* and attempted to reach Palestine, still under British rule. They were caught and the ship with all its passengers was returned to Germany. The following year, they tried once again, this time posing as tourists and booking passage on a luxury liner. When the ship docked in Haifa, they disappeared and remained there. Israel announced its independence two months later.

In Israel, Stolowitzky was raised as a Jewish boy. Gertruda Babilinska remained a devout Catholic. She never married and lived the rest of her life in Israel. Although her family in Poland urged her to return, she was too attached to her foster son to leave him. For his part, Stolowitzky loved his *mamusha* and considered her his mother. Even after he emigrated to the United States, he visited her regularly. In 1963, she was honored by Yad Vashem as a right-eous gentile and a tree was planted in Jerusalem in her honor. She died in

Michael Stolowitzky on the occasion of his foster mother Gertruda Babalinska's 90th birthday. Courtesy of Michael Stolowitzky.

1995 at the age of ninety-four and is buried in a cemetery in Tel Aviv, in a special section dedicated to righteous gentiles.

When Stolowitzky was eighteen, he served in the Israeli Navy, then studied at Tel Aviv University, earning a degree in tourism and working in the tourist industry. He came to the United States as Director of International Business Development for American Express. As of 2005, he was President of the American Tourist Society and consultant for American Express Vacations. Stolowitzky was married in Israel and had a son. He later divorced and remarried in the United States, maintaining residences in New York City and in Miami and regularly visiting Israel to see his son and his three grandchildren.

References

Stolowitzky, Michael. Telephone interview by the author, April 2006, Miami, Florida.
Rescuers: Stories of Courage. Produced by Barbra Streisand. Directed by Peter Bogdanovich. 106 min. 1997. Videocassette.

Strauss, Jacques (1935–), and Margot Kaiser (née Strauss) (1931–), and Sara (Nicole) Béar (1915–)

Born in Wurtzburg, Germany, Margot Strauss and her brother Jacques were separated from their parents at the beginning of World War II. They spent the war years being shifted from one family to another, one orphanage to another. But one woman kept appearing in their lives and ultimately saved them by her love.

Margot and Jacques's parents, Josef and Alice Strauss, left Germany with their children in 1936 in order to avoid Josef's imprisonment in Dachau concentration camp. Because he had once served in the French Foreign Legion, he was eligible for a visa to France. There, he studied kosher cooking and was hired as a chef on several French ocean liners. Two years later, his family joined him in France. But in 1940, France fell to the German Army and Alice Strauss was asked to serve as an interpreter for the Nazis. Although reluctant to do so, she had no choice.

Within a few months, the Germans accused her of spying for the British and while Josef was at sea, they took Alice Strauss and her children to an internment camp in Besançon in eastern France. Two months later they were taken to another camp in Tonnerre. There, Josef found his family and arranged for their transfer to Sens where they lived together in town.

As long as they remained with their parents, Jacques and Margot felt secure no matter what their living conditions were, but when the Nazis arrested Alice and Josef, the children, aged eleven and seven, were suddenly on their own. Not knowing what to do with them, the town police sent them to a hospital. From there, they were transferred to an orphanage, and shortly after to a Jewish children's home in Paris.

At this facility, they met a woman named Sara Béar, a young Turkish Jew in her twenties. She was a volunteer who came to the orphanage weekly to take Margot and Jacques for an outing since they had no relatives of their own like most of the other children. One day, as they were returning from their visit to her home, they saw the Gestapo (the German police) lining up all the children and pushing them into Gestapo vans. Realizing that the children were being taken for deportation, Béar quickly retreated with Margot and Jacques and kept them in her home. When her family returned to Turkey, Béar stayed in Paris to care for the Strauss children. They lived with her, went to school, and came to regard her as their second mother.

Margot and Jacques shortly before the war. Courtesy of Jacques Strauss.

The Gestapo came to their apartment in 1942 and accused Béar of helping Jewish children. Although they did not arrest her, Béar knew it was time to make other arrangements for her charges. After consulting a priest, the children got false identity papers and were housed with a Christian family outside the city. Béar also assumed a new identity as Nicole and became active in the underground.

By spring 1943, Margot and Jacques were moved again. Margot was placed in a Catholic convent school and Jacques in a nearby school for boys run by the monks. Other Jewish children were also hidden in these institutions, and when the Nazis began to search the schools, it was once more time to leave.

This time, both Jacques and Margot were moved back to Paris. Jacques was placed in a Christian home and Margot, almost in her teens, was sent to another Catholic school. Béar joined her there, as she also was forced into hiding for a while.

At this convent school, the Mother Superior wanted to baptize Margot, but the priest who had originally helped them, stopped the baptism. He insisted, "We have been entrusted with the care of these Jewish children and we shall return them to their parents as Jews—we have no right to do otherwise."

After Easter 1944, Margot and Jacques were moved for the seventh time. Now they were together and lived with a family in Paris. As the Allied bombings became more frequent, however, the family moved into the countryside with the children. In June, they heard about the Allied landing in Normandy

Sara Nicole Béar was a young woman when she first took responsibility for the Strauss children. Courtesy of The Hidden Child Foundation and Jacques Strauss.

and by August they had been liberated. With the Germans driven out, the children were returned to Paris and reunited with Sara (Nicole) Béar.

Back in school, with Béar as their guardian, life gradually seemed more normal. When they learned that their parents had been killed in Auschwitz, it was a devastating blow, but they were able to heal, knowing that Sara Béar loved them and would care for them.

Margot remained with Béar until 1953 and Jacques until 1958. When they were grown and educated, the Strauss siblings left Paris for the United States. Both married and raised their own families. Sara Béar also married and had three children, but Margot and Jacques always kept in touch with their foster mother.

Not until much later, did Margot (now Kaiser) and Jacques learn about Béar's numerous activities in the underground: how she sheltered refugees, distributed food to those in hiding, and collected money to support thirty Jewish children in gentile homes. Arrested three times by the Gestapo and threatened with deportation or torture, she never revealed anything she knew. In an article written in 2006, Margot Strauss Kaiser claimed, "There is no doubt that it is because of Nicole . . . that my brother and I survived the war."

Sara Nicole Béar was ninety-one in 2006.

Reference

Kaiser, Margot, as told to Michelle Kelly Wiens. "Sara 'Nicole' Béar." *The Hidden Child* 14 (2006): p. 3.

Sugihara, Chiune (1900–1986)

In 1940, before Japan had become involved in World War II, Chiune Sugihara (nicknamed Sempo) was a Japanese diplomat working in Kovno, Lithuania. Using his authority as Consul General, and despite the reluctance of his own government, he issued more than two thousand transit visas to Jews, enabling them to escape death. Explaining his actions, Sugihara stated, "I cannot allow these people to die, people who had come to me for help with death staring them in the eyes."

Chiune Sugihara was born on the island of Honshu in Japan and went to a prestigious school that specialized in training experts on the Soviet Union. Because he was fluent in the Russian language, he was assigned to a diplomatic post in Kovno, and was the first Japanese minister to Lithuania.

Sugihara first became involved in this rescue operation when he was approached by Dr. **Zorah Warhaftig**, a leader of Mizrahi, the religious

Zionist movement, and now in charge of refugee programs. Warhaftig had been searching for a way to help Jews stranded in Lithuania to escape the Nazis, and his plan had already gotten tentative agreement from the Soviet Union. The refugees would travel to Curaçao, in the Dutch West Indies, a place where no visa was required. They only needed transit visas —visas allowing the travelers to pass through other countries on their way to Curaçao. The Russians had tentatively agreed to this plan, but only on condition that the Japanese would also go along. That way, the refugees could travel by train to Russia's eastern provinces and embark by ship to Japan. From there, they could continue their journey to the Dutch West Indies.

When he heard the plan, Sugihara's first responsibility was to contact his own government and obtain their approval. But Japan's reply was unclear

> On September 1, 1940 . . . Consul Chiune Sugihara led his family to the Kovno railway station. The Russians had given him until that day to leave the country, and in the two months that had passed since they had annexed Lithuania, Sugihara had seen nothing to make him question their sincerity. It wasn't far from the Japanese Consulate to the station, but the departing diplomat had left plenty of time to cover the distance. He had no doubt his path would be jammed with Jewish refugees, striving even at this final moment to have the precious transit visa stamped on their papers. He was not mistaken. Sugihara did what he could—in the street, in the station, even through the window of the train car— until the moment the train actually began to pull away from the platform. Then he collapsed into his seat, drained and exhausted. During the past nineteen days, he had stamped and signed nearly six thousand visas entitling their bearers to remain in Japan for a maximum of twenty-one days while in transit between any two countries. Whether Tokyo would honor the visas, he did not know.
>
> —Marvin Tokayer and Mary Swartz, *The Fugu Plan*, p. 80.

and they were not enthusiastic. They instructed Sugihara to be sure that all the other paper work was complete and valid, and that refugees had enough money to maintain themselves while in Japan. Unsure of how to proceed and already scheduled to leave Kovno for a new post on August 31, 1940, Sugihara decided to grant the visas. With only a few weeks left before his reassignment, he spent almost all of his time issuing the necessary documents. He ignored all cautions from his government and issued visas even to those who had no other travel papers. In doing so, he saved many Jews. Among those saved were the rabbinical students at the well-respected Mir Academy in Kovno as well as Zorah Warhaftig himself. During those hectic last few days in Lithuania, Sugihara told himself, "Whatever punishment may be imposed upon me, I know I should follow my conscience."

After his Kovno position, Sugihara was assigned to Prague in Bohemia (Czechoslovakia) and then to Bucharest, Romania, Germany's ally. He remained in Bucharest until the war was over and when the Soviet army marched in to take the city from the Germans, he was arrested with other diplomats from enemy nations. Soviet authorities held Sugihara and his wife and daughters for three years before they were returned to Japan in 1947. That year, he was asked to submit his resignation from the Foreign Ministry because of his insubordination seven years before.

Chiune Sugihara in his office in Tokyo, Japan, in 1976. Courtesy of Rabbi Marvin Tokayer.

After his retirement, Sugihara held several jobs, including one for a Japanese trading company in Moscow from 1960 to 1975. He lived quietly with his family, unrecognized for his humanitarian work. In 1986, only one year before he died, Yad Vashem, the Holocaust Martyrs' and Heroes' Remembrance Authority in Jerusalem, honored Sugihara with the title Righteous Among the Nations for his aid to the refugees in Lithuania during World War II.

References

Paldiel, Mordecai. *Encyclopedia of the Holocaust.* s.v. "Sugihara, Sempo." New York: Macmillan, 1990.

Tokayer, Marvin, and Mary Swartz. *The Fugu Plan: The Untold Story of the Japanese and the Jews during World War II.* New York: Paddington Press, 1979.

Warhaftig, Zorah. *Refugee and Survivor: Rescue Efforts during the Holocaust.* Jerusalem, 1988.

http://www.ushmm.org/wlc/article.php?lang=en&ModuleId=10005594.

Sukiennik, Hannah (née Rydelnik) (1924–2001), and Genia Saionz (née Rydelnik) (1922–)

Hannah and Genia Rydelnik were two of the six children born to Szymon and Rachel Rydelnik. The family lived first in Zagarze Poland and then in Bedzin in Silesia. By the time they were liberated in 1945, the sisters had been in five labor camps, had escaped into the woods, and were saved by a Polish policeman.

When Germany invaded Poland in 1939, Hannah Rydelnik (later Sukiennik) had already completed her studies in *heder* (Hebrew school), primary school, and *gymnasia* (high school), and had begun her first year at a lyceum (post-secondary school). Her sister Genia (later Saionz) was just two years behind Hannah but both sisters' hopes for a career ended when Jews were forbidden to attend school.

Sukiennik saw the synagogue at Bedzin being burned, confirming her worst fears. Shortly after the fire, all Jews in Bedzin had to identify themselves by wearing an armband with a Star of David. The next blow occurred in 1940, when all Jews were required to move to one designated area, the ghetto. From the ghetto, it was easy for the Nazis to round up Jews and send them off to concentration camps where they were immediately killed or literally worked to death.

Before the liquidation of the ghetto, scheduled for August 1, 1943, the Rydelnik family, like so many others, prepared a bunker and tried to hide, but they found it impossible to remain there for long. When they emerged, they joined thousands of other Jews who were taken to an assembly point where a preliminary selection was made. The young and the strong were directed to one side for transport to labor camps. The old and the very young were sent off to the death camps. Hannah and Genia were directed to go with their parents, but at the last minute, they managed to move to

Movement of Jewish Population of Bedzin
1938: 27,000
1940: 24,495
1941: 13,000 Jews moved into slave labor camps in Silesia and Greater Germany
1942: 5,000 Jews from Bedzin sent to Auschwitz

the other side, with their brothers Milton and Maury. They were transported to slave labor camps and were saved from the gas chambers.

There was a string of labor camps in Upper and Lower Silesia, a heavily industrialized area of Poland that was annexed by Germany after the invasion. Most of these camps were for men but some were for women and a few utilized both men and women. Each camp was attached to a particular factory and the Jews were used as contract labor, shipped from one camp to another as they were needed. Hannah and Genia went together to Anneberg, where they were assigned to factory jobs. They were separated from their brothers Milton and Maury, and did not see them again until after the war.

From Anneberg, Sukiennik and Saionz were transferred to several other work camps, including Freiburg and Christianstadt—five camps in all. Sukiennik was trained to be a welder and it was this job that enabled her and her sister to finally escape.

One day, the administrators at the camp turned off the electricity that ran through the barbed wire fence surrounding their camp. Because Sukiennik was a welder, she had access to tools and was able to take advantage of this small window of opportunity. With pliers she snipped enough of the barbed wire to create an opening and she, Genia, and a friend slipped through and ran into the nearby forest. The women tried to remain hidden, but with no resources, they could not stay in the forest indefinitely. In their attempts to find food, they encountered a Polish policeman who agreed to hide them from the Nazis. They stayed with him until the area was liberated by the Russian Army in February 1945. But even then, their ordeal was not over. The Russian soldiers, rarely differentiating the Germans from their victims, chased after young women and raped them whenever they could.

Sukiennik and Saionz spent the last few months before the final peace treaty (May 1945) hiding from rapists before making their way back to Bedzin to search for family. They found that only their two brothers, Milton and Maury, had survived. Their parents, two married siblings, and their families had all been murdered.

Back in Bedzin, Sukiennik met her first husband, Isadore Goodman, and in 1946, the couple married. Together, they made their way to Munich, where their first child, Louisa, was born a year later. Genia also met a survivor, Moritz Saionz, whom she married. They came to the United States, settled in Philadelphia, and raised a family.

Hannah and Isadore Goodman arrived in the United States in 1949 with their two-year-old daughter and went to St. Joseph, Missouri. But Goodman, a tailor, found it difficult to get a job, and the family moved to Kansas City, where their second child, Stan, was born.

Goodman eventually opened a tailor and furrier shop and, when their son was still quite young, Hannah Goodman found a job in a fabric store and continued working there until her husband died in 1974. At that time, she took over the management of the tailor shop.

Milton and Maury Rydelnik, also tailors, came to New York and found jobs there, but soon, their brother-in-law Isadore Goodman convinced them to come to Kansas City. They did and both married women from the area and raised families.

In 1977, Hannah remarried to Ben Sukiennik, a man she had known for many years from the New Americans Club, a Kansas City organization of Holocaust survivors. It was not until many years later that Hannah Sukiennik began speaking out publicly about the Holocaust. In the late 1980s she was interviewed on the radio and in the 1990s agreed to an in-depth interview by the Midwest Center for Holocaust Education. Explaining the reason for her previous silence on the subject, she explained, "even today, there are some people who do not want to know."

References

Dodd, Monroe, ed. *From the Heart: A Mosaic of Memories—Life Before and After the Holocaust.* Kansas City: Kansas City Star Books and Midwest Center for Holocaust Education, 2001.

Gutman, Israel, ed. *Encyclopedia of the Holocaust.* s.v. "Silesia." New York: Macmillan, 1990.

Telephone interviews by the author. Laura Goodman and Stan Goodman, May 2006.

Sutin, Julius (1884–1974), and Jack Sutin (ca. 1925–)

Julius and Jack Sutin, father and son, first lived in Stolpce and then Mir, Poland. They stayed together during the war, fighting and hiding with the partisans in the forests of eastern Poland. Jack met his future wife, **Rochelle Schleiff Sutin** in the forests, and all three were able to survive and emigrate to the United States.

Julius Sutin came from a religious family. His father was a rabbi, but Julius and his father did not get along. After an early business failed, Julius studied art for a short time, although his family disapproved of it. Then he met Sarah, who was studying to be a dentist. Impressed by her, he learned to be a dental technician and when the two married, they went into practice together, first in Stolpce and then in the nearby town of Mir, near the Russian border.

Jack (whose Hebrew name is Yitzhak) was the only child of Julius and Sarah Sutin. He went to grade school in Mir, but because there was no high school there, he was sent to Baronowicze at the age of twelve and boarded with another Jewish family. Although it was difficult at first, Jack Sutin soon developed independence and leadership skills and these helped him during the difficult challenges of the war years.

In 1939, when the Germans occupied western Poland, Mir and Stolpce were ruled by the Russians. Now the school in Stolpce that had been closed to Jews came under the new Soviet system and Jack Sutin was able to attend. It was in the gymnasium (high school) at Stolpce that Jack first met Rochelle Schleiff. Although he would have liked to take her out then, she was a protected young girl and did not yet date. Still, he did not forget her.

Although the Sutin family were professionals and were prosperous by Russian standards, the Communist regime did not threaten or deport Jack's parents since they were the only dentists in town. By 1941, however, the Germans marched in and the situation was more dangerous. Within a short time, a *Judenrat* (Jewish Council) was established and its members were ordered to register all the young men for hard labor. Although Jack was on that list, his parents were still given preferential treatment as dentists and when the ghetto was established, they were given places in a professional building and allowed to continue their work.

Out on the roads, repairing the highways for the German occupation forces, Jack risked death every day as German soldiers passed by in their trucks and shot at random into the groups of Jewish workers. In addition, the roundups of Jews in the ghetto increased.

Julius and Jack felt that Sarah was protected because she was a dentist and would not be arrested. Julius was only a technician and thus more liable to be deported. Father and son decided to escape the ghetto.

In the fall of 1941, the two snuck outside the ghetto gates. Julius hid in Mir itself with a Christian family whose family members had all been his patients. Jack went six kilometers further and hid with a Polish farmer and his family, the Kurlutas. It was from them that he heard about the final liquidation of the ghetto and the death of his mother at the hands of the Polish police.

Julius and Jack returned to the ghetto, where a small number of Jews still remained, and joined the work crews. Then in May 1942, the entire remaining Jewish population was moved to an old castle (*zamek*) just outside of Mir. That summer, forty young Jews, most from the Zionist Youth Movement, decided to organize some resistance. They were able to accumulate a small number of weapons with the help of **Oswald Rufeisen**, a Jew who was posing as a German and was an officer in the German police force. Once they had the weapons, they decided to try and escape. They hoped to join the Russian partisans who roamed the forests, and fight the Germans.

Jack Sutin was able to escape undetected with many other young people on August 9, 1942. The following day, Julius escaped with another group. Those who remained in the ghetto were all killed on August 13, 1942.

Jack and his group of five young people at first went to his old contacts, the Kurlutas, for food but the Kurluta family could not support them all and they began begging at other farmhouses; if the farmer refused, they would wait until dark and take it anyway. They kept moving, never staying long in any one place. Gradually, more Jewish refugees from the ghettos joined them until they were a group of fourteen, including men, women, and some older people. Jack Sutin was their acknowledged leader, a fearless and successful raider who always brought back food for the group.

As winter was approaching, they began to think of a more permanent shelter and decided to build an underground bunker in the Nalibocka forest where they would be protected from the cold. While they built it, Jack demanded that they reserve an extra space for a girl named Rochelle Schleiff. Although he hardly knew Rochelle and had only met her once or twice, he dreamed about her one night in the forest. In his dream, his mother's voice was calling to him. She told him that he would meet Rochelle in the woods and they would remain together. He saw Rochelle's face clearly in his dream and was convinced it was true. Although his comrades thought he was crazy, they complied with his wishes when they were building the bunker and, in November 1942, the girl in his dream actually did show up and was taken in by the group. Jack felt that they had been fated to meet. He was not a demanding suitor and was kind and gentle with her. Despite Rochelle's reservations and suspicions, the two eventually fell in love.

Jack Sutin in the Neue Freiman DP camp in Germany circa 1947. Courtesy of the U.S. Holocaust Memorial Museum Photo Archives.

That winter, the group rarely left their bunker. They did not feel secure enough to conduct raids on German targets but confined themselves to stealing food to stay alive and punishing Polish farmers who were helping the Germans. Then the Germans began an all-out assault on both Russian and Jewish partisan positions and Sutin's group decided to join a larger unit for protection. With fifty partisans, they were able to spend more time attacking German targets.

That spring, Jack became seriously ill. He developed boils all over his skin that became infected and painful. Rochelle nursed him through this difficult time and they became more committed to each other. This commitment caused Rochelle to constantly fear for his safety and she even appealed to the partisan leader to let him stay behind a few times so his life would not be in danger. However, Jack still did his share of the fighting. Their group laid mines to blow up trains and truck transports, stopping the flow of supplies to the front.

When the Germans launched their final battle against the partisan units, Jack and Julius and their group knew they had no chance of beating the Germans. Instead they ran to hide in the swamps. Ultimately, the attack was not successful and most of the partisans survived; the Germans retreated toward Germany.

By the end of 1944, the war was over in eastern Poland. Julius and Jack were still alive and Jack now considered Rochelle to be his wife. They returned first to Stolpce, then to Mir. After staying in Mir for a while, living under Soviet rule, they moved westward, first to Lodz and then, in late 1945, into the American zone of Berlin and a displaced-persons camp where they discovered a few other relatives who had survived. The Sutins applied for visas to the United States, but while they waited, Jack became leader of the camp, working to organize and help the other refugees. While still in Germany, Rochelle became pregnant.

Their first child, a son, had been born prematurely while they were still in Lodz and had died. Now they were concerned that this baby might also meet the same fate, but fortunately she was a healthy girl. They named her Cecilia, after Rochelle's mother, and she accompanied Julius, Jack, and Rochelle Sutin to the United States in 1949. Two years later, in America, their son Larry was born.

The family settled in St. Paul, Minnesota, where they joined Rochelle's aunt and uncle. Shortly after their arrival, the local paper printed their story and quoted Jack Sutin as saying that one day he would write a book about his life during the war. Forty-five years later, that book, edited by his son, was in print. Julius died in 1974. He was ninety years old and although he had missed the publication of the book, he had lived to see his two grandchildren grow up.

Reference

Sutin, Jack, and Rochelle Sutin. *Jack and Rochelle: A Holocaust Story of Love and Resistance.* Edited by Lawrence Sutin. St. Paul, MN: Graywolf Press, 1995.

Sutin, Rochelle (ca. 1925–)

Rochelle Schleiff Sutin was born in Stolpce, Poland into a prosperous family. During the war, she was reduced to living in a hole in the woods and begging for food. Under these wretched conditions, she met and fell in love with Jack Sutin, who became her common-law husband even before the war had ended.

Sutin was the oldest of three daughters born to Lazar and Cila Schleiff. Lazar was a prosperous businessman who bought and sold lumber and owned several factories. His family lived in a large home, the only one in town with flush toilets, and his daughters were educated in good schools.

When the Germans invaded Poland on September 1, 1939, Stolpce became part of the eastern zone. It had been allocated to the Soviet Union in a secret agreement signed by Hitler and Stalin earlier that year. This postponed the horror of the Nazi's antisemitic policies for two years. However, the population was now subject to Communist rules and Lazar Schleiff, one of the more prosperous Jews, was singled out for special attention. His spacious and luxurious home was requisitioned for Russian officers, his business was appropriated by the state, and he was constantly questioned by the KGB (the Soviet secret police) and threatened with deportation to Siberia.

By 1940, Sutin and her sister Sofka were already in high school. The schools were now supervised by the Russians and the girls no longer experienced antisemitism, frowned on by the Soviet regime. Instead, they were ostracized because their father was considered a capitalist. Then in August 1941, the Germans broke their pact with Russia and marched across eastern Poland towards the Russian border. Knowing what they could expect from the Nazi occupiers, many Jews tried to flee but the Russian border was closed to Jews. The Schleiff family left Stolpce for the small town of Kruglice, where one of Schleiff's factories was located, and waited to see what would happen.

After a week, they sent Sutin back to find out if it was safe to return. Their house was still standing, but it was filled with many other Jews who had lost their homes in the bombing. The Schleiff family came back and lived in one room. They knew from the few Jews who had escaped western Poland that it was only a matter of time before they would all be sent to a ghetto.

As soon as the SS troops entered the city, the Jews were faced with new rulings limiting their movement, confiscating their property, and rounding them up for slave labor. One of the first actions of the SS was to collect the most prominent men of the town and execute them. Lazar Schleiff was among those first victims.

Sutin and her sister Sofka were conscripted to help clean the rubble from the streets after the bombing. Their mother was considered too old and their youngest sister, Miriam was too young. But eventually, Sofka refused to work, claiming, "They will kill us anyway."

With their father gone, it now became Sutin's responsibility to somehow care for the family. She continued working throughout the winter of 1941–1942. That spring, roundups and murders of Jews increased until one day, the entire ghetto was surrounded. Because Sutin was a worker, she was able to leave for work. She begged her sister and mother to try to come, too, and save themselves, but they refused. When that last roundup was over, Sutin's family was dead, but they had sent a message to her through a Polish classmate. They knew they would die, Cila Schleiff said, but she admonished her daughter to stay alive and "take revenge."

Devastated by the loss of her family, Sutin was determined to leave the labor camp where the remaining Jews were now incarcerated and try to escape to the forest. She and a friend, Tanya, did escape later that year and tried to join the Russian partisans. They discovered that the Russians that were hiding in the forests considered the Jews to be their enemies and were very reluctant to take them in. They did find one group of Russians who allowed them to stay with them in exchange for doing the cooking and mending and tending their fire. But it soon became clear that they could not remain without providing sex for the men. They left and searched for another refuge.

Once again alone and defenseless in the forests, the two girls decided to return to Stolpce and accept death from the Nazis, but fate intervened. They met two young Jewish partisans. One of them knew Sutin from her school days and told her that Jack Sutin was the head of a Jewish partisan group hiding in the forest. He had dreamed that Rochelle Schleiff would be coming to join them and had saved a bunk for her.

Although they were originally from the same town, Sutin hardly knew this man and could not believe that he remembered her and wanted her to join his group. However, she had few other options and agreed to go. There was no room in the bunker for Tanya but they found her a place with a sympathetic farmer.

At first, Rochelle had no feelings for this young man. She had been so traumatized by the death of her family and her recent escapes that she felt no emotions at all. She was merely grateful for a place to sleep and some food to eat. Gradually, she began to appreciate Jack Sutin's concern for her and to become fond of him. Still, she worried that he, too, would demand sex like the Russian partisans did and she briefly moved to another bunker. But he convinced her to return and by the winter of 1942, her love for him began to grow. Although they were not formally married until after the war, she celebrated her wedding anniversary on December 31, 1942.

In 1943, with the German Army beginning to suffer some reverses at the Russian border, Jack Sutin's group of partisans joined a larger Jewish group in the Nalibocka forest. They were with this group when the Germans launched an all-out attack on both the Russian and Jewish partisans. Rochelle and Jack Sutin and some of their comrades were able to hide in a swamp, knee-deep in water. They could not move for several days but they had escaped the worst of the onslaught and evaded the German dogs.

The German attack on the partisan units was not successful and most of the partisans survived. They became increasingly active in pursuing the German soldiers who were in full retreat by 1944. This situation presented a difficult challenge for Rochelle Sutin. She was in love with Jack and wanted to be sure he remained alive so they could be together after the war. Once in a while, she persuaded the leader of their group to allow him to remain behind for her sake, but he could not be protected from most of the skirmishes and the risks were considerable.

> [When the German prisoners were taken into the partisan compound] Everyone started beating them—with rifle butts, fists, boots. We beat them so much. I remember that they were lying on the ground just barely breathing. And I . . . I don't think I could ever do it again . . . I came up to one of the German officers [and] . . . started to kick him again and again in the groin. I was kicking and screaming, "For my mama! For my tate [Daddy]! For my sisters! I went on screaming out every name I could remember. . . . It was such a release! It was as if I had finally done what my mother had asked me to do.
>
> —Rochelle Schleiff Sutin (*Jack and Rochelle*, p. 143.)

When the war on the eastern front was over, Rochelle and Jack Sutin returned to Stolpce but found only destruction and hostility from the Polish population. From there, they went to Mir, then under Soviet rule, but life was difficult and the Soviet government was unconcerned with the suffering of the survivors. When they started conscripting the men into the Russian Army and the women to work in the mines, Rochelle collected some of the gold coins her family had buried when the war first began, and she and Jack made their way to Lodz. By then, Rochelle was already pregnant.

Still, the Sutins did not feel safe, and when they heard of a pogrom in nearby Katowice, fear brought on premature labor and the baby died. When the war had been won in the west, and Germany finally defeated, Rochelle and Jack left Poland and made their way into Germany, to the American zone in Berlin and then to a displaced-persons camp. There, Rochelle found an aunt and uncle who had also survived. She became pregnant again and this time, the baby was born healthy. They named her Cecilia, after Rochelle's mother.

The Sutin family finally received their visas to the United States in 1949. Their ship arrived in New York City on September 12 and they took a train to St. Paul, Minnesota where they were met by relatives.

Although life was difficult and lonely at first and Sutin felt that her relatives and new friends had no idea of the horrifying experiences they had lived through, still she knew that for the first time in many years, she was safe and had enough to eat. The Su-

Rochelle Schleif Sutin and her daughter Cecilia, in 1948 or 1949, at the Neue Freiman DP camp. Courtesy of the U.S. Holocaust Memorial Museum Photo Archives.

tin's son Larry was born in the United States in 1951. It was Larry who would transcribe and edit his parents' words and produce a book about their experiences. It was called simply *Jack and Rochelle.*

Reference

Sutin, Jack, and Rochelle Sutin. *Jack and Rochelle: A Holocaust Story of Love and Resistance,* Lawrence Sutin, ed. St. Paul, MN: Graywolf Press, 1995.

Sutzkever, Abraham (1913–), and Freyndke Sutzkever

Abraham Sutzkever, a Yiddish poet, and his wife Freyndke Levitan, both from Poland, lived through World War II first in the Vilna ghetto and then in the forest with the Jewish partisans. Throughout all those years, Abraham continued to write poetry that described his experiences and conveyed vivid images of life under the Nazis, while Freyndke risked her life to preserve it. They both succeeded in their efforts.

Sutzkever was born in Smorgon, a small Polish town (now in Belarus). His father died when he was seven while the family was exiled in Siberia during World War I. In 1922, Abraham and his mother moved to Vilna, a sophisticated and bustling city with a large Jewish population. Vilna offered many cultural opportunities for a young Jewish man. Sutzkever joined the Jewish Scout Movement, became part of an active, young literary circle, and began writing poetry. In Vilna, he also met and fell in love with Freyndke Levitan, dedicating one of his early poems, "On My Wandering Flute," to her.

Sutzkever's first published poem appeared in a literary magazine in 1934 and from that time, his poems, written in the Yiddish language, became more widely known and appeared in journals not only in Vilna but also in Warsaw and in the United States. His first collection of poetry, *Lieder* (Songs) was published in 1937.

The Nazis did not reach Vilna until 1941. As they did in every city they occupied, the Germans organized a ghetto and forced all Jews to take up residence there. Among them were Sutzkever, his wife, and his mother. Almost immediately, the roundups began, assembling Jews ostensibly for forced labor, but mostly for death. A description of one of these roundups can be found in Sutzkever's poem "Yom Kippur."

> *Because he wanted to smuggle a flower through the ghetto's gate*
> *my neighbor paid the price of seven lashes.*
> *How precious it is to him now—this blue vernal flower and its golden pupil!*
> *My neighbor bears the mementos with no regrets:*
> *spring breathes through and colors his tortured flesh—*
> *that's how much he wanted it to flourish.*
>
> —Abraham Sutzkever (translated by Seymour Mayne)

Sutzkever was chosen by the Nazis as part of a forced labor group that was assigned to sort the collections of books and manuscripts in the library of the Yiddish Institute (YIVO) in Vilna. Because the library was outside the ghetto, Sutzkever and others in his group found several opportunities to smuggle weapons and reading material back in. He also continued writing, and read many of his poems to his friends in the Writer's Association, a group formed inside the ghetto.

Sutzkever's first collection of poems about the war was written in the early days of the occupation, between June 25 and July 5, 1941, a period in which five thousand of Vilna's Jews were taken to Ponary Woods and shot. In a preface to one of those poems, "Faces of the Swamp," Sutzkever wrote that it was composed while "lying stuck in a broken chimney in my old apartment. . . . This way I hid from the snatchers who dragged off every Jewish male they could find." His poem also describes how his wife Freyndke fled from the Vilna ghetto with his poems. She carried them "through all the horrors and tragedies. They were with her through the first provocations, were covered with blood, in prison under Schweinenberg's whip."

Freyndke Sutzkever miraculously escaped and ran back into the ghetto with the poems, but Sutzkever had already left, during what he refers to as "the Roundup of the Yellow Permits." When he returned to the Vilna ghetto, he found his wife in the hospital, giving birth to their child. "In her labor pains," he wrote, "she was clutching the poems in her hands."

On September 12, 1943, Sutzkever secretly left the ghetto by underground passage with a small group of partisans, and hid out in the Naroch Forest with the Voroshilov Partisan Brigade. During that time, he kept a history of the partisan movement and also recorded all the crimes committed by the Nazis. Freyndke also managed to escape from the ghetto with her baby girl, along with another group of partisans, and joined Sutzkever in the forest.

In March 1944, four months before the war ended on the Russian front, a messenger delivered a manuscript containing some of Sutzkever's poetry to Moscow. As a result, Sutzkever, his wife, and daughter were taken from the forest and airlifted to Moscow in a tiny, two-passenger plane. Abraham sat beside the pilot while Freyndke and their daughter were strapped into the fuselage. The Soviets wanted to use him as an example of Jewish Resistance to Fascism but this political motive may have saved their lives. By the time the Germans surrendered to the Soviet Union four months later, on July 13, 1944, most of the Jewish inhabitants of Vilna had either been shot at Ponary or sent to concentration camps in Estonia or to the Sobibor extermination camp. Few returned. Of the fifty-seven thousand Jews who had lived in Vilna when the Nazis came, barely three thousand survived.

The Sutzkevers remained in the Soviet Union until Sutzkever was called as a witness in the Nuremberg trial in February 1946. They never returned to Russia, but sailed to Israel in 1947 on the illegal immigrant ship, the *SS Patria*. There, Sutzkever continued to write poetry in Yiddish and became founder and editor of a new literary journal, *Di Goldene Keyt* (The Golden Chain). As she had before and during the war, Freyndke Levitan Sutzkever supported him in all his endeavors.

The themes of both Sutzkever's prose and poetry revolve around the Holocaust and Israel and have been translated into many languages. In 2003, Abraham Sutzkever, still writing poetry, celebrated his ninetieth birthday.

References

Libo, Kenneth, and Michael Skakun. "Treasures from the Archives." *Forward* (November 7, 2003). Available at http://www/cjh.org/Forward.

Roskies, David. "Abraham Sutzkever: A Memoir." *Commentary Magazine* (2005).

Sutzkever, Abraham. *The Fiddle Rose: Poems 1970–1972.* Selected and translated by Ruth Whitman. Detroit, MI: Wayne State University Press, 1990.

Wisse, Ruth. "Essay." In *The Jewish Reader.* Amherst, MA: National Yiddish Book Center, 2001. Available at http://www.yiddishbookcenter.org (accessed April 2006).

Synnestvedt, Alice Resch (1908–)

Alice Resch Synnestvedt was born in the United States, raised in Norway, and spent the war years helping refugees in France. Working with Quaker relief organizations, she saved many Jewish children and helped others cross the border into Switzerland or Spain.

Synnestvedt's parents, Knut and Frida Resch, met in Germany, where they attended different schools. After graduation, Knut left for the United States and found a job with Westinghouse. In 1903, he sent for Frida. They were married and Synnestvedt and her younger brother Wilhelm were born in America.

When Synnestvedt was five years old, her father received an offer to help build a power station in his native Norway. He accepted, moving there with his family; except for a brief stay in the U.S. during World War I, he remained there. His children were educated in Norway and always considered themselves Norwegian.

After graduating from school, Synnestvedt left Norway for a trip through Europe to round out her education and decide on her future. She was introduced by a friend to the American Nursing School in Paris and, seemingly on the spur of the moment, she enrolled there as a student in 1929. Nursing was hard work but Synnestvedt found that she enjoyed it and was successful. After graduation, she also studied physical therapy.

As a nurse, Synnestvedt had no problem finding employment. She worked in a hospital and then began getting private assignments tending to sick patients at home or accompanying them to destinations outside France. Threats of war were looming and everyone was tense. One of Synnestvedt's diary entries on November 13, 1938 (right after *Kristallnacht*), decried the German persecution of Jews and noted, "It's terrible that we are running around having fun when the Jews of Germany are enduring such horrible persecution."

When World War II officially began less than a year later, and France joined the battle against Nazi Germany, Synnestvedt, with her background in nursing and her reputation for compassion and competence, was in a position to help. Through the American Hospital in Paris she was sent on assignments to help the wounded and then to tend to refugees fleeing from Germany and Spain, where the Spanish Civil War had just ended. Many of them were avowed Communists and were political refugees, but after the Nazi takeover of France, more and more were Jews—from France and from other European countries farther East—whose only crime was that they were born Jewish.

Synnestvedt met Helga Holbek early in the war and through her was introduced to the Quakers and their relief work. The two women soon found themselves in Toulouse, a city in the southwestern part of France, called "the free zone." Although "the free zone" was not entirely free, and the Nazi antisemitic laws were in effect there as well as in the north, it was not occupied by the German Army and therefore the atmosphere was more relaxed. Many Jews were living quietly with false identities and there was no overt harassment. However, there were many concentration camps in the area where those who had been identified as Jews were incarcerated. One of these camps was Gurs.

Synnestvedt was horrified when she first visited Gurs and saw the awful facilities, the lack of sanitation, and the hunger. The Quakers set up a food station in the camp and distributed clothing to the prisoners. One of Synnestvedt's assignments was to remove some of the younger children from Gurs and find refuges for them. She placed many in foster homes and personally brought forty-eight children to an orphanage in the nearby town of Aspet. Synnestvedt developed a special relationship with those forty-eight children, living with them for a while, playing with them, reassuring them, and comforting them. After she left, she brought them treats whenever she could and found clothing and other necessities to enhance their difficult lives. Long after the war, the children of Aspet remembered her and credited her with saving them.

Although the Quakers were supposed to be a neutral organization, offering relief but not taking sides politically, it was difficult to remain neutral. Synnestvedt and many of her co-workers were actively anti-Nazi. They would not jeopardize their vital work by joining the underground, but they did help clandestinely whenever they could, hiding many in their own apartments, helping them to evade the Germans, and then giving them food packages before they left on their final run to freedom. Synnestvedt personally escorted a group of children to safety in Switzerland when they were unable to cross the border themselves. Adults sometimes crossed the Pyrenees Mountains into Spain. Many of those that she helped save became lifelong friends.

The Quakers' most important ally in these endeavors was the French Catholic Church. Every monastery and convent in the area hid Jewish children and helped fleeing refugees. The archbishop of Toulouse, Jules-Gèrard Saliège, condemned those who worked with the Germans and urged his priests to help Jewish refugees escape the Nazis.

In 1943, the German Army came to the south of France in full force and the deportations of Jews increased considerably. As part of Quaker relief work, Synnestvedt distributed food to those on the trains as they passed through the station near Toulouse. They gave the refugees cooked rice and bottles of water to take with them but were not allowed to speak with the prisoners, enter the boxcars, or help them in

This letter from the Archbishop of Toulouse was read aloud in every parish church in the city.

August 22, 1943

There is a Christian morality and a human ethic which require us to heed certain duties and rights. They are part of human nature. They come from God. They can be abused, but not abolished. That children, men, women, mothers and fathers, are treated like animals, that family members are separated from each other and sent to unknown destinations, are sad spectacles which we must witness.

Why does the right to asylum no longer exist in our churches? Why have we been overcome? The Lord have mercy on us!

Holy Mother of God, pray for France! Frightful scenes have been played out in our parish in Noë and in Récébédoux. Jews are men and women. Foreigners are men and women. . . . They are our brothers like so many others. A Christian cannot forget this!

France, Beloved homeland! France, whose children, true to tradition, bear respect for humanity in their very fiber, chivalrous, generous France, I cannot believe that you bear responsibility for all of these terrible events.

With my affectionate devotion,
Jules-Gèrard Saliège
Archbishop of Toulouse

any other way. The Nazi soldiers followed the relief workers from car to car with guns pointed at their backs to make sure they did only what they were allowed to do, but Synnestvedt often did take handwritten notes from the deportees, who were crammed into the box cars so tightly that they could hardly breathe. Sometimes she recognized someone who had come through their relief station or had been at the camp at Gurs. It was frustrating and upsetting to know that these people were all going to their deaths and there was nothing she could do to stop it. Nevertheless, there were enough successful experiences to make the work rewarding.

The year 1943 was also the year Alice Resch Synnestvedt married. She had met her husband, Magnus Synnestvedt, while working in Toulouse and had occasionally used his apartment to hide refugees. He was a businessman who was involved with an invention that enabled engines to run on charcoal, an important project due to the severe shortage of gasoline. After many marriage proposals from him, she consented, and the wedding took place in Toulouse that November.

Alice Synnestvedt continued her relief work but waited anxiously for the end of the war, which seemed immanent. In June 1944, the U.S. Army landed at Normandy, and, shortly thereafter, U.S. planes came to Nice, a city on the Mediterranean Sea. They were quickly joined by the *Macquis*, the French Underground, and the population rejoiced as they watched the Germans retreating north.

By the end of the summer of 1944, all of France had been liberated, although the war was not yet over and fighting continued in isolated parts of France as the troops marched eastward toward Germany. Synnestvedt was now transferred to Caen in Normandy, to help the population recover from the fierce battle that had taken place there. While she and her friend Helga Holbek were there, they heard news of the war's end. Denmark and Norway were now also free.

It took some time for Synnestvedt to get permission from the French authorities to visit her parents and brother in Norway. While she waited, she worked in other relief organizations in Normandy and Paris. In January 1949, she became secretary of the Swedish organization *Rädda Barnem* (Save the Children). A year later, she was appointed head of the *Rädda Barnem* Children's Home for Jewish children three to six years of age. They recuperated there before joining their parents and moving to Israel. Synnestvedt's husband Magnus died in 1950.

Alice Resch Synnestvedt returned to Norway in 1960 to help care for her parents. After their deaths, she moved to Copenhagen. It took another twenty years before the children of Aspet, as well as others she had saved, began contacting her. In 1982, she traveled to Jerusalem to meet with some of them and their families. The following year, she was honored as a righteous gentile. She helped plant two trees on the Avenue of the Righteous approaching Yad Vashem, the Israel museum of the Holocaust. One tree was for her and one for her friend Helga Holbek, who had died in 1982. Many of the children she helped save were there with their spouses and children as well as several of her old co-workers. In a letter written to her brother describing this event she confessed, "I have to admit that neither Helga nor I felt that we had done anything dangerous or heroic—neither of us felt deserving of the honor."

In 1998, to celebrate her ninetieth birthday, Synnestvedt traveled to visit **Hugo Schiller**, one of her Aspet children, who lived in Myrtle Beach, South Carolina. Five years later, eight of those children came from North and South America, Europe, and Israel to Copenhagen to celebrate their benefactor's ninety-fifth birthday.

Reference

Synnestvedt, Alice Resch. *Over the Highest Mountains: A Memoir of Unexpected Heroism in France during World War II.* Pasadena, CA: Intentional Productions, 2005.

Szpilman, Wladyslaw (1911-)

Wladyslaw Szpilman of Warsaw was a well-known and popular pianist and songwriter before the war. He was never involved in politics and was not a religious Jew, but he was caught up in World War II and spent six years trying to avoid the Nazis. During that time he was saved three times—once by a Jewish policeman in the Warsaw ghetto, once by Polish Christian friends, and once by a German soldier.

At first, right after the German attacks of September 1939, Szpilman thought he could ignore the war and live his life as usual. He even continued going to the radio station every day during the bombings to perform his regularly scheduled live radio concerts. He was in the middle of a nocturne by Chopin when bombs hit the broadcasting tower and Polish radio went off the air.

Szpilman was one of a family of four children. In 1939 they were all young adults, still living with their parents in a Warsaw apartment. As the war progressed, they lost that family home and moved in with friends in order to be safe from the bombings and then from the nighttime roundups of Jews by the Gestapo. Little by little, life became more difficult. Szpilman and his brother Henryk went to do volunteer work for the war effort. His sisters, Regina and Halina, stayed home with their parents. They all hoped for a quick end to the fighting and an allied victory.

Instead, conditions became steadily worse. Nazi posters constantly listed new demands for the Jews and new limitations on their activities. Among those limitations was the stipulation that individual Jews could not keep more than 2,000 *zlotys*. Any additional money was to be held at the bank and would no longer be at their disposal. With normal life at a standstill and little work available for Jews besides unpaid labor, there was almost no source of money for the Szpilman family. They began selling off their possessions—furniture, jewelry, and extra clothing—in order to buy food.

After the establishment of the ghetto, options were more limited still. In the evenings, Szpilman got a job playing piano in a Jewish café frequented by the Jewish police and black marketeers. Although they could also have joined the Jewish police force working directly under Nazi supervision, both Wladyslaw and Henryk refused, seeing it as a form of collaboration.

As the war progressed, so did the Nazi plan for extermination of the Jews and, little by little, Jews were arrested, deported—supposedly to work camps—and killed. Most Warsaw Jews were taken to Treblinka, one of the most notorious death camps, where there were almost no survivors. In rare instances, someone escaped and brought back news of mass murder, but many of the ghetto residents, including the Szpilmans, could not believe it. By late 1942, however, rumors abounded that the Germans were planning to liquidate the ghetto and transport all residents to the gas chambers. The Szpilman family was arrested and, expecting the worst, joined the hundreds of other Jews who were being herded to the train station.

Wladyslaw Szpilman and his family, along with a growing crowd of Jews, waited for several days for a train to arrive. They were all hungry and thirsty. At one point, a child passed by selling candy for exorbitant prices. With his last *zlotys*, Szpilman's father bought a piece of candy, cut it into six tiny pieces, and distributed it to his family. That was the last meal they would have together. The next day, the train came.

As the Jews were boarding the boxcars urged on by the German soldiers that surrounded them, someone grabbed Szpilman by the collar and pulled him away, throwing him behind the cordon of Germans. As he struggled to get up and join his family, the man whispered to him, "What the hell do you think you're doing? Go on, save yourself!" Realizing, finally, that all those in the cars were going to their deaths and that, thanks to a Jewish policeman, he had a chance for life, he headed back into the ghetto. With the help of acquaintances, he managed to get a work permit that took him to the Aryan side to work each day. The workers were allowed to buy potatoes and bread before returning, so they would not starve. In addition to the sacks of potatoes that they brought back with them to the ghetto, they often smuggled in weapons for the Jewish fighters who were preparing for a final battle.

The deportations continued and parts of the ghetto were being eliminated as the population decreased. Szpilman realized that even with his work permit his days were numbered if he remained behind the walls. He decided to try and contact some Polish friends in the hopes that they would save him by giving him a place to hide. Although the penalty for hiding a Jew was death, he finally found a couple who agreed, and arranged first one hiding place and then another. In these illegal apartments, he had to remain quiet all day, lest the neighbors hear him and report it to the Germans. From one of his hideouts, Szpilman watched the Warsaw ghetto uprising in the spring of 1943 and saw the ghetto burning. He could not go out but had to depend on a Polish contact to bring him food. Sometimes the contact failed to come and many times he almost starved.

Alone and totally dependent on the good will of others, Szpilman waited for the war to be over. When the rebellion of the Polish Underground began in 1944, he was hopeful that it would be just a few more days, but the underground lost that first battle and the German army chased the Poles away, shot them, or burned them out of the houses where they were hiding. Szpilman miraculously survived when a fire destroyed most of the apartment building where he was staying. But now he had been abandoned by his contacts, who were either killed in the fighting or had run to safety. He was forced to creep out during the night to forage for food and water in the other apartments where no one lived any longer. Barely surviving, hounded by German soldiers, fearful of every sound, he managed to escape discovery, and with it certain death at the hands of the Germans.

One day, his luck ran out and he was discovered by a German officer. Expecting a speedy end to his life, he stood with his back against the wall and waited. The soldier asked who he was and what he did for a living. Szpilman answered, "I am a pianist." "Then play something," said the soldier, motioning to a piano in the next room of the abandoned apartment. Szpilman played.

The officer offered to help him escape to a village, but when Szpilman told him he couldn't, the German understood that he was a Jew. He found a secure hiding place for him, left him several loaves of bread and jam, and reassured him that it would all be over soon. In an effort to thank him, Szpilman offered his watch, the only possession he still had, but the officer refused. Instead, Szpilman said, "You have a long way to go home. If I survive, I'll certainly be working for Polish Radio again. . . . If anything happens to you, if I can help you then in any way, remember my name: Szpilman, Polish Radio."

It was not until weeks later that Wladyslaw Szpilman heard the loudspeakers in the streets announcing that the Germans had been defeated. It was winter 1945. He put on the warm coat that the German officer had left for him and went downstairs. To his horror, Polish militia began shooting at him. It took a while before he managed to convince them that, although he was wearing a German officer's overcoat, he was a Polish Jew.

Szpilman, finally a free man, walked through the ruins of Warsaw. His family had all been murdered, many of his friends were also dead, but he still had his music manuscripts, saved throughout the six years of his ordeal, and he still had his talent as a fine pianist. Within a short time, he was back playing at the radio station. His first postwar selection for Polish radio was the very same Chopin nocturne that had been interrupted in 1939. Shortly after the end of the war, while Warsaw was still in ruins, he wrote a book describing his experiences. He tried to find his German rescuer but did not know his name.

Szpilman's book was first published in 1946 in Polish. Because Poland was under Soviet rule at that time, and Soviet policy did not admit that there could possibly have been a good German, or that many Ukrainians, Poles, and Russians had collaborated with the Nazis, the book was not encouraged. It was out of print for many years. Only after the Iron Curtain was lifted and Poland became free was the book brought to Germany and published in German by Szpilman's son Andrzej. By that time, Szpilman had learned who his German rescuer was: Captain Wilm Hosenfeld. He also learned that Hosenfeld had been arrested and taken to a Russian POW camp at war's end. He was later brought to Russia and died there in 1949. But before his arrest, he had sent home his diaries condemning the war and asserting that Germany would have to pay for the terrible atrocities they were committing. Excerpts from that diary were included in the second edition of Szpilman's book, published in 1999 and translated into English as *The Pianist*.

Wladyslaw Szpilman remained in Poland throughout his life and was the Director of Music at Polish Radio until 1963. He also made many concert appearances and his musical compositions were well known throughout Poland.

Reference

Szpilman, Wladyslaw. *The Pianist*. Translated by Anthea Bell. New York: Picador USA, 1999.

T

Tec, Nechama (née Bawnik) (1931–), and Bawnik family

Nechama Bawnik Tec was only eight years old when the Nazis came to Lublin, Poland. She and her family survived the war solely through the help of Polish Christians, who sheltered them and allowed them to pose as relatives.

Roman and Estera Bawnik had been well off before the war. When Jews were barred from attending school, they could still afford to hire a private tutor, a young Jewish woman named Hela Trachtenberg, for their two daughters. But soon, Roman Bawnik's factories were taken over by the Germans and given to a German manager. Shortly after, the girls' tutor was forced to move into the ghetto. It was the beginning of many radical changes in the life of the Bawnik family.

Roman Bawnik was one of the few men who recognized the true danger of Nazism in those first years. He saw almost immediately that work was a matter of life and death and made sure that he, his wife, and his older daughter had jobs. Tec was still too young to work, but she was not too young to understand the brutality that surrounded her. Jewish patients in hospitals were killed or taken away to camps, orphans were dragged from their beds in late-night raids and shot. Then the Nazis proceeded to deport or kill the rest of the Jewish population of Lublin. Tec's aunt Ella along with her entire family disappeared in such a raid. Her uncle Josef was caught in a roundup and sent to a prison camp. His wife and two sons were killed and he, too, ultimately died. As the roundups continued, Roman Bawnik understood that in order to save his family, they would have to get false identities and disappear.

Their first hiding place was the chemical factory that Bawnik had once owned and where he now worked. The new manager, a sympathetic German, obtained papers identifying Roman Bawnik as a worker vital to the economy. For Tec, still a little girl, being cooped up all day while her sister and her parents went to work was depressing. After many months alone, her mother saw how unhappy she was and allowed her to spend some time in the ghetto, living with Trachtenberg, her old tutor. Although the ghetto population was dwindling and there were few children left, it was still better for Tec than remaining in the factory. She begged to be allowed to stay longer.

Then, one night, while she was with Trachtenberg in the ghetto, Estera Bawnik rushed in to awaken her daughter at 4:00 a.m. She had been warned of another roundup and ran with her to find a hiding place. They raced from one cellar to another, but there was no room for them. Finally they found one place that had room for only the little girl. Bawnik would find another shelter, she assured her daughter.

From their cramped hideout Tec could hear the Germans ordering everyone to come out into the square. They could hear the soldiers searching the houses and then shots were fired. Several hours later, Tec came out of hiding and began to make her way back to her tutor's house. She was horrified to see that a large number of babies had been shot in their carriages and many adults were lying dead on the street. She began to run and found Estera Bawnik waiting for her. Once in her mother's arms, she was able to cry. She felt guilty for having asked to stay in the ghetto. They all agreed that they would have to make new plans for their survival.

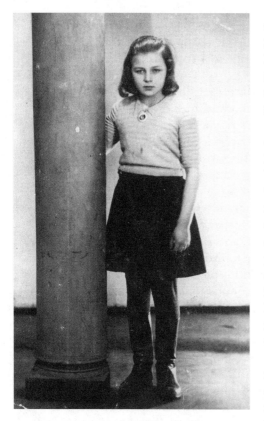

Nechama Bawnik Tec in 1942 in the Lublin ghetto. Courtesy of the U.S. Holocaust Memorial Museum Photo Archives.

With the help of a cousin, they traveled to Warsaw in November 1942, and each member of the family received false papers. Tec was given a new Polish identity: Christina, or Krysia. She had to memorize all the facts of her new made-up life as well as some of the basic Catholic prayers so no one would suspect her true identity.

Tec and her sister Giza were in less danger because they were blonde and spoke Polish well. Her parents looked more Jewish and spoke with Yiddish accents. The Bawniks feared that even with their authentic-looking papers, they would not be safe. For this reason, they first placed their daughters separately with a Polish family who claimed the girls as their nieces. Soon, another place was found for Tec's older sister and now each of the girls remained alone. Tec missed her family and was often hungry and frightened. She had to be on guard at every moment, being careful never to give herself away by a thoughtless remark or gesture.

Tec was overjoyed when her parents arranged for a new hiding place in Kielce where the family could be together. The Jews had all been deported from the city and the Bawniks stayed with a Christian family, the Homars. It was here, in the last years of the war, that Tec began to grow up and take on adult responsibility. Because it was not safe for her parents to go out, and her older sister had a full-time job working for the Germans, Tec was the one who went shopping with their Polish host. She learned how to bargain on the black market and get the best prices for everything. During the last year of the war, she began a business with her parents selling baked goods on the black market. Estera baked the rolls, Tec went out in the morning to sell them, and Roman Bawnik kept the accounts.

Only once did the Gestapo come to their home. They were searching for partisans, but Tec knew they would be happy to find Jews. She and Stefa Homar were able to get her parents into their hiding place just in time. The Germans searched the house; they even heard her father cough underneath the floor, but they never found them.

As the war neared its end, the Nazis became more zealous about rounding up Poles as well as Jews. They often shot people at random on the street, and began trying to eliminate the sale of black market goods. Tec was reported to the Gestapo by one of her customers. In order to avoid getting caught, she ran into the fields and hid there all day. Stefa was taken to the police station and tortured, but she refused to give Tec away. She insisted that her niece was a little girl and there had been some mistake. Stefa Homar returned home that night covered with cuts and bruises but proud that she had admitted nothing.

The Bawniks were extremely grateful to the Homar family for taking them in. They shared many things with them and grew to love them and their children. But they often heard the Homars speak about Jews in a derogatory way. Although Tec found this casual antisemitism painful at first, she gradually began to accept it as a part of Polish culture and not take it personally. She began to realize that despite what they said about Jews, they had risked their lives to save her family. She felt that they were good people.

At the beginning of 1945, everyone knew that parts of Poland had been liberated and it was only a matter of time before the Germans would have to retreat. When Allied bombs began falling on Kielce, both the Bawniks and the Homars rejoiced. The two families dodged snipers' bullets while crawling to the shelter across their courtyard and waited underground until all was quiet. When they heard men's voices speaking in Russian, they knew that at last they were liberated. Nechama Bawnik Tec was fourteen years old.

Shortly after liberation, the Bawniks quietly left Kielce. They understood that the Homars did not want to admit that they had saved Jews. Their neighbors would not have approved. Back in Lublin, they were devastated to find only a bombed-out ruin where their home used to be. Of the 40,000 Jews that had lived in Lublin, only three families had survived.

One year after the war ended, on July 4, 1946, there was an anti-Jewish pogrom in Kielce. The Poles attacked the Jews who had returned, killing forty-two and wounding about fifty more.

A few years after the war, Tec was able to reach the United States. She completed her education in New York, earning a Ph.D. in sociology from Columbia University. She married Leon Tec and had two children. It was not until the 1970s that she began to talk about her war experiences. Then her memories "finally burst like a flood." Her memoir, *Dry Tears: The Story of a Lost Childhood*, was praised as "a beautifully written and poignant account" and one that sheds light on the contribution of righteous gentiles in saving

Jews. Since its publication in 1982, Nechama Bawnik Tec has written several other books on the Holocaust. She taught at the University of Connecticut and her research on gentiles who rescued Jews was supported by the Memorial Foundation for Jewish Culture.

References

Tec, Nechama. *Dry Tears: The Story of a Lost Childhood*. Westport, CT: Wildcat Publishing, 1982.
Encyclopedia of the Holocaust. s.v. "Kielce."

Trachman sisters

The Trachman family—parents, five girls, and two boys—lived in Brzozow, Poland. When World War II began, the Trachman sons quickly fled to Russia. The parents and oldest daughter were killed, but four of the girls, Stepha, Halina, Dola, and Mania, found refuge in the nearby forest and survived.

Ben Zion Trachman, father of the family, was a well-to-do businessman, owner of two factories that he had financed by winning the Austrian State Lottery. A follower of the Bobover Hasidim (a pious family dynasty, originally from the town of Bobowa in Galicia, southern Poland) he was a deeply religious and charitable man. He had a beautiful voice and on the Jewish holidays, he served as cantor in the nearby town of Dynov.

Trachman's wife Rachel was also known for her charity, and her daughters were often sent to deliver baskets of food to the poor families in town, both gentiles and Jews. They were instructed by their mother to ring the bell and then leave promptly, so the needy families would not know who their benefactor was.

The Trachman children all attended public school in Brzozow, then completed gymnasium (high school). Although Polish public schools were open on Saturdays, the Jewish children did not attend on that day because it was the Sabbath. They would get the lessons from a Christian friend and make up all the work. The girls as well as the boys were tutored at home in Hebrew and Jewish subjects.

By the time World War II began on September 1, 1939, the two older Trachman daughters, Ruja (Raizl) and Stepha, were married and each had a child. The other three, Halina, Dola, and Mania

Mania Trachman Kraut (left front), Elizabeth Hoffman and her mother Stepha Trachman Hoffman (third from left) with Mania's husband (second row left) and two friends, in Germany several years after the war. Courtesy of Benzion Kraut.

were in their teens or early twenties and not yet married. Less than two weeks after the initial attack, the Germans occupied their area and, on September 15, the second day of Rosh Hashanah (the Jewish new year), they marched into Dynov where Ben Zion Trachman was leading services. His wife and daughters never knew exactly what happened. Perhaps he did not follow the Nazi orders quickly enough—or perhaps he refused to notice them while in the midst of prayer. The result was that Ben Zion Trachman was murdered. He was so riddled with bullets that, when his daughters went to find his body, they could not recognize him. Only his monogrammed handkerchief served as proof of his identity.

After Ben Zion Trachman was buried, his sons fled to Russia and his wife Rachel went to bed and never got up. She, too, was eventually killed by the Nazis in 1942.

Now the four Trachman sisters, Stepha, Halina, Dola, and Mania were alone. Their sister Ruja, an artist and pharmacist, lived with her husband and young son in Katowicz, where they were murdered by the Nazis. The four remaining sisters realized that if they wanted to live, they would have to hide. They decided to take a chance in the forests that surrounded the town.

Halina, Dola, Mania, and Stepha, with her baby girl, Elizabeth, spent the warmer months in the forest. They lived on raw potatoes that were brought to them by a young Polish woman who had once worked for the Trachmans. As the weather turned cold, however, Stepha worried about the baby and Mania went with her to help find a temporary home for Elizabeth.

They found a Christian family who agreed to take the baby and, although Stepha had no money, she promised to pay them after the war. Then the two women slipped out of town. Stepha and Mania walked all day, but as night fell they still had not yet reached the destination in the woods where they were to meet their sisters. They stopped for the night at a small, isolated house and asked for shelter and the woman agreed. In the morning, she brought them bread and coffee and offered them refuge in a bunker beneath her house. The sisters agreed, went in search of Halina and Dola, and the four of them settled in. "We never thought we would live," Mania told an interviewer many years later, but they did.

The woman who hid the Trachman sisters brought them food each day and also supplied them with used sweaters. The sisters spent their days unraveling the wool and then knitting socks and sweaters that their Polish benefactor sold. In this way, she had money to buy extra food.

For two years, the Trachman sisters lived underground. There was no water for bathing, little fresh air, and no medicine. They survived typhus as well as hunger and filth. Once they felt sure that the Nazis had discovered their bunker. The Germans came looking for Jews and passed over the trap door to their hideout, which had been carefully camouflaged. The terror-stricken women heard the soldiers jumping on the door above them and held their breaths, but the soldiers saw nothing suspicious and moved on. After they left, the sisters cried all day from fear and relief.

On September 1, 1944, exactly five years after the beginning of the war, the Russians had captured and overtaken the German positions and Brzozow was now liberated. The Trachman sisters left their bunker, left the woods behind, and returned home. They discovered that a stranger, assuming all the Trachmans were dead, had taken over their father's property. Their old home was still there, though it stood empty, as the Germans had removed all their furniture. They were able to collect some of the valuables they had left with gentile friends, however, and slowly they began to piece together their lives and make plans for the future.

Halina, who sold cosmetics before the war, left for Paris and obtained a license as a cosmetologist. She moved to the new state of Israel in 1948 and lived the rest of her life there. She never married and had no children.

Stepha returned to the Christian family who had sheltered her baby daughter and was able to reclaim her. After emigrating to New York City, she married Sigmund Hoffman, who died in the 1990s. Stepha Trachman Hoffman passed away ten years later.

Mania met her husband **Pinchas Zvi Kraut** while still in Brzozow. He was a distant cousin and quite a bit older, but the two fell in love. They left for Krakow, got married there, and continued to Austria, searching for other survivors from their family in the displaced-persons camp in Linz. From there, they moved to Munich, taking any jobs they could find in order to survive. In Munich in 1947, while they waited for a visa to the United States, their son Ben Zion (named after Trachman's father) was born. The visa was not forthcoming, but they were able to obtain a Canadian visa in 1951 and they arrived in Montreal early in 1952.

In Montreal the Krauts opened a small restaurant, where Mania worked tirelessly beside her husband for twenty-two years. They remained observant Jews and raised their only son in the Jewish tradition. Ben Zion Kraut studied first at McGill University and then at Yeshiva University. He became a professor of Holocaust studies. Before Mania Trachman Kraut died in 2005, she had three grandchildren.

No information is available concerning the fourth sister, Dola, or the Trachman brother, Samuel. Henry Trachman did manage to leave Russia and come to New York. He worked as a taxi driver and married but had no children. He died in the mid-1980s.

Stepha's daughter Elizabeth remained an only child. She was raised in New York City, married Marvin Glickman, and had two children.

References

Kraut, Ben Zion. Interview by the author, July 2006, Hempstead, New York.
———. "Mania Kraut." Unpublished eulogy.
Trachman Kraut, Mania. Interview by Chava Respith for Survivors of the Shoah Visual History Foundation, 1998.

U

Ullman family

Frank Ullman (b. 1913) and his wife, Emily Konijn Ullman (b. 1913), were part of a large Dutch-Jewish family from Utrecht that went into hiding during the war. Helped by the many support groups organized by the Dutch people, they were able to escape the Nazi dragnet. They and their families survived and Frank Ullman is still grateful "to the Dutch and especially to the Dutch Resistance who risked their lives in order to save ours."

Frank and his older brother Fritz were the sons of Marianne and Salomon Ullman. Their mother was born in Holland and their father, called Sally, was a businessman originally from Germany who came to Holland before Hitler's rise to power. When the Nazis invaded Holland in 1940, both the Ullman boys were already married and living in Amsterdam. Fritz had married a Catholic woman and had three sons. Frank married a Jewish woman, Emily Konijn, in 1936 and their first son, Leo, was born in 1939.

Emily Konijn was the youngest of three children. Her older sisters, Margaret Warendorf and Julie Marthe Jacobs, were also married to Jews and had children of their own. Their father died in 1932 but their mother, Berthe, lived through the war.

The first year under the Nazis did not seem so bad to Frank. During that year, the Germans hid their brutality under a thin veneer of civilization.

Frank Ullman at home. Courtesy of Frank Ullman.

Emilie Ullman near her home in Port Washington, New York, in 2001. Courtesy of Frank Ullman.

They refrained from using brute force, and began their antisemitic campaign slowly, with rulings discriminating against the Jews. Jews were not allowed to own bicycles, to use public transportation, or to shop anywhere but in a Jewish market. To identify themselves, they had to wear a Star of David on their clothing and had a large "J" stamped on their identity cards. Then they lost their jobs and were forced to live in one area of the city. Supposedly to help the war effort, the order was given for Jews to deliver all their jewelry and other valuables to Nazi government officials and to have all Jewish bank accounts closed. A law forbidding Jews to own radios then prevented them from following broadcasts about the war.

By 1941, Jews began to be rounded up and killed or transported to concentration camps. The following year, a letter went out to a number of the young men in Amsterdam ordering them to report for work in Germany. But the Ullman family did not trust the Nazis. Although they knew nothing yet about the gas chambers or the wholesale murder of Jews, they had already heard that the transports took not only young men but also women and children, the old, and the sick. The family agreed that it was time to go into hiding.

Frank, Emily, and their three-year-old son, Leo, were now living with Frank's parents and grandmother as well as with Emily's mother. Arrangements had to be made for all seven of them. First, false papers were obtained without the fatal "J" stamped on them, so that they could purchase the ration cards needed to buy food. These were prepared by the Dutch Underground. Then safe hiding places had to be found. They needed money for all this, however, and most Jews had no work.

Both Frank and his father had lost their jobs in the retail business, but Frank had a Muslim friend in Amsterdam who sold oriental rugs and agreed to allow Frank to sell for him on the black market. Within three months, Frank had accumulated enough funds to complete all his arrangements and have money for food and rent for his extended family. When they parted, his Muslim friend gave Frank his own prayer rug as a good luck charm, telling him that with this rug, "Allah will protect you and keep you out of harm's way."

The Ullmans' first concern was Leo and, with the help of a support group from the Dutch Reformed Church, he was placed in a home with the Schimmel family, a retired policeman, his wife, and two married children, who cared for him lovingly for three years. Frank's parents found refuge with a German woman in Utrecht, and Emily's mother also went into hiding.

Once everyone had found a safe haven, Emily and Frank disappeared, too, staying in the empty attic of a family that Emily had known through her volunteer work in the welfare office. They remained there for three full years. Frank never went out during that time. Emily, forced to seek medical help because of an infected tooth, managed to find a kind dentist who treated her secretly at night. He never asked for any money.

One day, Frank was listening to his secret radio in the attic when he heard the BBC (British Broadcasting Company) warn that there would be another *razzia* (roundup) of Jews in Amsterdam. Fearing that they would be discovered, Frank prepared a crawl space under the stairs. He camouflaged it with a door taken from the attic and covered the top with an assortment of tools and some potatoes so it would look like an old, neglected storage area. Squeezed in that tiny space, their hearts pounding, Frank and Emily heard the Nazi police enter and search their attic and then leave. They were not discovered.

As the weeks and months passed and the Nazis were closer to defeat, food shortages in Holland—as everywhere in Europe—became acute. There was hardly any food to be found in the city and both Jews and gentiles were close to starvation. Finally, the only available nourishment was sugar beets.

As soon as they heard that the war was over, in May 1945, Emily and Frank came out of hiding. Their first destination was to the intermediary who knew where their son had been placed. They were so weak they could hardly walk, but they managed to make their way to the Schimmel house and find Leo, safe and happy. They realized that all the people living on that street knew about the Jewish child at the Schimmels' home but no one ever gave him away.

The rest of the Ullman family had also survived the war in hiding, although there had been some difficult circumstances for some. Emily's sister, Margaret Warendorf, and her three children had been discovered by the Germans, sent to the Westerbork transit camp, and in the last months of the war deported to Bergen-Belsen, a death camp in Germany. Margaret's husband had escaped earlier to England. All remained alive and were reunited in Amsterdam. Emily's oldest sister, Julie Marthe Jacobs, had fled to the United States with her family and was safe.

Frank's parents, Marianne and Sally Ullman, had also been discovered in a *razzia* just before war's end. Since by then the trains to the camps were no longer running, the Nazis had to content themselves with putting the Ullmans into prison in Amsterdam. They were released immediately after the Nazi withdrawal. Fritz Ullman, too, was safe although he had been imprisoned for a short time in Westerbork and threatened with sterilization. Ironically, the only victims in the Ullman family were Marianne's brother, his wife, and six children. Converted to Christianity long before the war, they were devout Catholics. But the Germans' concern was with purity of blood and not beliefs. They were all transported from Westerbork to a death camp and murdered.

In 1946, Frank, Emily, and their son, now six years old, decided to leave for America. "Amsterdam was one big cemetery," said Ullman. "So many friends were dead, so much of the city destroyed." He received an affidavit from his cousin who had come to the United States before the war, and went into the retail business with him, opening up a successful chain of five-and-ten-cent stores in Long Island, New York.

Emily and Frank had another son, Henry, and both boys grew up in Port Washington, New York, married, and had children and grandchildren of their own. Leo kept in touch with his "war parents," and often visited them in Amsterdam. Frank retired in 1976 and he and Emily regularly shared their story of survival with the students at local schools and colleges. Emily Konijn Ullman died in 2000 at the age of eighty-seven. Fritz remained in Holland with his family and died in a car accident in 2002. Marianne and Sally Ullman also stayed in Holland as did Emily's sister, Margaret, her husband, and children.

In 2005, Frank was ninety-two and living independently near his sons and their families in Port Washington. He still had the prayer rug given to him by his Muslim friend.

References

Ullman, Emily. *Stories by Emily Ullman*. Port Washington, NY: Emily Ullman, 2000.
Ullman, Frank. Interview by the author, January 2005, Port Washington, New York.

Ungar, William (1913–)

Juggling his real identity as a Jew and his false identity as a Christian Pole, Wilo Ungar of Lvov, Poland, managed to live through the war years without being caught. In his hours of deepest despair, he kept up his courage by telling himself that he must stay alive for his wife, Wusia, and baby, Michael, who had disappeared in the early years of the war.

Ungar was born in 1913 in the Polish village of Krasne, one of the younger children in a large and loving family. He had a good education and served in the cavalry of the Polish Army between the two wars. His time in the army taught him to feel comfortable with non-Jews and was instrumental in saving his life on many occasions.

After his army service, Ungar returned home and continued his education in Lvov, a Polish city with a thriving Jewish population. He got a job teaching in a Jewish technical school, met and fell in love with a young woman, Wusia, and began to think about getting married when war postponed his plans.

In August 1939, just before the Germans attacked Poland, Ungar was called back to the army to help defend his country. Fearing the worst, he left his job, his family, and his intended bride and reported for duty. The old-fashioned Polish Army, with its cavalry, wagons, and antiquated rifles, was no match for the Nazi war machine and they were quickly overpowered. During one of the battles, Ungar was wounded and taken to a field hospital. At the army hospital he experienced the results of antisemitism first hand when a Polish doctor refused to treat his wound until all the Christian soldiers were tended.

After recovering from a compound ankle fracture, which had been set badly, he returned to Lvov on crutches and rejoined Wusia, who had given up hope of seeing him alive. After a long convalescence at home, Ungar returned to his old job and made plans to be married. By this time, Lvov had come under Russian rule. In line with Soviet policy, the Jewish technical school was now a Communist school, but all the teachers were allowed to remain.

After Ungar and Wusia married, they found a tiny room in a good neighborhood, and before long, the young couple was expecting their first baby. They were overjoyed and never thought that the war would prevent them from having a long and happy life together. As Ungar explained in his book, written more than fifty years later, "until then no one truly believed in the actual existence of pure Evil."

But evil came into their lives very quickly, along with the Germans. Nazi soldiers marched into eastern Poland in the summer of 1941, driving the Russians back across the border. Shortly after their arrival in Lvov, Ukrainians, allied with the Germans, began hunting Jews in the city's streets and shooting or arresting those they found. The Ungars stayed indoors as much as possible and felt that if they stayed out of the way, they would be safe. As time passed, however, life became ever more dangerous for Jews, even those who, like Ungar, had jobs and proper papers.

Although it was hard to be too depressed when expecting a new baby, the Ungars could not ignore the growing danger. A week after their son Michael was born, a pogrom organized by the Ukrainians raged througout Lvov, during which the Germans burned down all the synagogues. Soon German police began rounding up Jews and taking them to forced labor in camps outside the city. Most were never seen again. That fall of 1941, notices were put up demanding that all Jews live in one section of the city. Ungar and his wife were forced to leave their apartment and move in with relatives. Now, with all the Jews living in one area, roundups were simplified and were occurring daily, and although Ungar had been picked up several times, he always managed either to talk his way out or slip away unnoticed. But finally, it was their turn.

On a summer day in 1942, Ungar saw abnormal activity in the street, which was followed by a knock on the door. "There was no place to hide," Ungar recalled years later. "Even if there had been a place there was no time." Along with their entire family, the Ungars were herded outside and directed to go left or right. Ungar was sent to the right, Wusia and Michael to the left. He never saw them again.

Ungar appealed to every Pole and German who might have news of his wife and child, but with no success. Alone and worried, he continued working at the school, now run by the Nazis for Aryan youngsters, but he understood that his days, too, were numbered unless he could manage to save himself.

Salvation came from a Polish friend named Edward Wawer, who worked with Ungar at the school. One day Wawer offered Ungar his documents: a Polish birth certificate and identity papers. "I don't have any [hiding] place to offer you," he explained, "but I can do something that might be as good." Wawer's papers saved Ungar many times. During the years that followed, he wandered throughout Poland searching for a safe place with friends or relatives or strangers. Whenever he found a haven, it was temporary. As he discovered, there was no place in all of Poland where a Jew could be safe.

For a while he depended on his false identity papers to allow him to live outside the ghetto, but he always needed to be careful because someone might recognize him. At other times, he took refuge in the ghetto, hiding with other Jews or working in labor camps where he could obtain food in exchange for work, but he always went back to his hideout outside the ghetto. Whenever he got into trouble or was reported to the authorities, Ungar managed to escape. He began to feel that he was destined to live.

When he lost his false identity papers in mid-1943, during a narrow escape from Janowska concentration camp, he realized he had to go into hiding. He found refuge with a woman who had already helped him once before. She was Katherine (Katya) Wowkowa, a Ukrainian woman who was the superintendent in the building where he had lived with Wusia before they moved into the ghetto. Now that building was filled with German officials, but she remained at her post. Wowkowa agreed to let him hide in one of the coal bins in the cellar of the building. She brought him food every day and did not reveal his presence to anyone. Ungar stayed there, never leaving the building, while he listened to the bombs falling from Russian planes onto the city.

By July 1944, the front was moving westward beyond Poland and back into Germany. The Russian Army returned to Lvov, driving out the Germans, and Ungar felt secure enough to emerge from hiding. But he soon discovered that Jews were still not safe. Polish right-wing militia groups were killing Jews wherever they found them. When Ungar tried to re-enlist in the Polish Army to join the Russians in driving out the Nazis, he was told that Jews were not welcome in the Polish Army. Then he saw a Jewish friend killed in the hospital right after he had emerged from hiding. Ungar realized the war wasn't over quite yet. He returned to the apartment house where he had been hiding, but no longer in the coal cellar.

Ungar took possession of one of the large, empty apartments that until a few days ago had been occupied by a German. He was alive, but he was alone and discouraged, and he wanted only to forget his suffering. What better way to do that than to assume his former Christian identity? He would be Edward Wawer and forget that he was Jewish. The decision seemed simple enough, but Ungar could not sleep that night. He thought of his grandmother and how she always told him, "Remember your grandfather whom you are named after. Remember your good name." Then he began to recall his childhood and his family and the celebration of his bar mitzvah. When he arose the following morning, he knew he could never be anyone but Wilo Ungar, the Jew.

Resuming his life as best he could, Ungar began teaching again at his old school. After a short time, he obtained a permit to visit Krasne, his place of birth. He traced the route of his family and found that almost all of them had perished except for a niece, Manya, one brother, Max, and a few other scattered relatives. When they were given the chance to leave the Russian zone for repatriation, Ungar and Manya left Lvov. With a small group of refugees, they were smuggled across the border into Germany and from there, made arrangements to emigrate to the United States. They arrived in New York in May 1946.

At first, Ungar was not eager to start a new life. He stayed with his older brother George, who had left for America before he was born, and learned English. He got a job on an assembly line for a company that made envelope-making equipment and went back to school, studying at City College in Manhattan, where he received a degree in mechanical engineering. Slowly, his

William Ungar (center) his wife Jerry Ungar and a young friend at a Holocaust memorial ceremony in Great Neck, New York. Courtesy of Joan Mandel.

emotional wounds healed and he began seeking companionship in his adopted country. He found it in Jerry Schweitzer, a young woman who shared his values and his interests and the couple was married in 1950.

William (Wilo's American name) and Jerry Ungar had four daughters. Ungar established a successful business producing envelopes and forged ties with new friends and with the Jewish community where he lived in Great Neck, New York. He gave generously to many causes, both Jewish and non-Jewish, contributing large sums to his synagogue, to the Holocaust museum, and to a variety of other charities. He never forgot those who helped him in Poland and sent money and food regularly to Katya Wowkowa, who had risked her life to hide him.

In 1992, with the more relaxed political climate and the Soviet Union no longer in existence, Ungar, accompanied by his wife, returned to his old village and to all the other places that had once been so familiar. They found only graves. That trip may have given Ungar the incentive to write his life story. In 2000, Ungar finally set down the story of his war experiences in a book called *Destined to Live* and for the first time revealed to Jerry and his daughters that he had had another wife and child.

In spring of 2005, William Ungar, retired by then, was honored by the President of the United States at a special ceremony at the United States Holocaust Memorial Museum in Washington, DC. He was accompanied there by his wife, Jerry, their four daughters, and their seventeen grandchildren.

Reference

Ungar, William, with David Chanoff. *Destined to Live*. New York: University Press of America, 2000.

V

Veil, Simone (1927–)

Simone Jacob Veil, a French Jew, was deported from France to Auschwitz but never stopped believing that Jews had a future in Europe. After the war, she became active in French politics and later served as president of the European Parliament.

Veil was born in Nice, a southern French city with a large Jewish community. The youngest of three children, her father, André Jacob, was an architect and the Jacob family lived a comfortable life. But by 1941, under the pro-Nazi Vichy regime, Jacob was forbidden to work as a professional and their lives became more difficult. Still, as natives of France whose family dated back before the French Revolution, they believed that, unlike those Jews who had arrived more recently from Germany and other parts of Eastern Europe, they would not be deported. So they waited for a speedy end to the war.

In April 1944, the Nazis finally caught up with the Jacob family. Five months before the liberation of France, they were rounded up. Veil's father and brother, Jean, then nineteen years old, were deported to a concentration camp in Lithuania and died there. Veil later learned that they were in a transport of eight hundred Jews, only fifteen of whom survived.

Veil, her older sister, Madeline, and her mother were sent to Auschwitz-Birkenau, and the three women were assigned to hard labor. On near starvation rations, they dug ditches, carried heavy stones, and endured cold and suffering together. Veil later told an interviewer, "I had this will to live," and added, "I was always in the company of my mother and sister."

Auschwitz was liberated by the Russians in January 1945, but by that time, Veil, along with most of the other Jewish prisoners, had been removed from the camp. With thousands of others they were marched through the snow to Bergen-Belsen concentration camp in Germany.

Conditions at Bergen-Belsen were even worse than they had been at Ausch-witz. There was no food, no medical treatment of any kind, and no sanitation. Hundreds died every day, among them, Veil's mother, who succumbed to typhus just before the British liberated the camp in April 1945.

After the liberation, Veil did not feel happy; she felt only sadness. "We dared not believe, even at the very end, that our executioners had not succeeded in killing us to erase all trace of their crime," she said.

After the war, Veil, then eighteen, and her older sister, Madeline, resumed their lives and, like many other survivors, married early. Veil married a French Jew, Antonie Veil, and the couple opted to remain in France. Madeline became a psychologist, married, and had a child, but she and her fifteen-month-old son were tragically killed in a car accident in 1953.

After completing her studies in law and political science in 1957, Veil took a job as a civil servant in the Ministry of Justice. She was quickly promoted to magistrate and began a series of improvements for prisoners and illegitimate children. These reforms brought her to the attention of French President Valéry Giscard d'Estaing and he appointed Veil to a position in his cabinet as Minister of Health. She was one of the first women to hold a cabinet post in France and remained in Giscard d'Estaing's government from 1974-1979.

In 1979, Veil moved from French politics and served for three years as the president of the European Parliament. "I am placing my hope in Europe," she said when she accepted the post, "in a Europe that has overcome hatred and barbarism."

Active in the Jewish community as well, Veil became head of the Foundation for the Memory of the Shoah in 1999, when that organization was established by the French government. The foundation is one of the largest charitable organizations in France. Veil also holds honorary degrees from Israel's Weitzmann Institute, Bar-Ilan University, and the Hebrew University.

As of 2006, Simone Veil, almost eighty years old, was still active and outspoken. She called herself a "European activist" and was serving as a member of the Constitutional Council of France, an organization that reviews new laws to insure that they follow the standards set by the French Constitution.

Simone Veil has three children, twelve grandchildren, and four great grandchildren.

> *I can never say it often enough to make it clear, especially to the younger generations, what we were forced to endure: the SS did not think of us as human beings but as animals. They didn't only intend to kill us; they wanted to strip us of our humanity. We were not only assured of certain death, but destined to be effaced from human history. They intended to erase all evidence of their crime, to blow up the gas chambers at Birkenau till nothing remained; to that end they tried to burn the bodies of murdered Jews in the mass graves that litter the Ukraine, Poland, the Crimea, Lithuania, which we are just now beginning to uncover, one by one.... They intended to burn all our books, to efface all trace of our presence on earth, in order to make it seem as though we had never existed; we were condemned to be utterly forgotten by history. This very commemoration is itself a victory against Nazism and against forgetting.*
>
> —Mme. Simone Veil, in a speech delivered at the National Day of Remembrance of Heroes and Martyrs of the Holocaust in Greece, January 30, 2006.

Reference

Krishner, Sheldon. "The French Politician with the Nazi Tattoos." *The Canadian Jewish News,* March 2, 2006, p. 11.

Velmans, Edith (1925–)

Edith van Hessen Velmans, from The Hague in Holland, lost almost all her family during the war. Her constant optimism in the face of one disaster after another carried her through some of the worst times of her young life.

Velmans was the youngest child and the only daughter in her family. Her father, David van Hessen, was a representative of an American lumber corporation. Her mother, Adeleide Hilde Wertheimer, was originally from Germany, but moved to Holland after she met and married David. The van Hessens were middle class, liberal Jews who were at home in Dutch society in The Hague. They and their children, Guus, Jules, and Edith, had both Jewish and Christian friends, and they were surrounded by a large and loving family.

The first signs of impending disaster reached the van Hessen family in 1938 after *Kristallnacht* (the Night of Broken Glass), the first government-sponsored pogrom against Jews, which occurred in Germany on November 9. That was when Adeleide Hilde finally persuaded her mother to leave Germany and come to the safety of Holland. From then on, Omi (Grandma) was part of Velmans's life.

It was difficult for the Dutch to even consider that they might be involved in war. Holland had been neutral during World War I and no country had attacked them. The government now declared their neutrality again. Nevertheless, in the spring of 1940, the Germans marched in, defeated the small Dutch Army, and occupied the country. They took over all the government installations and quartered German soldiers in Dutch homes.

For Velmans, life continued as usual, at least for a while. She was a popular teenager and her days were filled with parties and boys and school plays and other activities. But gradually, the Nazi policies of segregation and isolation of Jews were instituted. First, Jews were forbidden on public beaches, in parks, and in cafes, then radios were confiscated. Velmans's Christian friends stood by her. Even when she was barred from school, her sunny, optimistic nature persisted and she always found ways to enjoy herself, although it was becoming progressively harder.

There was much sad news and many difficulties to overcome. Early in the war, Velmans's mother fell and broke her hip, necessitating a long hospital stay. Meanwhile, the homes of Jewish neighbors were confiscated for use by the Germans and Jewish friends and relatives slowly disappeared. Some were deported, first to Westerbork, a transit camp in the Netherlands, and from there to Auschwitz or Sobibor, death camps in Poland. Others went into hiding. Because the van Hessens knew someone on the Jewish Committee, they managed to stay off the lists marked for deportation and kept hoping that the war would end before they, too, would be dragged out of their homes and brought to a Nazi concentration camp.

In 1942, the danger for the Jews in The Hague could no longer be ignored. The van Hessens wanted, first of all, to save their children. Guus had gone to the United States before the German occupation, so he was safe, but Jules and Edith were young and vulnerable. Their parents feared they would be sent to labor camps and sought to protect them. Like so many other Dutch Jews, they obtained false papers and, with the help of Christian friends, the children went into hiding.

Velmans was sent to the zur Kleinmiedes, a generous Dutch family in the town of Breda. They had a daughter of their own named Ineke, slightly older than Edith and much less optimistic and cheerful. Although the family was very different from hers, Velmans was very grateful to them for taking her in and went out of her way to be helpful and friendly. Everyone thought it would only be a few months before the war was over and she could return home, but the months turned into years. Velmans, now with a new name and a new identity, felt isolated and repressed. Constantly worried about her family, she could not visit them or even write to them openly. Letters from her mother were written as if she were a friend and not a beloved daughter and Velmans had strict instructions to burn each letter after she had read it. It was the one order that she did not obey.

While Velmans was in hiding with the zur Kleinmiedes, her father was diagnosed with cancer of the jaw. Several operations and radiation therapy were only partially successful and he remained in a hospital in Utrecht. Her mother, in a different hospital, was still getting rehabilitated from a broken hip but was assumed to be safe from the Nazis. Her brother Jules, also in hiding, was ultimately caught by the Germans while attempting to escape from Holland by boat. He was sent first to Westerbork and then to Auschwitz/Birkenau. The family did not know what happened to Jules and heard nothing more from him.

During the last year of the war, Adeleide Hilde van Hessen was taken out of the hospital along with all the other Jewish patients and brought to Westerbork transit camp. Here she was reunited with her mother Omi, who had been transported there from a nursing home. After several months, they were sent together on a transport to Sobibor and murdered in the gas chambers. Her father, still in the hospital, succumbed to cancer a short time later.

As one blow after another fell on eighteen-year-old Velmans, she was determined not to let it change her outlook on life. Remembering the loving advice her parents had written her throughout her two and a half years in hiding, she clung to memories of her family and continued to be helpful and friendly to the zur Kleinmiedes, especially to Ineke, who was becoming as close as an adopted sister. During the war, she had been especially encouraged and bolstered by Ineke's mother, Tine zur Kleinmiedes, who never allowed her to give in to fear and insisted that she go out to the grocery store daily and face down the German soldiers who were posted in the town.

When Breda was liberated by the Polish and Canadian Armies, it was September 1944. They all thought the war would be over in days, but it took eight more months before the Germans were driven out of the northern part of the country. Amsterdam and The Hague were still in German hands and the fighting was continuing. During those last months, Edith was reunited with her cousin Paul, who had escaped to England and was now back with the British Air Force, and with her brother Guus, who had enlisted in the United States Army and was in Holland with his unit.

Velmans, now nineteen years old, knew it was time to move on and take charge of her life. More than anything else, she wanted to help those who had suffered so much more than she. She volunteered to work in a Jewish orphan home and began the search for old friends and relatives. She found that most of the Jews were gone. Of the sixty thousand people sent to Auschwitz-Birkenau from the Netherlands, only five hundred returned. The percentage was even less from Sobibor, where only nineteen from a total of thirty-four thousand survived. As Velmans began to grasp the extent of the horror to which her people had been subjected, she wrote, "if only we could pay back those executioners, that entire wretched nation. Murderers, worse than murderers they are." She added, "I never realized that there could be such suffering in the world, and that anyone could live through it." Nevertheless, her optimism prevailed. Just after the war was over, she wrote in her diary, "I want to be happy, I *will* be happy—I can take what life doles out even though all it brings is bad luck. You can take a lot. And life will turn out to be beautiful—if you can come up with something to give to others, instead of always taking."

In 1946, Velmans began her studies at the University of Amsterdam, then studied one year abroad in the United States before returning to Holland. She completed her degree in psychology and married Loet Velmans. Velmans was an old classmate of her brother Jules and had fought with the British in the Pacific. At about the same time, Ineke zur Kleinmiedes married Edith Velmans's cousin, Dolf, and Nina Fernandes, a close gentile friend from The Hague married her cousin Paul. This gave Velmans a great deal of satisfaction. As she later wrote, "The two families who had helped me survive, who had been my parents' lifeline in their darkest hour, were now my family, related to me by marriage. My name [van Hessen] ... was to be the name of their children and grandchildren."

When Edith van Hessen Velmans gave birth to twin girls in 1950 in an Amsterdam hospital, Tine zur Kleinmiedes was waiting to visit her. She told the nurses she was the babies' grandmother. In 1983, to celebrate her foster mother's ninetieth birthday, Velmans brought her *Tante* (Aunt) Tine to Israel, where she was honored by Yad Vashem as a righteous gentile. She died in 1994 at the age of one hundred.

Edith and Loet Velmans moved to the United States in the 1970s. They have three daughters and five grandchildren. In 1996, Velmans was knighted by Queen Beatrix of the Netherlands. In 1998, her memoir, *Edith's Story*, was published and received the Jewish Quarterly Wingate Literary Prize.

Reference

Velmans, Edith. *Edith's Story: The True Story of a Young Girl's Courage and Survival during World War II.* New York: Bantam, 1998.

Verdoner, Gerrit (d. 1947), and Francisca Kan (née Verdoner) (1937–), and Otto Verdoner (1939–), and Yoka Verdoner (1934–)

The Verdoner children, Yoka, Francisca, and Otto, were born in Holland and were hidden in three separate homes during World War II. Their mother died in Auschwitz, but their father, Gerrit Verdoner, survived and was able to collect his children and bring them to the United States before he, too, succumbed to illness, caused partly by the stress of the war.

Gerrit Verdoner and his wife, Hilde, were both born in Holland where their families had lived for generations. They were so assimilated into Dutch life that Yoka, their oldest child, was not aware that she was Jewish until the

Three generations of the Verdoner-Kan families on a visit to Holland to revisit their war experiences. (Kan is third from left. Otto, Verdoner's oldest son, is first on left.) Courtesy of Fran Kan.

Germans occupied the country. She only realized it when they barred Jews from the public schools in 1940 and Yoka was sent home.

Gerrit was a partner in a successful business that sold bicycles and bicycle parts in Amsterdam, and the family lived in a large home in Hilversum. When the Germans came in, they chose the Verdoner home for their officers' headquarters and the family was forced to move.

As the Nazis closed in on the Jews, the Verdoners made a desperate decision. In order to keep their children safe, they would send them away to live with other families. Because Gerrit worked for the Jewish Council and had many connections with the underground, he was able to place each of his children in a different home with sympathetic gentiles.

At the very beginning of 1943, Yoka went to Woubrugge, a town in the Dutch farming country, and lived with Dick and Ella Rijinders. Dick Rijinders was the mayor there and told everyone that he was caring for Yoka while her mother was in a sanatorium in Switzerland. Since she was almost nine years old, she could understand what the circumstances were and never made a mistake when she was questioned. She was treated kindly by the Rijinders, who had a young daughter of their own, and even though she was anxious to return to her home, she has fond memories of her stay with them.

Francisca, only five when she was placed with Jan and Fen Barens in the fall of 1942, was too young to grasp the complexity of her situation. She simply obeyed when her foster parents told her that she must call them Mama and Papa. At first the Barens lived in a seacoast resort town, Zandvoort, but after the Germans took over the town and fortified it in preparation for an Allied invasion, they moved to Amsterdam. Here they lived in one of the houses in the Jewish section of town. Many homes were now available there because so many Jews had already been evacuated.

The Barens's new house was quite near the zoo and Fran was allowed to visit there almost daily. She later wrote, "I was such a regular that the zookeepers knew me." Fran's visits to the zoo were among the few bright spots during those lonely and frightening years. Although the Barens were good people, loyal members of the Dutch Underground, and willing rescuers of Dutch Jews, they had no children of their own and did not understand much about them. Fran was punished and even beaten for small, childish infractions. She was also witness to the daily roundups of Jews, who were then taken by truck to the detainment center just two doors down from the Barens's home.

Fran was often awakened during the night by the noise of those trucks and their terror-stricken passengers waiting to be deported.

Otto, the youngest of the three Verdoner children, spent the war years with Wiete and Maria Hopperus Bume, who lived in the countryside and had a large family. Whenever strangers came near, Otto was told to run upstairs and hide. During the Battle of Arnhem in 1944, five-year-old Otto heard the noise of the fighter planes overhead.

With their children safe, Hilde and Gerrit Verdoner hoped that they could ride out the remaining years of the war. As a member of the Jewish Council, Gerrit was in charge of setting up the lists of those to be deported and thought he could protect his family. Ultimately, he failed in this attempt. While he was away on Council business, Hilde was caught in a roundup and taken to Westerbork, the transit camp from which prisoners were sent to Auschwitz. Although Gerrit kept hoping that she would be able to escape, Hilde refused to do so because she knew that would mean that the rest of her family, including her parents, brother, and in-laws, who were also imprisoned there, would be immediately sent to Auschwitz and certain death. Eventually, in early 1944, all were deported. Hilde, ill from typhus, was thrown into a boxcar and died either on the way to the camps or immediately after arrival. Gerrit's parents were also killed, although Hilde's parents were shipped to Theresienstadt and survived. Gerrit himself managed to find a hiding place at the last minute and remained hidden until the Allies came in the spring of 1945.

When liberation came to all of Holland, Gerrit Verdoner went to collect his children. After three years, Otto, now six years old, did not recognize his father, but was happy to be back. Fran and Yoka were collected soon after and the family was reunited, but without their mother, things were not the same for Fran and Yoka.

In addition to the difficulties of making a home for his children, Gerrit's attempts to resume his old life were upsetting and disappointing. During the German occupation, no Jew was permitted to own a business, so Gerrit's non-Jewish partner was put in charge of the entire bicycle factory. After the war was over, he was reluctant to share the business again. He even accused Gerrit of collaborating with the Nazis. Due to this outrageous accusation, he was detained briefly by the Dutch authorities before they discovered the truth.

Gerrit was angry and bitter after this incident and decided it was time to leave Holland. He had a sister and several cousins in the United States and so he emigrated to America with

> *Hilde Verdoner, mother of the three Verdoner children, was transported from Westerbork, the Dutch transit camp, to Auschwitz, on February 9, 1944, with a transport from the hospital, where she lay sick. She was killed in the gas chambers immediately after her arrival. Below is her last letter, written to her father, David Sluizer*
>
> *February 7, 1944*
>
> *Dear Father,*
> *My worst fears have been realized and I have been called up for transport.*
> *Do what you can!*
> *I have very little hope.*
> *Stay healthy and strong.*
> *Send me a note back as soon as possible if you find out anything.*
>
> *A thousand kisses,*
> *Hilde*

his children in 1946. He was probably already suffering from cancer when he arrived in New York.

Gerrit died in October 1947, leaving his children, then thirteen, ten, and eight, in the care of relatives. As adults, they found and translated their mother's letters from Westerbork and had them published. In the foreword to their book, *Signs of Life*, Fran and Yoka wrote that, after their father's death, "We spent periods of time living with various relatives and friends, sometimes together, sometimes apart, sometimes cared for with affection, sometimes with indifference at best."

Despite the sadness in their lives, the Verdoner children grew to adulthood and found their way in the United States. They all completed high school and went on to graduate from college. Otto is married to the daughter of a Holocaust survivor from Salonika, Greece. They live in Colorado and have two sons. Fran, now an artist, married Robert Kan, also a survivor from Holland. They are living in Delaware and have three daughters and five grandchildren. Yoka never married. She lived in Israel for many years, teaching English, and then returned to Holland for a while. As of 2006, she was living in California and had launched a career as a psychotherapist. The sisters wrote in their book, "Sometimes we wonder what our lives would have been like if there had been no Hitler, no war, no persecution, no policy of annihilation. We will never know."

References

Kan, Francisca Verdoner. "Reclaiming Amsterdam." *The New Light* 46 (Fall 2003), p. 18.

Verdoner, Yoka, and Francisca Verdoner Kan, eds. *Signs of Life: The Letters of Hilde Verdoner-Sluizer from Nazi Transit Camp Westerbork, 1942-1944*. Washington, DC: Acropolis Books, 1990.

Vitale family

Giorgio and Emma Segrè Vitale and their three daughters, Michelina (b. 1925), Georgina (b. 1926), and Emilia (b. 1938), from Turin, Italy, spent part of World War II in hiding, helped by friendly Italians, and managed to escape the Nazis. Back home after the war, they found that other family members had been caught, deported, and killed in the camps, but they had survived intact.

The Vitale children lived a carefree life, insulated from the problems that swirled around them. Their extended family, including two sets of grandparents and a large number of aunts, uncles, and cousins, was all embracing. They celebrated Jewish holidays and life-cycle events together, vacationed in the same seaside resorts, and helped each other in times of trouble. Giorgio worked in a successful business with his brothers selling electrical parts for cars, but even after the Vitales moved to Milan to supervise a new branch of the business, they visited regularly.

Involved in their own lives, the younger generation was hardly aware that Benito Mussolini, the Fascist ruler of Italy, had signed a pact with Nazi Germany. Suddenly, in September 1938, shortly after the birth of Emilia, they saw the headline in the paper: all Jews were barred from the public schools.

This announcement was a blow to the Vitale family, whose ancestors had lived in Italy for many generations. They were staunch patriots and counted many friends among their Christian neighbors. Although most of those friends did not change their attitudes, and private Jewish schools were quickly organized to serve Jewish children, increasing antisemitism began to develop in Italy. "Jews and dogs not allowed," was a sign that appeared in windows of cafes and stores. Owners of some shops proudly proclaimed their "Aryan" origins.

In 1940, when Italy entered World War II on the side of Germany, conditions worsened for Italy's Jews. Now every Jew was issued an identity card stamped with the words "of the Jewish race." Radios owned by Jews were confiscated, Jews were forced to move out of areas located near military bases, and young Jews were conscripted for forced labor and had to report after school. They were put to work maintaining parks, streets, and hospitals. In addition, countless nights were spent, together with all Italians, in bomb shelters as a protection against Allied bombing raids. During one such raid, Giorgio's business was destroyed. He and his Christian employees salvaged whatever they could and re-opened in another area.

> *[In Piea] . . . we listened hopefully every night on our shortwave radio to the BBC with the somber news of the painfully slow advance of the Allied forces from the south. We became part of the rural life of the little town. . . . Partisans were hiding in the woods all around the town, and the Germans were never far away. [They] went from house to house, at times rounding up the whole population in the square. . . . During one of the searches the Germans saw a patch of freshly dug ground in our vegetable garden. With machine guns pointed at my father, they made him dig so they could see what was buried there. It was our dog, which had died just days before.*
>
> —Georgina Vitale, *And Life Is Changed Forever* (p. 296).

As the bombing increased, schools were closed. Hoping to keep safe, the Vitales, along with many other families both Jewish and Christian, moved to their summer home, located in a small village and therefore not prey to Allied attacks.

When the schools closed in northern Italy, Georgina had only one semester of high school left. To make sure she completed her education, her parents sent her to Rome to live with an uncle. In that city, she was accepted into a Catholic school, where her cousin was already a student, and graduated.

In July 1943, Mussolini was thrown out of office and two months later Italy surrendered to the Allied Armies. All of Italy was ecstatic, thinking the war was over for them. Hitler, however, had other plans. With the U.S. Army located only in the southernmost part of the country, the Germans marched in from the north. Within a few hours of the surrender, they had occupied every city and began immediately to round up and deport Jews.

Through a friend who worked at the city hall in Turin, the Vitale family purchased false identity papers and settled in Piea, a tiny village twenty-eight miles from Turin. They were confident that they would only be there for a few months, trusting that the U.S. Army, already in Sicily and marching on to Naples, would soon drive the Germans out. That hope proved overly optimistic and the Vitales remained in hiding for two full years.

Italian ambivalence toward Nazi antisemitic policies is illustrated by an incident that occurred during the family's time in hiding. Georgina's high school diploma prepared her to teach the primary grades and she needed only to take a qualifying exam, given each year in September. Determined not to miss it, she traveled with her false identity papers to Turin, but showed her real papers to the officials administering the exam. She later wrote about that incident: "The instructors were confused and didn't know what to do. They looked at each other and . . . they gave me the exams, written and oral, and then I took the bus and went back to Piea." After the war, she received her diploma.

During their two years of occupation, the Germans multiplied their efforts to remove the Jews from Italy. In December 1943, the Nazis declared the Jews "public enemies of the country." They came searching for Jews even in tiny Piea, and the Vitales decided that they must separate. With yet another set of names and identities, Giorgio and Emma moved back to their old apartment in Turin, which they shared with a Christian family. Michelina and Georgina, now eighteen and nineteen years old, took their baby sister, five-year-old Emilia, and moved to Montanaro, another small village. They found a tiny room used to store furniture, where they remained for two months.

Those months in Montanaro were the most difficult of all. The weather was cold; there was no heat besides a tiny stove used for cooking. The toilet was outside and water had to be brought from across the street. By February, they decided to take their chances in Piea and the family reunited and stayed there. Although the Nazis came many times in search of Jews, the Vitales were never betrayed by their Italian neighbors who, they found out later, always knew they were Jewish.

When the war was over, the Vitale family, still together, moved back to their apartment in Turin and began to calculate the losses to their family and to the Jewish community. They learned that six thousand to eight thousand Italian Jews had been murdered, including some members of their own family.

By the end of 1945, life slowly began returning to normal. Michelina, engaged throughout the war, got married in the bombed out synagogue in Turin. Hers was the first Jewish wedding to be held since the war and the entire community was present for this event. Years later, her sister wrote, "It seemed to signify the rebirth of a people almost reduced to ashes by the evil schemes of a world gone mad."

Over the next five years, all the Vitale sisters were married and had children of their own. Giorgio and Emma remained in Turin and reestablished the business. Michelina and her husband also remained in Italy close to the family, and by 1946, their daughter, Paola was born. Georgina married her cousin Luciano, who had been in the United States during the war. Leaving Italy and her family was a difficult decision, but Georgina and Luciano finally married in 1948, left for New Haven, Connecticut, and eventually had four daughters. They brought their girls back to Italy for the first time in 1963, visited Turin, and introduced them to all their cousins and aunts. Then they took them to Piea, where the Vitale family had hidden during the war. From that time on, Georgina's daughters remained close to the Italian branch of the family and made regular visits. Georgina was widowed in 1972, but continued living in New Haven.

Emilia, the youngest sister, married a German Jew who had lived in Turin during the war. They had four children and, for a while, they stayed in Italy, but eventually decided to move to Israel. Emilia died there of cancer at the age of forty-six.

Reference

Glassner, Martin Ira, and Robert Krell, editors. *And Life Is Changed Forever: Holocaust Childhoods Remembered*. Detroit, MI: Wayne State University Press, 2006.

Vrba, Rudolf (1924–2006)

Rudolf Vrba was born in Czechoslovakia and transported first to Majdanek and then to Auschwitz in 1942. One of the first to successfully escape from the Auschwitz death camp, he gave an eyewitness account of Nazi atrocities to the free world.

Vrba was born in Topolcany, Slovakia, to Elias and Helena Rosenberg. His father owned a sawmill and Vrba, originally named Walter Rosenberg, was attending the gymnasia (high school) in Bratislava when the Germans first occupied his country.

In 1939, just before Germany invaded Poland, they annexed part of Czechoslovakia and created a pro-Nazi government in Slovakia. Their new policy, consistent with the Nuremberg laws in Germany, was to bar all Jewish students from public education and, at the age of fifteen, Vrba was expelled from high school and found a job as a laborer. As antisemitism became more virulent, he tried to escape the country, either to Hungary or to England, but was caught at the border, arrested, and sent to Majdanek concentration camp. From there he was shipped to Auschwitz.

From August 1942, Vrba shared the horrors of Auschwitz but worked in what most of the prisoners considered a "good job." He was part of a group that sorted all the clothing and personal possessions of the incoming prisoners. The gold was melted down into ingots and the clothing and other items were prepared for shipment to Germany.

In June 1943, Vrba was transferred again, this time to the Auschwitz-Birkenau death camp, and assigned as registrar in the quarantine section of the camp. Here, he was in a position to watch the nightly passage of trucks carrying Jews to the gas chambers. Vrba estimated that over one million Jews had already been murdered at Auschwitz. When he overheard German soldiers discussing the new shipment of Jews that were expected from Hungary, he was determined to escape and tell the world.

It took Vrba and another prisoner, Alfred Wetzler, nearly a year to plan and execute an escape. With the help of the camp underground, they dug a hole beneath a pile of wood that was being assembled for new construction. On April 7, 1944, Vrba and Wetzler entered the hole. Other prisoners covered the sides with boards and sprinkled the entire area with Russian tobacco soaked in gasoline. This technique, learned from Russian prisoners of war, was intended to divert the guard dogs that were used to track down escapees.

The men remained in their hideout for three days. When the Germans had given up the search for them, they waited until dark and walked out of the camp. It took the men two weeks to reach the town of Zilina in northern Slovakia and make contact with the Slovakian *Judenrat* (Jewish Council).

With the *Judenrat*, the men prepared a report to send to the Allies and to the Jewish leaders in Hungary, hoping to save this last intact Jewish community. The report, later referred to as the Auschwitz Protocol, contained detailed

The first death camp began operating at Chelmno in December 1941. By 1942, Belzec and Sobibor were established and then Treblinka. Majdanek was a concentration camp but was transformed into a death camp by the addition of gas chambers and ovens, also in 1942. Auschwitz, built in 1940, was originally a camp for Poles and then Soviet prisoners of war. In 1941, a second section was added, generally referred to as Birkenau or Auschwitz II, where the gas chambers were located. The first victims were Russian soldiers. It was transformed into a death camp for Jews by 1942. In all these camps, technical and scientific advances served the aims of mass murderers.

After the war, the name Auschwitz *became a code word, symbolizing Nazi brutality.*

Death Camp	Number of Jews Murdered
Majdanek	*200,000*
Sobibor	*250,000*
Chelmno	*320,000*
Belzec	*600,000*
Treblinka	*870,000*
Auschwitz	*1,500,000*

—Israel Gutman, ed. *Encyclopedia of the Holocaust.* Vol. 2. s.v. "Extermination Camps," pp. 461–630.

maps of the camp, the gas chambers, and the crematoria drawn by Vrba from memory. Preliminary information was sent out quickly, and by June, an official thirty-two-page report was sent to England, the United States, the Vatican, the Swiss Red Cross, and the Hungarian Jewish leaders. The British and American governments accepted the report as true and condemned the Nazis and their Hungarian allies, although they never bombed either the camp or the rail lines leading to Auschwitz. The biggest disappointment, however, was that the Hungarian Jewish leaders decided not to make the Auschwitz Protocol public. Reasons for this failure were never clear and by June 6, when two other Jews escaped from Auschwitz and came to Zilina, they reported that trainloads of Jews from Hungary had already arrived at Auschwitz and were being massacred.

As Vrba later told an interviewer with *The Ottawa Citizen* in 2005, "The strength of the Final Solution was its secrecy, its impossibility. I escaped to break that belief that it was not possible. And to stop the killings." By not going public with the news, Vrba explained, "already 200,000 of these I had tried to save, those whom I thought, indeed, I *had* saved were already dead."

Despite his disappointment at the results of his daring escape, it was estimated that his accurate information about the Auschwitz extermination camp did save at least a hundred thousand Hungarian Jews.

Once free and provided with false papers, Vrba joined the Czech partisans and officially adopted the name Rudolf Vrba. He received several medals for bravery by the Czech government.

Auschwitz was liberated by the Russians in January 1945, nine months after Vrba's escape. By May 1945, the war in Europe had ended and Vrba, now twenty-one, completed his education. He eventually earned a doctorate in chemistry and biochemistry at Charles University in Prague and then did post-doctorate work at the Czechoslovak Academy of Science.

In 1958, while part of an official scientific delegation to the West, Vrba defected from Communist Czechoslovakia and immigrated to Israel. After working at the Weizmann Institute for two years, he went to England, where he was a member of the British Medical Research Council for seven years. While in England, he published his personal memoir, *Escape from Auschwitz: I Cannot Forgive* (later reissued in the United States as *I Escaped from*

Auschwitz). After becoming a British citizen in 1966, he moved to Canada and settled there permanently—with the exception of a two-year stay at Harvard Medical School as a research fellow. On his return to Canada, he was hired as Associate Professor of pharmacology at the University of British Columbia.

Vrba was well known for his important research on brain chemistry and on diabetes and cancer. He died of cancer at the age of eighty-one and was survived by his wife, Robin, one daughter, Zuza Vrbowa Jackson, and two grandchildren. Another daughter died before he did.

References

Linn, Ruth. "Rudolf Vrba." *The Guardian,* April 13, 2006. Available at http://www .guardian.co.uk/secondworldwar/story/.

Martin, Douglas. "Rudolf Vrba, 81, Auschwitz Witness, Dies." *The New York Times,* April 7, 2006.

Vrba, Rudolf. *I Escaped from Auschwitz*. Fort Lee, NJ: Barricade Books, 2002.

W

Wagner, Kurt (1931–), and Heinz Walker (1930–)

Kurt Wagner and Heinz Walker, brothers born in Karlsruh, Germany, just one year apart, survived the war, but under very different circumstances: Walker was raised by his father, a pro-Nazi Christian, Wagner by his mother, a Jew. The brothers met for the first time thirty years after the war and, putting their parents' decisions behind them, slowly established a relationship.

The two brothers were sons of Ilse Ettlinger Walker and Julius Walker. Shortly after Hitler came to power in 1932, the Walkers, with the encouragement of an antisemitic government, were divorced and made a fateful compromise: to divide the children between them. Heinz Walker stayed with Julius, who had become a committed Nazi and member of the SA (*Sturmabteilung* or Storm Troopers) and was raised by his paternal grandparents. He remained in Karlsruh throughout the war, attending a public school. Julius Walker died of a brain hemorrhage before the war began. Heinz remained with his grandparents and, although the Walkers suffered from all the shortages endemic to wars and lived through a massive bombing of the city in 1943, he was never singled out or threatened. His gentile family succeeded in hiding the fact that he was half Jewish.

Kurt Wagner lived with his Jewish mother, his maternal grandparents, Sophie and Isaac Ettlinger, and his uncle Julius, and his life was very different. Barred from attending public school by the Nuremberg laws that had been promulgated by Hitler in 1933, Wagner attended a Jewish school at his local synagogue. He was seven years old in 1938, when he arrived at school to find that the synagogue had been burned to the ground, the result of a nationwide Nazi pogrom against the Jews that came to be called *Kristallnacht*, the Night of Broken Glass.

From that time on, conditions grew progressively worse for Germany's Jews. They were barred from all access to community services, forced to wear identifying Stars of David on their clothing, and put under strict curfew. By the time active fighting began in September 1939, the Nazis had begun to deport the Jews to concentration camps within Germany. One year later, when the German Army had invaded and occupied France, 895 German Jews were sent to Gurs, a French camp, to await their final destination and death. The Ettlinger family, including Wagner and his mother, uncle, and grandfather, was part of this transport (his grandmother had died a year earlier).

At the age of nine, Wagner was still young enough to remain with his mother at camp de Gurs, but that was barely an advantage. Conditions at Gurs were unbearable. Hunger and disease were widespread, sanitation was almost nonexistent, and there were no facilities for the children, who wandered around aimlessly in what has been described as "a sea of mud."

In order to alleviate the miserable lives of the refugees, several relief organizations began to operate at Gurs. One of these, the American Friends Service Committee, was sponsored by the Quakers. Among the workers was a Norwegian woman named **Alice Resch Synnestvedt**, who took on the project of helping the Jewish children at the camp. She found an orphanage in nearby Aspet that agreed to take forty-eight young refugees and care for them. Not all the parents were ready to let their children go, but Wagner's mother agreed.

Kurt Wagner stayed in Aspet at La Maison des Pupilles de la Nation for one and a half years. In 1942, he was one of six children who were sent to the United States. All six had relatives in America and thus were able to obtain visas. The ship arrived in Baltimore in August 1942. Only a few months later, his mother, uncle Julius, and grandfather Isaac were shipped to Auschwitz and murdered.

Wagner was taken to Chicago where his great uncle lived, but the man was not able to care for the boy. Instead, he was placed in a foster home for one year, where he lived with other refugee children. Then the Jewish Children's Bureau took him to a new home to meet Bella and Irwin Wagner. They had no children of their own and were happy to adopt Kurt. The adoption legalities were finalized as soon as the war was over, when it was ascertained that Kurt's mother was no longer alive, and Kurt Wagner embraced his new family. He became integrated with the community, graduated high school, and went on to college. In 1950, however, during his first year at college, Irwin Wagner died and Wagner was devastated. He was not able to continue his studies and instead joined the army.

By 1950, the United States was fighting the Korean War and Wagner was shipped to Alaska, where he spent two years on an army base. When he returned, he met Marilyn Fishman. They were married in 1954 and had two sons, Irwin and Stuart. But Wagner did not want his adoptive mother to be alone, and soon Bella Wagner joined her son's family. She lived with them happily until her death at the age of ninety-four.

Shortly after the war, Heinz Walker had searched for his brother and found him in the United States, living with his new adoptive family. Although Wagner had forgotten a good deal of the German language, they began a correspondence and the Wagners sent food packages to Walker, who was having a difficult time in postwar Germany. It took many more years before Wagner was ready to return to Karlsruh for a visit.

In 1978, Wagner, accompanied by his two grown sons, flew to Germany and visited Heinz Walker and his family. It was an emotional meeting. Wagner, still angry at his birth father for abandoning him and his mother, shared his feelings with Walker. Walker defended his father and related how hard it had been to grow up without a mother. Despite their differences, they established a friendship and Wagner met his father's sister and his cousin Gerhardt.

Over the next two decades, Walker and his wife, son, and two granddaughters made several visits to Chicago and all three generations met. Wagner hosted his brother in his home and the two became closer. In 2006, Kurt Wagner, now retired from a career in sales, was anticipating another visit to Karlsruh to celebrate his brother's granddaughter's wedding.

Reference

Wagner, Kurt. Telephone interview by the author, July 2006.

Wallenberg, Raoul (1912–1947?)

Swedish diplomat Raoul Wallenberg is probably the most famous of all the righteous gentiles of World War II. Using his credentials as a Swedish legation attaché, he created innovative ways to rescue individual Jews from deportation, saving the lives of tens of thousands of Hungarian Jews from the Nazis' final solution.

Wallenberg was a distinguished name in Sweden and the family included well-known bankers, diplomats, and officers. Despite the death of his father, an officer in the Swedish Navy who died before his son was born, Raoul grew up in a stable home. He lived with his mother, Maj Wising Wallenberg and stepfather, Frederick von Dardell, but he stayed in close touch with his father's family. His paternal grandfather, Gustav Wallenberg, guided his education and his career.

Wallenberg first decided to study architecture and went to the United States, where he graduated first in his class from the University of Michigan. Finding no opportunities for architects in Sweden, however, he became interested in banking and international business. His grandfather first sent him to South Africa for an apprenticeship with a Swedish firm, and then to Haifa, Palestine (now Israel), where he worked for a Dutch bank for six months in 1936. Here, for the first time, he met Jewish refugees and learned about Hitler's persecution of Jews. Wallenberg himself may have had a drop of Jewish blood from his grandmother's grandfather, named Benedicks, who had come to Sweden in the late eighteenth century.

Other jobs followed, mostly obtained through the influence of the Wallenberg family, who introduced him to a Hungarian Jew, Koloman Lauer. Lauer was the director of a Swedish-based import and export company specializing in food and delicacies. He needed someone like Wallenberg not only for his excellent language skills but also for his ability to move around freely in Europe. Within eight months, the two men were business partners and Wallenberg became joint owner and international director of the Mid-European Trading Company.

Raoul Wallenberg in his office in Budapest during the last year of the war. Courtesy of Thomas Veres and the U.S. Holocaust Memorial Museum Photo Archives.

During the early years of the war, Wallenberg was exposed to the antisemitism being perpetrated throughout the German-occupied parts of Europe. His travels in France and Germany on business had taught him how the Nazi bureaucracy worked. And while he was aware that Hungary was still a relatively safe place for Jews, he understood that it could fall to the Nazis at any time.

Wallenberg's suspicions proved correct. The German Army, sensing that Hungary's commitment to the Nazi cause was shaky, invaded that country on March 19, 1944, and began deporting Jews from the smaller towns. By spring of 1944, most people knew about Hitler's final solution and understood what awaited the Jews in Auschwitz and other concentration camps. Neutral Sweden had already established an operation for the rescue of Jews and needed someone to take charge of the project.

That summer, Wallenberg was asked to serve on the staff of the Swedish legation to Budapest; his assignment: save the remaining seven hundred thousand Jews of Hungary. Wallenberg had been recommended by his Hungarian partner, Kolomon Lauer, a member of the Swedish branch of the World Jewish Congress. His appointment had been approved by the American War Refugee Board, a committee established solely to help the Jews of Europe and funded by American Jewish organizations. Before accepting the post, Wallenberg insisted on free rein in his diplomatic dealings and in decisions about money. The Swedish king agreed and by July 1944 Wallenberg was in Budapest.

The Hungarian regent, Miklós Horthy, was ready to cooperate with Sweden and others who were trying to save Jews, but by October 1944, the Nazis forced the resignation of Horthy's men and appointed Ferenc Szalasi, an avid pro-Nazi Hungarian in his place. Szalasi reinstated the deportation and murder of the Jews of Hungary. Over the next three months, Wallenberg issued thousands of "protective passports" and, although technically these passes had no international standing, the Nazis respected them. The passports established a special connection with the individual passport holder, placing him or her under Sweden's protection. In addition, Wallenberg set up safe houses, ostensibly part of the Swedish Embassy, where Jews in danger could stay and escape the deportations. There were a total of thirty-one such protected houses sheltering fifteen thousand people, and Wallenberg employed six hundred Jews to manage the food supply, sanitation, and other needs of those in hiding. Among his protected Jews were **Tom Lantos** and **Kate Stern Lebovitz.**

Wallenberg did not limit his efforts to Budapest. He traveled to meet the Hungarian Jews who were being forcibly marched to the border of Austria.

He gave out food and medicine to the starving men and distributed protective passports that enabled him to take some of them back to Budapest. Wallenberg even removed people from the trains as they were departing to their deaths, distributing his passes to as many desperate refugees as possible. He also attempted to negotiate with the Russians to insure proper care of the Jews already liberated by the Soviet Army. It may have been this final concern that caused his disappearance.

The Soviets were very suspicious of their allies as well as their enemies. They suspected Swedish diplomats of spying for the Germans and then for the Americans. Seeing so many Swedish documents created distrust in the minds of the Soviets about Sweden's motives. In January 1945, Russian control of Eastern Europe was almost complete, and the war was virtually over on the Eastern front. Wallenberg, sure that his diplomatic status would protect him, asked for a meeting at Soviet Army headquarters. The meeting was granted. The last time he was seen in Hungary was a few days later, on January 17, with two Russian soldiers. He was quoted as saying that he did not know whether he was a guest of the Soviet Union or their prisoner.

Wallenberg disappeared behind the Iron Curtain. After several investigations, the Russian government reported that he had died in prison of natural causes in 1947. Other prisoners of Stalin claimed that they had seen him in various prisons after that. Although these claims were never proven, investigations by the United States, Britain, and Israel led to other information about Wallenberg's heroic actions. It was learned that just before the liberation of Budapest by the Russians, the SS and the Hungarian Nazis (the Arrow Cross) planned to blow up the ghetto. Because of Wallenberg's threats against the general who was ultimately responsible for the order, he managed to prevent this and save an additional hundred thousand Jews.

Since his disappearance, Raoul Wallenberg has been given honorary citizenship in the United States, named Righteous Among the Nations by Yad Vashem, the Holocaust memorial museum of Israel, and been recognized throughout the world. His body was never found.

References

"Raoul Wallenberg." http://www.jewishvirtuallibrary.org/jsource/biography/wallenberg.html.

Yahil, L. "Raoul Wallenberg: His Mission and His Activities in Hungary." *Yad Vashem Studies* 15 (1983): pp. 7-54.

Walters, Sam (1929–2007)

Sam Walters was born in Bedzin, Poland, a town near the German border. The youngest of three, he and his brothers were separated during World War II and ended up in three different countries.

Walters was born Shlomo Wolf Posmantier. His father, Hayyim David, was a butcher in Bedzin. He owned his own kosher butcher shop and also exported nonkosher meat. His mother, Gittel Posmantier, tended their home and the children with the help of a live-in nanny. Walters often accompanied his father to the synagogue where five thousand families prayed. With a population of over twenty-one thousand Jews, the Posmantier sons went to a Jewish public school.

Bedzin's location near the German border made this industrial city especially vulnerable to German attacks and they were quickly occupied by the Nazis after the invasion on September 1, 1939. One of the first of the antisemitic laws that was passed forbade Jewish children from attending school. At first, the Posmantiers hired a private tutor to teach the children secular subjects and a rabbi for Jewish learning, but as Nazi laws against the Jews became harsher, Posmantier's business was confiscated and tutors were no longer affordable.

The Germans did not establish a ghetto in Bedzin until 1943, but well before that, they were terrorizing Jews. They killed the leaders of the Jewish community and then the bakers so there would be no bread for the Jewish population. Early in the war, they began conscripting Jews for forced labor in local German-owned factories. Walters and his father ended up in Waldenberg, one of the satellite camps of Gröss Rosen. His father died there. Posmantier's last words to his son were, "Go forward. Don't look back."

Walters was fifteen years old when the Russians liberated Waldenberg in early 1945, and he walked back to Bedzin alone. There he learned that his mother had been murdered at Auschwitz and his brothers were alive but scattered. The thriving Jewish community of Bedzin had disappeared and Walters was one of the youngest among the handful of its residents who had survived. All the young men and women who had bravely attempted a rebellion in the city had been killed. The synagogue had been burned early in the war. Walters could not resume his old life. He made his way to Landsberg, Germany, where a large displaced-persons camp had been established by the Allies and remained there for four years while waiting for a visa to the United States. During that time he learned some plumbing and welding skills in preparation for earning his living. Meanwhile, one of his brothers settled in France and the other went to Israel.

In 1949, Walters arrived in Kansas City and took his father's advice: he went forward. He changed his name from Shlomo Posmantier to the more Americanized Sam P. Walters, taking Posmantier as his middle name. Although he wanted to continue his education, he was not able to afford college. He took courses in English to improve his language skills and quickly found work, first as a welder and later as a sales representative for a jewelry company.

By 1957, eight years after his arrival in the United States, Walters was well established in his new country but missed his family. He traveled first to France and then to Israel to visit his brothers. While in Israel he met Ann Finkelstein, also a Holocaust survivor. Walters and Finkelstein were married in Israel and then returned to Kansas City. Their daughter Tovah was born two years later.

Walters and his family remained in Kansas City, where he became involved in public service. He was an active member of B'nai Brith and, through his synagogue, he established a fund for children. In the late 1990s he told an interviewer that he believed he survived in order to help other people.

Although never able to continue his formal education, Walters filled in the gaps with lectures and concerts. "I'm involved in humanity," he said.

Walters died in January, 2007. By then, his daughter had become a doctor, was married, and had a son.

References

Dodd, Monroe, ed. *From the Heart: Life Before and After the Holocaust—A Mosaic of Memories*. Kansas City: Kansas City Star Books and the Midwest Center for Holocaust Education, 2001.

Gutman, Israel, ed. *Encyclopedia of the Holocaust*. s.v. "Bedzin." New York: Macmillan, 1990.

Warhaftig, Zerah/Zorah (1906–2002)

Zorah (or Zerah) Warhaftig of Belarus, was an anti-Nazi activist even before the war. He fled from the German advance in 1939 and in still-unoccupied Lithuania, devoted himself to helping refugees from Poland escape the double threat of Nazi and Soviet brutality. His efforts helped to develop an unusual route to safety.

Warhaftig was born in Volkovysk, a town in western Byelorussia (now Belarus). He was the son of a great Torah scholar and followed in his father's footsteps, studying at several different yeshivahs (academies of Jewish learning) in Warsaw. After becoming a rabbi, he also took a law degree at the University of Warsaw.

Warhaftig's early affiliation with *Mizrachi*, the movement of religious Zionism, led to a commitment to help Jews resettle in Palestine, but in the wake of the Nazi invasion of Poland in 1939, he was forced to take up other activities. Even before the outbreak of the war, Warhaftig had been an active member and then co-chair of the Committee to Boycott Nazi Germany. Because of this affiliation, he knew he had to leave as soon as the Germans marched into Poland. Warhaftig escaped on foot to Lithuania, still an independent nation, and in Kovno, the Lithuanian capital, he became head of the Palestine committee for Polish refugees. England, however, was allowing only a trickle of Jewish immigration into Palestine.

Then, in June of 1941, Soviet troops marched in and took over Lithuania. They began to deport many Jewish refugees to Siberia and other undeveloped areas in eastern Russia as slave laborers. The Jews, faced with a choice of returning to Nazi-occupied Poland or becoming prisoners in the Soviet Union, desperately searched for asylum, but few countries were interested in accepting them. Warhaftig, aware of the Nazis' treatment of the Jews of Germany, and anticipating a Holocaust, began investigating other ways to rescue Jews. He heard that two Dutch yeshivah students had obtained permission from the Dutch consul to travel to Curaçao, in the Dutch West Indies. Realizing that Curaçao was open to immigration, Warhaftig now persuaded Russia to allow the refugees to travel east. From there, they could go by ship to Japan, cross the Pacific to the United States and continue to the Dutch West Indies. Russia tentatively agreed on one condition: that the Japanese would also grant transit visas.

Armed with this conditional acceptance, Warhaftig approached the Japanese consul **Chiune (Sempo) Sugihara** and convinced him to issue Jews the lifesaving exit visas. Sugihara, following his conscience rather than orders from his own government, worked with Warhaftig to save several thousand people, including a shipload of yeshivah students from the Polish city of Mir.

Warhaftig also took this route. He left Kovno on one of the transports he had arranged and arrived safely in Tokyo. From there, he was able to go to Shanghai, still a free city. Finally, in 1942, he received a visa to the United States. Once safe in the United States, he became vice president of *Ha-Po'el Ha-Mizrachi* (the workers' wing of *Mizrachi*) and joined the executive committee of the World Jewish Congress. Through this organization, he worked to locate Jewish children who had been hidden in European monasteries during the war, and arranged for their passage to Palestine. And in 1947, Warhaftig, now married and with children of his own, fulfilled his lifelong dream and came with his family to Jerusalem.

Plunging into the politics of the emerging Jewish state, he was soon chairing the legal department of Palestinian Jewry's provisional government. Immediately after Israel gained its independence in 1948, he was elected to the Knesset (Israel's parliament) as a member of the National Religious Party and was re-elected nine times, serving between 1949 and 1981. In June 1967, after the Six-Day War, Warhaftig consulted extensively with Muslim *imams* (Islamic religious leaders) and *qadis* (Islamic community leaders), Jewish rabbis, and Christian priests. Two months later, he set up a council to ensure regular consultations. He then wrote a decree guaranteeing religious autonomy for Jews, Muslims, and Christians in the newly conquered section of East Jerusalem, and drafted a constitutionally binding edict protecting their respective holy sites.

In addition to his political activities, Warhaftig's interest in education led him to establish a center for Jewish law at the Hebrew University of Jerusalem. He himself took a doctorate in law from that institution and lectured students there until 1963. In 1970, he chaired the presidium at Bar-Ilan University, an institution with a diverse student body. Zorah Warhaftig's commitment to Bal-Ilan's diversity led to his "confession of shame," written in 1995, when a Bar-Ilan graduate murdered Yitzhak Rabin, the Israeli prime minister.

After his retirement from politics, Warhaftig remained a prolific author on Jewish law, Talmudic literature, politics, and history. His writings include *Refugee and Survivor*, a memoir about his war experiences. He died on September 26, 2002, at the age of ninety-six. His three sons and one daughter still live in Israel.

References

Joffe, Lawrence. "Zerah Warhaftig." *The Guardian*, October 9, 2002. Available at http://www.guardian.co.uk/israel/ (search on warhaftig).

Gutman, Israel, ed. *Encyclopedia of the Holocaust*. s.v. "Warhaftig, Zorah." New York: Macmillan, 1990.

Wasserstrom family

The Wasserstrom family, Alter Zelig (1903–1992), his wife Chaja (1903–1992), and their two children Manya (b.1928) and Avraham (b.1934), fled to the Ukraine from Lublin, Poland, disguised as Roma to avoid capture by the Nazis in 1939. When the Germans crossed the border into Russia, they fled again. They were able to survive six years in Russia before they were allowed to return.

Both Alter Zelig and Chaja were professional tailors and owned their own small shop. Faced with the virulent antisemitism of the Poles they thought at first that the Germans might be an improvement. Alter Zelig remembered that they were kind and pleasant when they invaded in World War I and expected this experience to be the same. Once the German Army came in, however, they sent their elite SS forces to Lublin. Almost immediately the SS began seizing Jews at random, abusing them, sending them to concentration camps, and even killing them. They would arrest Orthodox Jews and force them to eat forbidden foods like pork or do other things that were against Jewish law. The Jewish community was terrorized and quickly realized that this would not be like World War I.

Alter Zelig was an active Socialist who knew how to defend himself, but there was no defense against such arbitrary authorities. He spoke with a neighbor, a butcher who also had a wife and two young children, and they decided to leave Poland together. The butcher had a horse and wagon and the two families packed it with essentials and headed toward the Bug River, the border between Poland and Soviet-occupied Ukraine. They had heard that there was a bridge they could cross to get beyond the reach of the Nazis. Traveling by wagon through German-occupied Poland was dangerous. The two families thought of a plan to evade the danger. They painted and decorated their wagon to look like a gypsy caravan. Then the women dressed themselves to appear like gypsies and set out. For most of the journey, no one bothered them, but one zealous German soldier did stop the wagon "Jude?" ("Jew?") he asked. Alter Zelig replied in German, "Nein. Dorten Jude," ("No. Those are Jews,") and pointed to a wagon behind them. The soldiers waved them on.

When they reached the border, they found the bridge closed and had to investigate other possibilities. They learned that it was possible to bribe the German border guard through a local intermediary and in one day the arrangement was made. In exchange for money, plus the horse and wagon and all its contents, the two families would be permitted to cross to the Russian side. They had to promise not to return.

Setting out in a small rowboat, the Wasserstroms saw the rifles of the Nazi soldiers aimed at them as they crossed the river. But as they neared the other bank, Russian soldiers appeared aiming rifles and ordered them to go back. Caught in the middle, the women made a quick decision. They began pinching their children hard so that they would cry. The howling of the children evoked Russian sympathy for their plight and they let them go ashore.

The Russian soldiers treated the families well and then loaded them, along with other refugees, onto a truck to take them to a refugee camp. Alter Zelig and his friend decided not to go, however. Instead, when the truck stopped briefly, they took their wives and children and found a place to live in a Ukrainian village near the Polish border. After only a few months, they were taken from there into the Soviet Union proper.

In this new place, the Wasserstroms settled in. Both parents found work as tailors and Alter Zelig was happy to be living in a Communist country. But within a short time, he had begun to see the problems of the Soviet Union, most especially the food shortages. He complained to his co-workers and was promptly arrested by authorities and sentenced to five years in Siberia.

Now Chaja had to assume the full burden of supporting the children. Life was difficult. Then in 1941, the Germans were once again threatening them. Breaching the treaty that Hitler and Stalin had made in 1939, the German Army conquered Soviet-occupied eastern Poland, continued into the Ukraine, and then crossed the border into Russia. The Wasserstroms could hear the German guns just outside their village.

Chaja Wasserstrom felt they should stay and wait for German occupation so they could rejoin their extended family in Lublin, but the Russians had another idea. They sent soldiers to the homes of all the residents to evacuate them to a safer place. They were saved from the Germans a second time.

The Wasserstroms, Chaja, Manya (later called Mary), and Avraham (Abe), now found themselves in the Soviet Republic of Mordovskaya. Food was scarce here, too. Even bread was rationed and the children often went hungry. Chaja barely managed by sewing clothes for the peasants in exchange for food. They had completely lost track of Alter Zelig.

In the village where the Wasserstroms lived, Russian soldiers often came for rest and recuperation. In 1942, one of those soldiers was a Jew. When he heard that there were Jews in the town, he came to see them and struck up a friendship with the Wasserstroms, exchanging stories and war experiences with them. When the soldier's leave was up, he left, and did not keep in touch. When he was sent for a second recuperative period, it was to Tashkent. He never saw Chaja Wasserstrom or the children again but he did meet Alter Zelig.

Alter Zelig had been released from a Siberian prison and went to Tashkent with a friend where the climate was warmer. One day, they sat on a park bench and conversing in Yiddish, Alter Zelig told his friend about his family and his concern that he might never see Chaja, Mary, and Abe again. A solider sitting on the next bench overheard the conversation and recognized the names as the same family that had once befriended him. He told Wasserstrom where they were and a few short weeks later, the family was reunited.

Together again, the Wasserstroms now moved to another new village just outside the city of Kyubiszev. But the Communist authorities again interfered in the family's life, jailing Alter Zelig for refusing to accept Russian citizenship. While he was in jail, many gypsies, also refugees from the Nazis, came to their village. For a short time, a gypsy family shared the Wasserstroms' tiny apartment and the families became friends. Often the gypsy woman would take Abe with her when she wandered around the village reading palms. During those trips, they sometimes were able to smuggle extra food to Abe's father who was starving in prison.

When beatings and starvation had no effect on Wasserstrom's decision, the authorities released him. The family continued to live in the same village until 1945, when the war was over and the Russians allowed all the Poles to leave.

Back in Poland, however, the authorities were not allowing Jews to return to Lublin. Instead, they were relocated to lower Silesia, where they were given an apartment confiscated from the German occupants. Since Abe spoke no Polish, he was registered in a Russian school, which had been set up for the children of the Russian officers who were overseeing the area.

After one and a half years under Russian occupation, Alter Zelig was more convinced than ever that Communism was not as good as he believed and he sought new opportunities. In 1947, a friend in Sweden arranged for visas for the Wasserstroms. For three years the family lived in Stockholm, then, through another friend, they were able to obtain visas to Canada.

The Wasserstroms lived in Montreal from 1950 to 1960. Mary and Abe completed their schooling there while their parents worked in the tailoring trade. Abe also worked part-time as a furrier's apprentice to earn money for college.

Mary met Murray Nagel in Montreal. After they were married in 1957, they moved to Nagel's home in Brooklyn, New York, and Mary encouraged her brother to apply to colleges in the United States. Abe did and was accepted at New York University. He graduated in 1964 with a degree in engineering and was soon employed as a specialist in heating and ventilating. One year after his college graduation, Abe met his wife, Fay Frankel, an Israeli originally from Russia, who was visiting relatives in New York. They were married in Tel Aviv in 1965, settled in New York, and had three children and then four grand-children. He now lives in Florida.

Mary Wasserstrom Nagel and her husband moved to Freehold, New Jersey. They had one daughter and one grandson.

Alter Zelig and Chaja Wasserstrom joined their children in New York. They continued working as tailors until their retirement.

Reference

Wasserstrom, Abe. Telephone interview by the author, April 2006.

Weil, André (1906–1998)

André Weil, an assimilated French Jew from Paris, was vacationing in Finland when World War II erupted. A series of unfortunate decisions and coin-cidences ultimately determined his fate and separated him from his homeland for most of his life.

Weil, a recognized mathematician, lived and worked at a university in Paris and was married to **Evelyne Gillot Weil**. The couple was not involved in politics or foreign affairs and, ignoring the threats of war, left home for a holi-day. When war broke out in September 1939, his wife's first thought was to return to her home and her young son from a previous marriage, Alain, who had been left with her mother while they were away. Weil felt differently. He wanted to remain in Finland and see what would happen. Although France was committed to helping Poland in case of an attack, one could never be sure.

The couple agreed to part temporarily, but, before Evelyne left, the Weils took an excursion on a rowboat on a lake near the Russian border. Weil had poor eyesight and carried a pair of binoculars with him that he used to scan the horizon and view the scenery more clearly. With the threat of war all around them, the Finnish authorities became suspicious. Thinking he might be a spy, they watched his activities and, after a few days, arrested him.

With his wife back in Paris and no one to vouch for him, Weil was sent to jail in Lapland, in northern Finland, and was kept there for several months. When it became clear that he was not a spy, the authorities were not sure how to deal with him. He was transferred to a prison in Denmark and from there

> *[After the occupation of Paris] Assisted by Paris police, the SS conducted periodic roundups of Jews. Those found were sent to the Drancy, France, transit camp for deportation. A mammoth hunt in 1942 collected 13,000 Jews, including 4000 children—many of whom had been separated from their parents. After being penned up in a sports stadium for one week, the crying children were then crammed into cattle cars and delivered to Auschwitz.*
>
> —David J. Hogan, Editor-in-chief.
> *The Holocaust Chronicle*, p. 197.

sent to England. The English, allied with the French, took him back to France with a police escort. But once home, he was jailed again, this time for draft evasion. Faced with the choice of joining the army or remaining in jail, Weil enlisted. Despite his poor eyesight, he was made a lieutenant and immediately sent to Dunkirk to help stop the German advance.

By the time Weil arrived at the front, the fighting was over. On June 4, 1940, he was evacuated from Dunkirk with 338,000 other soldiers of the French, British, and Belgian armies, to prevent their total destruction by the Nazis. The troops remained in England, taking shelter from the nightly bombings by the German Air Force, and waiting for another opportunity to fight.

But Weil, concerned about his parents, his wife, and stepson, was anxious to get back home. He knew that Paris had fallen to the Nazis on June 14, 1940, and he had not heard from anyone in his family. In 1941, he managed to get space on a ship taking wounded soldiers back to France and landed in Marseilles. He tracked down his family and told them all to join him there, hoping to get a visa to the United States. Failing that, he would accept a visa to any other country in order to avoid the war and the roundups of Jews that were becoming more and more frequent.

All of these options proved difficult if not impossible. Most borders were closed to European Jews and few ships were sailing. Weil took his family from Marseilles to Casablanca in North Africa and from there tried to arrange passage to Martinique, a Caribbean island that was a part of France. Before sailing, his luck turned. With the intervention of a Frenchman whom he knew, he was put on a preferred list of professors, writers, and artists who were given temporary visas to the United States. The Weil family arrived in the United States at the end of 1941.

Work as a mathematics professor was difficult to find. Weil was offered nonpaying positions to help acquaint him with the American university system, but he had a family to support. His wife gave birth to their first child in the United States and their funds were running out. Then an offer came from Brazil. The University of São Paulo had heard of him and invited him to join the faculty there. He accepted, and with his parents, his wife, and now two children, he sailed from New Orleans to South America in 1942.

André and his wife Evelyne Weil in 1950 at a conference in the United States. Courtesy of Sylvie Weil.

Weil remained in Brazil for six years before returning to his native France. Once back home, however, he found that his decision to leave in the middle of the war had not served him well. Because of his questionable war record he was not able to find employment at any of the French universities. With a wife, a stepson, and now two daughters to support, Weil had no choice but to return to America. He worked at the University of Chicago and then at Princeton University. His parents, back in Paris, helped to raise his children. His wife established a residence in France but went back and forth regularly. Weil, however, was not able to return to Paris permanently until his retirement. Although he pursued his career successfully, his life had been forever changed by the war against the Jews.

Reference

Weil, Sylvie. Interview by the author, December 2005, New York, New York.

Weil, Evelyne (née Gillot) (1910–1986), and Louise Gillot (1877–1965)

Evelyne Weil and her mother, Louise Gillot, both Parisian Jews, never considered themselves to be heroes. Nor did they think much about being Jewish. When war came, however, they were able to call up inner resources and face adversity with courage.

Weil was born Evelyne Gillot, one of five children. Her mother, Louise, an assimilated Jew, had married a gentile. She was widowed early and raised her children alone. After an early and brief marriage to a Christian man, her daughter, Evelyne, divorced. The son of that marriage, Alain De Possel, was still very young when she met and married **André Weil**, a noted mathematician and academic and a Jew.

The couple was vacationing in Finland when Germany attacked Poland in 1939. France's earlier commitment to come to the aid of Poland made war virtually certain and Weil hurried back to rejoin her son and her mother. Unsure of what might happen, her husband André remained in Finland. Temporarily jailed as a spy, he was later released and ultimately served briefly in the army before being evacuated to England with the defeated French troops.

Weil lost contact with André for many months. She was with her mother and her son when the Germans marched into Paris, and, fearing the city would be burned, she fled south along with thousands of others. The roads were clogged with refugees. There was no transportation and little shelter. But Louise Gillot remembered that she had friends in Sablé, a small town southwest of Paris, and so the three headed there. Sablé was a simple, unsophisticated place with simple people who had literally never seen a Jew and did not know that Weil or her mother were Jewish. They accepted their presence in the town and the two women found a tiny house to rent.

Weil and her mother were not the only refugees in Sablé. Over the course of 1940, the town became a center for both Jews and non-Jews who were running from the Nazis. Centers were set up to accommodate them: soup kitchens, overnight lodgings, first aid were all made available for these transients who stayed one or two nights and then moved on to the south, away from the Nazi presence and the threat of bombs. Weil found a way to be useful in this unfamiliar situation. She distributed food, provided diapers for babies, and helped bathe children. When there was no room in the refugee centers, she

put people up in her own attic. Although the work was difficult and demanding and food was scarce, the Nazis had not occupied the town and the small
family managed to survive through 1941.

Then one day Weil heard from her husband. He was now in Marseilles, a
southern city that was still part of free France, and urged Weil to bring her
family and join him and his parents, Salome and Bernard Weil. Weil prepared
to leave with her son but Louise Gillot refused. She would take her chances
and remain in Sablé.

Crossing the border from the German-occupied North to the southern part,
which was still under French control, was challenging and dangerous but it
could be done. Weil had been given an address in the town of Vierzon. At that
house, they were told, someone would be available who, for money, would
smuggle them across the Cher River. When Weil and Alain arrived there,
however, the residents denied having any knowledge of such an arrangement.
At a loss, Weil took her son and sat down in a nearby café. There was nowhere
to go and the two remained at the table for many hours. Finally, the owner
came and asked them if they were waiting "to pass." Hesitantly, Weil said she
was. "Wait until closing time," said the man, and we'll arrange it.

That night, they met several other women who wanted to cross and the
young woman who would take them. She instructed them briefly, stressing the
fact that they must not run. They set up a meeting time and she left. A few
hours later, the small group assembled and met their guide. She had arranged
to take them just when the officer in charge would go to dinner. The second in
command was her boyfriend. While the group waited on one side of the
bridge, the young woman went to her boyfriend and kissed him. At the same
time, she motioned with her hand that they should go across the bridge. They
crossed, trying hard to follow her instructions and not to run. After they were
out of sight of the bridge, they did break into a run, hurrying to get to the safe
house that had previously been designated. A short time later, when the
woman came, she scolded them for running but it didn't matter now. They
were safe.

Weil, with her son Alain, continued by train to Marseilles where André Weil
was waiting. They wanted to leave the country but could not obtain a visa. To
distance themselves further from the Nazis, they sailed to Casablanca, then
under French control, and waited for a visa to anywhere in the world. Late in
1941, through the help of a friend, they were placed on a list of privileged
people who would be allowed into the United States. Once in America, Weil
gave birth to a daughter, Sylvie. When her husband found work as a mathematics professor in Brazil, she followed him there. Another daughter was born.

The Weils remained in Brazil for six years, but Weil missed France and the
family returned to their native country in 1948. Although her husband was not
able to find work in France and had to go to the United States, she set up
her home once again in Paris, regularly traveling back and forth to America to
visit him.

Louise Gillot remained safely in Sablé throughout the war, where no one
ever knew she was Jewish. Although she returned to Paris, she bought a
summer home in the town that had saved her life, and her grandchildren
spent many vacations there with her.

Reference

Weil, Sylvie. Interview by the author, December 2005. New York, New York.

Weil, Peter (1931–)

Born in Karlsruh, Germany, Peter Weil and his parents moved to Paris when he was two years old, fleeing from Nazi antisemitism. When the Nazis invaded France in 1940, the Weils fled again and Peter was on the last ship to leave that country before the French surrendered to Germany.

When the edicts of 1933 decreed that he could no longer practice law, Weil's father, along with many other Jews, left his native land in search of a more hospitable environment. Once settled in Paris, his father built a successful business making pillows and comforters and the family lived in a beautiful apartment in Neuilly-sur-Seine, a prosperous Paris suburb. Weil was an only child and his parents lavished attention on him.

But there was no escaping the effects of the war that was threatening all of Europe. Even before Germany invaded France, suspicion and prejudice pursued the Jews living there and the Weils decided to move into the countryside. Friends owned a farm near Vichy, a city about seventy-five miles south of Paris, but even there, their status as both foreigners and Jews put them at constant risk.

In the spring of 1939, six months before the official outbreak of war, the French government issued a decree that all male "enemy aliens" in France between the ages of nineteen and thirty-nine had to report to internment camps. The irony of this ruling was not lost on the Weils. In 1933, they had been declared stateless in Germany. Now in France, they were considered Germans and thus enemy aliens. Weil's father complied with the order and was interned in a concentration camp near Blois, a small city in central France.

With his father gone, Weil, now eight years old, moved with his mother to a guesthouse near Blois with another Jewish family whose father had been interned. They were allowed to visit the camp once a week and to bring food and clothing. Weil joined his mother on those regular visits and, during the week, went to school. Because no public school in France would accept Jews, he went to a Catholic school in the area. Many Jewish children attended his school, but they were never formally identified. The Jewish students followed the regular schedule of morning prayers and learned the catechism with all the Catholic children.

During the time they were living in Blois, Peter and his mother had to regularly descend into an air raid shelter for air raid drills in anticipation of the impending war. But besides this danger, there was the even more immediate danger of deportation. It was only a matter of time before Weil's father would be sent back to Germany because of his status as a foreign national.

The Weils had one chance to escape the Nazi deportations. In 1937, well before the war had begun, they had planned a vacation trip to the United States and had applied for visas. Weil's mother now decided that she would travel to Paris, go to the American Embassy, and try to obtain those visas. She was only partially successful.

In the fall of 1939, just after the outbreak of war, the American Embassy issued one visa, for Weil's father. His mother did not have the necessary papers to obtain hers at that time, but since his father was the one who was most at risk, obtaining a visa for him was vital. Now he had to find a way to leave the internment camp.

Weil's family had been prosperous before the war, and still had some money. His father used the money to purchase a new Peugeot automobile. He offered to give it to the commandant of the concentration camp with one proviso: that the commandant would first drive him to the port of Le Havre where his ship, the *Ile de France,* was embarking. The commandant agreed and Weil's father sailed to America and safety.

Weil and his mother were still trapped in France, waiting for Swiss relatives to arrange the proper papers for them and worrying that they might not be able to leave. The Germans were advancing further south every day. They occupied Vichy, and Weil and his mother kept moving south, keeping just ahead of the occupying troops and the falling bombs.

Peter Weil was nine years old when he and his mother finally obtained their visas and sailed from Marseilles. Theirs was the last American passenger ship to leave France. They arrived in the United States on February 11, 1940. In June 1940, France officially surrendered to Germany.

After they were settled in their new country, Weil's mother suggested that he write to President Roosevelt and tell him about his "adventures" in France. The President responded with a gracious letter, welcoming the Weil family to the United States.

Peter Weil grew up as an American. He graduated from the Wharton School of the University of Pennsylvania and went on to obtain his MBA from New York University. He married an American woman, had three children, and a successful career working as an importer in the steel industry. After retiring, he began selling industrial real estate in New Jersey. More than sixty years later, Peter Weil still felt "grateful that I am here and have been able to live freely as an American and a Jew."

Reference

Weil, Peter. "Moving to Freedom." *The New Light* 45, no. 3 (Spring 2003): p. 41.

Weilheimer, Richard (1931–), and Ernest Strassburger (1935–)

Richard and Ernest Weilheimer were brothers, born in Ludwigshafen, near the city of Mannheim, Germany. Their mother died during World War II and their father was killed by the Nazis. But the two boys were able to survive thanks to the help of French relief organizations and righteous gentiles. Ernest took the name Strassburger when he was legally adopted by an aunt and uncle.

The Weilheimer parents, Maximillian and Lilly Wetzler were observant Jews but also well-entrenched in German culture. Maximillian was the secretary of the Jewish community and Lilly, whose father was a cantor and a learned Jew, was a kindergarten teacher and a recognized violinist before she married and had children.

By the time their son Richard was old enough to attend school, Hitler had already come to power and German schools were no longer open to Jewish children. He attended a Jewish kindergarten. When the Nazis outlawed any schooling for Jews, he was taught at home by his maternal grandfather. Despite the increasing oppression and the limitations imposed by antisemitic laws, the Weilheimers, along with many other Jews, felt they could weather the storm. They were certain that Hitler's Third Reich would soon end. Then came *Kristallnacht*, The Night of Broken Glass.

Kristallnacht was a government-organized pogrom against Jews that took place throughout Germany and Austria. The Nazis claimed that it was a spontaneous response to the murder of a minor German official by a young Jewish student, Herschel Grynszpan, on November 7, 1938. Grynszpan was protesting his parents' deportation from Germany to Poland. Two days later, coordinated attacks on Jews, on synagogues, and on Jewish businesses occurred, as well as mass arrests of Jewish men.

The night of the attacks, Nazis in uniform, along with a crowd of civilians, stormed the homes where Jews lived. They pounded on the Weilheimers' door and took away Lilly's father and husband. Now alone with her two little boys, Lilly took them and ran from the apartment. Taking the back streets, she walked across town to the homes of relatives, looking for a safe place to stay. She found that they, too, had experienced the same intrusions and the men of each family had been taken. No one knew where they were or what would happen. Finally, Lilly returned to her own home and found the apartment completely destroyed. The Nazis had returned while they were gone, smashed all their furniture with an ax, destroyed all their linens by spilling chemicals and molasses on them, and had broken everything else. Fearful for her life and her children's lives, Lilly hid in the attic for a week. Then her father returned and she felt safe enough to go down to their apartment.

Weilheimer and Strassburger, only seven and four years old, were too young to understand the ramifications of this terrible night. They did not know that German insurance companies had been instructed by the government to refuse all claims made by Jews as a result of *Kristallnacht*, or that England and France had acquiesced to Germany's takeover of Czechoslovakia in return for a promise that there would be no more aggression. But they did know that their father had disappeared.

Several more weeks passed before Maximillian Weilheimer was released and came back home. Within a year, Germany had invaded Poland and, in spite of Hitler's promises, war began.

The Weilheimers followed the news as the German Army marched into Poland, then Norway, Denmark, the Low Countries (Belgium and Holland), and France. At the same time, they began deporting Jews from their area of Germany. On October 22, 1940, the Weilheimer family was given one hour to pack, gather enough food for three days, and get ready to leave for relocation. They were allowed one suitcase each. All their other possessions were confiscated by the German government.

The family, including the four Weilheimers and Lilly's mother, were piled onto a truck and driven to the railroad station. Her father was too sick to travel and had to be left behind. On arriving at the station, they found many people in a panic. A few were so terrified at what the Germans might do to them that they committed suicide rather than board the train.

> *A description of Camp de Gurs as seen through the eyes of a nine-year-old:*
>
> *The flimsy barracks were no longer suitable for human habitation. They had been intended as temporary shelters, hastily constructed from wooden boards covered by a single sheet of tarpaper, and by now they had been totally neglected. They were filthy, with great gaps in the roofs and sides. Many boards had split and the tarpaper was torn, allowing the rain to seep down and the wind to whistle through. . . . we had to sleep on the damp, bare ground. There were no mattresses, blankets or other necessities other than what we had brought in our suitcases.*
>
> Richard Weilheimer (*Be Happy, Be Free, Dance*, p. 35.)

These trains were not yet the cattle cars that so many later deportees would experience. They were old passenger trains with the seats removed so many more people could fit. They seemed bad enough, however, for those being forced inside.

After a three-day journey, the passengers found themselves in Vichy, France (generally referred to as "unoccupied France"), and were met by the workers from the American Friends Service Committee, an American Quaker organization, who gave them food.

Next, they were loaded onto trucks and finally arrived at their destination: a camp at the foot of the Pyrenees Mountains called camp de Gurs. Gurs had originally been a holding camp for Spanish prisoners and refugees from the Spanish Civil War and a few Spaniards still remained. Now, in a run-down group of barracks in a sea of mud, sixty-five hundred German Jews were deposited. The French authorities were hardly prepared for such a large group of refugees and, in fact, resented the Germans dumping their unwanted Jews on French soil.

The problems of overcrowding, lack of food, and inadequate sanitation created instant misery. Diseases were rampant and there was no medicine available. Weilheimer and Strassburger, still too young to be sent with the men, remained in the women's barracks with their mother, while Maximillian was alone in the men's barracks. They saw each other only occasionally.

Although life was bleak for everyone, the barracks were soon organized and leaders elected. These leaders attempted to set up religious services, a school for the children, and committees to prepare and present entertainments. Such attempts at social and cultural normalcy, however, could not eliminate the serious problems endemic to Gurs: hunger, disease, an infestation of rats, and mud so thick that the inmates had to remove their shoes to walk through it. Soon, the children were suffering from malnutrition and Weilheimer had sores on his body that would not heal.

French and American relief organizations came into camp de Gurs to bring additional food and clothing to those interned there. The American Friends Service Committee and the Oeuvre de Secours aux Enfants (OSE), a Jewish group, were the most active. Women from the Friends Service Committee set up a supplementary kitchen in one of the barracks and distributed milk to the children. When they saw the misery close at hand, they were determined to find a more wholesome and safer place for the youngest ones.

The refuge they found was a children's home in the nearby town of Aspet called La Maison des Pupilles de la Nation. This orphanage had room but little money and not enough food for those who were already there. The Friends Society promised to supply food for both the newcomers and the French orphans if they would open their doors to the children from Gurs. The agreement was made and forty-eight boys and girls, ranging in age from five to thirteen

The Weilheimer brothers at the Maison des Pupilles de la Nation, a children's home near Camp de Gurs. Ernest is on the left. Richard is behind him. Also included in the photo are Hugo Schiller and Kurt Wagner (formerly Walker). Courtesy of the U.S. Holocaust Memorial Museum Photo Archives.

years, were sent to Aspet in February 1941. Among them were Weilheimer and Strassburger.

At first it was very difficult for all the children. They were separated from their parents for the first time and placed in a strange environment where they could not understand the language. Their adjustment was helped considerably by **Alice Resch Synnestvedt**, one of the nurses for the American Friends Committee. She stayed with them for the first six weeks and after that, returned periodically to visit the children and bring them treats or clothing. Weilheimer and Strassburger also received letters regularly from their parents, assuring them that they would soon be together again and encouraging them to study and be good. Lilly never wrote to tell her boys that she was ill with breast cancer. After she died, on July 17, 1941, the boys were informed of her death by the head of the school, but they could not return to see their father, and he was not allowed to visit them. Each grieved alone, in his own way.

By 1942, rumors were confirmed that the "final solution" for Jews was in place. The Nazis, with the full cooperation of French police, now began rounding up Jews, including children, and shipping them in boxcars to Auschwitz. The American Friends and the OSE quickly went into action, removing the Jewish children from the orphanage at Aspet and finding an individual hiding place for each one with a French family.

At the same time, the United States agreed to take in a thousand Jewish children so the Friends Service Committee made the arrangements and chose which children would go. In general, they selected those who had relatives in America. Six children from Aspet, including Strassburger and Weilheimer, were among the first shipment of 250 children.

Just before they left on the last ship out of Europe, embarking from Marseilles, Maximillian managed to obtain a pass to see his children off before they sailed. Once again, he promised they would be together soon. He kissed them goodbye and they never saw him again. In November of that same year he was deported to a labor camp, later transferred back to Gurs, then to Drancy, a holding camp in northern France, and finally to Sobibor, where he was murdered in the gas chambers.

Weilheimer and Strassburger sailed to the United States and, after a short orientation period, were introduced to their relatives, the Sterns and the Strassburgers, two of their mother's sisters who had emigrated to America before the war. They also reunited with their grandmother, who had been released from Gurs early through the efforts of a son, and shipped to the safety of America. Each boy was taken in by one family. Ernest was adopted legally by the Strassburgers. The Sterns would have liked to adopt Richard but he was reluctant. He wanted to retain his parents' name. However, he grew to love his aunt and uncle and considered them his parents.

Both boys adjusted to life in New York. They lived only a block from each other and were together a great deal, allowing Weilheimer to fulfill his promise to his parents that he would take care of his little brother. During those years, Weilheimer met a friend from Aspet, **Hugo Schiller**, who lived in the same neighborhood, also with an aunt and uncle.

Following graduation from high school, Weilheimer expected to look for a job, but his plans were postponed when he was drafted into the army for the Korean War. After his two years of army service in Korea, he found a job as a window decorator. He enjoyed the work but soon realized there was little room for growth. When he left, he had the opportunity to join a company that manufactured scarves and other ladies' accessories and did well. In 1957, Weilheimer fell in love and married Sheila Fishbein and the couple soon had two sons.

Strassburger graduated high school and went on to City College of New York, earning a degree in business administration in 1958. He served in the U.S. Army Reserve for six months and when he came out, he met his wife, Esther Hutterer. The two were married in June of 1959 and had three sons before Esther died of cancer. Strassburger managed a successful career, first in advertising and then in real estate and took care of his boys alone for over a year. Then he met and married Doris Nadler and they had a fourth son.

Both Strassburger and Weilheimer became grandfathers and their family continued to expand. It was the birth of Weilheimer's first grandchild that motivated him to tell the story of his life. He named his book *Be Happy, Be Free, Dance! A Holocaust Survivor's Message to His Grandchildren*.

Reference

Weilheimer, Richard. *Be Happy, Be Free, Dance! A Holocaust Survivor's Message to His Grandchildren*. Pasadena, CA: Intentional Productions, 2005.

Weinstein, Edi (1923–), and Asher Weinstein (d. 1972)

A series of near-miraculous escapes helped Edi Weinstein and his father, Asher Weinstein, of Losice, Poland, to survive the war. One of the younger Weinstein's most dangerous and daring escapes was his flight from Treblinka, the notorious death camp, where 870,000 Jews were murdered.

The Weinstein family, parents and two sons, Edi and Srulik (Yisrael), lived in Losice, a Polish town near the Bug River. Asher Weinstein earned a living buying eggs and poultry from the nearby farms and selling them in town. Edi Weinstein's boyhood was typical of many young Jews of that period: he went to a *heder*, a Jewish religious school, from the age of three. When he was older, he attended a yeshivah. By the time he was fifteen, he was already working.

When World War II broke out, Losice was first bombed by the Germans, then occupied by the Russians in a secret agreement between Germany and the Soviet Union. But within a few weeks, the boundary was reassessed and the Russians retreated, making way for German occupation. The Weinsteins had fled briefly to a neighboring town where they had relatives, but soon returned; crossing into Russian territory also had its problems. Few could envision the cruelty of Nazi antisemitism and Jews assured each other that the casual violence of the soldiers would subside.

Violence did not subside, however. By 1940, the Jews of Losice were conscripted for slave labor to work on extending railroad tracks and building roads. They were forced to work twelve hours a day and were killed by German police and soldiers for the smallest infractions. Edi Weinstein was first sent to Niemojki railroad station with four hundred other Jewish men to build a concrete platform. When that project was completed, he was sent further from home, where he labored quarrying stone from a mountain, laying tracks, and doing other heavy work. But after being clubbed by a guard, he decided to escape. Weinstein first ran from the camp, then enlisted the aid of a peasant who drove him part way home. He walked the rest of the way back to Losice. This was the first of many escapes.

Weinstein's next assignment was to help build a barracks for German soldiers, then to repave the road leading to the frontier with Russia. It slowly became apparent that the Germans were planning to invade the Soviet Union and the attack would be launched from Losice. They had used Jewish slave labor to prepare for battle.

Many of the families of Losice, including the Weinsteins, ran west once again, trying to avoid the fighting, but within a week the front had moved far to the east. The family returned to their home and to the Nazi rulings that quickly eliminated their most elementary rights. Among other orders, Jews were not allowed to own any metal implements, jewelry, furs or woolen items. These were all confiscated without compensation. Then, on December 1, 1941, came the decree that Jews must live in a ghetto and were not allowed out except to work. Food was strictly limited and people began to go hungry. As thousands of families, deported by the Nazis, began arriving from western Poland, hunger became worse. More and more Jews died of starvation.

Just a few months after the establishment of the ghetto, Asher and Edi were shipped off to Wolfer und Göbel, a work camp much further from home.

Not only could the workers not return home at night, but food was barely adequate for survival and corporal punishment was commonplace. After twenty-three days, Edi was determined to escape. With a friend, he slipped behind some buildings at the end of the workday, while the workers were boarding the trucks back to camp. They hid overnight in a loft and the next day, walked the twenty miles back home.

Each time Edi returned to Losice, he managed to find another work assignment. Most kept him close to home. He was there when the Losice ghetto was liquidated in August 1942 and all the remaining Jewish inhabitants were led at gunpoint to the railway station. Carts were provided for women and children, but the men had to run all the way. Whoever lagged behind was shot by the soldiers. As Edi and his brother marched through the nearby villages they saw corpses lying in the streets and realized that the Jews in all the towns were being evacuated. They were separated from their mother during that march and never saw her again. Only later did Weinstein learn that she was killed in the gas chambers at Treblinka.

The journey to the death camp took three days, during which the prisoners were given neither food nor water. Some of the prisoners were so thirsty that they tried to lick up the mud and water from the streets. They were instantly shot by the German guards.

When the hundreds of marchers finally were able to board the trains, Weinstein could see that they would suffocate in those crowded conditions. Each boxcar had scant ventilation and they were so crowded that no one could sit down. He and his brother Yisrulik quickly made their way out of one car and found another that was less crowded. Their aunt and her three children were in that car and they all remained there for the four-hour journey to Treblinka.

Edi and Srulik's first sight of Treblinka was of corpses piled up on the station platform. He soon learned they were the bodies of those who had died from suffocation in the trains themselves. He recognized many of the dead as his own aunts and cousins. The corpses now had to be carried away, dumped into a large, open trench, and burned. The Weinstein brothers were among those assigned to this task. No sooner was this completed then guards took them into the forest where other bodies had to be disposed of in the same way. At last, they were led back to the camp and told to wait on line for food and water.

While they waited, Edi was shot by a Nazi guard and fell to the ground. A bullet had entered his chest and exited through his back. Srulik was quickly at his side, binding the wound and finding a clean shirt for him. He concealed his brother under a pile of clothes that had been taken from the dead prisoners and went in search of water. He never returned and Edi assumed he had been shot and killed.

Edi remained hidden among the clothing for several days, aided by other prisoners from Losice. Although his pain was unbearable and he had no medical care, he survived, and took his place with other Jews from Losice sorting clothing and disposing of corpses whenever a new transport came in. During one of those work assignments, he saw five babies, still alive, lying next to an open trench filled with burning bodies. He watched, horrified, as the soldiers tossed them into the pit. He later wrote that it was one of the images of the war that he will never forget.

Edi had escaped from several other camps and he began to think about how he might escape this one as well. The opportunity came when he was assigned to load a freight car with the used clothing that the inmates had sorted and bundled. He and two other prisoners managed to hide under the piles of clothes and when the train began its journey west, they were on it. Tucked in their belts were gold coins that they had confiscated from the dead bodies. Edi had been in the hell of Treblinka for seventeen days.

After jumping from the train, Edi sneaked back into the Wolfer und Göbel camp, where he was reunited with his father, Asher. Within a short time, both escaped this camp and returned to Losice, where a little ghetto had been established containing a small number of Jews who worked for the Nazis. However, they understood that it was only a matter of time before they would be arrested again and taken back to Treblinka. Using the gold coins that Weinstein had smuggled out of Treblinka, father and son, with another man, found a hiding place with a Polish farmer. After a few months, the farmer feared that the neighbors had discovered he was hiding Jews and asked them to leave. With the help of an estate manager who knew Asher, the men were able to dig a new bunker in a drained and abandoned fishpond and remained there for a year, slowly spending their stash of coins to purchase food. They had several more narrow escapes before they were finally liberated by Russian solders in July 1944.

Returning to Losice after their liberation, Asher and Edi found only a handful of Jews who had survived the Nazi death machine. Of the eight thousand Jews who had lived in their town, only twenty-five had returned and some of these were from the surrounding towns. Despite rampant Polish antisemitism, Edi decided to join the Polish Army and help complete the German defeat. He was soon sent to Warsaw on an assignment and on the way, stopped to visit his father, now living in Lodz. But when he heard about the continued killings of Jews by Poles, he changed his mind about serving in the Polish Army. Instead, Asher and Edi left Poland for occupied Germany, where displaced-persons camps had been set up by the Allies.

In 1947, while still in the displaced-persons camp, Edi wrote the story of his war years in Yiddish. It was first translated into Hebrew and, in 2002, into English, under the title *Quenched Steel: The Story of an Escape from Treblinka*.

Edi married another survivor, Jean Zucker Windsheim, in 1948. Asher also remarried that year. In 1949, the two newly married men and their wives left for the United States. Asher died peacefully in 1972.

In America, Edi and Jean had two sons, Larry and Michael, both of whom are college graduates with doctoral degrees. In 1993, after the Iron Curtain was lifted, Michael accompanied his parents on a trip to Losice and Treblinka. Edi found many changes there and realized that the present inhabitants have no memory of the thousands of Jews who once lived there.

Reference

Weinstein, Edi. *Quenched Steel: The Story of an Escape from Treblinka*. Jerusalem: Yad Vashem, 2002.

Weiss, Alexander (1915–1996)

Alexander Weiss, from Bogada Desus in Transylvania, served in a Jewish labor brigade in the Romanian Army during World War II. He survived the brutal work and the attempted murder of all the conscripts and died in the United States in a car accident.

When Weiss was born, Transylvania was a province of Romania. After the war began, the Nazis arranged to transfer that territory to Hungary, but Weiss, whose father was a tailor, grew up as a Romanian. He and his ten siblings all considered themselves Romanian Jews.

Weiss was recruited into the army even before the war began. Because Romania's government was fiercely antisemitic, however, Jews were not accepted into the regular army. Instead they served in labor battalions, as they did in Hungary. The men in these labor battalions lived under terrible conditions and suffered serious punishment for the smallest infractions. They had to perform difficult, physical labor and enjoyed none of the privileges of regular soldiers serving their country.

Weiss's unit was assigned to cut down trees and carry them down a mountain. Anywhere from twenty to thirty men worked together. The taller, stronger men carried the biggest trees; they worked harder and died sooner. The smaller men tended to survive longer and Weiss was a small man.

As the Soviet Army began beating back the German troops and their Romanian allies, and the war neared its end, the Jewish men looked forward to returning to their families, but the Nazis had other plans. All the Jewish survivors from the Romanian labor brigades were placed in a trench and executed. Weiss was shot through the throat but did not die. He understood enough to maneuver himself from the front to the back of the trench, where he would be somewhat protected from the Germans' bullets. A German soldier, seeing that he was still alive, told Weiss to remain in the trench and stay perfectly still. Later, he was able to escape. Because of the help of this soldier, Weiss could never hate all the Germans; he knew some were good people.

After the war, Weiss went back to Bogada Desus, now part of Romania again. He met **Irene Abraham**, whose family he had known before the war, and she became his wife. The couple lived under Communism from 1945–1965. During that time, Weiss worked as a buyer for a supply company. Their children, Angie and Mark, were born in Romania.

In 1965, the Weiss family was permitted to leave Communist Romania and went to Italy. They lived in Rome for six months, and then got papers to join Irene's uncle, Rav Rosman, and his family in Michigan. The Rosmans had come to America before the war and the family had a successful line of dry cleaning businesses. Weiss became a manager for one of their stores. When Weiss was sixty-five, Rosman gave him ownership of the store and he continued working for another ten years, managing the business and doing the tailoring work, a profession that he had learned from his father and of which he was always very proud.

At the age of seventy-five, Weiss retired and sold the store, but he continued to work as a tailor from the basement of his home until his death in a car accident at eighty-one. When his wife, Irene, saw him get injured in the accident, she had a stroke and died shortly thereafter.

Weiss's daughter, Angie Weiss Gill, became a successful physical therapist living in Riverdale, New York. She married and had two children. His son, Mark Weiss, remained in Michigan. A successful doctor, he specialized in intervention radiology. He married and has four children. Weiss's parents and most of his siblings died in the Holocaust.

Reference

Gill, Meshullam (Mickey) (son-in-law of Alexander Weiss). Interview by Yaakov Taitz July 2006, Riverdale, New York.

Wells, Leon W. (1925–)

Leon Wells, the sole survivor of his large family, was born in Stojanov, Poland. He lived through the cruelty of the Janowska labor camp outside Lvov and worked as part of the death brigade, burying and burning the bodies of thousands of Jews who were murdered by the Nazis. His diary, reporting on one small part of that ordeal, was used as testimony in the Nuremberg Trials.

Leon Wells (born Weliczker) was the second child and the oldest son in a family of seven children. His father was a timber merchant and his mother, a well-educated woman, was from a family of scholars. They lived in Stojanov, a town about sixty miles from Lvov near the Ukrainian border, and had a large, extended family there.

In 1933, Wells's family moved to Lvov and settled into a large apartment. At that time, Wells was eight years old, his older sister, Ellen Lea, was ten, his brothers, Aaron and Jacob, were nine and seven. There were three younger sisters, Rachel, Judith, and Bina, the baby. Ellen and Leo went to school in Lvov and to Hebrew school in the afternoons. They were good students and Wells had completed his first year of gymnasium, the equivalent of high school, when World War II broke out in September 1939.

At first, Lvov was occupied by the Russians, who marched in by previous arrangement with the Nazis in a secret pact made in August 1939. The first thing the new Soviet administration did was to annex that part of Poland to the U.S.S.R. Then they deprived all entrepreneurs of their businesses and forced people to live in smaller quarters. Wells's father now lost his livelihood and was given work as manager of a notions store. Here, he was introduced to the Soviet customs of black marketeering and bribery, the only way that workers could make a living in Soviet society.

Although life was difficult, education was free and, with no discrimination against Jews, Wells and his sister advanced quickly in school and had already been accepted to a technical college in Moscow for the fall 1941 term. In June 1941, the Germans broke the Nazi-Soviet Pact and marched into Lvov, driving the Red Army back behind their original boundaries. Now the Jews were faced with a new set of problems, even more serious than those presented by the Russians.

As the Russians retreated, the Ukrainians, old enemies of Russia and of the Jews, viciously attacked the Jewish community. When the Germans finally restored order, the Ukrainians worked hand in hand with the Nazis, tormenting, threatening, and often murdering Jews for no reason.

Under Nazi rule, at first only the men and older boys were conscripted for forced labor. After several experiences with Ukrainian and German brutality, Wells, still only sixteen, tried to hide from the police when they came searching for workers, but could not evade them for long. Then he was arrested and brought to the Janowska camp, just outside the city of Lvov.

The horrors of this camp were well known and, in a book first published right after the war, Wells described the methods used by the camp guards to humiliate and torture the prisoners. He also enumerated the different jobs available in the camp and how one work group might be arbitrarily chosen to dig their own graves, lie in them, and be slaughtered by the guards. Those who became too sick to work were also executed.

One day, Wells himself was chosen for death. He described how the prisoners dug a large trench and were shot two at a time. Just before it was his turn, a guard asked him to return to the camp to retrieve a dead body. Weak and sick, he slowly dragged the corpse, falling further and further behind the guard. Suddenly he realized no one was watching him and he bolted and ran away. He hid in the camp, waiting to see if the guard would report him but he did not. Everyone assumed he had been killed according to the order and he took the opportunity to sneak out and run back to his family.

Wells was so ill that his parents took him to the hospital where he was treated for typhoid and pneumonia. He stayed for a month before being released. When Wells was well enough to travel, his younger brother, Jacob, took him back to Stojanov, where all his sisters were staying with their grandfather. The Nazis had not bothered the Jews of that small town, and they felt he would be safe from recapture there. But within months, the roundups that the Jews of the cities were experiencing came to Stojanov as well. While Wells was in a small village working for a peasant on assignment from the *Judenrat* (the Jewish governing committee), all his sisters and several aunts, uncles, and cousins were taken away. He later learned they were murdered in Belzec death camp. That same day, he learned that his mother had been arrested in Lvov. Totally desolate, he attempted suicide but was stopped by his relatives who made him promise not to attempt to kill himself again.

By November 1942, the remaining handful of Stojanov's Jews were forced to resettle in the nearby community of Radziechow. Within a month, they were ordered to move again, to other towns. He realized that the Jews were being herded into ever-smaller areas and would soon be squeezed out altogether.

Wells decided to return to Lvov and see if the rest of his family was still alive. He was able to find his brothers, Aaron and Jacob, who told him that their father had already been arrested and they themselves were waiting for death. Wells realized that he had a purpose: he would stay with his younger brothers, help support them, and encourage them to stay alive. He cleaned up the apartment that they shared with several others, built a hiding place for them in the cellar, and found work. All this made him feel better but ultimately did not prevent their arrest. His brothers were separated from him and taken to be killed. Wells was sent back to Janowska and more backbreaking work. Lvov was now *judenrein* (free of Jews).

After a few other work assignments, Wells and several hundred other men were sent outside the camp to work building bunkers, where they would eventually be living. Just beside the bunkers were long trenches. People were brought to the area to be slaughtered by Nazi rifle fire. After they had all been shot, the death brigade swung into action, dragging the bodies into the trenches, stacking them like logs, and setting fire to the remains.

Wells and the others in the death brigade fully expected to be killed within a few days so they would not be able to report on what the Nazis were doing. This did not happen, however. Instead, they continued this work from May

> *[Death brigades, called* Sonderkommando *(special units), existed in all the death camps and in many concentration camps as well. They were] selected from among the prisoners . . . to perform especially onerous tasks, including searching the dead for valuables, moving bodies to the crematoria or open pits, and cleaning the gas chambers. They received better housing and food, but these were short-lived privileges since the Sonderkommando members were gassed and replaced at regular intervals.*
>
> —David J. Hogan, Editor-in-chief.
> *The Holocaust Chronicle,* p. 378.

through November 1943. They buried and burned the bodies, sorted the clothes and valuables that the dead had worn, then dug up the burned bones, refined, and reburied the ashes. The men became efficient at their jobs and their German overseers rewarded them with extra food and other privileges. There was even an orchestra that played while they worked. During those months, Wells was able to keep a diary of daily events, which later served as an eyewitness account of German atrocities.

Over the months, the men of the death brigade established their own camaraderie and began to plan their escape together. The plan was an elaborate one and, although it did not work out quite as expected, most of the prisoners did manage to escape. Wells and several companions ran back to Lvov where they briefly found a hiding place with a Polish friend. From there, they were transferred to an underground bunker at the home of another Pole who was hiding twenty-two Jews beneath his barn. Wells remained there until April 1944, when Lvov was liberated by the Russians.

Leaving the bunker, Wells had no place to go. He knew that all his family was dead, but wandered back to their old apartment anyway. The new tenants recognized him but were hardly welcoming. He eventually heard that there was a Jewish registry in Lvov, where they were distributing bread and there he met some other survivors. Wells became the 184th Jewish survivor to register. Lvov, once a community of one hundred fifty thousand Jews had been totally decimated.

Slowly, Wells began to live again. He found a job and an apartment, made friends with other survivors, and started to plan for the future. One of his new friends was a woman named Halina Wind (see **Halina Preston**) who was part of a small group who had survived for fourteen months in the sewers of Lvov.

When the war was finally over in the west, Russia agreed to release Polish citizens who had fled from the Nazis, as well as those who the Soviet government had sent to Siberia. Wells took advantage of that brief amnesty to leave Soviet Russia and go to what was then still free Poland. He settled first in Silesia in June 1945 and by February 1946 had crossed into the American Zone in occupied Germany. Here he enrolled in a technical college and began to study engineering. He soon was offered a scholarship to a school in Switzerland and completed a Ph.D. there before emigrating to America in the summer of 1949.

While he was studying, Wells, with the help of a Polish Jewish historian, was able to publish the journal he had kept at Janowska concentration camp. His book gave details of the work he had done in the death brigade and described the camp commanders and those who were murdered there. It was first published in Polish and was used as testimony in the Nuremberg trials. Wells was also asked to identify one of the commanders of the Janowska camp who was trying to hide under a different identity. The man was later condemned to death.

In 1963, fourteen years after his arrival in the United States, Wells's book, expanded and translated into English, was published under the title *Janowska Road*. It was later republished by the Holocaust Library as *The Death Brigade*.

Leon Wells eventually settled in New Jersey. He published several other books and was an advisor for the Holocaust Library, a publisher in New York.

Reference

Wells, Leon Welizcer. *The Death Brigade*. New York: Holocaust Library, 1983.

Werber, Jacob (1914–2006)

Jacob Werber, the youngest of eight children, was born in Radom, Poland. The only survivor in his family, he was one of the first to be arrested and spent five and one-half years in Buchenwald. Before the war was over, he had lost his own daughter to the Nazi murderers, but was able to save seven hundred Jewish children.

Werber was already a young man of twenty-five when World War II began with the German invasion of Poland. He had a wife and a one-year-old daughter and worked in the family's fur business. A few months after the Nazis occupied Radom, Werber was arrested. He was falsely accused of two crimes: being a Communist and hoarding furs, and was sent to Buchenwald, a concentration camp for men in Germany. The population of the camp included political prisoners, ordinary criminals, Jehovah's Witnesses, homosexuals, and others who were considered enemies of the state. The early transport was made up of 3,200 people, mostly non-Jews. Of that original transport, only eleven were still living by the end of the war.

Conditions were so harsh that the Germans assumed a prisoner would be dead after three months and automatically notified the *Judenrat* (Jewish Committee) in his town of the death. Accordingly, the German authorities wrote a letter to the *Judenrat* of Radom, advising them that Werber had died and his ashes could be purchased from the proper authority. The Werbers bought what they believed to be Jacob's ashes and observed the traditional week of mourning for him. The Werber family went to their deaths believing that the youngest son had predeceased them all. But Werber managed to stay alive through five and one-half long years of near starvation, unspeakable atrocities, and physical labor.

At first, he worked in the quarry, considered the most grueling of all the work. Then he became a porter, chained to a wagon loaded with heavy material, which was brought back and forth from the work sites. When he got an infection from the chains that attached the wagon to his body, he spent a brief time in the hospital. During those few weeks, the porters were all selected for death but he had escaped that selection. After his recuperation, he was taught bricklaying and then worked in construction, carrying stones and bricks. It was during this time that he saw one of the worst examples of how the Germans used Jewish prisoners.

In Buchenwald, human skin was used to make lampshades and Werber was witness to it. While working with another prisoner to repair the house of the Commandant, he saw the Commandant's wife, Ilse Koch (later tried as a war criminal), as she commented on the tattoo on the chest of his fellow worker. Just weeks later, that prisoner was pulled out of line and murdered. His skin was sent to the tannery at Buchenwald to be prepared, but the prisoners who worked there (mostly Jehovah's Witnesses) would not do the work. Those who refused to work were killed and the skin was ultimately sent to an outside tannery. The next time Werber was called in to do repairs in the Commandant's home, he saw a new lamp and recognized, in the parchment shade, the familiar tattoo.

During the first years at Buchenwald, the criminal element dominated. Criminals ran the camp for the Nazis and viciously controlled the other prisoners. But gradually, the political prisoners, many of them academic or community leaders, were able to take control. They formed an underground that exposed those who were selling food meant for the prisoners and took control

At Buchenwald concentration camp, Jacob Werber and two other men were punished for a minor infraction by being hung by their hands. Werber, lying on the ground, has just been cut down. Courtesy of Jacob Werber.

of work assignments. This underground was in place and already well organized when the first large shipments of Jewish prisoners came to Buchenwald in 1944. Many of them were children.

Werber's job at that time was to receive the prisoners as they entered, register them, and take them to the showers. In the course of his duties, he saw that the children were terrified to enter the shower rooms, fearing that they would be gassed. There were no gas chambers at Buchenwald. Prisoners might die of hunger, be shot by the guards, or be beaten to death, but there had never been any mass executions there. It was only from these children that Werber learned of the existence of the gas chambers of Auschwitz and Treblinka. In order to reassure them, Werber and the other prisoners in charge took off their clothes and entered the showers with the children.

The underground organization in Buchenwald was determined to save these children. They knew that two years before, a shipment of gypsies had come to the camp and the German soldiers had taken all the children to the forest and shot them. In order to avoid that possibility, the children's records showed them to be older than they were. They were assigned to various jobs but never worked. The underground also arranged to give extra food to the children. They accomplished this by postponing the reporting of those who had died each night so they could continue to receive the extra rations for another few days. The food that would have gone to those who died was divided among the children.

Buchenwald's children were kept in a barracks in a section of the camp referred to as "the small camp." When the German guards approached, they were warned that those prisoners had typhus, a highly contagious disease. The Germans always avoided areas with typhus for fear that they would contract the disease.

As the war neared its end, the underground organization in Buchenwald became stronger and the Germans now depended on them for the daily running of the camp. In those last months of the war, they started a clandestine school for the children using some of the prisoners who had previously been teachers. Guards were posted outside the barracks where the children were taught. If a Nazi guard approached, a signal would be given and the children scattered. Werber told the children stories about Palestine and shared his dreams of a future Jewish state with them. One young boy challenged Werber, asking, "Why do we need to learn when we will never grow up to use our education?" Werber assured him that he would live to grow up and join his brothers in Israel.

Sixty years after the liberation of Buchenwald, Werber explained to an interviewer that by the time the Americans came, "we had liberated ourselves." The prisoners had weapons, which they had smuggled in from the munitions factory where many had worked. As rumors spread that the Americans were near, the prisoners' underground organization took over the camp and succeeded in killing a few German and Ukrainian guards and capturing the rest. The Commandant was caught telephoning for help and was handed over to the Americans. The report sent by the American Army noted that "the leadership of the camp is in the hands of a well-organized committee comprising all nationalities represented."

At the liberation of Buchenwald, Jacob Werber (on far right, indicated by an "X") accompanied the children he had helped to save. Courtesy of Jacob Werber.

When the war was over, Werber first handed over his seven hundred children to safety. Then he began to learn the sad news of his family. His wife and baby daughter were dead. His entire birth family, parents, siblings, aunts, and uncles were also gone, all two hundred murdered in Treblinka by the Nazi war machine. He found only one nephew, Sydney Lipman, and two nieces still alive. Heartbroken but determined to live, Weber met **Mildred Drezner**, a young woman from Radom, at a displaced-persons camp in Germany, and in January 1946 they were married. Searching for a future, Werber remembered an older brother in America. Max Werber had emigrated before his youngest brother Jacob was born and the two brothers had never met. With an American-Jewish soldier as an intermediary, Werber contacted his brother, who arranged for the proper papers and, by 1946, Werber and his wife Mildred, her father, **Joseph Drezner,** and Jacob's nephew, Sidney Lipman, had arrived in Beacon, New York, the home of Max Werber.

Those first few weeks in Max's home were tense and difficult, and the two families were unable to overcome the estrangement caused by the great gap in their ages and experiences. Within three weeks, Jacob Werber had found a job as a furrier and moved down to New York City with his wife. Gradually, he learned English and worked his way up. He established his own novelty business and made a large profit selling Davy Crocket hats.

In a report dated April 1945, issued by the U.S. Army Fourth Armored Division (604-2,2-daily reports) the officer leading the liberation of Buchenwald Concentration Camp reported on the camp, making no differentiation between Jewish and non-Jewish prisoners:

Concentration Camp Buchenwald (4775) occupied by 21,400 political prisoners; about 7000 French. Others are German Anti-Nazis, Russians, Poles, Spaniards. About 20,000 have been evacuated during the past three days. Medical Sit: 3,000 sick, many in critical state; 3,000 invalids incl. blind. Hospital and doctors present but no medicine or med. materials or disinfectants on hand. No operations can be made. Situation desperate. Help urgently required.

Food sit sufficient for 2 days but no bread at all on hand—special assault groups had been organized to over-power the guards. Before our arrival the guard posts were taken and 125 SS were captd and are still in the custody of the camp. The leadership of the camp is in the hands of a well organized committee comprising all nationalities represented.

Modern Military Archives, Washington; June 1944–May 1949. Reprinted from Saving Children with the permission of Jacob Werber.

The Werbers lived first in a small apartment in the Bronx. From there, they moved to Brooklyn, then to Queens, and finally to an affluent Long Island suburb and a beautiful spacious home. They had two sons. Martin was born in 1947 and David three years later. But Werber never forgot the children of Buchenwald.

In the year 2000, a reunion of "Werber's children" was organized in Tel Aviv. Of the original seven hundred, two hundred came. They arrived from countries all over the world and all still remembered Jacob Werber and how he had saved them during the war.

Reference

Werber, Jack. *Saving Children: Diary of a Buchenwald Survivor and Rescuer.* New Brunswick, NJ: Transaction Publishers, 1996.

Werber, Jacob. Interview by the author, May 2006, Great Neck, New York.

Wiesel, Elie (1928–)

Elie Wiesel may be the primary spokesman of the Holocaust. Perhaps the most well-known of all the survivors, Wiesel, originally from Sighet, in Transylvania, continued to speak and write in the name of the living and the dead and raised his voice to defend both Jews and non-Jews.

Eliezer Wiesel was born in Sighet, a town in northern Transylvania, originally part of Romania. An intelligent and studious boy from an observant Hasidic background, Wiesel was deeply religious and took every opportunity to study Jewish law and the mystical books of the Kabbalah. His parents earned a living as shopkeepers and, as the only son in his family, Wiesel was encouraged to become a scholar.

His quiet childhood lasted until 1943. That year, the war first came to the little town of Sighet, when the Hungarians, who had assumed jurisdiction of northern Transylvania in 1940, began deporting all foreign Jews. One of those first deportees was Wiesel's teacher, Moshe the Beadle. Moshe managed to escape from the deportation trains and returned to report what had happened. He described how the Jews were forced to dig huge trenches, to undress, and stand at the edge. German and Hungarian soldiers then shot them and they fell into the mass grave. Moshe's story was so horrifying that the people could not believe it. "How could any army kill thousands of innocent men, women, and children?" they asked. It must be a lie.

The people of Sighet continued to doubt the stories they heard about the murder of Jews. Even after the German Army marched into Hungary in 1944, they assured each other that the Nazis couldn't kill everyone and that the war would be over before they could reach Sighet. But in spite of their denials, the Nazis did come and the familiar pattern of events began. First came the order to wear the Star of David, then all Jews were herded into ghettos, and then they were deported. The Wiesel family, along with all the inhabitants of Sighet, were sent on a train to Auschwitz/Birkenau. At that point, he and his father were separated from his mother and three sisters, who were immediately sent to the gas chambers and murdered.

In his book *Night*, Wiesel describes how he and his father were disinfected, had their heads shaved, were taken through the showers, and given ragged uniforms to wear. "Within a few seconds," he wrote, "we ceased to be men. . . .

Elie Wiesel in the 1980s. Courtesy of Photofest.

The student of Talmud, the child that I was, had been consumed in the flames." From that time, Wiesel's faith in God was severely shaken.

Within a few days, the Wiesels, father and son, were transferred from Birkenau, the death camp, to Auschwitz, a work camp. They understood that as long as they were healthy enough to work, their lives would be spared. From Auschwitz they were brought to Buna, a satellite work camp near Auschwitz. They were driven mercilessly, beaten for no reason, and given rations barely adequate to keep them alive. Nevertheless, Wiesel and his father managed to survive and to stay together throughout that long year.

As the war neared its end and the Russian Army was approaching, the German soldiers made arrangements to evacuate the camp. At that time, Wiesel was in the hospital recovering from an infected foot. He could have remained there but he feared that those who did not leave would be put to death by the Germans. Also, he did not want to be separated from his father. With his foot still sore and bleeding, he set out on a forced march through snow, ice, and bitter cold.

After more than three days of marching, and with no food or water, the group was loaded onto trains and, for ten days, traveled in unheated boxcars, again with no food. They ate the snow to assuage their thirst and got weaker every day. Many died along the way. When Wiesel and his father finally arrived at Buchenwald concentration camp, not far from Weimar, Germany, there were only a handful of prisoners left alive. One hundred men had boarded their train; twelve got off.

> *Let us not forget that there is always a moment when the moral choice is made.*
>
> ***
>
> *Often because of one story or one book or one person, we are able to make a different choice, a choice for humanity, for life.*
>
> —Elie Wiesel

At Buchenwald, on January 29, 1945, Wiesel's father died from hunger and dysentery. The war was nearly over by then and Wiesel, now sixteen years old, was alone, the sole survivor of his family. He was transferred to the children's block and remained there until liberation on April 10, 1945.

Following his recuperation and a few years in a French orphanage, Wiesel studied at the Sorbonne in Paris. After Israel declared its statehood, he became a foreign correspondent for an Israeli daily newspaper. He remained in France for ten years and then moved to the United States in 1956.

It was not until 1956 that Wiesel was able to write about the war. His first book, *Night* (originally written in Yiddish), describes his personal experiences with his father at the camp, but all of his writings—over thirty books in all—are about the Holocaust and about the fragility of the human condition in the face of suffering. Although Wiesel was always aware that many others suffered during World War II, he insisted on the uniqueness of the Jewish experience. "While not all victims were Jews," he pointed out, "all Jews were victims."

After Wiesel moved to the United States, he received many honorary degrees. He was awarded the Congressional Medal of Honor in 1985 and the Nobel Peace Prize in 1986. He was the chair of the U.S. Holocaust Memorial Council between 1980 and 1986 and in that capacity was able to introduce Holocaust material into the schools in a number of states and to make people more aware of the Holocaust and its effects.

In 2005, Wiesel was the Andrew Mellon Professor of Humanities at Boston University, a post he had held since 1976. He was always a strong voice of conscience in the world, speaking out against the atrocities in Rwanda, in Bosnia, and anywhere that particular ethnic groups have been singled out by government policies. He insisted that "to remain silent and indifferent [in the face of injustice] is the greatest sin of all."

Although he never returned to a religious life of study after the war, his moral imperatives reflect Jewish sensibility and a Jewish sense of justice.

References

Abrahmson, I., ed. *Against Silence: The Voice and Vision of Elie Wiesel,* 3 vols. New York: Holocaust Library, 1985.

"Elie Wiesel." Available at http://xroads.virginia.edu/~CAP/HOLO/ELIEBIO.HTM

Wiesel, Elie. *Night.* Translated by Stella Rodway. New York: Bantam Books, 1960.

Wiesel, Irene Friedman (1913–1993), and Susan Gonosky (née Friedman) (1940–)

Born in Budapest one year after the beginning of World War II, Susan Friedman Wiesel Gonosky only had the dimmest, most fragmentary memories of those years of suffering. But she learned her family story from her mother, Irene Friedman Wiesel, who lived through the death of her husband in the

Hungarian labor brigades, the Nazi invasion of Hungary, and her daughter's last-minute rescue.

Irene and Arthur Friedman, Hungarian Jews, were living in Budapest when Germany attacked Poland on September 1, 1939. But war seemed far away from Hungary. The following year, the Friedmans had a baby girl, Zsuzsi (Susan), and continued with their lives, hoping the fighting would bypass their country. But then Hungary came down strongly in favor of the Nazis, who had already taken over Czechoslovakia, Austria, and Poland, and were attacking the Soviet Union. Hungary, too, began to adopt antisemitic policies and in 1942, Arthur Friedman was taken away as a slave laborer for the Hungarian Army. Neither Irene nor her daughter ever saw him again and Gonosky, only two years old, had no memory of her father.

With the war coming closer and her husband gone, Wiesel found two part-time jobs. She worked for the Jewish Agency and also for a Jewish newspaper, published in Budapest. Because she could not care for her daughter, she sent her to cousins (the Roths) and Gonosky lived with that family in a small town outside Budapest. Wiesel assumed that her daughter would be safer there, but when she found out that the Jewish community was confined to a ghetto, she immediately made plans to rescue her. With the help of Anna Vargas, a gentile woman who cleaned the building where Wiesel worked, she succeeded. Vargas traveled to the Roths, took Gonosky, and cared for her in her home. In less than a year, however, the situation in Hungary had changed again. Wiesel lost her jobs and took her daughter back with her.

After three years of success on the battlefield, the tide was turning against Germany. Hungary, Germany's ally, began to consider making a separate peace. In order to avoid that eventuality, the Nazis marched into Hungary and occupied the country in March 1944. Now they began deporting Hungary's Jews as well.

During that last year of war, several Hungarian Jews were busy negotiating to save at least some of their number from the gas chambers of Auschwitz and the bullets of Nazi soldiers. Among them were **Rezso Kasztner** and **Joel Brand,** who had been trying to work with the Nazis, exchanging Jews for supplies badly needed by the Germans. Kasztner managed to rescue approximately eighteen hundred people in this negotiation before it fell apart. Wiesel and Gonosky were among those rescued on what came to be called "the Kasztner train."

Gonosky was only four years old when she and her mother boarded Kasztner's special train that took them to Bergen-Belsen. They remained in a separate section of the camp for six months; only two incidents stayed in Gonosky's memory from that time. Both conjure up destruction. It was raining and Gonosky kept pulling on her mother's raincoat until she tore it. A second recollection is of a small shot glass that she played with. It was her only toy at Bergen-Belsen and she broke it by accident.

The next stop for the Kasztner Jews was Switzerland, where they remained for two more years. Once the war was over, they were able to travel to Paris, where Wiesel found her late husband Arthur Friedman's surviving brother. From there, they arranged their papers and sailed to New York, where Wiesel's parents were waiting for them. Ironically, the Irene and Arthur Friedman had the opportunity to leave Hungary for the United States in

1938 with her parents but had not gone because Arthur's mother was still alive and did not want to be left alone. Now, eight years later, in July 1946, Arthur Friedman's mother was dead of natural causes, Friedman himself had been killed in the war, and his widow and child were alone.

America was good to both mother and daughter. Within a short time, Wiesel married David Wiesel, also a Holocaust survivor, and a cousin of the famous **Elie Wiesel**. Gonosky was officially adopted by her stepfather and grew up in Brooklyn. She was educated in Jewish schools and then attended New York University and Teacher's College of Columbia University, where she received a master's degree in special education for hard-of-hearing children. For many years, she worked as a lip-reading teacher in the New York City schools.

In 1964, Susan Friedman Wiesel married Arthur Gonosky. They had a son and, as of 2006, three grandchildren. Irene Friedman Wiesel died in New York in 1993. Although Susan Gonosky had very few memories of the war, she remained conscious of her status as a survivor and always understood that she was lucky to emerge unscathed from a war that killed one and a half million Jewish children.

Reference

Gonosky, Susan. Interview by the author, February 2006, Miami Beach, Florida.

Wiesenthal, Simon (1908–2005), and Cyla Wiesenthal (1908–2003)

Both Simon Wiesenthal and Cyla Mueller Wiesenthal were from Buczacz, Poland. The Wiesenthals survived first under the Russians and then the Nazis. After World War II ended, Simon Wiesenthal was determined to bring to justice those responsible for the deaths of six million Jews and the sufferings of countless more.

Simon and Cyla Wiesenthal grew up in Buczacz, near Lvov, in eastern Poland (now the Ukraine). They were married in 1936 and Simon, who had studied architecture, had already set up a small architectural company in Lvov, when Germany invaded Poland in 1939. With the partition of Poland between the Germans and Russians, Wiesenthal and his family quickly experienced the impact of the Soviet occupation. His stepfather was arrested and died in prison, his stepbrother was shot, and Wiesenthal had to give up his work as an architect and take a job as a mechanic in a bedspring factory in order to support himself and his wife. He was able to save himself, his wife, and his mother from deportation to Siberia by bribing an NKVD (Soviet Secret Police) commissar.

But there was worse to come. When the Germans marched eastward and displaced the Russians, Wiesenthal and his wife were taken for forced labor to Janówska, a nearby work camp. There he worked in the repair shop for the eastern railroads and gathered important information that he later passed on to the Polish Underground. In return for this information, he obtained false papers for Cyla, who was able to pass as Irena Kowalska, a Polish Christian.

Cyla was spirited out of the camp to Lublin, where she worked for a while as a nanny for a Polish family. Then she returned to Lvov to try and visit Simon, still in Janówska. They managed a brief visit through the barbed wire fence, then the Polish Underground found a job for her in Lvov in an electrical plant. Before the end of the war, Cyla was deported to Germany as a slave laborer, along with other Poles, and liberated from there in 1945. Simon's mother was deported to the Belzec death camp and murdered.

In 1943, with the help of the deputy director of the camp, Wiesenthal escaped from Janowska but was recaptured in June 1944. He tried to kill himself but was too weak to do so. Instead, after interrogation by Nazi officials, he was selected for extermination. But German plans to murder him, along with the remaining Jewish prisoners, were interrupted at the last minute by the advancing Soviet Army. Instead of shooting them, Nazi guards led their prisoners westward through Poland to Buchenwald and finally, to Mauthausen, near Vienna. Wiesenthal was one of a very few prisoners to survive that forced evacuation. By the time he arrived at Mauthausen he weighed less than a hundred pounds and was barely alive. The Americans liberated the camp on May 5, 1945.

After regaining his health and some of his strength, Wiesenthal immediately began preparing evidence of Nazi war crimes and atrocities for use by the United States Army in the Nuremberg trials. He first worked for the U.S. Army's Office of Strategic Services and Counter-Intelligence Corps and also took a job as head of the Jewish Central Committee of the U.S. Zone in Austria.

Wiesenthal's relatives had all been killed by the Nazis. He believed that Cyla was dead, too. He did not know of her final deportation to Germany and was told that the building she had been living in was demolished by bombs. Because of Wiesenthal's suicide attempt, Cyla had also been told that her husband was dead. She learned that he was alive through a chance meeting with a friend and they were reunited in Austria at the end of 1945.

With no other family members remaining, the Wiesenthals settled in Vienna, where their daughter, Pauline, was born in 1946. By 1947, Simon's work with the U.S. Army was completed and he set up the Jewish Historical Documentation Center in Linz, Austria. Working with thirty volunteers, the center continued assembling evidence for future Nazi war crimes trials. At the same time, Wiesenthal held a salaried position doing relief work and social work. He never again worked as an architect. Cyla chose to distance herself from her husband's

Excerpt from "Pope John Paul II and the Jewish People," —a news release issued by Rabbi Marvin Hier, head of the Simon Wiesenthal Center in Los Angeles, California, after the Pope's death in April, 2005.

On December 3, 2003, together with a small delegation of Center trustees, I returned to the Vatican . . . to present the Pope with the Wiesenthal Center's highest honor, our Humanitarian Award. On that occasion, I recapped his remarkable accomplishments: "As a youngster, you played goalie on the Jewish soccer team in Wadowice . . . in 1937, concerned about the safety of Ginka Beer, a Jewish student on her way to Palestine, you personally escorted her to the railroad station . . . in 1963, you were one of the major supporters of Nostra Aetate, *the historic Vatican document which rejected the collective responsibility of the Jewish people for the crucifixion . . . in 1986, you were the first Pope to ever visit a synagogue . . . the first to recognize the State of Israel . . . the first to issue a document that seeks forgiveness for members of the Church for wrongdoing committed against the Jewish people throughout history and to apologize for Catholics who failed to help Jews during the Nazi period . . . the first to visit a concentration camp and to institute an official observance of Yom HaShoah, Holocaust Remembrance Day at the Vatican."*

work but she supported his efforts throughout their sixty-seven years of marriage.

Wiesenthal is best known for his role in tracking down the infamous Nazi, Adolf Eichmann. He obtained information from eyewitnesses that he subsequently gave to the Israeli Mosad (Secret Service). Mosad agents captured Eichmann in Buenos Aires, Argentina, in 1959. He was put on trial in Israel, was found guilty of mass murder, and executed on May 31, 1961. Other notorious Nazi criminals whom Wiesenthal was instrumental in catching included Karl Silberbauer, the Gestapo officer who arrested Anne Frank, and nine of the sixteen SS officers who had participated in the extermination of Lvov's Jews. Wiesenthal also wrote several books about his experiences.

Inspired by his activities, the Wiesenthal Center was set up in Los Angeles in 1977 as an institute for Holocaust remembrance and with an attached Museum of Tolerance. The Wiesenthal Center has branches throughout the world.

Cyla died in 2003 and Simon in 2005. In his obituary, *The New York Times* called him "a stubborn sleuth on the trail of history's archfiends." He is remembered as the conscience of the Holocaust. "If we ignore the past," he said, " . . . then the past will return. Only by remembering can we and our children and their children build a just future . . . in which human life never loses its value."

References

Blumenthal, Ralph. "Simon Wiesenthal Is Dead at 96; Tirelessly Pursued Nazi Fugitives." *New York Times,* Wednesday, September 21, 2005. p. C18.
Van der Vat, Dan. "Cyla Wiesenthal." *Guardian,* November 14, 2003. Available at http://www.guardian.co.uk/obituaries/story/0,,1084887,00.html.
Wiesenthal, Simon. *Justice, Not Vengeance.* Translated by Ewald Osers. London: Mandarin, 1990.
http://www.jewishvirtuallibrary.org/jsource/biography/Wiesenthal.html.

Wizenberg family

The Wizenberg family was scattered throughout France during the Nazi occupation. They all survived, but each experienced his or her own unique trauma. Although they were reunited when Paris was liberated, the war against the Jews changed their lives irretrievably.

Joseph and Madeline Wizenberg were both born in Poland. Joseph first emigrated by himself to Paris in the 1920s, using false papers. A few years later, he brought his fiancée and then other family members to Paris. Joseph and his father were skilled cabinetmakers and started a small furniture factory.

The Wizenbergs soon began their own family: Charles was born in 1933, Berthe in 1934, and Rachel in 1937. Régine was born in September 1939, just days after the Nazi invasion of Poland. Madeline Wizenberg went into labor in the cellar of their apartment house during an air raid, and her fourth child was delivered there with the help of a midwife.

By 1940, France had been defeated and the anti-Jewish laws that were established in Germany in 1933 were now introduced in France. Berthe, the oldest of the Wizenberg daughters, remembered that when her kindergarten class made their weekly visits to the local park, as the only Jewish child in the class, she was barred from entering.

In 1941, each Jewish family was told to present themselves to the French police in their area to make sure their papers were in order. Most of the families obeyed, but Joseph Wizenberg held back. He decided he would pretend to be sick that day. If everything turned out all right, he would go the following day.

Wizenberg's caution proved to be well founded. As each family reported to the local police, the men were arrested and sent to Pithiviers, a labor camp near Paris, and the women and children were sent home. When Joseph heard the news, he set up a hiding place for himself by removing the mattress from a convertible sofa in their apartment. Whenever anyone knocked at the door, he would jump into the empty space underneath the couch. Then the children would replace the cushions and sit on it until the visitor left.

This could not continue for long. Joseph needed to earn money to support his family. He once again bought false papers, this time identifying him as a Polish Christian worker, and continued working and returning to his home, an apartment in a fine building in Paris. But when the order came for every Jew to wear an armband identifying him or her as *Juif* (Jew) he knew he had to take steps to insure the safety of his family.

Wizenberg searched for separate places for each of his children, reasoning that if one was caught by the Nazis, the others might still survive. He placed Charles, then eight years old, on a farm with the parents of the concierge of their building. Then he found a Catholic orphanage run by the nuns at a convent not far from Paris that was willing to take Berthe and Rachel, aged seven and four. The youngest, Régine, only a toddler, was placed with another family who worked on a nearby farm. Their mother, Madeline, along with the Wizenberg grandparents and an uncle, hid out in the country home of a Christian friend on the outskirts of Paris. Madeline was already pregnant with their fifth child. When he was born, the baby, named Maurice, was quickly given into the care of Christian friends so that his cries would not endanger the rest of the family in hiding there.

Joseph Wizenberg himself continued working in a furniture factory, sheltered by Chapelet, a Christian acquaintance who had learned cabinet making from him. Now overseeing a furniture factory, Chapelet not only gave Wizenberg a job, but allowed him to return after all the workers had left, and sleep there. He could not make any noise, turn on any light, or cook, but he did manage to keep out of the hands of the authorities most of the time. His regular salary enabled him to send money to each of the homes where his children were being sheltered.

Twice Joseph Wizenberg was arrested and sent to labor camps. Both times he was able to escape and return to his factory hideout. Neither he nor his wife could visit the children, and the children did not know whether or not their parents were alive. During their three years at the orphanage, no one knew that Berthe and Rachel were Jewish except the Mother Superior. Their last name was changed to one that sounded less Jewish. At the convent, there was never enough to eat and the girls experienced constant hunger.

To Those My Eyes Have Seen Depart . . .

My Eyes search for you
Where are you my beloved
Flown away in the smoke
Dissolved in the gray skies
Where have you disappeared
You one day
Ripped . . . torn . . .
Taken away far from us
From a wandering home always moving
Forever . . .

Your lamentations . . . your cries . . . silent
When bent under the meager load
You were taking along (some warm cloths . . .
A mattress . . . attached in haste)
Surrounded by policemen like criminals
Innocent you lowered your head . . .
Where are you
You who never came back?
Your fate is known by an indifferent world
But my heart grieves and yearns for you
Your tomb is nowhere
. . . it is in the depth of my eyes.

—written and translated by Berthe Wizenberg Fleischer

In addition, Berthe felt intense pressure to behave, so as not to be singled out or to make trouble. And even at her age, a sense of responsibility for her younger sister weighed heavily on her.

In late 1944, as soon as Paris was liberated, Joseph Wizenberg collected his family and they returned home. But life was not the same as it had once been. Wizenberg had been daring and courageous throughout the war, sheltering and supporting his family, sneaking through the dark streets at the risk of his life to visit his wife and deliver money for his children. Now that it was all over, he was sick and exhausted, and no longer able to work. Madeline, too, was sick. With no medical care throughout the war years, her physical condition had deteriorated and she became a semi-invalid. The Wizenberg children realized they would have to take on some of the responsibility for earning a living.

It was Charles and Berthe, then twelve and eleven years old, who first shouldered the burden of family support, selling black market cigarettes in local bars. Then, while going to school during the day, they did piece work at home making pocketbooks. In addition, Berthe, as the oldest of the Wizenberg daughters, cared for the younger children. She mothered Régine and Maurice as best she could, and helped with Jacqueline, the youngest, born after the war. Although their mother tried to start a business of her own, it failed. The family, with only Charles and Berthe to depend on, was living in poverty.

By the time they were in their teens, Charles and Berthe were working full time making pocketbooks. They had finished grade school, but did not attend the lycée (high school). Berthe did continue studying piano, which she loved, and Charles played the violin. And although Berthe was proud of the fact that she was helping her family, she felt trapped. When her maternal aunt came from America to visit them, she offered to sponsor Berthe as a new immigrant to the United States. Although she was reluctant, she knew she needed to get out on her own and build a life for herself. With her mother's encouragement, she agreed. In 1955, her papers came.

At first, Berthe Wizenberg disliked New York. She could not speak any English and she hated her job in a handbag factory. She planned to stay for only a year, but she began to take night school courses in English, typing, and shorthand. Then she met Herbert Fleischer, a young American man who wanted to marry her. Despite his offer of marriage, Berthe was determined to return to Paris. Fleischer pursued her and brought her back, and they were married in 1956.

As soon as she could, Berthe sponsored Charles and his young family, and then Rachel. Charles began his career in New York by opening a small pocket-book factory. Soon, he left that behind and pursued his dream: to become a successful jazz violinist in America, a dream he realized. Charles Wizenberg and his wife have one son. Rachel found work as a secretary, married an American, and also raised a son.

Régine married a French Catholic and she and the Wizenberg parents remained in France. Berthe later brought her two youngest siblings to New York as well, but Maurice ultimately returned to France. He pulled away from the family and became an Orthodox Jew. Madeline and Joseph Wizenberg visited the United States many times, but always returned to Paris. Madeline died in 1986 and Joseph in 1991.

Berthe continued her education in New York, first getting a high school equivalency diploma, then a college degree from Queens College (part of the City University of New York). She became a teacher of French and comparative literature, working in several colleges and high schools in the New York area. She also worked as a piano teacher. Berthe and Herbert Fleischer have two daughters.

One thing Berthe Wizenberg Fleischer missed when she was young "was having the right teachers and the right education." She tried hard to give her daughters that opportunity. She has also struggled to continue her own education. While she worked full time as a teacher and raised her daughters, Francine and Vivian, she earned a master's degree in philosophy and completed the course work for her doctorate.

After her retirement, Berthe had mixed feelings about having left her native France. "The French people saved us," she stated thoughtfully in an interview. "They saved me, but still, I never felt completely French."

Reference

Wizenberg Fleischer, Berthe. Interview by the author. November 2005, Flushing, New York.

Wollheim, Norbert (1913–1998)

Norbert Wollheim of Berlin, Germany, administered the *Kindertransport*, a pre–World War II effort that saved the lives of seven thousand Jewish children. A survivor of Auschwitz, Wollheim emerged from that experience still committed to helping the Jewish community and, after the war, he became a leader of the displaced persons in the British zone of Germany.

Wollheim grew up in Berlin with his parents and an older sister. He attended public school and was active in a Jewish youth group. His goal was to become a lawyer and he enrolled in law school in 1931. But one year later, when the Nazis came to power in Germany, Jews were no longer permitted to study law.

Seeing the developing antisemitism under Hitler, Wollheim took a job with a Jewish import-export firm, thinking it might help him to leave Germany, but his community needed him and he could not leave. He was first asked to organize groups of Jewish children to attend summer camp in the neighboring countries of Denmark and Sweden. These camps, it was believed, would remove Jewish youth from the difficult, tension-filled lives most were forced to live under Nazism. A few weeks at summer camp, however, was only a temporary respite from the growing threat. The increasing danger to Jewish lives was made clear on November 9, 1938. That night, there was a nation-wide, government-approved pogrom against all Jews. Called *Kristallnacht* (the Night of Broken Glass), it resulted in the destruction of Jewish businesses, the burning of synagogues, and the killing of Jews.

Many Jewish men were arrested on *Kristallnacht* and thousands of Jews sought new ways to leave Germany and Austria. Although most countries were not anxious to accept Jewish refugees, Great Britain had offered to take in ten thousand children from the areas directly threatened by Hitler: Germany, Austria, Poland, and Czechoslovakia. Wollheim, already experienced in orga-nizing children's camps, was now asked by the Jewish community to admin-ister this new program. It involved overseeing the entire process—from the initial application, to communicating with the parents, setting up transporta-tion, and finding counselors to accompany the children, who ranged in age from five to nineteen.

Wollheim personally came to the train station to see the children off and usually traveled with them to England before returning to organize the next group. It was difficult for the parents to part from their children. When it was time for the train to leave, Wollheim would make a formal announcement: "Ladies and gentlemen, the time has arrived to say goodbye." The children would then be ushered onto the train, sometimes tearfully. Most never saw their parents again.

Between 1938 and 1939, Wollheim organized twenty transports and saved seven thousand children. He sent off the last *Kindertransport* on August 29, 1939, two days before Germany invaded Poland.

Wollheim had decided not to accompany that last transport to England because he saw that war was immanent and did not want to leave his young bride alone. He had married Rosa the year before and the couple was expect-ing their first child, born later in 1939. They remained in Berlin and Wollheim continued to work for the Jewish community, administering a Jewish voca-tional school, until the Nazi authorities summoned him for slave labor. It was 1941.

While he was working, Wollheim's parents were rounded up and deported to Auschwitz in December 1942. They were immediately sent to the gas chambers and killed. Just four months later, on March 11, 1943, he, his wife Rosa, who was pregnant again, and their three-year-old son were arrested and forced into a cattle car holding one hundred people. It was so crowded they could hardly breathe. Wollheim recognized several friends from his old youth group who had been arrested at the same time. It was Friday evening, the eve of the Sabbath, when the train pulled out of the station. The Wollheims began singing Hebrew Sabbath songs. Some of his friends joined him and one woman even managed to light Sabbath candles.

The next day, the train arrived in Auschwitz with its cargo of one thousand people and they were sorted: Rosa and their son were sent to the gas chambers, Wollheim was sent to work. He was assigned to one of the satellite camps of Auschwitz called Monowitz. Here, a synthetic rubber factory run by the German industrialist I. G. Farben, was operating, and Wollheim was given a job in construction. Work was difficult, death was a constant threat, and there was barely enough food to sustain the men. Wollheim remained in Monowitz until January 18, 1945, when the Nazis evacuated Auschwitz and marched all their prisoners away from the advancing Soviet Army. They were forced to walk through the snow to Gleiwitz, another concentration camp. From there, they were sent by train on a journey into Czechoslovakia, then Austria, back to Czechoslovakia, and finally to Germany. They traveled for days with no provisions; each night more people died. They had begun the journey with six thousand men. When their train pulled into Berlin at last, only two thousand prisoners remained alive.

> *I remember very well that morning of May 3, 1945, when we saw the American flag ... hanging from the trees in the forest near Schwerin, and then we realized that we had been just reborn, and had received a new lease on life. I remember we embraced each other. I was in a small group of people, and we were laughing and we were crying ... [it]was a tremendous feeling of relief, but also of burden because we realized that this moment for which we had waited years and years, we couldn't share with those of us who had deserved it— our own families. And we realized also something else ... that we had no home left to go to. ... that was the moment of tremendous elation, but of also tremendous sadness.*
>
> —Norbert Wollheim in an interview in the United States, n.d.

Those two thousand men were now brought to a camp at Sachsenhausen-Oranienburg, but when the Allies began bombing, they were taken once more on a march. It was May 2, 1945. Both the Germans and their prisoners knew the war was coming to an end. The soldiers were less committed to guarding the men and Wollheim was able to flee from the Nazi guards. He made his way to nearby Schwerin where he encountered the American Army.

When the war ended, Germany was divided up into four administrative zones, each governed temporarily by one of the allied nations: England, France, the Soviet Union, and the United States. Once he was liberated, Wollheim knew that he did not want to return to the part of Germany that was occupied by the Soviet Union. Instead, he settled in Luebeck, a city located in the northern part of Germany, not far from the Baltic Sea, in the British sector.

As soon as he arrived in Luebeck, Wollheim began organizing a Jewish community of eight hundred displaced persons. When he heard of the bigger displaced-persons camp at nearby Bergen-Belsen, he traveled there and visited with that camp's leader, **Josef Rosensaft**. Together, Wollheim and Rosensaft set up the Central Committee of Liberated Jews in the British Zone. Elections were held and Rosensaft was chosen as chairman with Wollheim as vice-chairman.

By the end of 1945, Wollheim had met Friedel, also a German Jew and a survivor whom he had known in the Youth Movement. He and Friedel were married and soon had two children, Peter and Ruth. He continued as a leader of the Jewish refugees in Germany until the Wollheims, with the sponsorship of the **Fabian family,** friends from Germany, emigrated to the United States in 1952. They settled in New York City where Wollheim found work as an accountant.

Norbert Wollheim rededicated the Jewish cemetery in Lübeck, Germany, in 1948. Courtesy of the U.S. Holocaust Memorial Museum.

Even before coming to America, Wollheim had begun a lawsuit against the I. G. Farben factory for compensation for his twenty-two months of slave labor in Monowitz. In 1953, the suit, the first of its kind, was settled in his favor, paving the way for others and ultimately, for compensation for all those who were consigned to slave labor during the war.

In New York, the Wollheims raised their children and Wollheim continued his commitment to the Jewish survivor community. He was active in the World Federation of the Bergen-Belsen Survivors, the American Gathering of Jewish Holocaust Survivors, the Conference on Jewish Material Claims against Germany, and was a president of his synagogue in Fresh Meadows, New York, a suburban community in Queens (New York City). When he died in 1998, Wollheim was mourned by members of all these organizations as well as by his two children, one grandchild, his third wife Charlotte, and her two sons.

References

Berenbaum, Michael. *A Promise to Remember: The Holocaust in the Words and Voices of its Survivors.* New York: Bulfinch, 2003.
http://query.nytimes.com/gst/fullpage.html?res=9A0DEFDE113FF930A35752 C1A96E958260

Y

Yoran, Shalom (1922–), and Maurice Sznycer (1920–)

Shalom Sznycer Yoran of Raciaz, Poland, never forgot his mother's last words to him during the war. She told him to avenge his parents deaths and to "let the world know" what had happened to the Jews in Poland. In 1946, after he and his brother Maurice Sznycer spent three years fighting with the partisans in the forests, he wrote down all their experiences. That book, *The Defiant*, relates his family's harrowing story from the first day of the war until the final victory.

Yoran was born in 1922 and his original Polish name was Selim Sznycer. His father, Samuel, owned and managed a lumberyard and they lived nearby in a spacious home. Both his parents came from large families—his mother, Hannah, was one of fourteen children—and Yoran and his older brother, Maurice (originally named Musio), spent a great deal of time with aunts, uncles, and cousins.

Sznycer was sixteen and Yoran was fourteen when war broke out. Because their town was not far from the Polish-German border, bombs fell almost immediately and the bombardment continued for three days. When it was over, most of the inhabitants of Raciaz had decided to flee east toward Warsaw. On the way, they saw the defeated Polish Army in retreat.

But the Sznycer family did not succeed in escaping the Germans, who soon occupied all of western Poland; they returned to Raciaz to find their home ransacked. Within a month, their lumber business was confiscated and they saw at first hand the German attitude toward Jews. Jews were threatened and taunted, dragged off to forced labor, killed at random, and forced to give up their possessions to the Nazi soldiers and police.

With another family, the Sznycers began considering escape. Eastern Poland had been occupied by the Russians following the Soviet-German treaty and it was safer there for Jews. Their final decision was made after the Nazis gathered

The Sznycer family before the war. Shalom Yoran is to the left of his parents and Maurice Sznycer to the right. Courtesy of Joan Mandel.

most of the Jews in the Raciaz synagogue, forced them to undress, and watch while the soldiers desecrated the Torah. The following morning, the family packed two suitcases and left, making their way on foot from one town to another, trying to avoid German soldiers. When they arrived at the frozen Bug River, the border between German-occupied Poland and Soviet-occupied Poland, they paid a guide to help them cross. On December 29, 1939, the family arrived in Semiatic, a town near Bialystok, then in Russian territory.

The Sznycers wandered from place to place, trying to find work, constantly forced to move further east because of Russian rulings concerning refugees. Yoran, by now fifteen, became an apprentice in a photographers' cooperative and by 1940 began to earn a salary. Gradually, the family members found better jobs and were able to make a home for themselves. But then the Germans broke their pact with the Soviets and marched into Russian territory. Once again, German bombs fell on their home and they fled, this time settling in Kurzeniec, a small town with over one thousand Jews. The Germans ordered the Jews to form a *Judenrat* (Jewish Council) and provide slave labor from among their own people. Soon the Sznycers found themselves in a camp working for the Germans. But there was worse to come.

Within weeks, a large number of Jews from Kurzeniec were rounded up and taken out of town. No one knew where they were going. Only one person, a young boy who had managed to slip away and hide, returned from that *aktia* (action). When he reentered the town, he reported that all the Jews had been ordered to dig a trench. Men, women, and children were lined up in front of the hole and shot. They fell face down into their graves and were covered up with earth.

At first, the Jews thought it only happened to those who were identified as Communists, but as more and more reports came in, they realized that that was the fate of every Jew. Yoran and Sznycer wanted to escape and join the partisans who were fighting in the surrounding forests. But the boys needed guns in order to fight. At this time, Yoran was working as a messenger at the town hall. When a group of Germans arrived to speak with the mayor, Yoran took the opportunity to steal a pistol from their glove compartment. Although the German soldiers were furious when they found it missing, they never discovered who did it.

The Sznycer brothers were anxious to join those who were fighting the Nazis but both the *Judenrat* and their own parents were against it. Their father told them that they must stay together and they obeyed. But then the Nazi soldiers surrounded their town and the remaining Jews of Kurzeniec were rounded up. Samuel Sznycer was in the synagogue for morning prayers, but Yoran, Sznycer, and their mother, Hannah, ran into the cornfields to escape and hid until the Germans had left. Before separating, Hannah whispered to Yoran that he must go and fight and stay alive. He must avenge his parents' death and tell the world what the Nazis had done. When Yoran and Sznycer emerged, their mother was nowhere in sight. Only later did they hear from others that both Samuel and Hannah had been murdered in this last *aktia*.

Sznycer and Yoran now ran to the forests. They met others and lived with them in an underground bunker camouflaged with leaves. They stole or begged for food from the local farmers, sometimes enduring days of hunger and thirst. Sometimes they were reduced to drinking water from a pigsty. Once caught by gentiles, Yoran was stripped of his clothing. His attackers attempted to stab him, but he miraculously escaped, running barefoot and naked in the snow.

As the war neared its end, their group joined with the Russian partisans, most of whom were escaped prisoners of war. Sznycer and Yoran went on many missions to blow up train tracks in order to stop the German supplies from reaching the front. With four other partisans, they set fire to a munitions factory and saw with satisfaction that the Germans were now afraid of them.

By 1944, the Nazis were in full retreat. Yoran and Sznycer were welcomed

Letter from a German commander about the partisans

This once-secret document stored in a museum in Minsk is now at the Ghetto Fighters Museum in Israel. It was given to the author in this English translation by Varda Yoran and gives concrete evidence of German policy against the Jews and of the effectiveness of the Jewish Partisans who fought the Nazis during World War II.

Minsk, July 31, 1942

From: The Commissioner General for White Ruthenia Division Gauleiter/G.-507/42g–(must be cited in reply)

To: The Reichskommissar for the East Gauleiter Heinrich Lohse Riga

Concerning: The struggle against the Partisans and Action against Jews in the General District White Ruthenia

In all the clashes with partisans in White Ruthenia it has become clear that Jewry, in the Polish as well as the formerly Russian part of the General District, with the Polish resistance movement in the East and Moscow's Red Army men is the main carrier of the partisan movement in the East. Therefore, the treatment of the Jews in White Ruthenia, in view of the danger to the whole economy, has become a primarily political problem which must be solved in light of political, not economic considerations. In intensive talks with SS Brigade Leader Bonner, and the outstandingly effective director of the SD SS Obersturmbannfuehrer Dr. jur. Strauch, we have liquidated about 55,000 Jews in White Ruthenia in the past ten weeks. In the Minsk rural area Jewry has been destroyed totally, without thereby endangering the productive capacity. In the mostly Polish Lida area 16,000 Jews were liquidated, in Slonim 8,000 Jews, etc. Through the takeover by rear area troops—as already reported—our preparations for the liquidation of the Jews in the Glebokie district were interfered with. The Rear Area Command has, without coordinating with me, liquidated 10,000 Jews, whose systematic destruction had already been planned by us. In Minsk city, about 10,000 Jews were liquidated on 28th and 29th July, of whom 6,500 Russian Jews, mostly aged, women and children; the rest consisting of Jews unable

Continued on next page

Continued from previous page

to work, who had been sent to Minsk in November of last year from Vienna, Bruenn, Berlin and Bremen, by command of the Fuehrer.

The Sluzk area, too, has been relieved of several thousand Jews. The same goes for Novogrodesk and Milejka. Radical measures are planned for Baranowicz and Hansewicz. In Baranowicz about 10,000 live in the city alone, of whom 9,000 will be liquidated next month. In Minsk city 2,600 Jews from Germany have remained. In addition, all 6,000 Jews and Jewesses from Russia are still alive, having survived the Aktion *because they serve the units employing them as labor force. Minsk will continue to have the most Jews in the future as well, since the concentration of armament industries and the needs of the railways require this. In all the other districts the maximum number of Jews in the labor force will be set by the SD and myself at 800, and possibly 500, so that at the end of the* Aktions *already mentioned we will be left with 8,600 Jews in Minsk and about 7,000 in the ten remaining districts, including the Jew-free Minsk rural area* (Minsk-Land). *The danger that the partisans will in the future be able to draw on the Jews will thus no longer exist. To me and to the SD it would be most preferable, once the economic requirements of the army are no longer a factor, to eliminate the Jews in the General District of White Ruthenia once and for all. For the time being the economic needs of the armed forces, who are the main employers of Jews, will be taken into account.*

To this uncompromising position vis-à-vis the Jews must be added the difficult task of the SD in White Ruthenia, charged with constantly escorting new transports of Jews from the Reich *to their destination. This makes extraordinary demands on the physical and moral endurance of the men of the SD, and interferes with the other tasks they are assigned in the White Ruthenia territory.*

I would therefore be grateful if the honorable Reichskommissar would find it possible to stop the transport of Jews to Minsk at least until the partisan danger is finally overcome. I need the SD 100% in the mission of fighting the partisans and the Polish resistance movement, which both require all the resources of the not overly strong SD units.

Continued on next page

into the Russian Army and fought against the Germans. When the Germans left Polish territory, the two brothers came to surrender their arms to the officials but the Russian officers told them they were needed to protect Russia. Yoran and Sznycer said nothing, but quietly slipped away and joined their Jewish comrades. They fled from Poland into Hungary and then into Italy. There, Yoran met some members of the Palestine Brigade, a Jewish division from Palestine that had fought under the British flag. The Jewish soldiers of the Palestine Brigade gave him a false identity and smuggled him into Palestine in 1946.

Yoran and Sznycer separated in Italy. Sznycer and another friend headed for Paris where they planned to study at the Sorbonne. Sznycer took the French name Maurice and eventually became Professor Maurice Sznycer, an expert in ancient Semitic languages. At the age of eighty-four, he was still teaching at the Sorbonne once or twice a week and was often called upon to decipher ancient inscriptions in Ugarit, Phoenician, and Aramaic. Many of his books and articles have been published. Sznycer married a Holocaust survivor from Poland and the couple had one daughter, who became a dermatologist, and then a granddaughter who studied law in Paris.

In Palestine, Selim Sznycer took a Hebrew name, Shalom Yoran. He joined his grandmother and several aunts and uncles in what would soon become the Jewish state, resumed his education, and married. He served seven years in the new Israeli Air Force, took a degree in aeronautical engineering, and was instrumental in building the Israeli aircraft industry. When he was fifty years old, Yoran retired and moved with his wife, Varda, to the United States, where he became chairman of a private aircraft trading and service company.

In 1990, Yoran discovered the manuscript that he had written about the war years right after he arrived in Israel. He remembered his mother's request that he tell the world and, with the help of his wife Varda, he reviewed and translated his manuscript into English. It was published in 1996.

At the age of eighty-two, Yoran was still active in philanthropic and educational work. In 1997, he was awarded the Flame of Truth award by the Tel-Aviv University Fund for Higher Education, where he had established an annual endowment fund in the name of his parents. He was on the board of the Museum of Jewish Heritage in New York and often spoke to school groups about his experiences. He always felt "lucky to be among those who resisted" the Nazis and is convinced that if more people had fought back instead of succumbing to brutality, history might have been different.

References

Yoran, Shalom. *The Defiant: A True Story*. New York: St. Martin's Press, 1996.
Yoran, Varda. Interview by the author, January 2006, Great Neck, New York.

Continued from previous page

After accomplishing the Aktion *against the Jews in Minsk,* Obersturmbannfuehrer *Dr. Strauch informs me tonight with just indignation that suddenly, without instructions from the* Reichsfuehrer *SS and without informing the* Generalkommissar, *a transport of 1000 Jews from Warsaw had arrived.*

I ask the honorable Reichskommissar *(as already prepared via telegram) to suspend such transports, in his capacity as the highest authority in the East. The Polish Jew, just as the Russian Jew, is an enemy of the Germans. He represents a politically dangerous element, whose political danger far exceeds his value as skilled worker. Under no circumstances must, in an area of civil administration, factors in the army or air force be permitted to bring in Jews from the* Generalgouvernement *(Poland) or elsewhere, without permission of the Reichskommissar, thereby endangering the totality of the political work and the security of the General District. I am fully in agreement with the commandant of the SD in White Ruthenia, that we will liquidate every Jew transport which has not been requested or announced by our services, so as to prevent further disturbances in White Ruthenia.*

The General Commissar for White Ruthenia
(signed) Kube

Z

Zaks sisters

The four Zaks sisters of Sosnowiec, Poland, were the only survivors from a family of nine. Mania, Tola, and Rozia stayed together during most of the war and found Cesia and her son afterward. The young women came together to America and raised families of their own. Their help and comfort for each other under the worst of circumstances was a sustaining force throughout their lives and enabled them to overcome hunger, cold, and human degradation.

The Zaks family consisted of a son, Romek, and six daughters. They lived in Sosnowiec, a Polish city near the German border, where their father owned a grocery store. The Zaks children enjoyed their lives and their studies. The girls ice-skated and watched their brother play soccer. They went on vacations to resorts or to visit family in nearby towns. Their home "was always filled with songs and laughter."

Regina, the oldest, was the first to marry, in 1935. Cesia, the next in age, married three years later and moved to Kielce. Romek was still in his teens and the other girls were younger when the Germans invaded Poland and life changed forever.

Romek was the first to fall victim to Nazi terror. While he was visiting an uncle and cousin, the Germans approached their street and shouted for all Jewish men to come outside. Not knowing what to expect they came out, along with thirty-eight other men from the building. With no warning or reason, all the men were shot and killed where they stood and were quickly buried in a mass grave.

The family was devastated by the loss and horrified by the senseless brutality and increasing deprivation. One by one the civil liberties of the Jews were taken away. Jews were not permitted to use public transportation or parks. The Jewish badge was introduced and all schooling was forbidden to Jewish children.

Mania Zaks (second from right) in her seventh grade school photo shortly before the war. Courtesy of the U.S. Holocaust Memorial Museum Photo Archives.

By 1940 the Nazi raids began. They were always unexpected, often in the middle of the night, and ended up with a random group of Jews being arrested. During one of those raids, Mania Zaks was taken away to the Oberaltstadt labor camp nearby. Less than two years later, the rest of the family was ordered to assemble at a central meeting place. A "routine check," said the Nazi officials. But it turned into a major roundup.

Hundreds of people were surrounded by soldiers and held with no food or water for two days and nights. Finally, an SS officer ordered them all to line up. The young and healthy were sent to the right, to work, and Tola was chosen for that line. On the other line were the Zaks parents, their married daughter, Regina with her husband and child, and the two youngest girls, Rozia and Cyma. They were to be deported to an unknown destination.

Although the Jews of Sosnowiec still knew nothing about Auschwitz or the other death camps, no one wanted to leave their homes. While waiting to be loaded onto the trains, Rozia, Cyma, and their parents managed to escape and returned home. By then, they were the only four members of the family that remained. Later that same year, a ghetto was established, and the Zaks, along with the other remaining Jews, became completely cut off from the outside world.

In the ghetto, Nazi raids became ever more frequent. Like many other families, the Zaks built a bunker between two walls to hide when they heard the soldiers approaching. But the Jewish population was dwindling and they knew it was just a matter of time before all Jews would be deported.

Rozia resisted her parents' suggestion that she volunteer to work in Oberaltstadt. Still in her early teens, she wanted to stay with the family. But her father convinced her that work was her best chance of survival. When he delivered her to the Nazis, her father told Rozia to be strong. "You must live," he told her, "for we will be waiting here for you." Rozia was taken to the Oberaltstadt labor camp and discovered her sisters Tola and Mania there. Two weeks later, the ghetto was emptied and the Zaks parents with Cyma, their youngest child, were shipped to Auschwitz and murdered in the gas chambers.

In the camp, the sisters stayed together, bolstering each other's spirits and reminding each other that when the war was over they would be reunited with their family. They endured illness, constant hunger, brutality, and deliberate degradation by the guards. The prisoners were forced to crawl in the snow, to drink water from the mud puddles, or to remove their clothes and stand naked before the guards, who laughed and called them names. Rozia later wrote that "the brutalities and inhumane treatment left wounds and mental anguish that nothing could erase."

Despite the harsh treatment and unmitigated cruelty, the girls survived and were liberated by the Russian Army on May 8, 1945.

It took a few weeks before they could return home. When they did, they found their house occupied by others and their parents and siblings dead. Only Cesia, their older sister and her son were still alive. Cesia's husband, Bernard, was dead but her son, born in 1940, had been hidden by a kind Polish family and was saved. They all moved in together and decided that Rozia, now the youngest of the sisters, should continue her schooling. They were unsure of where to send her, however. Rozia had not attended school for six years. After some inquiries they found a children's home nearby that had its own school for refugee children.

But there was no future for Jews in Poland. Antisemitism was still rampant and most of the people they knew were dead. Cesia took Rozia from the orphanage and helped her join a Zionist youth group that was preparing to live on a kibbutz in Israel. The youth group moved to Germany to await illegal transportation to what was then Palestine, still under British rule, and Rozia's sisters followed her there. Eventually, they all decided to stay together and go to America, where they had an uncle. They registered Rozia, still under eighteen, as an orphan and she left for the United States in September 1947. Shortly after her arrival, she was brought to her uncle's home in Cleveland, Ohio. Once again, Cesia, Mania, and Tola followed. Rozia was the only one of the girls who was able to attend school in the United States, but all the sisters married and lived on the same street in Cleveland, Ohio, recreating the warm and loving family they remembered from their own childhoods.

Reference

Kaplovitz, Rose Zaks. "The Story of My Life." In *Children Who Survived the Final Solution*. Edited by Peter Trajan. New York: iUniverse, 2004.

Zar, Rose (1923–)

Born in the Polish town of Piotrkow, Rose Guterman Zar was able to escape the ghetto and avoid the death camps that killed most of her family. She took her father's advice and hid "in the mouth of the wolf," working for the chief commandant of the Nazi SS.

Bela and Herman Guterman, Zar's parents, were business people; Herman dealt in leather goods and had a small shoe factory. Zar, along with her brother Benek, the Gutermans' two older children, were educated in the Polish gymnasium, where they learned languages, science, and art. Pola, Zar's younger sister, was only six years old, but had already begun her education when World War II broke out in 1939.

As soon as the Germans marched into Piotrkow the violence began. There were random beatings and killings and a host of restrictive laws. Slowly, the Nazi net surrounding the Jews tightened: confiscations of property and businesses, the establishment of the ghetto, and then the beginning of the roundups, taking Jews off to camps, supposedly for resettlement and work. The Guterman family remained intact through those first years. They adapted to the new rules and managed to get work cards, insuring that they were still useful to the Germans and would not be deported. But Herman Guterman knew it was just a matter of time and he assessed the chances of survival for each member of the family.

Guterman's two older children could pass as Polish Christians. They spoke Polish perfectly, did not look Jewish, and were old enough to live independently. Herman and Bela Guterman would stay with Pola, who was too young to be on her own. They would take their chances that Herman's skills would save them all. For Zar and her brother he purchased false papers identifying them as Christians and made an elaborate plan for their escape. They were to leave Piotrkow separately and meet in another village. He gave them money and advice, learned from the time he had escaped the Russian Army and fled into Poland. "If you're ever on the run and have to hide," Guterman told his children, "the best place is right in the mouth of the wolf."

Amid threats of a final roundup and transport, Zar and Benek left for the train station, but almost immediately their plans went awry and had to be changed. They ended up in Warsaw, where each of them found work. Benek was accepted as an apprentice barber and Zar, under her false name Wanda Gajda, took a job as a helper and housekeeper for a small shoemaking business. At first it was difficult to listen to all their antisemitic comments and jokes about Jews, but she forced herself to laugh and even join in. Still harder was when she watched her boss cutting up the parchment from holy Torah scrolls to use for the inner soles of the shoes they were making. But she was able to continue her work and not reveal her distress. Zar finally had to leave when a combination of sexual advances by the male workers and a suspicion that she was Jewish led her to fear for her life.

Discouraged, lonely, and unemployed, Zar sneaked back to Piotrkow. She was anxious to find out what had happened to her family and to her boyfriend, Mayer Zarnowiecki. Zarnowiecki had refused to try to hide with false papers, asking, "With a face like mine, who needs papers?" They both knew he looked too Jewish to pass. Now, in the remains of the ghetto, Zar found him and her father, both working as slave laborers. Among only a handful of Jews who had escaped the final roundup, the two men looked terrible. Guterman told his daughter how the family's hiding place was discovered and they were taken to

Rose Zar (far right) visiting a Jewish cemetery with other survivors in Piotrkow Tryblinalski, Poland, in 1945. Courtesy of the U.S. Holocaust Memorial Museum Photo Archives.

the railroad station. At the last minute, he was pulled from the crowd because his skills were required. Although he insisted that he would not leave his wife and daughter, the SS beat him and led him away. Bela and Pola were pushed onto the train to Treblinka. They were murdered in the gas chambers there.

Zar wanted to stay in the Piotrkow ghetto with the remaining Jews and share their fate, but her father insisted that she go back. "I no longer care what happens to me," said Guterman, "but you must survive. . . . It is your duty . . . to your mother . . . to me . . . to the Jewish people."

Zar went from Warsaw to Krakow, where she was able to find a bed to sleep in and a job as a cleaning woman for the SS headquarters. She quickly advanced from janitor to assistant nurse in the hospital and had just begun to feel less frightened, when she was reported on the false charge of smuggling. Her accuser was a man whose advances she had rejected. She was fired from the hospital, but had made several friends among the administrative staff and they soon found her another post. Because she worked hard, she was chosen as a housekeeper for the Commandant of the SS forces in Krakow. The Commandant's wife, Mrs. Roemer, was coming to join him.

When Mrs. Roemer discovered that her new housekeeper was educated and spoke German, the two women became friends. After the Roemers had a baby, they chose Zar to be the baby's nurse, and she was in complete charge of the little boy for more than a year. During that time, she was suspected of being a Jew several times, but was determined never to show fear. Using a combination of courage and bravado, she never gave herself away by any word or

608 ZIELENZIGER, ERIC (1920-)

gesture and always managed to escape. When the Gestapo came to search for her in her rooming house, she was able to move in with the Commandant and his wife. No one would ever suspect that a Jew was living there.

Zar remained with Commandant and Mrs. Roemer, living comfortably and enjoying a certain amount of independence. But secretly, when the Roemers were out, she listened to the BBC, the British radio station, and waited for the war to be over. Although she knew that her boss and his wife wanted her to return with them to Germany, she was not planning to do that.

At last, early in 1945, the Russian Army approached Krakow. During that final bombardment, Zar escaped into the shelter below their apartment house with the other tenants. The Commandant had already sent his wife and son home and went looking for her before the German retreat. All the people in the shelter heard him knocking at the door, but she begged them not to open it. Finally, he left without her. The next day, Zar, known to everyone as Wanda Gajda, went back to the Commandant's apartment, took some of his fine furniture, and found her own apartment.

After five long years of hiding and pretending and many close calls, Zar was finally free. But she knew her life could not continue as before. Her mother and sister were dead. Her father, she learned, had been transported to Blizin, a subcamp of Auschwitz, in 1944. He died there. Benek was the only other member of her family who survived. Zar's boyfriend Mayer had been in Buchenwald, then Silben, and finally Theresienstadt concentration camp, but remained alive. He and Zar were married in 1945, but before escaping to the West, they helped smuggle 135 Jewish children from Soviet-occupied Poland to Germany and eventually, to Israel.

Settling first in Germany, in the American zone, Rose and Mayer Zar (shortened from Zarnowiecki) worked as head educators for the Jewish refugee children in Lindenfels, Germany. In 1951, they came to the United States and settled in South Bend, Indiana. Zar studied special education and worked in a school for mentally retarded children and also as a Hebrew school teacher. The Zars had three children and, as of 1983, one grandchild. In the 1980s, Zar wrote a memoir of her war experiences. It was dedicated to her family and her husband's family, all killed during World War II. Remembering her father's good advice, she named her book *In the Mouth of the Wolf.*

Reference

Zar, Rose. *In the Mouth of the Wolf.* Philadelphia: Jewish Publication Society, 1983.

Zielenziger, Eric (1920-)

Eric Zielenziger, a native of Berlin, Germany, spent five hundred days hiding from the Nazis in his adopted city of Amsterdam. When the war was over and he emerged, his parents and all his friends were dead and "Amsterdam seemed like one big cemetery." Alone, he made his way to the United States and built a new life and a successful career.

Eric was born in Berlin, the only child of a successful economist and journalist who had been press secretary to Berlin's mayor. After Hitler's rise to power, however, the Zielenzigers realized that Nazi policies posed more than just a

Eric Zielenziger at home in Great Neck, New York. Courtesy of Eric Zielenziger.

passing setback for Jews. They left Germany for France in 1933 and, in 1934, settled in Holland. In Amsterdam, Eric's father found a position as the director of the Jewish Central Information Office, an organization created by World Jewry to fight antisemitism, and Eric grew up in an open and tolerant Dutch society. He graduated high school and found a job with an import company.

After the war erupted in 1939, the threat to Holland seemed more imminent and, early in 1940, the Jewish Central Information Office began moving its headquarters to London. The Zielenziger family was scheduled to follow within the next few months, but in May 1940, the German Army marched into Holland and Belgium. They quickly occupied Amsterdam and bombed the port of Rotterdam heavily. It was too late to leave.

Living conditions deteriorated quickly. One of the first demands on the Jews was that they were forced to surrender their textile ration coupons, used for purchasing clothing. They were required to obtain the yellow star marked *Jood* (Jew) that had to be worn on their outer clothes. Shortly afterward, Eric lost his job when a German administrator walked into the offices of the Jewish-owned firm and took over. Within a few months, long lists of young people were ordered to assemble at the railway station. They were to be taken to an unknown destination to participate in the *Arbeitseinsatz* (labor initiative).

Zielenziger was exempt from that first roundup as well as subsequent "labor initiatives" because he was now employed in the emigration department of the

Jewish Council, helping Jews find visas to other lands. He had a travel permit issued by the German SS so he could move freely around the country and carry on this work. In the course of his duties, he watched the trains moving out of Amsterdam, packed with Jews on their way to Westerbork, the Dutch transit camp where the Jews of Holland waited for deportation to Poland. Once, in an official capacity, he went to Westerbork himself. When he saw the conditions there, Zielenziger realized that he would never submit to deportation and that, if he wanted to survive, he would have to go into hiding.

On June 20, 1943, Zielenziger received a warning from friends that the Gestapo, with the Amsterdam police, would be searching Amsterdam for any remaining Jews. The entire city was under curfew so everyone had to remain at home, ready to be picked up by the Nazis. Zielenziger decided this was the time for him to disappear. He had other friends who had gone into hiding and knew whom to approach for help. In his mind, he began to work out a plan, but first, he and his parents had to evade this new roundup.

Carefully, the Zielenzigers prepared the apartment. They cleaned and scrubbed it until it was spotless and then placed a Nazi newspaper on the table so it would appear as if a German sympathizer lived there. Then mother, father, and son hid in a crawl space under the ground floor of their apartment. They heard the Gestapo come and knock on the door. When there was no answer the soldiers left and went around the back. They entered and walked across the kitchen. Zielenziger heard the sound of their boots above him. Then he heard one of the soldiers comment on the Nazi newspaper and they left.

The family stayed hidden under the floor until after dark. They returned to the apartment to sleep and the following morning, Eric Zielenziger ventured out. He was immediately stopped by a Gestapo agent and asked to show his identity card. It had the letter "J" stamped on it, showing he was a Jew. But he also had his SS travel permit. When the agent saw that document, he let Zielenziger go, never noticing that his permit had expired in March. "I owe my life to this oversight," said Zielenziger.

At great risk, the Zielenziger family remained in their apartment for a few more months. On September 29, on the eve of Rosh Hashanah, the Jewish New Year, they learned that there would be another roundup of Jews, perhaps a final roundup. The Zielenzigers agreed that Eric would go into hiding and his parents, now armed with an Ecuadorian passport that had been purchased for them, would try to leave the country. "We thought our separation would not last long," Zielenziger later wrote. "Mussolini had fallen; the Allies had landed in Sicily. My father believed we would soon be free."

Zielenziger's parents packed a suitcase and said goodbye. Zielenziger himself took a few articles of clothing and, with the help of the building's caretaker, hid in the boiler room of their apartment house. The next morning, he heard that his parents had been arrested during the night. He crept back to his apartment for some more clothing, barely escaped the curiosity of two German women who were his upstairs neighbors, and was able to reach Reverend Smelik's house that night.

Smelik was Zielenziger's contact with the underground. He gave him some ration coupons for bread, potatoes, and some other foods and an address in

South Amsterdam. There he would find the Blums, a young Christian family who had agreed to hide him for the duration of the war.

Zielenziger was given a small room in the Blum's apartment. Although he and the Blums often spent time together talking about their lives and about the progress of the war, he did not leave the house for over a year. Whenever a guest came, he would disappear into his small room. The Zielenzigers had left money with Reverend Smelik, and it was used to pay the Blums a modest rent and purchase his food. But as the war progressed, there was less and less to eat. Because the Blums had a baby to feed by this time, Zielenziger moved to another home, where he remained for the next six months, until the end of the war.

When the Allies began attacking Germany, German occupation became harsher. Electricity and gas went out all over Amsterdam and the ration system almost collapsed. In order to obtain fuel to burn, people pulled out beams from abandoned houses and chopped them into logs. It was in this way that half of Amsterdam was destroyed. During the last months, the only food available was sugar beets, which were cooked until they turned into molasses. Allied planes constantly flew over Amsterdam and even though the bombs posed a danger to all, Zielenziger later wrote that "their zooming noise was music to our ears."

The Dutch were liberated on May 5, 1945, when Germany surrendered unconditionally. Right after that, the Dutch Underground fighters appeared, wearing orange armbands and blue overalls. Zielenziger borrowed a bicycle and rode back to the Blums, bringing them a bouquet of flowers. He then went to thank the Reverend Smelik.

Hearing that his mother had survived Bergen-Belsen, he quickly made arrangements to rent a furnished room where they could live. He waited for every train. Although he met several other friends who were returning from the camps, his mother failed to appear. Finally, he learned that she had been liberated in April, but had subsequently died from typhus. His father had perished in the camp. His grandmother, also, had been deported and killed by the Nazis.

Heartbroken, and feeling that Amsterdam held nothing for him except sad memories, Zielenziger, now twenty-five years old, decided to move to the United States. He arrived in New York in 1946, met his wife, Ruth, and raised a family of two sons. He spent his working life in the international commodity trade, dealing primarily in spices.

After his retirement, he and his family traveled back to Europe to visit Bergen-Belsen, Berlin, and the German towns where his grandparents used to live. In 2004, Zielenziger also went to Amsterdam and visited his rescuer, Mrs. Blum, now a ninety-year-old widow. With his help, she was honored as a righteous gentile by Israel's Ambassador in Holland. When Mrs. Blum wrote to thank him, she revealed that her husband, Fritz Blum, was also a Jew. He had never told anyone, not even his children.

Reference

Zielenziger, Eric. "500 Days in Hiding." *The New Light* 47 (fall 2004): p. 17.

Zielinska, Ruth, and Elizabeth Mundlak (née Zielinska) (1940–)

Ruth Zielinska and her baby daughter Elizabeth Zielinska Mundlak of Czestachowa, Poland, were separated during World War II. Mundlak was carried out of the ghetto in a garbage bag and brought to a Catholic orphanage. She was adopted by a Polish family whom she grew to love. Ruth Zielinska spent most of the war posing as a Christian and working for the Germans. After the war, she found her daughter, but their reunion was traumatic.

Elizabeth Mundlak, a dark-haired little girl with blue eyes, was born Aliza Asz in Czestochowa, Poland. Her parents, Ruth and Shimon Asz, made the decision to save their baby by sending her out of the ghetto with a gentile doctor who worked for the underground. Before they parted from their daughter, they dyed her dark curls blond so no one would suspect she was a Jewish child.

Mundlak was first brought to an orphanage as an abandoned child, but was quickly adopted by a Polish family. Victoria and Marion Mundlak, her adoptive parents, had a ten-year-old son Andrew, and Mundlak quickly became part of the family. It was not until several weeks had passed that they discovered that their blonde daughter's hair was really black and realized that she must be a Jewish child. They had a family meeting and all agreed that they would keep her in spite of the risk.

Any Polish family harboring a Jew, whether a child or an adult, faced death, and the family was careful not to reveal what they knew to anyone. Mundlak's "father" was part of an underground cell and he was able to deal speedily with the neighbors who threatened to give him away unless he gave them money.

Mundlak, still very young, knew nothing of this, nor did she remember her birth family. Her father was killed by the Nazis, but her mother, Ruth, who took the name Jozefa Zielinska, was able to survive. She obtained false papers as a gentile, escaped from the ghetto, and reached Austria. There, she was conscripted as a Christian slave laborer and worked as a hotel cleaning woman. Once, she was detained by the Gestapo on suspicion of being a Jew and held while experts on racial characteristics measured and examined her. Zielinska was declared to be "a perfect Aryan specimen."

Following this ordeal, Zielinska, with the help of a friend, was able to arrange for new documents and she escaped to neutral Switzerland. She waited through the last few months of the war worrying about her daughter Aliza. At the first opportunity, she returned to Poland to find her.

At the end of 1945, a strange woman appeared at Mundlak's home and embraced her. Mundlak, with no memory of her birth mother, was frightened and confused. But her biological mother and her adoptive mother were both wise and considerate. At first, Zielenska pretended to be an aunt and visited frequently. Mundlak suspected that this woman would remove her from the only life she knew and the parents she loved. She later confessed, "I hated those visits and I was scared."

After many months, Zielinska was offered a job in another country and the decision was made to take her daughter with her. Although then six-year-old Mundlak protested and pleaded she could not change the decision.

Zielinska kept her false name and it became Mundlak's name also, along with Elizabeth, the name the nuns had given her when she first arrived at the orphanage. When Zielinska married, her new husband, Julian Ritterman, legally added their name to his own so everyone in the family would have the same last name. Within a few years, Zielinska had another daughter, Danielle, and Mundlak adjusted to her new parents. She always considered herself lucky to have two loving families and she kept in touch with her wartime parents.

After living under the Communists for many years, the Zielinska family had an opportunity to leave Poland. In 1957, they moved to Venezuela. There, Elizabeth, only nineteen, met Alexander Mundlak, a mechanical engineer and also a Holocaust survivor from Poland. They were married and had one son, Simon. After her marriage, Elizabeth Mundlak studied chemical engineering and became a lecturer at the University in Caracas. While in that position, she was awarded a scholarship for a Ph.D. in environmental engineering at the Polytechnic Institute in New York.

Mundlak's husband died suddenly of a heart attack when he was forty-nine. She remained with her parents and her in-laws in Caracas until the older generation died. Then she retired and joined her son in the United States for part of each year.

In 1996, on a visit to Israel, she decided to visit Andrew, her wartime brother, in Poland. They had a warm reunion and Mundlak learned about the lives of her adoptive parents who had already passed away. During that visit, she also met a woman who was active in an organization of child survivors. Mundlak, too, became an active member and was encouraged to make films about the Holocaust. Her first film was *Caribia and Koenigstein: Ships of Hope*. The film tells the story of two ships filled with refugees that were given asylum in Venezuela. Her second effort was a documentary about her own survival, filmed in Czestachowa, about Jewish life in that city before World War II. It was shown in 2002.

References

Mundlak, Elizabeth Zielinski de. "Black Roots in the Hair of a Blond Cherub." In *Children Who Survived the Final Solution*. Edited by Peter Tarjan. New York: iUniverse, 2004.

de Zoete family

Hendrik Edward (known by his Hebrew name, Chaim) de Zoete and his wife, Sofia, were originally from Holland but spent many years in Indonesia, where their three daughters, Mirjam (b. 1931), Judith (b. 1932), and Hadassah (b. 1933) were born. They returned to Holland in 1936 and survived the German bombings, the invasion, and the cruel and difficult years of Nazi rule.

Chaim de Zoete was a pharmacist in the Dutch Army. He was sent to Indonesia, then a Dutch colony, and the family lived there for eight years. Sofia Pollack de Zoete, a nurse and an accomplished linguist, stopped working when she married, and raised her three daughters.

The de Zoetes returned to Rotterdam in 1936 and Chaim de Zoete worked for the municipal pharmacy, supplying medicines to hospitals and welfare patients. They lived in a spacious apartment and the girls attended a private Montessori school.

The de Zoetas with their three daughters shortly before World War II forced them to separate and go into hiding. Courtesy of Mirjam de Zoeta Geismar.

The German invasion of neutral Holland on May 5, 1940, took most of the population by surprise. Bombs fell over Rotterdam and, although their house was not damaged, the pharmacy where de Zoete worked was completely destroyed. He was put in charge of setting up a new pharmacy, but within months, Nazi laws forbade Jews from working at all.

With no money coming in, the de Zoetes had to move out of their large apartment house. They settled in Voorburg, a small town that seemed safer and was less expensive than Rotterdam. But even here, they had to curtail most of their activities. According to the new laws, Jews had to identify themselves with a Star of David that was sewn onto their outer clothing. All Jewish children were forbidden to go to the public schools; they could go only to Jewish schools. They could not own bicycles, enjoy the public parks, or go to concerts. Shopping for food was strictly limited to a few hours a day. Life became bleak.

At first, only Jews who were not native to Holland were arrested and deported. By 1942, however, Dutch Jews were also rounded up by the Nazis and sent to Westerbork, a holding camp, before being deported to Auschwitz, Bergen-Belsen, and other concentration camps in Germany and Poland, where most met their deaths. Of the estimated 150,000 Jews living in Holland when World War II began, 90,000 were eventually murdered by the Nazis, a full sixty percent of the Jewish population.

Chaim de Zoete was suspicious of the Nazis from the beginning and, as a result, he planned early, securing hiding places for his family. In August 1942, when he was ordered to report to the railroad station for a forced labor assignment, he ignored the order and instead, put his plan into action. Mirjam, eleven years old, had to cut off her long braids because they made her "look Jewish." She was told to remove the Star of David from her clothes and was sent alone to an address in Voorburg where she remained for two weeks before being brought to another family, Nan and Jan van Gelder. Judith and Hadassah, aged ten and nine, were each sent to different homes where they were hidden.

Each of the girls had many addresses during the remaining three years of the war. After six months with one family, Mirjam had to leave quickly because the grandfather was arrested and they feared he would be forced to confess that his daughter was hiding a Jewish girl. She was then taken to

Haarlem and placed with a woman, Nel van Vliet, and her grown daughter, Sonja. There were two paying boarders who had their own rooms and three other Jewish children besides Mirjam who were in hiding: a twelve-year-old boy, his sister, two years younger, and a four-year-old boy. They all shared the same crawl space under the floor where they went each night, from 7:00 p.m. to 7:00 a.m. It was too low for them to walk around but they could sit. They remained there for twelve hours every night and sometimes during the day as well. If a neighbor or someone else knocked on the door, the children would have to scurry into their hideout and wait there until the unexpected guest had left.

Mirjam stayed in this home until the end of the war and shared the suffering of all in what the Dutch called "the hunger winter." Many times during that winter of 1944–1945, she and her foster aunt's daughter left the shelter of their safe house to beg for food from the nearby farmers, or trade their possessions for something to eat. Judith and Hadassah also moved several times, and Judith ended up sharing a hiding place with many other children in the home of a butcher and his family.

The de Zoete parents were able to stay together, but went from one hiding place to another, twenty-five different addresses in all, until they found safety in the Reformed Breeplein Church in Rotterdam South. They were hidden by the minister, Dr. Brillenburg Wurth, and his wife, with the help of the church custodian, Mr. de Mars, and his wife. Their refuge was a narrow space under the roof where they remained for almost two years. There was only room enough to lie down and Chaim and Sofia spent the final years of the war lying next to each other. The minister brought them food there, but they could stand up for only one hour a day, in the middle of the night, when no one was likely to be in the church.

When the war ended, the de Zoetes collected their children and returned to Rotterdam, but there were no victory celebrations, only mourning. Most of their family had been deported and killed in the camps, including Mirjam's favorite cousin (also named Mirjam) and four young cousins who had been betrayed by a Dutch Nazi and handed over for deportation. Each visit to a family member brought tears and sadness.

In addition to the overwhelming losses, there were the practical challenges of returning to their former life. The de Zoete family had no home and no money. The girls had lost three years of school and needed extra help to catch up. But they did resume some normalcy. Always Zionists, the de Zoete daughters affiliated with a Zionist Youth Movement and prepared to go to Israel.

Mirjam, at the age of sixteen, went first. She arrived with a group of young people in 1947 and because they had

> I don't think we ever went a whole day without food, but some days we only got one piece of bread in the morning and mashed tulip bulbs for dinner. We were always hungry. In the very last month of the war, it became known to the Americans that a lot of the Dutch people were starving. They flew over Holland in airplanes filled with metallic boxes full with food. [They sent us] crackers, bread, butter and many more food items. They dumped them out of the plane on to the soccer fields. When after so many years of hunger we tasted our first piece of bread with butter, we thought that that was the best thing we ever ate.
>
> —Mirjam Geismar in unpublished e-mail to her grandson

official passports and visas, they were allowed in by the British. They went first to a children's village, where they studied Hebrew and other subjects for half the day and worked for the other half. The following year, after Israel gained independence, the rest of the family came.

Life in Israel was difficult at first, but Chaim de Zoete found a job as a pharmacist and they settled in Jerusalem. As each of the girls turned eighteen, she joined the new Israeli Army. After serving the required two years, Mirjam went with her army group to start a new kibbutz. She left within a short time, however, and in 1950, she married David Geismar, also a Dutch Jew who had been in hiding during the war.

David and Mirjam Geismar settled in a cooperative community in Israel called Arbel and remained there for five years before leaving to start their own business. David Geismar opened an electrical appliance store, but found it difficult to maintain because he was called into the army each year for reserve duty. Finally, in 1957, he closed the business for good and the Geismars, with their two children, emigrated to the United States, where David's mother was already living. He opened a business and the couple had two more children.

As the children grew older, Mirjam became more active in the Connecticut community where they lived. She took courses in emergency medicine and volunteered for the EMS. Later, she worked as a nurse's assistant and often spoke to schools and other groups about growing up during the Holocaust.

The rest of the de Zoete family remained in Israel. Judith studied nursing and worked in that profession for many years. She married Nathan Cohen, also a Dutch child survivor, and had three daughters and eight grandchildren. Hadassah volunteered to continue with the Israeli Army and served well beyond her required time. She married Zigi Mandel, a child survivor from Poland, and had two sons and four grandchildren. The de Zoete parents lived in Israel but died in Holland, the place they loved so much. Chaim died in March 1969 while on a visit there, and Sofia died twelve years later, also during a visit to Holland.

More than twenty years later, in 2003, David Geismar died on a visit to Israel. After his death, Mirjam continued to speak about the Holocaust, telling her audiences, "If it wasn't for all the gentiles who helped me and risked their lives to save us, we wouldn't be here today." People complain that "they didn't do enough," Geismar told an interviewer, "but it was very hard. Think: would you have done that? Would you risk your life for someone else?"

Reference

de Zoete Geismar, Mirjam. Telephone interview by the author, June 2006.

Zola, Edward (1923–)

Edward Zola, a Jew from Sighet in Transylvania, was part of a contingency of young Jewish men who were taken to labor camps during World War II. He was one of only a few hundred Jews from his town who survived the war. All were under forty years old. There were no longer any old people or any children remaining and Zola did not see a Jewish child again until he came to the United States.

Zola's name was originally Moshe Lazar Davidovits, and he was the youngest of eight children: five girls and three boys. His oldest sister and brother, Regina and Louis, both emigrated to America before the war. The others remained in the town of Sighet, where their father, Yaakov Mendel Davidovits, operated a factory and store for the manufacture and sale of woolen clothing. The Davidovits family was observant and belonged to a Hasidic group that had its own synagogue. It was the same synagogue that **Eli Wiesel's** family attended. There were many synagogues in Sighet, a town of thirty thousand people. Approximately forty percent of the population was Jewish.

Sighet, in the province of Marmatiei, had been part of Romania after World War I, but by agreement with Germany, it came under Hungarian rule in 1940. At that time, the Hungarian Army, a staunch ally of the Nazis, marched into Marmatiei (now renamed Maramaros-Sighet) and in solidarity with Nazi policy, immediately began to promulgate antisemitic laws. Jews were no longer allowed to own their own businesses. All Jews were required to show identification and those who were not citizens were deported to Poland. Another law decreed that if a Jew were traveling, he or she had to get permission from the local police in order to remain for the night. It was also forbidden to listen to the BBC, the British radio station. Zola and his family depended on fragments of news that came to them at their synagogue, where they continued to pray regularly.

Conditions for the Jews worsened week by week, but once the Germans were driven back from Stalingrad, the Davidovits family clung to the hope that the war would end soon. It seemed as if Hungary was losing the will to fight. However, Germany was still trying to achieve their "final solution" for the Jews and attempted to kill as many as possible even as their armies were retreating. In March 1944, the Germans occupied Hungary and that Passover, the family had their last seder (ritual holiday meal) together. "My father was so overwhelmed that he could no longer remember the melodies for the prayers," said Zola. "We all just sat and cried."

Exactly one week later, sixteen-year-old Zola was rounded up with all the other boys his age and taken to a labor camp. Although this seemed terrible at the time, it actually saved him from what might have been a worse fate. The following week, all the Jews remaining in Sighet were forced into a tiny area, referred to as the ghetto. Space was in such short supply that fifteen to twenty people had to live in each room. Within a month, Zola's family, his parents, his married sister Charna with her husband and two children, and his sisters Frieda, Joan, and Lily, were all transported to Poland. After three days on overcrowded freight trains with no food, water, or toilet facilities, they arrived in Auschwitz. Yaakov and Rachel Davidovits, Zola's parents, were killed that first day. Charna and her family were also sent to the gas chambers. The others were taken to work and survived the war. But Zola did not know at the time what had happened to his family.

Zola remained in the labor camp where life "was full of misery." Each morning the prisoners lined up for roll call and they were asked who was sick. Those who raised their hands were sent away with the guards and simply disappeared. The others began to understand that an admission of illness was a death sentence. "We quickly learned never to raise our hands," said Zola.

As the war neared its end, the Nazis tried to move their slave laborers closer to Germany, where they could continue their work for the Third Reich. Late in 1944, Zola and his group were forced to march to Budapest, the Hungarian capital. There, they were joined by thousands of other Jews. The entire group was herded westward, through the snow of the Austrian Alps. Many of the prisoners were barefoot, but the German guards made no allowances. Those who could not keep up were shot on the spot. They slept on the ground, in the snow, and were awakened at 6:00 a.m. Whoever could not get up was killed and each morning there were more dead bodies.

After marching for many months, the Jews arrived in Mauthausen, a concentration camp in Austria. Zola described this camp only as "horrifying" and "filled with indescribable torture." Just when the prisoners thought they could not bear any more suffering, they were forced once again to march, this time to a sub-camp called Gunstkirchen, also in Austria. The Americans were already in the area when the remaining Jews, already half-starved, were abandoned without food or water. Mad with hunger, some resorted to cannibalism, eating the flesh of their dead comrades. When the U.S. Army arrived, on March 5, 1945, Zola was so weak and sick that he was taken straight to a hospital to recuperate. It took him three months before he was able to understand that he was actually free.

Regaining his strength, Zola made his way back to Sighet, hitchhiking on Russian trucks, and taking his meals at the soup kitchens that the Joint Distribution Committee had set up for penniless refugees. He arrived two days before Yom Kippur, the holiest day in the Jewish year, and Zola went straight to the only synagogue in town that was still standing. A remnant of Jews who had returned was there at the service, anxious to hear news of others who had survived, but he could tell them nothing. Zola also found his sisters, Frieda, Joan, and Lily. The Davidovits girls had reclaimed their father's shop and they all lived together. Eugene Davidovits, Zola's brother, had survived the labor camps but had been denounced as a spy by Hungarian Christians who did not want Jews returning to Sighet. He was taken off to Russia but was eventually released and was able to emigrate to the United States.

After Eugene was released from prison, the Davidovits siblings went to a displaced-persons camp in Germany. Once registered there, their brother, Louis Davidovits, who was serving in the American Army, contacted Zola. Their sister Regina also came to Germany to see the family and to help arrange for visas to the United States. It was decided that Zola would apply on the German quota, using the name of his mother's brother, Ernst Zola. He retained that name once he arrived in New York City, in 1947, just around Christmas.

Edward Zola made a new life in New York after the war. Courtesy of Joan Mandel.

Zola was twenty-five years old when he began a new life in the United States. His first job was selling men's belts. Anxious to start a family of his own, he married Pearl Turner, also from Sighet—although the two had not known each other there—and he and Pearl had two children, Robin and Jeff. When Pearl died of breast cancer, Zola was bereft.

Many years later, Zola remarried. His second wife, **Ruth Klausner**, is a Holocaust survivor from Holland. The Zolas settled on Long Island and Zola eventually had five grandchildren. Zola's sisters and brothers all married and raised families in the United States.

Reference

Zola, Ed. Interviews by Joan Mandel, November and December 2005, Great Neck, New York.

Zoreff, Meir-Lev, and Jakov Zoreff (1940–)

Meir-Lev Zoreff and his wife Sonia of Kovno, Lithuania, lived through some of the most horrifying days of World War II under the brutal Nazi occupation. Zoreff lost his wife and almost lost his infant son in one of the roundups conducted by the Germans. But at war's end, he returned from the camps and from serving in the Soviet Army, found his son, and picked up the pieces of his life.

Zoreff was born Leib Goldsmidt. As a young student, he pursued a career in the theatre. His bride, Sonia, was a music student. Soon expecting their first child, they both worked during the day and attended school at night. Their whole future seemed to lie ahead of them until World War II began and all their dreams were shattered.

By the time Jakov was born, the Goldsmidts were living in the Kovno ghetto. Food was in short supply and death was everywhere. The Goldsmidts did not circumcise their son because they wanted to give him to non-Jews in hopes of saving his life. The mark of circumcision would be an unmistakable sign that the child was Jewish. But Sonia's mother and sister felt that he should be circumcised no matter what, and they had the procedure done while his parents were at work. "Maybe he will survive," said his grandmother. "If, God forbid, he should not, then let him die as a Jew."

Leib and Sonia Goldsmidt were angry but they could do nothing. They tried as much as possible to provide food for their child and, at first, they were aided by Sonia's sister, Judith, then only fourteen years old. Because she was small and thin, she found ways to squeeze through the narrow opening of the ghetto walls and find food on the Aryan side. With Judith's help they did not starve. Jakov reached the age of two.

During those years, Goldsmidt had been conscripted by the Nazis for slave labor. He went out of the Kovno ghetto every day to work under terrible conditions. One day, along with a group of Jewish prisoners, he was brought to a ranch near Kovno. A sadistic young Nazi waited there for them and forced them into an icy lake where they had to remain for hours. When they were allowed out at last, he ordered them to lie on the frozen ground. All the prisoners became sick and that was the reason that Goldsmidt was at home the day the Nazis ordered the roundup of children and the elderly.

It was March 28, 1944. As soon as he heard the rumor that the Nazis were collecting all children and old people, Goldsmidt prepared a hiding place for his wife and son underneath their fireplace. Because they lived at the far end of the ghetto, they had the time to do this. When the hideout was completed, they gave little Jakov a shot of Luminal, a sedative, and kept him underground for two days. Goldsmidt later wrote, "We took him out at night. He didn't cry; he ate whatever there was. The next morning he extended his arm to get the injection and crept back into the hole as if he understood."

With his wife and son hidden, Goldsmidt watched with mounting horror as crying children were rounded up and thrown onto trucks. The mothers' pleas, the barking dogs, the shouts of the drunken Ukrainian police waving axes and iron rods, and the cries of the children being snatched from their hiding places all combined to create a nightmarish scene. Most of the parents were away at their jobs at forced labor. When they returned, they found that their children were gone.

Jakov had been spared, but the Goldsmidts knew it was only a matter of time. They spoke with a friend, Ruth Rosenthal, who had rescued other children from the ghetto. She could hide Jakov in a monastery. With few other choices, his parents agreed and Sonia Goldsmidt carried her son in a basket to the door of the monastery and left him with a nun. For the time being, Jakov was safe, but Sonia faced a new danger. Outside the ghetto, she was arrested by the Gestapo (the German police) and, when she refused to tell them where her child was hidden, they killed her.

Less than three years old, Jakov woke up bewildered and in a strange place. Frightened, he kept called for "Mama Sonia" and "Papa Leib." The nun told him that if he stopped saying those words, she would let him out and allow him to play with the other children. Jakov asked her if he could "repeat Mama and Papa's names only in his heart, quietly, just to himself." Moved by his request, the nun agreed. She answered, "Yes, in your heart, you can repeat these names so you'll never forget them."

Jakov did not forget. A year later, when the Nazis had surrendered, one of his mother's sisters, who had been hidden by a Catholic woman, came to find him and brought him to her home. Shortly after, Goldsmidt returned. He had spent many months at Dachau concentration camp. After his liberation by the Russians, he joined the Russian Army to help drive out the Germans. At last, he was free. When Jakov saw him, he "jumped on me as if we had separated only yesterday, and not a year earlier."

Goldsmidt married Sonia's younger sister, Judith, and she became a mother to Jakov. The family emigrated to Israel and Goldsmidt took a Hebrew name, Meir-Lev Zoreff, and began to pursue a career in theatre once again. Zoreff became an actor and appeared regularly with both the Kamary and Habimah theatres in Tel Aviv. He and Judith had another son and a daughter. Jakov grew up as an Israeli child, but for many years he would wake up at night calling for "Mama Sonia."

In the 1990s, Meir-Lev Zoreff retired from a successful career. By then, his son Jakov was a father of three and then a grandfather. They all remained in Israel.

Reference

Zoreff, Meir-Lev. "Survival in Kovno." *The Hidden Child* 13 (2005): p. 10.

Zuckerman, Yitzhak (1915–1981)

Yitzhak Zuckerman of Vilna was one of the most important Jewish activists in Poland. Beginning with his early days in the Zionist Youth Movement, he believed that Jews should be proud nationalists and he devoted himself to education toward that end. But when World War II broke out, he became a leader of the Jewish Fighting Force and was one of the heroes of the Warsaw ghetto uprising.

Born in 1915 in Vilna, Poland, Zuckerman completed Hebrew high school in that city, became an ardent Zionist, and a member of *HeHalutz* (The Pioneer) and *HeHalutz haTza'ir* (Pioneer Youth). Soon he was asked to work in the central office of the movement in Warsaw. He was in Warsaw in 1939, when Poland was invaded by Germany, but left for the east with some of his comrades to avoid Nazi occupation. Zuckerman continued to organize new Zionist Youth groups, but now was forced to operate clandestinely because Eastern Poland, under Russian occupation, had made Zionism illegal.

In April 1940, under orders from his movement, Zuckerman returned to Warsaw to organize and promote underground activities there. In Warsaw, he set up an underground press, established a Jewish high school to promote Zionist ideals of self-sufficiency and independence, and organized conferences and seminars to educate and encourage Jews. He even set up secret training farms to prepare young Jews for a life in a future Jewish state. Antek (his underground name) Zuckerman was one of the most successful underground leaders in all of Poland. During those years of activism, Zuckerman met Zivia

Yitzhak Zuckerman testifying for the prosecution at the trial of Adolf Eichmann. Courtesy of the U.S. Holocaust Memorial Museum Photo Archives.

Lubetkin (see **Zivia Zuckerman**), also a member of the Zionist Movement and a hero of the Warsaw ghetto, and eventually married her.

By 1941, news reached the Jews of Warsaw that the Germans had taken over the Russian-occupied parts of Poland and had murdered tens of thousands of Jews there. With the realization that masses of Jews were being killed, Zuckerman decided it was more expedient to concentrate on defense rather than education. In *Chapters from the Legacy*, one of the books he published after the war, he explained, "there was no point [in educational activities] unless such activities went hand in hand with an armed Jewish resistance force."

Zuckerman was among the few who were committed to military resistance by the Jews and he was a moving force in initiating contacts with various Jewish Underground factions in ghettos throughout Poland. He received little support at first, but as mass deportations began in July 1942, more and more people realized they would not be able to save themselves and were spurred on to die fighting. Young Zionists from the various movements formed the core of this group, called, in Polish, *Zydowska Organizacia Bojowa* (ZOB), the Jewish Fighting Force.

Most of the rebellions in Polish ghettos were short-lived or were complete failures. The Warsaw ghetto uprising was the exception. The ZOB began preparing for the rebellion in January 1943, led by Zuckerman and a few others. By April they were ready and at this point, Antek Zuckerman was told to leave the ghetto to be the liaison with the Polish Underground. In this role he was able to help smuggle in weapons to the ghetto fighters and also to arrange rescue operations.

The rebellion by Jews in the ghetto began on April 19, 1943, and lasted for twenty-seven days. It was the first such rebellion against the Germans to break out in Poland and it caused a great deal of damage to the German Army. Ultimately, however, the Jews, poorly armed and untrained, could not hold out. Once the Nazis had killed most of the insurgents and burned down the ghetto, Zuckerman put together a team that came through the Warsaw sewer system and led the handful of survivors, including his future wife, Zivia Lubetkin, to safety.

Hiding in Aryan Warsaw, Zuckerman became active in the Jewish National Committee. This group helped Jews in hiding and kept in contact with the Jewish partisan units and when possible, with Jews in some of the forced labor camps. Most Jews from Warsaw had been deported to Treblinka, a death camp from which very few returned. German records show that 300,000 Jews from Warsaw and its surroundings were gassed in Treblinka.

When the Polish Underground finally began to fight against the Nazis in August 1944, Antek Zuckerman joined them and commanded a group of Jewish fighters, but that attempt was also unsuccessful. Liberation did not come to Warsaw until January 1945, when the Soviet Army marched in.

At first, Zuckerman remained in Poland, doing relief work among the small number of Jews who had survived. By 1946 he was hard at work reviving his old Zionist Movement, *HeHalutz*, and organizing the refugees to apply for visas and get to Palestine. By 1947, he and Zivia, now married, left for Palestine themselves. They were among the founders of Kibbutz *Lohamei ha-Ghetta'ot* (the Ghetto Fighters' Kibbutz) and also sponsored the Ghetto Fighters' Museum, dedicated to the memory of the fallen fighters. Zivia and Yitzhak Zuckerman had two children.

Zuckerman wrote many books about his war experience before his death in 1981 at the age of seventy-six.

References

Gutman, Israel, ed. *Encyclopedia of the Holocaust.* s.v. "Zuckerman, Yitzhak" and "Z.O.B." New York: Macmillan, 1990.

Lubetkin, Zivia. *In the Days of Destruction and Revolt.* Tel Aviv: Hakibbutz Hameuhad and Am Oved Publishing House, 1981.

Zuckerman, Yitzhak. *Chapters from the Legacy.* Northern Galilee, Israel: Ghetto Fighters House, 1982. (In Hebrew and Yiddish.)

Zuckerman, Zivia (1914–1978)

Zivia Lubetkin Zuckerman, a native of Beten, Poland, and the daughter of a grocer, was one of the leaders of the Jewish uprising in the Warsaw ghetto. When the Nazis bombed Warsaw on September 1, 1939, marking the official beginning of World War II, she was caught in the Soviet-occupied part of Poland and could have remained there, outside the reach of Nazi persecution. Instead, as a member of a Zionist Youth Movement, she agreed to go to German-occupied Warsaw and help organize the youth. Arriving there, she was horrified to see the treatment of Jews by the German soldiers and was determined to restore honor to her people.

By 1940, the Nazis had rounded up all of Warsaw's 500,000 Jews and forced them into one small, run-down area of the city: the ghetto. In addition, large numbers were rounded up from neighboring towns and herded into Warsaw. A wall was built around the ghetto in November 1940, and from that time on, no Jews were allowed to leave except for work assignments, and only under the supervision of armed guards.

Surrounded by misery, hunger, and fear, Zuckerman, along with other members of the Zionist Movement, first attempted to organize the young people. Zuckerman was often referred to as "Mother of the Ghetto" because of her work establishing schools for children and lectures for adults. She also helped form new Zionist youth groups. Although she knew that most of the children would not survive, she insisted that while they were alive, they must live with dignity and honor. Zuckerman's first name, Zivia, became so well known in the ghetto that it was used as a code word for the Jewish community in secret messages sent outside the ghetto.

Slowly, Zuckerman and her comrades in the movement realized that the Germans intended to kill all the Jews and were convinced that they must mount a rebellion. Even though they understood that they could never win against the might of the German Army, they wanted to show the world that Jews would not go to their deaths "without uttering a cry of protest."

Zuckerman became famous among this Jewish network of fighters. As part of her work with the underground, she was frequently sent out of the Warsaw ghetto to warn other Jews of the fate in store for them. She instructed them not to show up when the deportation orders came, to hide their children, and

Zivia Zuckerman was one of many survivors who testified against Adolf Eichman at his trial in Jerusalem in April 1961. Courtesy of the U.S. Holocaust Memorial Museum Photo Archives.

to resist the Germans by any means possible. Sometimes she, along with other young Jewish women, disguised themselves as Poles and pretended to flirt with the German soldiers. In this way they hoped to gain information about troop movements or the arrival of shipments. They might even be able to steal a pistol or a stick of dynamite and smuggle it back to the ghetto. Because Jews were not allowed to have weapons, one of the biggest challenges of the Jewish Fighting Force was trying to accumulate enough firearms to launch a rebellion.

Finally, in April 1943, after several skirmishes with German soldiers, the ghetto fighters felt they could wait no longer. When they heard that the Germans planned to liquidate the ghetto and send the remaining Jews to death camps, they began a major resistance against the Nazis. With only a few hundred young men and women, a small stash of stolen guns, and homemade bombs, they began a fight against 2,842 Nazi soldiers, augmented by an additional 7,000 police and secret service men. Unbelievably, they managed to repeatedly drive the Germans out of the ghetto.

The Warsaw ghetto rebellion was the first successful citizen rebellion to be launched against the German Army. Zuckerman later wrote that she was "amazed by our first victory over the enemy" and "intoxicated. . . . A feeling of pride had filled our hearts." But ultimately, they could not win against such a superior force. The Germans, rather than face a house-to-house struggle, set fire to the entire ghetto to force the fighters out. Retreating from each building as the fire consumed it, the ghetto fighters, their numbers dwindling, continued fighting, finally hiding in a bunker at 18 Mila Street. On May 8, after three weeks of intense fighting, the Germans discovered this last hiding place and blew up all the entrances. Most of the remaining Jewish fighters were killed, including the commander, Mordecai Anielewicz.

Miraculously, Zuckerman was not in the bunker when it was attacked. When she and a few others returned and discovered what had happened, they made a decision: it was time to escape. Following a prearranged plan, the fifty remaining fighters climbed down into the Warsaw sewers. They carried their wounded comrades on their backs and tied their weapons around their necks. Zuckerman was chosen to lead the group.

Zivia Lubetkin Zuckerman later described the horror and exhaustion she experienced as the band of survivors trudged for hours in the darkness, filth, and slime of the sewers. "My feet seemed to move automatically in this dark shaft," she recalled "and the echoes of a remote dream returned . . . of the distant land of Israel : . . of a life of dignity."

Of the fifty that left the ghetto with Zuckerman, only thirty-five managed to escape. As they emerged from the sewer into a street outside the ghetto, they were met by a rescue truck and whisked away to the safety of the forest. That rescue was organized by **Yitzhak** (Antek) **Zuckerman.**

Until the end of the war, Zuckerman led guerrilla detachments in Poland. Along with other Jewish fighters, she joined the Polish revolt in 1944, shortly before the Germans surrendered to the Russian Army. In 1946, one year after the war was over, Zivia Lubetkin and Antek Zuckerman married and moved to Israel, where they helped found Kibbutz *Lohamei ha-Ghetta'ot* (Ghetto

---

And There You Were
                In memory of Zivia Lubetkin

And there you were next to
the TV in a tightly packed circle,
everyone watching, following
a small research submarine
sunk at the bottom of the sea.
Tense the way you are.

It was a well-done documentary
about people in distress.
On the small screen
two experienced sailors
were trapped in the depths, their radio out of order.

We saw the ships. Summoned from Scotland.
And over a vast expanse of sea
fast ships, huge planes rushed
from Canada with the latest rescue equipment,
the whole great effort
for the sake of two young men on the verge of despair.

You held your breath. I saw you were moved like us
by the courage of those boys
in a terrible test of endurance.
Until they were saved.
And I nearly made a fool of myself
saying: Hey! what's the matter—
why all the fuss? I knew someone,
a frail girl, who was deep
in an ocean—not Pacific at all, not the Atlantic,
sunk for seven years without
a wireless. Without any radio without a single
connection to the air
outside.

Ships moved above her without
stopping
huge planes traveled without the slightest
change of course.
She called from the depths. They heard her wrestling
   with the elements
black
red
blue

Continued on next page

Continued from previous page

Struggling for oxygen. For a last breath. Until
the boy came. We know him,
that boy who came from the end of the shaft

to lead her hand in hand blinded by gas
to exit from Warsaw's sewer.
Luckily it was only half streaming
with excrement. And on to some refuge . . .

—Abba Kovner

Fighters' Kibbutz). She thought that few in Palestine would know about her part in the Warsaw ghetto uprising. However, reports of this courageous episode in Jewish history had spread quickly. Shortly after Israel declared its independence in 1948, Zivia Lubetkin Zuckerman was honored by the Jewish state for her role in defense of the Jewish people.

Zuckerman died on July 11, 1978, after a long battle with cancer. She left behind her husband, Yitzhak, two children, Shimon and Ya-el, and one grandson, Eyal. When she got older, she recounted her war experiences in her memoir, *In the Days of Destruction and Revolt*, first published in Israel a month after her death.

Reference

Lubetkin, Zivia. *In the Days of Destruction and Revolt.* Translated by Ishai Tubbin. Northern Galilee, Israel: Ghetto Fighters House, 1981.
Taitz, Emily, and Sondra Henry. "Zivia Lubetkin Zuckerman." In *Remarkable Jewish Women: Rebels, Rabbis, and Other Women from Biblical Times to the Present,* pp. 150–153. Philadelphia: Jewish Publication Society, 1996.

Zugman, David (1930–)

For David Zugman of Sokol, Poland, the horrors of World War II were so vivid that the only way he could live a normal life was to block out the memories completely. But because he had written a letter to relatives describing the events in detail shortly after they occurred, he did have a record of how his mother was killed and how he escaped death.

David Zugman was an only child, born in Sokol, a town near Lvov in eastern Poland (now part of the Ukraine). His father was a grain merchant and his mother was a popular dressmaker who made clothes for all the Polish and Ukrainian women in their town. Right after the war broke out, Sokol was occupied by the Soviet Union according to a secret pact made between Russia and Germany. On June 23, 1941, however, the Germans broke that agreement and marched across the Bug River into Soviet Territory. Zugman, then eleven years old, marked that date as the beginning of his nightmare.

Within a few days, all Jewish men were ordered to report to the town center "under penalty of death." The Nazis told their families that the men had been transported for work detail, but Zugman's father was shot to death along with all the others.

A year later, in 1942, a ghetto was established in Sokol and Zugman and his mother had to leave their home and all their belongings behind and move into cramped quarters. Although food was scarce, Zugman got enough to eat because his mother continued making dresses for the Christian women of Sokol and was paid in food. Even as he and his mother were waiting for the transport to the camps, Zugman recalled that the husband of a customer came to the station to retrieve the fabric that his wife had given her to make a dress.

Both Zugman and his mother were able to escape from the cattle car en route. Many Jews died attempting to escape but the Zugmans survived and returned to the ghetto. They lived by selling the possessions they had left with their Christian landlord before moving into the ghetto.

In less than a year, however, the liquidation of the ghetto began. After this final *aktion* (roundup), Sokol would be *Judenrein*, free of Jews. In order to save themselves, the Zugmans, with a small group of thirty Jews, hid in a bunker. They remained underground for twelve days. When their food and water were gone, they emerged and split up. Zugman and his mother went to their old landlord, but he was afraid to hide them, since the Nazis killed anyone protecting Jews.

The Ukrainian police found mother and son hiding in a stack of corn but let them go and they made their way to an area called Wolyn. Wolyn was controlled by Ukrainian partisans and Germans rarely went there. Several Jewish families lived in Wolyn and for five months, Zugman's mother worked as a dressmaker there, supporting herself and her son. After those five relatively peaceful months, the Ukrainian Partisans (the Bandrovtes) began to kill Poles and Jews and the Zugmans went into hiding again, begging for food each day.

Finally, the Ukrainians caught up with them. Exhausted, cold, and ridden with lice, they were dragged from their hiding place beneath a haystack. Because of frostbite, Zugman's feet were swollen and he could not walk. He was thrown into a wagon and along with his mother, another woman, and her baby, was taken to a deserted spot in the middle of a field. There, both women and the baby were shot and thrown into a well, still alive.

Zugman, in a trance, watched the executions and then passed out. When he woke, he was in a bed and his feet were being warmed. He had been rescued by a Baptist family who revived him and healed his frostbite. Then they sent him away.

After many weeks of misery, wandering alone from house to house, begging for food and a night's lodging, Zugman was taken in by a family of Jehovah's Witnesses. They allowed him to stay in their attic for five months, feeding him, and talking to him about their religion. Before long, he began to believe their doctrine.

Eastern Poland and the Ukraine were liberated by the Russians in August 1944 and, although fighting still continued in the West, the war ended for Zugman. He returned to Sokol and joined the less than thirty Jewish survivors of their town.

Still a child, he was taken in by another survivor, Doctor Kindler, who had helped deliver Zugman fourteen years before. Although Zugman told Kindler that he had become a Jehovah's Witness, the doctor was not dissuaded and insisted that young Zugman "come and live with us anyway."

With Kindler and his family, Zugman sneaked across the Russian border into Krakow in western Poland then into Bucharest. Their destination was Palestine but a series of events and chance meetings turned up an uncle in New York and Zugman was removed from the group of children planning to emigrate to the Jewish state and placed in an Italian boarding school.

> *Never again will we wait for bombs that never came to hit the gas chambers. Never again will we wait for salvation that never arrives. Now we have our own air force. The Jewish people are now capable of standing up to those who seek their destruction. . . .*
>
> —Ben Caspit, Israeli Journalist (written during the Israeli action against Lebanon, July 2006).

From there, he was sent to Montreal, Canada, by the Canadian Jewish Congress with a group of a thousand orphans. In Montreal he lived with a foster family and completed his high school education. In 1950, his papers came through and he joined his uncle Henry and his family in New York City.

In a short time, Zugman was earning a living and had rented a room. Working and going to school at night, he graduated City College as a CPA. In 1960, he married. The Zugmans soon moved to Florida where he ultimately became a partner in an accounting firm.

Zugman had put his war experiences behind him. He had forgotten everything. But then he found the letter he had written to his uncle. It was in Ukrainian and Polish, languages that he no longer spoke. He had the letters translated and rediscovered the terrible events surrounding the death of his mother. He included a translation of that letter in a brief account of his life, written in 2004.

Reference

Zugman, David B. "On a Wing and a Prayer." In *Children Who Survived the Final Solution.* Edited by Peter Tarjan. New York. iUniverse, 2004.

GLOSSARY

aktia—A round-up of Jews for deportation.

Anschluss—The annexation of Austria into Hitler's Third Reich in March 1938.

Anti-Defamation League (ADL)—An organization under the sponsorship of B'nai Brith, an American Jewish Service organization. The ADL fights antisemitism and all other forms of hatred or intolerance.

Armia Krajowa—The Polish underground army, known to be antisemitic.

Arrow Cross—The Hungarian Nazi Party.

Aryan—A racial category of light-skinned peoples, considered by the Nazis to be superior to all other races.

Auschwitz—The most notorious of all the concentration camps. It became a metaphor for Nazi atrocities during World War II.

Axis—The political, military, and ideological alliance of Germany with Italy and later Japan.

Banderas—A partisan group composed mostly of Ukrainians, named after its founder, Stefan Bandera. The group was known to be fiercely antisemitic.

bar mitzvah/bat mitzvah (plural: b'nai mitvah/b'not mitzvah)—A rite of passage for Jewish boys and girls at age thirteen. A bar mitzvah or bat mitzvah marks the fact that the child is now responsible for fulfilling the commandments.

Blitz, the—The German bombing of London during World War II.

Blitzkrieg—"Lightning war," a series of strikes launched by Germany during World War II.

B'nai Akiva—literally, "The Children of Akiva," a religious Zionist youth organization.

Bobover Hasidim—A group of Hasidim who followed the Bobover Rebbe, a spiritual leader from Bobov, a town in Galicia (southern Poland).

CANDLES—The acronym for Children of Auschwitz Nazi Deadly Lab Experiments Survivors, an organization and museum based in Terre Haute, Indiana, dedicated especially to information on Mengele's twins.

CENTOS—A federation of associations in Poland that existed before World War II for the care of orphans.

death brigade—A group of prisoners singled out by the Nazis in the camps to deal with the dead: remove them from the gas chambers, place them in the crematoria, and bury the ashes.

death march—Mass evacuation of prisoners from the concentration camps. The march was organized by the Nazis in an attempt to remove evidence of their brutality before their final defeat by the Soviet and Allied forces.

DP Camps—Displaced persons camps set up after World War II, mostly in Germany, Austria, and Italy, to help refugees and homeless Jews.

ETZEL—The abbreviation for *Irgun Tzva'i Leumi (National Military Organization)*, an armed right-wing group of jews that fought the British in Palestine in the 1930s and 1940s. This organization no longer exists.

General Gouvernement—The central part of Poland, an artificially created political unit under the supervision of the Nazi occupiers. The western part of Poland was annexed to Germany, and the eastern part was allotted originally to the Soviet Union.

Gestapo—The Nazi state secret police force.

Gymnasia—German and Polish high schools.

Ha'apalah—Illegal Jewish immigration to Palestine, carried on clandestinely by Jews from Israel after World War II and before Israel's independence in 1948. Also known as *Aliyah Bet*.

Hadassah—An American Zionist women's organization that raises money for Israel, especially for medical care and children's homes.

Haganah—The Israeli Defense Force.

HaPo'el HaMizrachi—A Zionist political party for observant Jews.

HaShomer HaTza-ir—"The Young Watchman," a Socialist-Zionist youth movement popular among Jews in Eastern Europe.

Hasidim—"Pious ones." Hasidim are a group of Orthodox Jews who believe in expressing their love of God with song, dance, and mystical practices. They were widespread from the late eighteenth century, especially in southern Europe. Although scattered during World War II, they continue to be a vital and influential part of Judaism.

heder—"Room," specifically a Hebrew school, usually for younger children.

HeHalutz Hatza-ir—The Young Pioneers, a Zionist youth organization.

HIAS—The Hebrew Immigrant Aid Society, which helped Jews to immigrate into the United States after the war.

Hitler Youth—A Nazi-sponsored German youth organization popular with young German boys and girls.

imam—An Islamic religious leader.

International Refugee Organization (IRO)—A temporary relief organization established in 1946 by the United Nations to aid refugees from Europe and China with food, medical care, vocational training, and preparation for resettlement. The agency was discontinued in 1952.

Iron Curtain—The Soviet Union's efforts to seal itself and its satellite nations off from the West and other non-Communist nations; the term was first used by Winston Churchill after World War II.

Jehovah's Witnesses—A sect of Christians constituting a small minority in Europe during World War II. They were considered a political threat, and some were taken to concentration camps.

Jewish Agency—An organization established in 1943 by the Jews of Palestine to rescue Jews in Europe. After the war they were active in aiding immigration into the Jewish state and helped the absorption of new immigrants.

Jewish Brigade—The Jewish Armed Force, consisting of volunteers from Palestine, which was then occupied by the British. They functioned under orders from Great Britain but flew their own Jewish flag.

Jewish Central Information Office—A Jewish organization created by world Jewry to fight antisemitism.

JOINT—The American Joint Distribution Committee. An American Jewish organization that was active during and especially after World War II.

***Jude/Jood* (German/Dutch)**—"Jew." Under Nazi rule, this word (or simply the letter *J*) was stamped on every Jew's identity card.

Judenrat—A committee formed in each Jewish community by order of the Nazis. Leaders of the *Judenrat* were responsible for registering all Jews and supplying lists for forced labor and deportation.

Judenrein—"Free of Jews." Nazi Germany's goal was to rid Europe of all Jews.

Kabbalah—Mystical books of Jewish wisdom written in the thirteenth century.

Kaddish—The memorial prayer for the dead, recited by Jewish mourners at the funeral and on the anniversary of the death.

kapos—Prisoners in the concentration camps who were selected by the Germans to oversee and discipline other inmates. Many were criminals and treated other prisoners harshly, but others tried to mitigate their suffering.

Kasztner train—A train filled with Hungarian Jews who had been chosen by Reszo Kasztner to be saved from deportation and death by the Nazis. This was part of a proposed deal to supply equipment for the German war effort on the Russian front. Although the agreement failed, approximately 1,800 Jews were saved.

Kibbutz—A collective settlement in Israel.

Kibbutz *Lohamei ha-Ghetta'ot*—literally, Kibbutz of the Ghetto Fighters, a kibbutz organized by survivors of the Warsaw Ghetto.

Kindertransport—A rescue effort organized by Jews with the cooperation of the British government. England agreed to accept a thousand children from Germany, Austria, Czechoslovakia, and Poland who were in danger because of the pending war. Many of the children were placed in private foster homes. Others were sent to orphanages. The *Kindertransport* stopped when war broke out on September 1, 1939.

klezmer—The word is derived from the Hebrew *kli zemer*, a generic term denoting a musical instrument. In Eastern Europe, klezmer was a type of music that incorporated folk tunes from various countries with traditional Jewish music. A variety of instruments was used, but most often a clarinet was the lead instrument.

Knesset—The Israeli parliament.

Kristallnacht—"Night of Broken Glass," a nationally sponsored pogrom promulgated against the Jews of Germany and Austria on November 9–10, 1938, in which Jewish shops were looted, synagogues burned, and many Jews beaten, imprisoned, or killed.

labor brigades—Military brigades made up mostly of Jews, established by pro-Nazi governments in Romania, Czechoslovakia, and Hungary. Jews in the brigades served the regular army by digging trenches and tank traps, repairing roads, and burying the dead. Most were abused and treated like prisoners, and many died.

Ladino—The language of the Sephardic Jews, based on a combination of old Castilian and Hebrew.

lager (**German**)—A prison block in a concentration camp.

Macquis—The French underground operating during World War II.

Mamushka/Mamusha—Polish words for "mama."

March of the Living—A symbolic march to Auschwitz set up for survivors and their children, friends, and supporters to celebrate the ultimate failure of Hitler's "final solution."

matzah—Special unleavened bread made without any yeast and eaten for the entire week of Passover.

mensch—in German, "man;" in Yiddish, "a good, upright person."

Molotov-Ribbentrop Pact—A secret nonaggression treaty between the Soviet Union and Nazi Germany, signed in August 1939, in which Germany agreed to Soviet occupation of parts of Eastern Europe bordering on Russia. In return, the USSR agreed not to interfere with Germany's invasion of Poland.

Mosad—The Israeli Secret Service, active in tracking down Nazi war criminals after the war.

mufti—An Arab Muslim leader.

Nansenhjelpan—A Norwegian aid group.

Nazi—The abbreviated form of *Nazionalsozialistische Deutsche Arbeiterpartei* or National Socialist German Workers' Party.

NKVD—The Soviet secret police, later called the KGB.

Nuremberg Laws—A series of racial laws enacted by the Nazis in Nuremberg in 1935, effectively depriving all Jews of citizenship and civil rights.

Nuremberg Trials—Trials of the Nazi leaders that took place after the war to punish those active in mistreating Jews and others.

Obersturmbannfuehrer—The head of a unit of German storm troopers.

OSE—*Oeuvres de Secours aux Enfants*, a French-Jewish aid organization that maintained children's homes and helped hide Jewish children.

Passover—The Jewish holiday commemorating the exodus of the ancient Israelites from Egypt. During the seven days of Passover, Jews may not eat bread or any leavened food.

Pastors' Emergency League—An organization of pastors and ministers in Germany who stood against Nazi policies and resisted Hitler's vision of the church as subservient to the government.

Po'alei Tziyyon—"Workers of Zion," a Zionist political labor party in Eastern Europe.

Qadi—An Islamic community leader.

Radda Bärnem—"Save the Children," a Swedish organization.

razzia—"Round-up," the equivalent of *aktia* in the Dutch language.

Reichskommissar—"National Commissar," a German title.

Reichstag—The German Parliament.

Reichsvertretung der Deutscher Juden—An organization of German Jews set up under Hitler's rule.

righteous gentiles—Non-Jews who risked their lives to save Jews for no monetary gain.

Roma—A tribe of people believed to have originated in India or Egypt, formerly referred to as gypsies.

Romaniote Jews—Jews whose ancestors lived in the old Byzantine Empire, later Turkey and Greece.

Rome-Berlin Treaty—A political agreement between Hitler and Mussolini, pledging mutual support in war. It was signed in 1936.

Schule **(German)**—School.

SD—The abbreviation for *Sicherheitsdienst des Reichsfuehrers*, the security service of the SS. The SD acted as an intelligence service for the Nazi government and was a major force in implementing the "final solution."

seder—The ceremonial meal of Passover that retells the story of the exodus from Egypt.

Sephardic Jews—Jews whose ancestors lived in Spain or Portugal and were expelled in 1492 and 1497.

Shabbos goy—A gentile who performs small tasks that Jews were not permitted to do on the Sabbath, such as turning on lights, making fires, and so on.

Shah—The ruler of Iran until the 1970s.

Shoah—The Hebrew word for the Holocaust.

shokhet—a ritual meat-slaughterer (usually also a butcher) who killed livestock according to Biblical law so it would be kosher.

Sinti—A tribe of people believed to have originated in India or Egypt, formerly referred to as gypsies. The Sinti formed a majority of the gypsy peoples in Austria and Germany.

Sonderkommando—See *death brigade*.

Soviet-German nonaggression treaty—See *Molotov-Ribbentrop Pact*.

SS—*Schutzstaffel* or protection squad, known as the German Special Forces. It acted as Nazi Party police and were a major force in the mass murder of Jews during the war. The SS was considered the most racially pure of all branches of the German Army and was the backbone of the Nazi regime.

Star of David—A six-pointed star and a symbol of the Jewish people since the Middle Ages.

Talmud—A compendium of books commenting on and explaining the laws of the Bible, written and edited in the second to the sixth centuries C.E.

Tante **(Dutch and German)**—Aunt.

Torah—The first five books of the Bible (the Pentateuch) written in Hebrew on parchment and assembled as a scroll. The Torah is considered the holiest of all Jewish texts and can be found in every synagogue. Parts of it are read or chanted as a regular part of the Sabbath service.

Transnistria—An undeveloped area in the Ukraine east of the Dniester River and west of the Bug River. It was used as a dumping ground for deported Jews by the pro-Nazi Romanian government.

UJA—United Jewish Appeal, an American-based philanthropic organization that collects and contributes money to Jewish causes in Israel and throughout the world.

UNRRA—The United Nations Relief and Rehabilitation Administration.

Vichy France—The puppet pro-Nazi government centered in the city of Vichy in the southern part of France.

Wezembeek—Originally a sanitorium for Jewish children with tuberculosis in Brussels. After the Germans invaded Belgium, it became a home for Jewish orphans and children whose parents had been deported.

Yad Vashem—The Holocaust museum of Israel, located in Jerusalem.

yarmulka—A small skullcap worn by observant Jewish men.

Yeshivah—A Jewish academy of learning for older children and adults.

Yiddish—The language of the Jews of central and Eastern Europe, based on a German dialect and including a mixture of Hebrew, Polish, and other languages.

YIVO—The Yiddish Institute and Library in Vilna, now relocated to New York City.

Yom HaShoah—A day memorializing the victims of the Holocaust. It is commemorated in Israel and also among Jewish communities throughout the world and falls in the spring, shortly before Israel Independence day.

Yom Kippur—The Day of Atonement, considered the holiest of all Jewish holidays.

Zegota—The Polish code name for the Council for Aid to Jews in Occupied Poland, a secret organization that functioned during World War II.

Zionists—Those who believe that Israel is the ancient homeland of the Jews, and that Jews should return to live there in their own state.

zloty—The Polish unit of currency.

ZOB—*Zydowska Organizaria Bojowa*, the Jewish fighting force in Poland.

RESOURCE GUIDE

Further Reading

Bauer, Yehudah. *A History of the Holocaust*. Revised edition. New York: Franklin Watts, 2001.

Bullock, Alan. *Hitler: A Study in Tyranny*. New York: Harper and Row, 1964.

Chary, Frederick B. *The Bulgarian Jews and the Final Solution, 1940–1944*. Pittsburgh: University of Pittsburgh Press, 1972.

Conot, Robert E. *Justice at Nuremberg*. New York: Harper and Row, 1983.

Dawidowicz, Lucy. *A Holocaust Reader*. New York: Behrman House, 1976.

Dobroszycki, Lucjan, and Barbara Kirshenblatt-Gimblett. *Image before My Eyes: A Photographic History of Jewish Life in Poland before the Holocaust*. New York: Schocken Books, 1977.

Dwork, Debórah. *Children with a Star: Jewish Youth in Nazi Europe*. New Haven, CT: Yale University Press, 1991.

Eidelman, Jay M., general ed. *Ours to Fight For: American Jewish Voices from the Second World War*. New York: Museum of Jewish Heritage, 2003.

Evans, Richard J. *The Third Reich in Power*. New York: Penguin Press, 2005.

Fenelon, Fania. *Playing for Time: An Extraordinary Personal Account of the Women's Orchestra in Auschwitz*. New York: Atheneum, 1977.

Frank, Anne. *The Diary of a Young Girl*. The Definitive Edition. Edited by Otto H. Frank, Mirjam Pressler, and Susan Massotty. New York: Doubleday, 1995.

Fromer, Rebecca Camhi. *The Holocaust Odyssey of Daniel Bennahmias, Sonderkommando*. Introduction by Steven B. Bowman. Tuscaloosa: University of Alabama Press, 1993.

Gilbert, Martin. *Atlas of the Holocaust*. New York: Morrow, 1993.

———. *The Holocaust: A History of the Jews of Europe during the Second World War*. New York: Henry Holt, 1985.

Goldhagen, Daniel Jonah. *Hitler's Willing Executioners*. New York: Knopf, 1996.

Gutman, Israel, ed. *Encyclopedia of the Holocaust*. 4 vols. New York: Macmillan, 1990.

Hogan, David J., ed. *The Holocaust Chronicle: A History in Words and Pictures*. Lincolnwood, IL: Publications International, 2000.

Jong, Louis de. *The Netherlands and Nazi Germany*. Cambridge, MA: Harvard University Press, 1990.

Kenrick, Donald, ed. *In the Shadow of the Swastika: The Gypsies during the Second World War*. Hertfordshire, UK: University of Hertfordshire Press, 1999.

Klemperer, Victor. *I Will Bear Witness*. New York: Random House, 1998.

Kranzler, David. *Japanese Nazis and Jews: The Jewish Refugee Community of Shanghai, 1938-1945*. New York: Yeshiva University Press, 1976.

Landau, Ronnie S. *The Nazi Holocaust*. Chicago: Ivan R. Dee, 1992.

Langer, Lawrence. *Art from the Ashes: A Holocaust Anthology*. New York: Oxford University Press, 1995.

———. *Holocaust Testimonies: The Ruins of Memory*. New Haven, CT: Yale University Press, 1991.

Levi, Primo. *Survival in Auschwitz*. New York: Macmillan, 1961.

Lipstadt, Deborah E. *Denying the Holocaust: The Growing Assault on Truth*. New York: Free Press, 1993.

Marrus, Michael R., and Robert O. Paxton. *Vichy France and the Jews*. New York: Basic Books, 1981.

Matsas, Michael. *The Illusion of Safety: The Story of the Greek Jews during World War II*. New York: Pella Publishing, 1997.

Meed, Vladka. *On Both Sides of the Wall*. Translated by Steven Meed. New York: Schocken Books, 1993.

Moore, Bob. *Victims and Survivors: The Nazi Persecutions of the Jews in the Netherlands 1940-1945*. New York and London: Arnold, 1997.

Morse, Arthur. *While Six Million Died: A Chronicle of American Apathy*. New York: Hart Publishing, 1968.

Plant, Richard. *The Pink Triangle: The Nazi War against Homosexuals*. New York: Henry Holt, 1986.

Pringle, Heather. *The Master Plan: Himmler's Scholars and the Holocaust*. New York: Hyperion, 2006.

Ramati, Alexander. *The Assisi Underground: The Priests Who Rescued Jews*. New York: Stein & Day, 1978.

Rashke, Richard. *Escape from Sobibor*. Boston: Houghton Mifflin, 1982.

Ringelblum, Emanuel. *Notes from the Warsaw Ghetto*. New York: McGraw-Hill, 1958.

Rudashevski, Yitzhok. *The Diary of the Vilna Ghetto: June 1941-April 1943*. Northern Galilee, Israel: Ghetto Fighters House, 1972.

Sarfatti, Michele. *The Jews in Mussolini's Italy: From Equality to Persecution*. Translated by John Tedeschi and Anna Tedeschi. Madison: University of Wisconsin Press, 2006.

Sergeant, Harriet. *Shanghai*. London: John Murray, 1998.

Spiegelman, Art. *Maus: A Survivor's Tale*. Vol. 1. New York: Pantheon Books, 1973.

———. *Maus: A Survivor's Tale*. Vol. 2. New York: Pantheon Books, 1986.

Steiner, Jean-Francois. *Treblinka: The Extraordinary Story of Jewish Resistance in the Notorious Nazi Death Camp*. New York: MJF Books, 1967.

Suhl, Yuri. *They Fought Back*. New York: Crown, 1967.

Thomas, Gordon. *Voyage of the Damned*. New York: Stein and Day, 1974.

Tokayer, Marvin, and Mary Swartz. *The Fugu Plan: The Untold Story of the Japanese and the Jews during World War II*. New York: Paddington Press, 1979.

Trunk, Isaiah. *Judenrat: The Jewish Councils in Eastern Europe under Nazi Occupation*. New York: Macmillan, 1972.

Volavkova, Hana, ed. *I Never Saw Another Butterfly: Children's Drawings and Poems from Theresienstadt Concentration Camp, 1942.* New York: McGraw-Hill, 1964.

Wiesel, Elie. *The Night Trilogy.* New York: Hill and Wang, 1987.

Zuckerman, Yitzhak. *A Surplus of Memory: Chronicle of the Warsaw Ghetto Uprising.* Berkeley: University of California Press, 1993.

Films and Videotapes on the Holocaust

Anne Frank: The Whole Story. Directed by Robert Dornhelm. Culver City, CA: Social Studies School Service, 2001.

The Camera of My Family: Four Generations in Germany, 1845–1945. Directed by Catherine Noren. New York, NY: ADL Media, 1988.

The Century of Simon Wiesenthal: Freedom Is Not a Gift from Heaven. Directed by Willy Lindwer. Teaneck, NJ: Ergo Media, 1995.

The Cross and the Star. Directed by John Michalczyk. First Run Films, 1999.

Daring to Resist. Directed by Barbara Attie. Women Make Movies, 2000.

Diplomats for the Damned. An A&E Television Production. New Video Group, 2000.

Double Crossing: The Voyage of the St. Louis. Produced by the Holocaust Memorial Foundation of Illinois and Loyola University of Chicago. Ergo Media, 1992.

Elie Wiesel Goes Home. Directed by Judit Elek. Choices, 2002.

Europa, Europa. Directed by Artur Brauner and Margaret Menegoz. Orion Home Video, 1992.

Genocide. Directed by Arnold Schwartzman. Simon Wiesenthal Center, 1981.

Into the Arms of Strangers. Directed by Mark Jonathan Harris. Hollywood, CA: Warner Bros., 2001.

Kovno Ghetto: A Buried History. Produced and directed by the History Channel. New Video Group, 1997.

Let Memory Speak. Directed by Batia Bettman. Washington, DC: U.S. Holocaust Memorial Museum, 1999.

Nuremberg. Directed by Stephen Trombley. Culver City, CA: Social Studies School Services, 1997.

One Survivor Remembers. Directed by Gerda Weissmann. Produced by HBO and the U.S. Holocaust Memorial Museum. Direct Cinema, 1996.

Pianist, The. Directed by Roman Polanski. Universal Studios, 2003.

Power of Good. Directed by Matej Minac. National Center for Jewish Film, 2002.

Primo. Directed by Richard Wilson. Kultur International Films, 2004.

Rescuers: Stories of Courage—Two Couples. Directed by Tim Hunter and Lynne Littman. Hollywood, CA: Paramount, 1998.

Schindler's List. Directed by Steven Spielberg. Hollywood, CA: Universal Pictures, 1993.

Sugihara: Conspiracy of Kindness. Directed by Robert Kirk. WGBH Boston Video, 2005.

Unlikely Heroes. Directed by Richard Trank. Moriah Films, 2003.

Uprising. Directed by Jon Avnet. Warner Home Video, 2001.

Weapons of the Spirit. Directed by Pierre Sauvage. Friends of Le Chambon Foundation, 1994.

Web Sites

CANDLES Holocaust Museum: www.candlesholocaustmuseum.org
The Ghetto Fighters Museum (Israel): www.gfh.org.il/eng/

Hidden Child Foundation: www.adl.org/hidden/start.asp
Holocaust History: www.holocaust-history.org
Jewish Partisans Education Center: www.jewishpartisans.org
Nizkor Project: www.nizkor.org
Oracle Library Think Quest: www.library.thinkquest.org
One Thousand Children: www.onethousandchildren.org
Simon Wiesenthal Center: www.wiesenthal.com
United States Holocaust Memorial Museum: www.ushmm.org
Yad Vashem (Israel): www.yadvashem.org

U.S. and Canadian Organizations Representing Speakers on the Holocaust

United States

Arkansas

Knowing Our Past Foundation
6834 Cantrell Rd.
Box 383
Little Rock, AR 72207
(501) 312-2288

California

Chambon Foundation
8033 Sunset Blvd.
Los Angeles, CA 90046
(323) 650-1774

The Holocaust Center of Northern California
121 Steuart St.
San Francisco, CA 94105
(415) 777-9060

Jewish Partisans Educational Foundation
2107 Van Ness Ave.
San Francisco, CA 94109
(415) 563-2244

Colorado

Holocaust Awareness Institute
University of Denver
2199 S. University Blvd.
Denver, CO 80208
(303) 871-3037

Connecticut

Holocaust Child Survivors of Connecticut
20 Tubbs Spring Ct.
Weston, CT 06883
(203) 226-3092

Florida

Center for Holocaust and Human Rights Education
Florida Atlantic University College of Education
777 Glades Rd.
Boca Raton, FL 33431
(561) 297-2021

Florida Holocaust Museum
55 Fifth St. South
St. Petersburg, FL 33701
(727) 820-0100

Holocaust Documentation and Education Center, Inc.
13899 Biscayne Blvd.
Suite 404
North Miami, FL 33181
(305) 919-5690

Georgia

Georgia Commission on the Holocaust
Kennesaw State University
100 Chastain Rd.
Drop Box 3308
Kennesaw, GA 30144
(678) 797-2085

The Lillian and A. J. Weinberg Center for Holocaust Education
William Breman Jewish Heritage Museum
The Selig Center
1440 Spring St. NE
Atlanta, GA 30309
(404) 870-1872

Illinois

Holocaust Memorial Foundation of Illinois
4255 West Main St.
Skokie, IL 60076
(847) 677-4684

Kansas

Midwest Center for Holocaust Education
5801 W. 113th St. Suite 106
Shawnee Mission, KS 66211
(913) 327-8190

Maine

Holocaust Human Rights Center of Maine
P.O. Box 4645
Augusta, ME 04330
(207) 993-2620

Maryland

Baltimore Jewish Council—Holocaust Programs
5750 Park Heights Ave.
Baltimore, MD 21215
(410) 542-4834

One Thousand Children, Inc.
P.O. Box 4710
Silver Spring, MD 20914
(301) 622-0363

Michigan

Holocaust Memorial Center
28123 Orchard Lake Rd.
Farmington Hills, MI 48334
(284) 553-2433

Minnesota

Jewish Community Relations Council of Minnesota and the
Dakotas Holocaust Research Center
12 North 12th St., Suite 480
Minneapolis, MN 55403
(612) 338-7816

St. Cloud State University Center for Holocaust and Genocide Education
Miller Center 235
720 Fourth Ave. South
St. Cloud, MN 56301
(320) 308-4205

Missouri

Holocaust Museum and Learning Center/St. Louis
12 Millstone Campus Dr.
St. Louis, MO 63146
(314) 432-0020

Nevada

Jewish Federation of Las Vegas
Holocaust Education Center
2317 Renaissance Dr.
Las Vegas, NV 89110
(702) 732-3228

New Jersey

Center for Holocaust and Genocide Studies—Ramapo College
Ramapo College Library
505 Ramapo Valley Rd.
Mahwah, NJ 07446
(201) 684-7409

Drew University Center for Holocaust/Genocide Study
Embury Hall
Madison, NJ 07940
(973) 408-3914

Holocaust Education Center of the Delaware Valley
Goodwin Holocaust Museum
Weinberg Jewish Community Campus
1301 Springdale Rd.
Cherry Hill, NJ 08003
(856) 751-9500 extension 249

Holocaust Resouorce Center at the Allen and Joan Bildner Center
Bildner Center for the Study of Jewish Life
12 College Ave.
New Brunswick, NJ 08901
(732) 932-3052

New Mexico

New Mexico Holocaust and Intolerance Museum and Study Center
415 Central Ave. NW
Albequerque, NM 87102
(505) 247-0606

New York

Holocaust Resource Center of Buffalo
1050 Maryvale Dr.
Cheektowaga, NY 14225
(716) 634-9625

American Society for Yad Vashem
500 Fifth Avenue 42nd floor
New York, NY 10110
(212) 220-4304

Hidden Child Foundation/ADL
605 Third Avenue
New York, NY 10017
(212) 692-3900

Holocaust Memorial and Tolerance Center of Nassau County
Welwyn Preserve
100 Crescent Beach Rd.
Glen Cove, NY 11542
(516) 571-8040

Holocaust Resource Center and Archives—Queensborough
Community College/CUNY
222-05 56th Ave.
Bayside, NY 11364
(718) 281-5770

Holocaust Resource Center of Temple Judea of Manhasset
333 Searington Rd.

Manhasset, NY 11030
(516) 621-4725

Center for Holocaust Awareness and Information (CHAI)
Jewish Community Federation of Greater Rochester
441 East Ave.
Rochester, NY 14607
(585) 461-0912

North Carolina

North Carolina Council on the Holocaust
Department of Public Instruction
Office of the State Superintendent
6301 Mail Service Center
Raleigh, NC 27699
(919) 807-3432

Ohio

Center for Holocaust and Humanity Education
Hebrew Union College/Jewish Institute of Religion
5101 Clifton Ave.
Cincinnati, OH 45220
(513) 221-1842 (fax)

Oregon

Oregon Holocaust Resource Center
Pacific University
2043 College Way
Forest Grove, OR 97116
(503) 359-2930

Pennsylvania

Holocaust Center of the United Jewish Federation of Greater Pittsburgh
5738 Darlington Rd.
Pittsburgh, PA 15217
(412) 421-1996

World Federation of Jewish Child Survivors of the Holocaust
P.O. Box 741
Conshocken, PA 19428
(610) 527-1039

Rhode Island

Rhode Island Holocaust Memorial Museum
401 Elmgrove Ave.
Providence, RI 02906
(401) 453-7860

South Carolina

South Carolina Council on the Holocaust
3023 Whitehall Rd.

Columbia, SC 29204
(803) 782-9294

Tennessee

Tennessee Holocaust Commission
2417 West End Ave.
Nashville, TN 37240
(615) 343-2563

Texas

Dallas Holocaust Museum
211 North Record St.
Dallas, TX 75202
(214) 750-4672

Holocaust Museum Houston
5401 Caroline St.
Houston, TX 77004
(713) 942-8000

Virginia

The Holocaust Commission of the United Federation of Tidewater
5000 Corporate Woods Dr., Suite 200
Virginia Beach, VA 23462
(757) 965-7613

Washington

Washington State Holocaust Education Resource Center
2031 Third Ave.
Seattle, WA 98121
(206) 441-5747

Washington, D.C.

U.S. Holocaust Museum
100 Raoul Wallenberg Pl. S.W.
Washington, DC 20024
(202) 488-0400
In addition to speakers, the museum has ongoing exhibits, recorded and written
testimony of survivors, photo archives and educational programs.

West Virginia

West Virginia Holocaust Education Center and Foundation
P.O. Box 1125
Morgantown, WV 26507
(304) 291-3732

Canada

Holocaust Center of Toronto
4600 Bathurst St.

Toronto, ON M2R3V2
(416) 635-0925

The Montreal Holocaust Memorial Center
5151 Cote Ste. Catherine Rd.
Montreal, Quebec
Canada H3W 1M6
(514) 345-2605

Vancouver Holocaust Education Center
#50-950 West 41st Ave.
Vancouver, BC V5Z 2N7
(604) 264-0497

INDEX

Boldface page references indicate main biographical entries. Italicized page references indicate photographs. Page numbers followed by "*m*" or "*b*" indicate maps or box inserts, respectively.

ABOUT THE AUTHOR

EMILY TAITZ is an independent scholar who has authored or coauthored numerous books and essays, particularly on Jewish women and Judaism. She is the author of *Judaism* (Greenwood, 2005) and *The Jews of Medieval France* (Greenwood, 1994), among other works.